TCHAIKOVSKY'S
COMPLETE SONGS

Russian Music Studies
Malcolm Hamrick Brown, founding editor

for
Joseph Miller
and
Vasily Petyarkin

Tchaikovsky at Frolovskoe, 1890. Courtesy Russian State Tchaikovsky Museum at Klin.

Tchaikovsky's Complete Songs

*A Companion
with Texts and Translations*

Richard D. Sylvester

INDIANA UNIVERSITY PRESS
Bloomington & Indianapolis

Published with the generous support of the
Indiana University Press Music Fund

This book is a publication of

Indiana University Press
601 North Morton Street
Bloomington, IN 47404-3797 USA

http://iupress.indiana.edu

Telephone orders   800-842-6796
Fax orders   812-855-7931
Orders by e-mail   iuporder@indiana.edu

The paper used in this publication meets the minimum requirements of
American National Standard for Information Sciences—Permanence of Paper
for Printed Library Materials, ANSI Z39.48–1984.

Manufactured in the United States of America

Library of Congress Cataloging-in-Publication Data

Tchaikovsky, Peter Ilich, 1840–1893.
  [Songs. Texts. English & Russian]
  Tchaikovsky's complete songs : a companion with texts and translations /
Richard D. Sylvester.
    p.   cm. — (Russian music studies)
  Includes bibliographical references (p.), discographies, and indexes.
  ISBN 0-253-34041-1 (cloth : alk. paper)
    1. Songs, Russian—Russia—Texts. I. Sylvester, Richard D. II. Title.
III. Russian music studies (Bloomington, Ind.)

ML54.6.T24 S9 2002
782.4'3'092—dc21   2001024858

1 2 3 4 5 07 06 05 04 03 02

Contents

Acknowledgments   ix
Preface   xi
Transcriptions from Cyrillic   xiii

Songs

Three Early Romances   1
    Songs 1-3   1
Six Romances, Opus 6 (1869)   9
    Songs 4-9   11
One Romance (1870)   29
    Song 10   29
Six Romances, Opus 16 (1872)   33
    Songs 11-16   35
Two Romances (1873)   50
    Songs 17-18   52
Romances of 1875   57
    Opus 25, Songs 19-24   59
    Songs 25-26   75
    Opus 27, Songs 27-32   79
    Opus 28, Songs 33-38   94
Six Romances, Opus 38 (1878)   108
    Songs 39-44   112
Seven Romances, Opus 47 (1880)   127
    Songs 45-51   130
Sixteen Songs for Children, Opus 54 (1883)   151
    Songs 52-67   154
Six Romances, Opus 57 (1884)   190
    Songs 68-73   192
Twelve Romances, Opus 60 (1886)   205
    Songs 74-85   207

Six Romances, Opus 63 (1887)   237
Songs 86-91   239
Six Mélodies, Opus 65 (1888)   251
Songs 92-97   253
Six Romances, Opus 73 (1893)   268
Songs 98-103   271

AFTERWORD   283

DUETS
Six Duets, Opus 46 (1880)   287

SINGERS & RECORDINGS   297
BIBLIOGRAPHY   329
INDEX OF SONG TITLES IN RUSSIAN   337
INDEX OF SONG TITLES IN ENGLISH   340
INDEX OF NAMES   344

ACKNOWLEDGMENTS

Research for this book was supported by travel grants from the Colgate University Faculty Research Council in October 1996 and January 2000, and a grant in May 1998 from the International Research & Exchanges Board, with funds provided by the U. S. Department of State (Title VIII program) and the National Endowment for the Humanities. I am most grateful for their support; none of them is responsible for the views expressed. I also wish to thank my colleagues at Colgate University who have helped and encouraged me in so many important ways, especially Jane Pinchin, Alice Nakhimovsky, and Chris Vecsey. I could not have undertaken this book without them.

My debts to colleagues in Russia are many. I am grateful to the Russian Academy of Theatrical Art (GITIS) in Moscow for their hospitality, and especially to Natalia Plyusnina. I have been welcome over the years at the Library of the Union of Theatrical Workers; the director, Vyacheslav Nechayev, and his staff have helped me in innumerable ways. Eleonora Mamedova-Sokolova of the Bakhrushin and Chaliapin Museums has been a resourceful and valued friend in all matters pertaining to the Russian vocal scene. Irina Medvedeva of the Glinka Museum welcomed this project and put me in touch with Galina Belonovich, Director of the Tchaikovsky Museum at Klin, and her colleague Polina Vaidman, who have generously contributed to the documentation that underlies this book. Lyudmila Korabelnikova of the Arts Institute, Mikhail Agin of the Russian Academy of Music (Gnesin Institute), Tamara Skvirskaya of the St. Petersburg Conservatory, and Irina Navolokina of the Russian State Archive of Sound Recordings gladly assisted me when I asked for their help. Lyudmila Dedyukina of the Moscow Conservatory Library kindly supplied books, information, and tea during my visits to the Conservatory. To Alexander Abramovich Makarov, a friend of many years, I am grateful for introductions to Tatyana and Olga Reizen, Konstantin Lisovsky, and Zara Dolukhanova: to each of them I owe thanks for their warm hospitality and readiness to answer my questions.

Indispensable help on the sources of Tchaikovsky's songs came from Maria Hatjigeorgiou (Greek folk songs, Song 16), Roman Koropeckyj of UCLA (Lenartowicz, Song 31), Robert Rothstein of the University of Massachusetts at Amherst ("Legend," Song 56), and Wayles Browne of Cornell University (Serbian folk poetry, Song 77). If any errors have crept into my reporting of their meticulous scholarship, the responsibility is entirely mine. For help with Italian texts my thanks to Pat Avila, Valentina Versace, Andreanna Campana, and Ross Ferlito; to Martha Dietz for help with German texts and encouragement from the beginning; and to Jean Post and Edward Lobb, who went through the French songs with me line by line.

I am grateful for the courteous help rendered on numerous occasions by staff members of the Colgate Library, especially Ellen Bolland and Ann Ackerson of the Division of Interlibrary Loan, and by the staff of the Slavic and Baltic Division of the New York Public Library.

For information about recordings not in my own collection, I am deeply indebted to Greg Audette, Ian Harvey, Don Seibert, Bill Thomas, Victor Han, Richard Kummins, Vin Reda, Bernhard Vogel, and Joseph Miller, serious collectors all, who have been uncommonly generous in sharing their rarities and their expert knowledge with me. My thanks to S. A. Viholainen and the Melodiya Record Company in Moscow for providing digital transfers of recordings from their archives and granting licensing rights to include them on the compact disc that accompanies this book. Richard C. Burns of Syracuse and James Bona of Colgate cheerfully gave indispensable technical support in preparing the master digital tape.

Laurel Fay, Nancy Ries, Edward Lobb, and Ronald Rebholz read portions of the manuscript and brought their wisdom to fundamental issues of interpretation and presentation. I owe very much to them and to all the friends who heard my ideas and gave advice during my work on this book: Gaines and Jean Post, Shimon Markish, Caryl Emerson, Robert Maclennan, Charlotte Douglas, Vladimir Zak, Svetlana Golybina, Nina Drozdetskaya, Olga Kazakova, Edythe Haber, Leona Egan, Slava and Lora Paperno, and Pavel Palazchenko. My special thanks to Joseph Swain and other Colgate colleagues in all disciplines who encouraged me to talk about these songs at a Colgate Humanities Colloquium in October 1999. They were an ideal audience who helped me solve questions of presentation at a critical time in preparing this book.

Malcolm Hamrick Brown of Indiana University gave shape to this book at the outset. For his sage advice and unfailing encouragement, I am profoundly grateful to him.

I owe most of all to Joseph Miller, who originally showed me the need for a book of texts of Russian songs with parallel translations, and who gave invaluable practical advice at every stage, and to Vasily Petyarkin, who saw that such a project should begin with Tchaikovsky, and whose understanding of Russian songs has been a constant source of illumination. To these two friends who first imagined it, and who have stood by to inspire, instruct, criticize, and spur me on, this book is gratefully dedicated.

R. D. S.

Moscow – Hamilton, New York
January 2001

PREFACE

The purpose of this book is to bring together in one place the texts of all the songs written by Tchaikovsky. They have never been collected or examined as song lyrics, either in Russia or the West.

The texts are presented in their entirety, as they appear in each song, in the original Cyrillic. In addition, I have included a transcription of each text into the Latin alphabet, and, printed line by line alongside it, a translation into plain, unrhymed English. My translations are not "singing" versions, but they will allow a reader who does not know Russian to follow the words from start to finish as set by the composer to be sung. In most cases, it has been possible to locate the source text chosen by the composer for each song. Where the source differs from the lyrics of the song, departures have been pointed out in some detail, in order to bring the song into sharper relief as an independent work of art. Such rewordings are frequent in the case of Tchaikovsky, who sometimes tailored the text freely to achieve the musical effect he desired.

Historical and descriptive information—dates, names, other significant settings of the text, key signatures, voice range, and so on—is provided at the end of each song. Recordings of the song are also listed there, by the singer's last name. Where a singer's name appears in **bold letters**, a recording of the song by that singer can be heard on the CD that accompanies this book. Information about the singers and a list of their recordings are placed together in an appendix called Singers & Recordings.

The order of the songs and the consecutive numbering of them used here follow the 1940 academic edition of Tchaikovsky's songs which is the basis of the present compilation. These are volumes 44 and 45 of his *Polnoe sobranie sochinenii* [Complete Collected Works, abbreviated *PSS*], Moscow and Leningrad, 1940. Throughout the commentary, in lieu of footnotes, the names of works cited appear in *italics*, with page numbers as necessary. Information about these and other sources will be found in the Bibliography.

Ever since the pursuit of scientific study was divided into strict compartments at the universities—music, philology, history, and so on—inquiry into subjects which fall between these hard and fast divisions leads directly into uncharted territory. Such is the case with the subject undertaken here. Specialists in Russian literature (the field in which I received my training) may know that various poems by Pushkin or some other poet have been set to music by this or that composer, but rarely has it occurred to them that the musical setting of the poem could reveal anything about it as a poem. Usually, the opposite is true: a musical setting, if noticed at all, is seen as a mere footnote; or if there has been any tampering with the text, as a debasement, an opportunity to pounce on the composer, as Vladimir Nabokov pounces on

Tchaikovsky in his commentary to Pushkin's *Eugene Onegin*. Rarely has academic insularity been practiced with such zest. Of course, admonishments in a commentary written by the author of *Pale Fire* are not to be missed. But as opera criticism, they are really beside the point: *Onegin* remains one of the most satisfying of all 19th-century operas, performed more often today than ever before.

In the same way, for musicologists, the words under the notes on a vocal score are simply part of the score, and usually the least important part of it, though historians of music have been less narrow in this respect than historians of poetry, owing to the central importance of vocal music. But as a rule, Russian songs have been seen as peripheral to the study of poetry by the literary critics, and by musicologists as a minor genre in the work of composers whose importance in the history of music is seen to lie in their symphonies, operas, and other compositions more massive in scale than the song. Smaller, however, does not mean lesser, but only different, as Nicolas Slonimsky reminds us in his extended entry on Tchaikovsky in *Baker's Biographical Dictionary of Musicians*, 7th ed.: "... besides his stage works, symphs., chamber music, and piano compositions, he composed a great number of lyric songs *that are the most poignant creations of his genius*" (my italics).

I hope this collection of Tchaikovsky's song lyrics will provide a basis for further study of the songs as musical compositions. There is some good scattered commentary on them in Russian (*Al'shvang, Ovchinnikov, Vasina-Grossman*), in French (*Lischke*), and English (*Abraham, David Brown*), but they have not been fully understood. What is missing in English is informed commentary by a musicologist who knows Russian songs and actually *likes* them—all kinds of them, not just folk songs or the songs of "the Five." As I have tried to show in my commentaries, Tchaikovsky's romances need to be seen for what they are— highly original songs that largely come out of the Russian urban romance tradition and are aimed, like his operas, at a wide audience.

Singers and the public have always understood them best. I hope this book will encourage new singers to sing them, and lovers of music to listen to them. Since the advent of the compact disc, many of them have been freshly recorded by outstanding artists in Russia and beyond; some excellent historical recordings have been issued on compact disc as well. More accessible than ever, Tchaikovsky's songs only remain to be discovered, or rediscovered, by performers and public alike.

Transcriptions from Cyrillic

Except in the Bibliography, where authors and titles are transliterated according to the simplified Library of Congress system, Russian names are spelled in this book as we are used to seeing them, even if that entails some inconsistencies. For example, Tchaikovsky and Chekhov begin with the same Cyrillic letter, but I have retained the older spelling for Tchaikovsky's name because it is more familiar than "Chaikovsky." In cases of individual artists who adopted a non-standard spelling, I use that: Rachmaninoff (not Rakhmaninov), Chaliapin (not Shaliapin), Hvorostovsky (not Khvorostovsky).

Most of the troublesome details in transliterating from Cyrillic arise in connection with the sound "yot" (explained on page xiv). There is nothing new in my solution to these problems. First, the *endings* of Russian names. Both surnames and given names that end in "yot" are spelled with a -y: Tolstoy (not Tolstoi), Polonsky (not Polonskii), Afanasy (not Afanasii), Aleksey (not Aleksei), Nikolay (not Nikolai). Only in the case of a name like "Nikolay" might there be a doubt: Nikolay rhymes with "lie," not "lay," and "Migay" rhymes with "guy," not "gay." A related problem occurs *within* a surname, like that of the composer Taneev. To indicate how the name is pronounced, I spell it "Taneyev," not Taneev; similarly, Dostoyevsky (not Dostoevsky). Finally, I spell the letter "ë" the way it sounds, though I realize this is not standard linguistic practice: Fyodor (not Feodor or Fëdor), Pyotr (not Piotr or Pëtr). I beg the indulgence of colleagues who believe a reform of these conventions is long overdue, but for readers who are not specialists in these matters, these compromises are perhaps more helpful than consistency which looks strange.

Even a consistent *transliteration* system, however, like the Library of Congress system, does not reflect the way Russian words actually *sound*, given the phonetics of the Russian language. To follow the words of a song as sung on recordings or in performance, a reader who does not already know Russian needs a *transcription* of the words rather than a transliteration. For this book I have devised such a system. With each song, there is a transcription of the lyric in Latin letters, side by side with a translation into English. The purpose of these parallel texts is to enable readers who do not know Russian to follow the words, and what they mean, as they are being sung.

My transcriptions take the Library of Congress system as their starting point, but modify spelling to reflect the phonetics of the word as spoken (or rather, as sung: the differences are discussed in *Richter 1994*). My aim has been to limit the number of these modifications, and to keep them reasonably consistent. They are not an attempt to describe every nuance of pronunciation, but rather an attempt to show better than the LC system does what the words sound like. In my transcription, the composer's name would be spelled

"Chajkófskij," and the writer would be "Chékhaf." Unlike LC transliteration, these spellings show which syllable in the word is stressed (this is important in Russian), as well as the automatic changes that take place in voicing and devoicing of consonants, and in reduction of the vowel "o" to "a" when it is not stressed.

The reader does not have to understand anything about Russian phonetics to follow the transcription of a song. The use of English letters to represent Russian sounds has obvious drawbacks, but on the other hand, learning a set of phonetic symbols would take as much time as learning the Cyrillic alphabet (a few hours) and would be another barrier to the general reader. The system used here is designed to be immediately comprehensible. Nevertheless, it will look strange at first. What follows is a brief look at the details with examples.

First, and most important, the sound "j" (called "yot" from Greek "iota"). It is exceedingly common in Russian. It can come at the beginning, middle, or end of a word, but Russian does not have a single letter to spell it, hence all the problems encountered above with regard to spelling Russian names (the problem is addressed differently in the transcriptions than in the body of the text). It represents the sound "y" in "you," "bayou," or "boy." In my transcriptions, I spell this sound with the letter "j" (an argument has been made for modifying the LC system by using "j" in this way, and I adopt that solution here: see *Edgerton*). Lest there be any doubt, the reader should interpret the letter "j" in transcriptions of songs in this book as sounding like the German "Johann," never like French Jean, Spanish Juan, or English John.

I retain the LC convention of an apostrophe for the "soft sign" used in Russian spelling. The reader is not expected to react to this apostrophe in any way, but should understand that its use has nothing to do with the meaning of an apostrophe in English. It can be ignored, unless the reader decides to learn some Russian, at which point its meaning will become clear in the first lesson.

In cases where spelling and speaking are at variance, I transcribe the sound rather than the spelling for obvious reasons. There are few such inconsistencies in Russian, but they occur in some very common words and endings.

I have kept the LC convention of using "y" to stand for the tense Russian vowel that is a variant of "i" as in "Bill" or "sit," only deeper. To master this sound, one needs to work with a Russian speaker. For an amusing illustration of the facial contortions required to pronounce this vowel in stentorian voice from the rostrum of the Hall of Columns in Moscow, see the photograph of Nicolas Slonimsky in his autobiography *Perfect Pitch* (*Slonimsky 1988*, plate 29).

The vowel system is very easy. The vowels are a, e, i, o, u, plus the deeper variant of "i" just mentioned. Every vowel is a syllable, and every syllable has one vowel in it. Russian words are stressed on one of the syllables only. When a, e, and o are not in the stressed syllable, they are "reduced" in spoken Russian, but in singing the only reduction that occurs is "o" to "a".

a	as in "Mahler"
e	as in "bell"
i	as in "beet"
y	as in "Bill"
o	as in "coat" but deepened toward "call" (as in "kot"= "tomcat")
u	as in "flute"

Consonants are transcribed as in the LC system except for "j". My transcriptions do not show the difference between plain and palatalized consonants, but it is not necessary to understand the distinction in order to follow a song.

b	as in "boy"
d	as in "dill"
f	as in "father"
g	as in "Gogol"
j	as in "Johann"
k	as in "kaftan" (but without any breath of air)
l	as in "bull"
m	as in "Moscow"
n	as in "noble"
p	as in "Paul" (no breath of air)
r	trilled once, as in Italian "Roma"
s	as in "soul"
t	as in "Tomsk" (no breath of air)
v	as in "Volga"
z	as in "Zachary"

Some Russian consonants require two or more letters in transcription:

ch	as in "China"
kh	as in "Bach" or Scottish "loch"
sh	as in "shoot"
shch	as in "fresh chips"
ts	as in "bats" or "pizza"
zh	as in "azure" or French "Jean"

Some examples of Russian names follow in the table below:

1) The "LC" column shows Library of Congress transliteration, used in the BIBLIOGRAPHY of this book.

2) The "Traditional" column shows the spelling used in the commentary throughout the book.

3) The "Song Text" column shows the transcription used for each song text in the book, devised to approximate the way the words actually sound.

Cyrillic	LC	Traditional	Song Text
Петербург	Peterburg	Petersburg	Peterbúrk
Киев	Kiev	Kiev	Kíjef
Новгород	Novgorod	Novgorod	Nóvgarat
Толстой	Tolstoi	Tolstoy	Talstój
Достоевский	Dostoevskii	Dostoyevsky	Dastajéfskij
Танеев	Taneev	Taneyev	Tanéjef
Невский	Nevskii	Nevsky	Néfskij
Хомяков	Khomiakov	Khomyakov	Khamjakóf
Тютчев	Tiutchev	Tyutchev	Tjútchef
Сергей	Sergei	Sergey	Sergéj
Николай	Nikolai	Nikolay	Nikaláj
Елизавета	Elizaveta	Yelizaveta	Jelizavéta
Татьяна	Tat'iana	Tatyana	Tat'jána
Федор (Фёдор)	Fedor	Fyodor	Fjódar

Readers who want to sing these songs will, I hope, understand that these transcriptions do not teach the pronunciation; but a course in Russian, even a short one, will.

I had the privilege of spending some time with Jessye Norman when she came to Colgate University to receive an honorary degree in 1996. I asked her if she ever planned to sing any of Tchaikovsky's songs in Russian. She answered "Yes! There are some I want to sing. But first I have to brush up on my Russian conversation. I never sing a language I don't converse in!" She illustrated this with a story about reviewing her Hungarian conversation before recording Bartok's *Bluebeard's Castle*. Her point was not the need for total fluency, but the need in performance to be totally at home in the sounds and intonations unique to the language.

The best thing that singers can do to prepare to sing Tchaikovsky's songs is to take a Russian class, or get a Russian coach, and above all, like Jessye Norman, learn some Russian conversation.

Tchaikovsky's
Complete Songs

1 *Мой гений, мой ангел, мой друг*
My genius, my angel, my friend

This song is the earliest composition by Tchaikovsky performed today. In its modest way, it already shows some of the qualities of the mature composer's art: a lovely melody and laconic means, used to achieve a musical end that is completely convincing in its sincerity.

In the case of a very early work like this one, questions of origin and intention loom especially large and threaten to overwhelm the work itself, so that even if it has any merit, that is hardly the main point. Such has been the fate of this song. A copy of it in Tchaikovsky's hand is his earliest known manuscript still extant. Discussion has centered on the meaning of the word "Dedicated" followed by a row of dots that stop at the edge of the paper (this page is reproduced in *PSS*, vol. 44). Who, if anyone, is meant by this is not known, but the dots have been counted and matched to a name (*Poznansky 1991*, 48), and an effort has been made to rule some possibilities out (*Vaidman 1988*, 46-7). The composer's younger brother, Modest Tchaikovsky, who was not even ten years old when the song was written but who is ultimately the source of the view that the dedication (or non-dedication) has a bearing on how the song is to be understood, gave two different dates for its composition, and dismissed it as "a mere empty amateur effusion."

This is a song that has succeeded thanks to the singers, who are the only ones to have taken it seriously as a song since its publication in 1940. The text is a poem by Afanasy Fet from a cycle called "To Ophelia." What becomes clear in performance is that its subject is a close relationship between the poet and a kind of muse figure, a guardian angel you can talk to, whose invisible presence brings inspiration and essential companionship to heart, mind, and soul: there is an implied conversation going on. This is a theme that occupied Tchaikovsky throughout his life.

His text is identical to Fet's original poem, but he chose to repeat the last line of the poem at the end of the song, breaking it up into three exclamations, one for "genius," one for "angel," and a final one for "friend," this last word elaborated into a melisma of tender adoration. It is quite fitting that this shy song to an adored and idealized friend who brings inspiration has turned out to be the one that stands at the beginning of Tchaikovsky's book of songs.

> Не здесь ли ты лёгкою тенью,
> Мой гений, мой ангел, мой друг,
> Беседуешь тихо со мною
> И тихо летаешь вокруг?

И робким даришь вдохновеньем,
И сладкий врачуешь недуг,
И тихим даришь сновиденьем,
Мой гений, мой ангел, мой друг...
Мой гений! Мой ангел! Мой друг!

Ne zdés' li ty ljókhkaju tén'ju,	You're here, aren't you, light spirit,
Moj génij, moj ángel, moj drúk,	My genius, my angel, my friend,
Besédujesh tíkha sa mnóju	Whispering to me in conversation
I tíkha letájesh vakrúk?	As you quietly circle in flight?
I rópkim darísh vdakhnavén'jem,	You favor me with shy inspiration,
I slátkij vrachújesh nedúk,	Your powers heal my sweet affliction,
I tíkhim darísh snavidén'jem,	You grant a quiet dream to my imagination,
Moj génij, moj ángel, moj drúk...	My genius, my angel, my friend...
Moj génij! Moj ángel! Moj drúk!	My genius! My angel! My friend!

TEXT. **Afanásy Fet**, 1842. Untitled, the first of four poems in a cycle called "To Ophelia." First set by Tchaikovsky; later by several minor composers.
METER. Ternary. Amphibrach, 3-foot:
> *You're here with me, are you, light spirit,*
> *My genius, my angel, my friend...*

MUSIC. Date unknown: probably 1857 or 1858. Without opus number. C Minor. 3/4, Larghetto. For Low Voice: g–e^2 flat. Published 1940 in *PSS*, Vol. 44 (also in *Sovetskaia muzyka*, 1940, No. 5/6). Listed in *Ivanov* (Part I, 367) as published by Leibrok in St. Petersburg, with a censor date of 1860, but this is probably erroneous: no copy of it has been found.

RECORDINGS. Borodina, Descamps, Fischer-Dieskau, Hvorostovsky, Isakova, Krasnaya, Leiferkus, Maksakova, Söderström, Tear.

2 *Песнь Земфиры*
Zemfira's Song

The text of this song is from Alexander Pushkin's narrative poem Цыганы (*The Gypsies*). Pushkin heard gypsies sing Zemfira's song when he was in Kishinyov. He had the music written down and published it with his Russian translation of the original Moldavian song in 1825. The song immediately became popular. There are many different settings of it before and after Tchaikovsky's, of which an 1832 version by Verstovsky (who edited the music for Pushkin's publication) was especially popular and is still sung today. Several operas have been written to Pushkin's poem, beginning with Mikhail Vielgorsky (1838, unfinished), Leoncavallo (*Gli zingari*, 1912) and, most famously, by Rachmaninoff (*Aleko*, 1892).

Pushkin's brilliant narrative poem, with its harsh corrective to easy romantic assumptions, has some sections written in dramatic form, as here in the song. Aleko, in Byronic flight from civilization, has taken Zemfira as his lover and joined her gypsy caravan with a trained bear in tow. Zemfira has grown tired of him and taken a young gypsy lover. Her defiance of his knife is prophetic: he later finds her with her lover and stabs them to death. He is banished from the camp by the old gypsy, her father. In the song, Aleko's first two lines (spoken, not sung) are taken from an earlier scene in the poem.

Tchaikovsky wrote the song for some kind of performance, probably for students at the Moscow Conservatory. This may explain the spoken lines from Pushkin's poem written into the score (these are shown below in italics); perhaps too it accounts for the exclusion of a stanza of the song, and the change of one word, нож (knife), into меч (sword). The best recordings are the ones that include these spoken lines: Elisabeth Söderström, with her accompanist Vladimir Ashkenazy as Aleko, and Nina Rautio, with Sergei Leiferkus. This latter version gets rid of the sword and restores Pushkin's knife.

Алеко
Или под сенью дымной кущи
Цыгана дикого рассказ?

Старый муж, грозный муж, режь меня,
Старый муж, грозный муж, жги меня:
Я тверда, не боюсь
Ни огня, ни меча.
Режь меня, жги меня.

Ненавижу тебя,
Презираю тебя;
Я другого люблю,
Умираю любя.

Алеко
Молчи. Мне пенье надоело,
Я диких песен не люблю.

Земфира
Не любишь? мне какое дело.
Я песню для себя пою.

Старый муж, грозный муж, режь меня,
Старый муж, грозный муж, жги меня:
Я тверда, не боюсь
Ни огня, ни меча.
Режь меня, жги меня.

Он свежее весны,
Жарче летнего дня;
Как он молод и смел!
Как он любит меня!

Алеко
Молчи, Земфира, я доволен…

Земфира
Так понял песню ты мою?

Алеко
Земфира!

Земфира
Ты сердиться волен,
Я песню про тебя пою.

Старый муж, грозный муж, режь меня,
Старый муж, грозный муж, жги меня:
Я тверда, не боюсь
Ни огня, ни меча.
Режь меня, жги меня!

ALÉKO
Ili pat sén'ju dýmnaj kúshchi
Tsygána díkava rasskás?

ALEKO [pondering the nature of fame,
after listening to Zemfira's father tell the
legend of Ovid's exile among them]—
Or is it a tale told by a wild gypsy
Under a smoky tent?

Stáryj músh, gróznyj músh, résh menjá,
Stáryj músh, gróznyj músh, zhgí menjá:
Ja tverdá, ne bojús'
Ni agnjá, ni mechá.
Résh menjá, zhgí menjá.

Old husband, cruel husband, stab me,
Old husband, cruel husband, burn me:
I am firm, I don't fear
Either fire or sword.
Stab me, burn me.

Nenavízhu tebjá,
Preziráju tebjá;
Ja drugóva ljubljú,
Umiráju ljubjá.

I detest you,
I despise you;
I love another,
I die loving.

ALÉKO
Malchí. Mne pén'je nadajéla,
Ja díkikh pésen ne ljubljú.

ALEKO
Be quiet. I'm tired of your singing,
I don't like wild songs.

ZEMFÍRA
Ne ljúbish? mné kakóje déla.
Ja pésnju dlja sebjá pajú.

ZEMFIRA
You don't? why should I care.
This song is for myself.

Stáryj músh, gróznyj músh, résh menjá,
Stáryj músh, gróznyj músh, zhgí menjá:
Ja tverdá, ne bojús'
Ni agnjá, ni mechá.
Résh menjá, zhgí menjá.

Old husband, cruel husband, stab me,
Old husband, cruel husband, burn me:
I am firm, I don't fear
Either fire or sword.
Stab me, burn me.

On svezhéje vesný,
Zhárche létneva dnjá;
Kak on mólat i smél!
Kak on ljúbit menjá!

He's fresher than spring,
Hotter than a summer day;
How young and bold he is!
How he loves me!

ALÉKO
Malchí, Zemfíra, ja davólen...

ALEKO
Be quiet, Zemfira, I've had enough...

ZEMFÍRA
Tak pónjal pésnju ty majú?

ZEMFIRA
So you understand my song?

ALÉKO
Zemfíra!

ALEKO
Zemfira!

Zemfíra	Zemfira
Ty serdítsa vólen,	*Be angry if you like,*
Ja pésnju pra tebjá pajú.	*This song is about you.*

Stáryj músh, gróznyj músh, résh menjá,	Old husband, cruel husband, stab me,
Stáryj músh, gróznyj músh, zhgí menjá:	Old husband, cruel husband, burn me:
Ja tverdá, ne bojús'	I am firm, I don't fear
Ni agnjá, ni mechá.	Either fire or sword.
Résh menjá, zhgí menjá!	Stab me, burn me!

TEXT. **Aleksándr Púshkin**, from Цыганы (*The Gypsies*), 1824. First set by Mikhail Vielgorsky in 1825; by Aleksey Verstovsky in 1832. Other settings by Aliabiev (1860), Gurilyov (1849), Anton Rubinstein (1868, in German), and Pauline Viardot (1882).

METER. Ternary. Anapest, 2-foot:

> *He's as fresh as the spring,*
> *He's as hot as July,*
> *He's so young, he's so bold!*

The longer 3-foot lines at the beginning of the song are slight rearrangements of Pushkin's original. The spoken lines (shown in italics) are iambic tetrameter.

MUSIC. Date unknown: formerly thought to be late 1850s or early 1860s, but since revised to a date soon after Tchaikovsky came to the Moscow Conservatory in 1866. Without opus number. A Minor. 4/4, Allegro non tanto. For Middle or High Voice: e^1–a^2.

Published 1940 in *PSS*, vol. 44 (also in *Sovetskaia muzyka*, 1940, No. 5/6). Since the 1940 publication, which was based on a copy by another hand, an autograph manuscript has been found: *Vaidman 1988*, 36-38, discusses the differences and includes a photograph of the manuscript.

RECORDINGS. Dolukhanova, Kazarnovskaya, Krasnaya, Milashkina, Podleś, Rautio, Söderström.

Vielgorsky: Gerasimova.

Verstovsky: Borisenko, Obraztsova, Obukhova, Preobrazhenskaya, Sharubina.

❦

3 *Mezza notte*
Midnight

When Tchaikovsky was in New York as principal guest conductor for the opening of Carnegie Hall in 1891, he told the *New York Herald* in an interview: "I was seventeen years of age when I made the acquaintance of my singing master, Piccioli, and his influence over me was enormous. Up to this day I hear the melodies of Bellini with tears in my eyes" (*Yoffe*, 54). It is possible that Piccioli gave Tchaikovsky this text, and encouraged him to write the song. It is his first published composition.

This period of Italian mania recalls Glinka's early career. When Glinka was taking lessons in composition in 1828 from a man named Zamboni in St. Petersburg—the son of the famous buffo Luigi Zamboni, who sang the first Figaro in Rossini's *Barber of Seville*—his teacher gave him some anonymous Italian texts as song assignments. Half a century later, when Tchaikovsky was in Venice in 1877, his publisher Jurgenson asked him to translate these songs for an edition of Glinka's unpublished works. Since that time, more of Glinka's Italian songs have been discovered, but the four singing translations into Russian done by Tchaikovsky in Venice are still used today (*Glinka*, 334).

The text below is a slightly emended version of the copy in *PSS*, which contains some minor anomalies.

Poco è l'ora omai lontana,	Soon it will be time,
Palpitando il cor l'aspetta,	My beating heart awaits her,
Già rimbomba la campana...	The booming bell already tolls...
E tu dormi, o mia diletta?	Are you sleeping, oh my beloved?
Ti fuggì forse dal cor:	You can't escape your heart:
Mezza notte è il nostro amor,	Midnight is our love,
Notte è il nostro amor.	Night is our love.
Pari a nota di liuto	Like a note made by a lute
Nel silenzio di quest'ora	In the silence of this hour
Odo il timido saluto	I hear the shy greeting
Di colei che m'innamora	Of my inamorata
E ripeto a quel tenor:	And on the same note repeat:
Mezza notte è il nostro amor,	Midnight is our love,
Notte è il nostro amor.	Night is our love.

Amor misero e verace	Love that's poor and true
Delle tenebre si giova,	Takes advantage of the dark,
Tace il mondo ed ei non tace,	The world is still, but love's not still,
Ma il suo gemito rinnova	It renews its moan unceasingly
Fin che spunta il primo albor:	Till the first light of dawn:
Mezza notte è il nostro amor,	Midnight is our love,
Notte è il nostro amor.	Night is our love.

TEXT. Authorship unknown.

MUSIC. Date unknown: early 1860s. Without opus number. G Major. 6/8, Leggiero. For Soprano or Tenor: c^1 sharp–a^2.

First published in Leibrok's "Musée Musical" series in St. Petersburg; no date. The title page reads: "Mezza Notte. Romance pour soprano ou ténor avec accompagnement de piano composée par Tschaykowsky."

The song is Tchaikovsky's first published composition. It was discovered in 1926 in the Jurgenson archive. Published in 1940 in *PSS*, vol. 44.

RECORDINGS. Dolukhanova, Kazarnovskaya, Krasnaya, Larin, Milashkina, Söderström.

⤜⤛

6 Romances, Opus 6 (1869)

In January 1866, after receiving his diploma from the St. Petersburg Conservatory, Tchaikovsky, in his mid-twenties and sure at last that he wanted to devote his life to music ("music is the only road for me," *DG*, 36), left for Moscow where he was to take a position as a teacher of music theory. He was hired by the brother of Anton Rubinstein, founder of the first Russian conservatory in St. Petersburg, where in 1862 Tchaikovsky had enrolled as a member of its first class. Now Nikolay Rubinstein was organizing a similar institute in Moscow. When the Moscow Conservatory opened in September 1866, Tchaikovsky was on the faculty as a professor of harmony and composition. He taught there and took part in all its activities for the next twelve years.

Like everyone who worked professionally with him, Nikolay Rubinstein took a liking to Tchaikovsky right away. He even invited him to live (for free) in his apartment, a place which was never dull, owing to a steady flow of students, musicians, writers, and other visitors passing through. Rubinstein was director of the Moscow branch of the Russian Musical Society and knew everyone in the artistic and literary world. He was dynamic, sometimes tyrannical, both as director of the conservatory from its founding right up to his death in 1881, and as a virtuoso pianist who could thrill an audience or terrify the faint of heart among his pupils. Only six years older than Tchaikovsky, he treated him like a younger kinsman, with equal doses of rousing support and ruthless criticism.

Leaving Petersburg was hard for Tchaikovsky at first, but he grew to like Moscow for its theatrical life and its warmer, more relaxed style. He met people who would be important to him the rest of his life, singers like Elizabeth Lavrovskaya, writers like the dramatist Alexander Ostrovsky, with whom he collaborated on the libretto for his first opera, and poets like Aleksey Pleshcheyev, who wrote more of the lyrics he used in his songs than anyone else. Among all these new friends and colleagues, the most important, after Rubinstein, was Peter Jurgenson, his publisher.

The early Moscow period from 1866 to the end of 1869 culminates in the romances of Opus 6. During this period Tchaikovsky established those patterns of work to which he held throughout his life. Unlike his two greatly gifted contemporaries in St. Petersburg, Borodin and Musorgsky, he devoted himself entirely to music, and generally did not rest until he had seen a composition through to completion. This is the period of his first symphony ("Winter Dreams," Op. 13), and some early piano pieces, including the fascinating Romance in F minor—a work which begins hauntingly rather like a slow, sad tango and then turns into a swaggering Spanish dance—Opus 5, which he dedicated to Désirée Artôt, a singer from Paris, a "goddess of opera" with whom he became infatuated in 1868 when she was singing in Moscow. From the very beginning he was determined to write for the theater. During this period he composed two operas, *Voyevoda* (*The Governor*) and *Undine*, and undertook plans for two others. But even though the former was put on at the Bolshoy Theater, he was not satisfied with it, nor with *Undine*, which was turned down. He decided to destroy them, though fragments of both survive and some of the music found its way into later works like *Swan Lake*.

Of everything he wrote during this period, the one clear success was the overture-fantasy "Romeo and Juliet," suggested to him by Mily Balakirev, leader of the "national" school in St. Petersburg, otherwise known as "the mighty handful," the "moguchaya kuchka," as their spokesman the critic Stasov called them, or the "Five," comprised as they were of Borodin, Musorgsky, Cui, Rimsky-Korsakov, and Balakirev. Tchaikovsky was drawn to Balakirev's fine knowledge of native Russian folk songs and, following his example, he did his own harmonization of fifty Russian folk songs in 1869. He wanted to be liked by them; perhaps especially he wanted to win the approval of Balakirev. But Balakirev was hostile to the Rubinsteins, scornful of the conservatories, intolerant even of Russian urban popular music as opposed to real peasant folk music, and would have liked to win Tchaikovsky away from these influences altogether. Tchaikovsky went more than halfway to meet the "Five" on their own terms, but in the end he was too original and had too much of his own music in him to be constrained and dictated to by the narrow, unyielding genius of Balakirev, the pedantry of Cui, or the doctrinaire pronouncements of Stasov. He was Russian through and through and he understood better than most what they all owed to Glinka, but to him this did not mean that he had to turn his back on Mozart or Schumann or anyone else.

When he finished "Romeo and Juliet" to Balakirev's satisfaction (it would later have to be revised, however), he immediately sat down to write some songs for his own satisfaction. These six songs, written in one week, between 23-30 November 1869, evidently did satisfy him completely (which was rare). In the romances of Opus 6, his talent as a song writer suddenly appears fully realized. It is not a cycle, but a set of different songs, to lyrics that have the freshness of appearing in a song for the first time. His characteristic approach to the text is already present—an attempt to use words "musically," not hesitating to adjust them in small ways if need be for his purposes, repeating words or phrases when the music calls for it. To let the music "finish saying" what the words suggest, he always preferred a good poet to a great one, seeking lyrics that for him could be the means to a musical end.

Early in 1870 Jurgenson published Opus 6 in a handsome edition. It was reprinted many times during Tchaikovsky's lifetime.

4   *Не верь, мой друг*
    Don't believe, my love

Op. 6, No. 1

There could be no better choice of a "good" Russian poet than Aleksey
Tolstoy (1817-1875), cousin of the novelist. Eleven of Tchaikovsky's romances
would be to texts by Tolstoy, including some of his best songs to come. He
liked Tolstoy's poetry for its "musicality"; it is not surprising that he chose one
of his poems as the lyric for the first song in Opus 6.

Having made that choice, he then proceeded to arrange the text for the
purposes of making it into the song he imagined musically. Here is the Tolstoy
poem Tchaikovsky took as his source:

> Не верь мне, друг, когда, в избытке горя,
> Я говорю, что разлюбил тебя, —
> В отлива час не верь измене моря,
> Оно к земле воротится, любя.
>
> Уж я тоскую, прежней страсти полный,
> Мою свободу вновь тебе отдам —
> И уж бегут с обратным шумом волны
> Издалека к любимым берегам.

> Don't believe me, love, when in fullness of grief
> I say I do not love you any more, —
> Don't believe the ebbing sea's inconstancy:
> It will return to land, loving as before.

> Full of passion, I long for you again,
> Again I'm ready to surrender to you —
> And rushing back the loud waves run
> From far away to their beloved shore.

As a text on the page, Tolstoy's poem works very well, with its tension
between what is being talked about (romantic love, the ebb and flow of passion)
and the reasoned, self-possessed way in which the argument is delivered—"consider the tides: there is your answer to why I am sometimes cool and distant, yet
bound to surrender to you again, to love you with all my former passion."

But Tchaikovsky's ends and means are different. Reasoning is not a part of
it, but rather the logic of feelings. This is a love song, but an unusual one,
proceeding as it does from sadness in the face of limits—limits that are painful
but as inevitable as a force of nature. To bring this out, Tchaikovsky repeats
several times the phrase "don't believe," and ends the song with a reprise of

the entire first stanza. Tolstoy's two-part poem becomes a three-part song, the basic emotion being one of tender pleading in the face of a truth that is painful, an emotion quite different from that of the original poem. By the end of Tolstoy's poem, we have forgotten about the "fullness of grief" which was its starting point. In Tchaikovsky's song, however, that note is there at the outset, sustained throughout the first section, and returned to in the third, concluding section of the song. Passion—the incoming tide—is expressed dramatically in the second, middle section of the song, in a crescendo that culminates in the loud piano chords that express, quite unmistakably, the crash of waves that have reached the shore. Here the song returns to where it started. By doing so, the song becomes a musical expression of the idea that the tide goes out, comes back, goes out again, and promises to return. In this there is a consolation essentially different from that in the text Tchaikovsky took as his source.

He made four minor changes in the text, aimed either at bringing it closer into line with everyday speech or making it easier to sing phonetically. The most telling of these are in the first line. In place of Tolstoy's "don't believe me, love," Tchaikovsky has "don't believe, my love," a miniscule change with an ounce less egotism in an already self-centered text. He substitutes в порыве горя (f parýve górja, in a fit of grief), for Tolstoy's в избытке горя (v yzbýtke górja, in fullness of grief), a more literary phrase. This change of wording is also easier on the ear, with softer labials that minimize the tense vowel "y". The slight rearrangement of words in line 7 is an improvement, too, for Tchaikovsky's purposes, less rhetorical, more natural.

A note on the word друг in the title ("drug" in transliteration, "druk" in transcription). The phrase мой друг, which I have translated here as "my love," can also be translated "my friend," as it was in Song 1. In Russian, nearly every noun denoting a human being is marked male or female, but this word is universal in its gender. It is used to address one's nearest and dearest of either sex, whether lover, family member, or close friend. It has a strong resonance in Tchaikovsky's songs, where it occurs frequently from his first song to his last.

> Не верь, мой друг, не верь, когда в порыве горя,
> Я говорю, что разлюбил тебя, —
> В отлива час не верь, не верь измене моря,
> Оно к земле воротится, любя.
>
> Уж я тоскую, прежней страсти полный,
> Свою свободу вновь тебе отдам —
> И уж бегут обратно с шумом волны
> Издалека к любимым берегам.
>
> Не верь, мой друг, не верь,

не верь, мой друг, не верь, когда в порыве горя
Я говорю, что разлюбил тебя —
В отлива час не верь, не верь измене моря,
Оно к земле воротится, любя.

Ne vér', moj drúk, ne vér',	Don't believe, my love, don't believe,
kagdá f parýve górja,	when, in a fit of grief,
Ja gavarjú, shto razljubíl tebjá, —	I say I do not love you any more, —
V atlíva chás ne vér', ne vér'	Don't believe, don't believe the ebbing
izméne mórja,	sea's inconstancy,
Anó g zemlé varótitsa, ljubjá.	It will return to land, loving as before.
Ush ja taskúju, prézhnej strásti pólnyj,	Full of passion, I long for you again,
Svajú svabódu vnof' tebé addám —	Again I'm ready to surrender to you —
I uzh begút abrátna s shúmam vólny	And rushing back the loud waves run
Izdaleká k ljubímym beregám.	From far away to their beloved shore.
Ne vér', moj drúk, ne vér',	Don't believe, my love, don't believe,
ne vér', moj drúk, ne vér',	don't believe, my love, don't believe,
kagdá f parýve górja,	when, in a fit of grief,
Ja gavarjú, shto razljubíl tebjá, —	I say I do not love you any more, —
V atlíva chás ne vér', ne vér'	Don't believe, don't believe the ebbing
izméne mórja,	sea's inconstancy,
Anó g zemlé varótitsa, ljubjá.	It will return to land, loving as before.

TEXT. **Alekséy Tolstóy**, 1856. Untitled. First set by Tchaikovsky; later by over twenty other composers, including Rachmaninoff (Op. 14/7, 1896) and Rimsky-Korsakov (Op. 46/4, 1897).

METER. Binary. Iambic, 5-foot:
> *And rushing back the waves come crashing loudly*
> *From far away to their beloved shore.*

MUSIC. 1869. Op. 6, no. 1. C-sharp Minor. 4/4, Moderato assai. For High Voice: c¹ sharp–f² sharp. Dedicated to **Aleksándra Ménshikova** (1840-1902), a soprano at the Bolshoy in Moscow from 1866-69, then at the Mariinsky in St. Petersburg from 1869-1880. A good actress, with an expressive coloratura; Cui compared her to the famous Adelina Patti (*Pruzhansky*, 325).

RECORDINGS. Borodina, Descamps, Krasnaya, Kruglikova, Kudriavtseva, Leiferkus, Milashkina, Mkrtchyan, Petina, Price, Rodgers, Rozhdestvenskaya, Söderström, Tear, Tyler, Varady, Vishnevskaya, Zimmermann.

Rachmaninoff: Söderström.

Rimsky-Korsakov: Martynov.

5 *Ни слова, о друг мой*
Not a word, my friend

Op. 6, No. 2

The idea of irrevocable loss—in this case "days of bright happiness," once present, now gone forever—is one of the most common themes in Russian songs. Variations on it are found in several of Tchaikovsky's romances. Here he expresses it with singular force, as laconically and eloquently as possible, free of soul-wrenching "gypsy" emotionality the theme sometimes brings with it.

The imagery used here goes back to Thomas Gray's *Elegy Written in a Country Church-yard* (1750), a poem widely known in Russia after Zhukovsky translated it in 1801. That marked the beginning not only of Zhukovsky's career, but of the whole "golden age" that reached its high point in Pushkin's poetry and Glinka's music. The philosopher and poet Vladimir Solovyov traced back to Zhukovsky's famous translation the beginning of what he called "truly human poetry" in Russia (*Solov'ëv*, 156)—that is, poetry about ordinary people rather than about God, the Cosmos, Russia, and the Tsar.

This text by Moritz Hartmann in Aleksey Pleshcheyev's translation is appealing precisely because it is an example of "human poetry." Hartmann revisits the elegy, but with epigrammatic force. He restates its meaning in purely individual terms, scaling everything down, from the stage-set of gravestones and trees—Gray's elegy is about a whole village—to one gravestone and one tree, one man and one woman, one "друг" and another, two friends together (on this word, see the previous song). Where Gray looked on a grave with its inscription of "uncouth rhymes" that "implore the passing tribute of a sigh," Hartmann rules out the expected sigh—"not a word, not a sigh"—in favor of the stark truth itself, read on the face of one friend by another, who knows better than anyone how to read what is written there.

It is a challenging text to set to music, but it has a dramatic immediacy which Tchaikovsky would have found appealing. The declamatory beginning delays the moment when the full melody is stated and the voice can give expression at last to sorrowful cantilena. At the end of the first line of text, the stressed "o" in the word вздоха (vzdókha, sigh) is elongated by being sung over three different notes, a mournful melisma which drove Tchaikovsky's fiercest critic César Cui to pronounce this a blatant infraction of the rules of declamation. But it sets the word in maximum relief, in a way that recalls the melismatic style of Russian folk laments (*Malcolm Brown 1983*, 62, and *Taruskin 1993*, 38). The middle section of the song, which is the second stanza, moves stepwise up the scale for the first two lines. At this point (marked *forte* for both voice and piano) the melody is articulated fully as the voice sings the climactic lines of the text "there were days of bright happiness and this happiness is no more." Then the voice moves lower and repeats the last phrase softly. We recognize this climactic section as the melody heard at the outset in the piano introduction, reinforcing the satisfying sense of musical shape Tchaikovsky gives to the song.

He discarded the title and changed one word in the text: in line 6, instead of "I read in your tired *gaze*," he preferred "in your tired *heart*." He makes the two-part poem into a three-part song, thereby gaining something essential to his conception of how this lyric should be rendered musically. The poem itself builds up to the statement of total loss, and ends there; we are left to contemplate the awful meaning of the word "silence" in the title. But the song returns to the hushed reverence of the beginning, ending in sorrowful stasis with the image of the willows bending low. This is an entirely different resolution, a note not of stark regret but of compassion. The agnosticism of the German original is completely missing in the Tchaikovsky song, with its feeling of Orthodox spirituality in the way the song ends. The epithet грустные (sad) and the gesture expressed in the verb склоняются (bending down) suggest characteristic Russian images of compassion in icons by masters like Andrey Rublyov and Theophanes the Greek—images that express an all-forgiving tenderness.

Ни слова, о друг мой, ни вздоха...
Мы будем с тобой молчаливы...
Ведь молча над камнем, над камнем могильным
Склоняются грустные ивы...

И только, склонившись, читают,
Как я, в твоём сердце усталом,
Что были дни ясного счастья,
Что этого счастья — не стало!
Что этого счастья — не стало!

Ни слова, о друг мой, ни вздоха...
Мы будем с тобой молчаливы...
Ведь молча над камнем, над камнем могильным
Склоняются грустные ивы...
Склоняются грустные ивы.

Ni slóva, o drúk moj, ni vzdókha...	Not a word, my friend, not a sigh...
My búdem s tabój malchalívy...	Let us be silent together...
Vet' mólcha nat kámnem,	As in silence over the stone,
nat kámnem magíl'nym	over the stone of the grave,
Sklanjájutsa grúsnyje ívy...	The sad willows bend low...
I tól'ka, sklanífshis', chitájut,	And thus bent low, they read,

Kak já, f tvajom sérttse ustálam,	As I read in your tired heart,
Shto býli dni jásnava shchást'ja,	That once there were days of bright happiness,
Shto ètava shchást'ja ne stála!	And that happiness has gone forever!
Shto ètava shchást'ja ne stála!	And that happiness has gone forever!

Ni slóva, o drúk moj, ni vzdókha...	Not a word, my friend, not a sigh...
My búdem s tabój malchalívy...	Let us be silent together...
Vet' mólcha nat kámnem,	As in silence over the stone,
nat kámnem magíl'nym	over the stone of the grave,
Sklanjájutsa grúsnyje ívy...	The sad willows bend low...
Sklanjájutsa grúsnyje ívy...	The sad willows bend low...

TEXT. **Aleksѐy Pleshchѐyev**, 1861. Title: Молчание (Silence); a translation of "Schweigen" by the Viennese poet **Moritz Hartmann** (1821-1872). First set by Tchaikovsky; later by several other composers, including Cui (Op. 11/1, 1877).

METER. Ternary. Amphibrach, 3-foot:
As willows bend over the gravestone,
So let us be silent together...

MUSIC. 1869. Op. 6, no. 2. E Minor. 9/8, Andante ma non troppo. For High Voice: d^1–g^2. An arrangement of the song for low voice and orchestra was written by Sergey Taneyev in the 1890s (pub. 1957: *MN*, 434). Dedicated to Tchaikovsky's friend and colleague **Nikoláy Kashkín** (1839-1920), who taught piano and music theory and history at the Moscow Conservatory. Author of an important but controversial memoir about Tchaikovsky (in *Proshloe russkoi muzyki*; partial English translation in *Poznansky 1999*).

RECORDINGS. Borodina, DeGaetani, Dolukhanova, Estes, Ghiaurov, Hvorostovsky, Kasrashvili, Krasnaya, Kruglikova, Kurenko, Kuuzik, Larin, Leiferkus, Levko, Lisovsky, Martynov, Mkrtchyan, **Obukhova**, Reizen, Rodgers, Rosing, Serkebayev, Slobodskaya, Vedernikov, Vishnevskaya.

Pleshcheyev's Source Text

Schweigen

Kein Wort und keinen Hauch —	Sie neigen sich und lesen,
Wir wollen schweigen.	Wie ich auf deinen Wangen:
Die Trauerweiden, die sich neigen	Es ist ein Glück gewesen
Auf Leichensteine, schweigen auch.	Und ist vorbeigegangen.

(*Hartmann*, 113)

6

И больно, и сладко
It's painful, it's sweet

Op. 6, No. 3

Tchaikovsky's favorite composer was Mozart. It was a passion that began in his early childhood and lasted all his life. His first raptures over music were induced by an elaborate kind of music box called an "orchestrina," a large mechanical instrument from Germany which could play fixed tunes and was intended to reproduce the sounds of a whole orchestra. His father brought one of these serious toys home when Tchaikovsky was a child of four or five. On this instrument he first heard "Vedrai, carino" from Mozart's *Don Giovanni*. From the time he first started going to hear the Italian opera in St. Petersburg, he went to every production of Mozart's operas he could, often going back night after night to hear the same performance again; in 1875 he translated the libretto of *The Marriage of Figaro*; his fourth suite for orchestra, Op. 61 (1887) is based on themes from Mozart and is called "Mozartiana." In 1890, when composing his opera *The Queen of Spades*, he said that he felt immersed in the 18th century and it was as if all music had reached its peak with Mozart and stopped there. In May 1893 he transcribed themes from Mozart's 4th Fantasy into a vocal quartet to his own words, telling his publisher Jurgenson he expected no money for it because "very little of this is mine"; he heard it performed by Lavrovskaya's students at the Moscow Conservatory in October 1893, just a few days before he went to St. Petersburg for what was to be his last concert. At that concert, by the way—famous because it was the premiere of his 6th Symphony, conducted by him a few days before his death—the program included two dances from Mozart's opera *Idomeneo* (the program of this concert is reproduced in *DG*, 593-4).

In its opening phrase, this song recalls Cherubino's "Non so più" from *The Marriage of Figaro*, and it has the Mozartean spirit of a comic aria about romantic attraction which is at once funny and touching. As soon as Alexandra Kochetova sang it in March 1870 at a concert of the Russian Musical Society, Tchaikovsky reported in a letter that it was "causing a furor" (*DG*, 68). Maybe the audience, unfazed by this sort of thing in Mozart, was enjoying the pleasant shock of hearing it all in Russian. Certainly everyone was talking about it and demanding to hear it sung again. It is not easy to sing: the voice has to negotiate two octaves with ease, and the tempo has to be managed with the right feverishness so that the key phrase, the fifth line in each stanza, which is to be sung slower, can stand out in exquisite torment.

Tchaikovsky found the text in the poetry of Countess Yevdokiya Rostopchina (1811-1858), a woman who belonged to Moscow's highest society.

Admired by Pushkin, Zhukovsky, and Lermontov, she had her own voice as a poet and made out of the materials of society life lyrics that were witty or sad, but contained genuine feelings. Composers like Glinka, Dargomyzhsky, and others found them ideal to set to music. Tchaikovsky made some adjustments to the verb forms in stanzas 2 and 3, making them more colloquial. He highlighted the key phrase of the song (the song's title) by repeating it. He discarded the fourth stanza of the poem altogether, no doubt to shorten the text. But also, for his purposes—to write a song in the spirit of his favorite composer— it is a digression that would only spoil the sudden throwaway line at the end of the poem. The omitted stanza will be found below.

И больно, и сладко,
Когда при начале любви,
То сердце забьётся украдкой,
То в жилах течёт лихорадка,
И больно, и сладко;
То жар запылает в крови...
И больно, и сладко!

Пробьёт час свиданья, —
Потупя предательный взор,
В волненьи, в томленьи незнанья,
Боишься, желаешь признанья, —
И в муку свиданье!
Начнёшь и прервёшь разговор...
И в муку свиданье!

Не вымолвишь слова...
Немеешь, робеешь, дрожишь;
Душа, проклиная оковы,
Вся в речи излиться готова...
Нет силы, нет слова,
И только глядишь и молчишь!

И сладко, и больно...
И трепет безумный затих;
И сердцу легко и раздольно...
Слова полились бы так вольно,
И сладко, и больно,
Но слушать уж некому их.
И сладко, и больно,
И сладко, и больно.

I ból'na, i slátka,
Kagdá pri nachále ljubví,
To sérttse zabjótsa ukrátkaj,
To v zhílakh techót likharátka,
I ból'na, i slátka;
To zhár zapylájet f kraví...
I ból'na, i slátka!

Prabjót chas svidán'ja, —
Patúpja predátel'nyj vzór,
V valnén'ji, f tamlén'ji neznán'ja,
Baíshsa, zhelájesh priznán'ja, —
I v múku svidán'je!
Nachnjósh i prervjósh razgavór...
I v múku svidán'je!

Ne výmalvish slóva...

It's painful, it's sweet,
When you first fall in love,
Now secretly your heart starts pounding,
Now a fever's flowing in your veins,
It's painful, it's sweet;
Now your blood's blazing hot...
It's painful, it's sweet!

The rendezvous hour strikes —
Lowering your telltale gaze,
Excited and in agony, not knowing,
You fear and desire a confession, —
A meeting that's torment!
You start to speak and break it off...
A meeting that's torment!

You can't say a word...

Neméjesh, rabéjesh, drazhísh;	You're dumb, you're shy, you're shaking;
Dushá, praklinája akóvy,	Your soul's cursing its shackles,
Fsja v réchi izlítsa gatóva...	Ready to pour itself out...
Net síly, net slóva,	No strength, not a word,
I tól'ka gljadísh i malchísh!	You're just staring in silence!

I slátka, i ból'na...	It's sweet, it's painful...
I trépet bezúmnyj zatíkh;	And the mad trepidation has passed;
I sérttsu lekhkó i razdól'na...	And your heart feels light and open...
Slavá palilíz' by tak vól'na,	Words could flow so freely now,
I slátka, i ból'na,	It's sweet, it's painful,
No slúshat' ush nékamu íkh.	But no one's there to hear them.
I slátka, i ból'na,	It's sweet, it's painful,
I slátka, i ból'na.	It's sweet, it's painful.

TEXT. **Yevdokíya Rostopchiná**, 1854. Title: Слова для музыки (Words for music). Earlier set by Dubuque (1865).

METER. Ternary. Amphibrach, lines of 2 and 3 feet:

> *It's sweet and it's painful,*
> *The mad trepidation has passed...*

MUSIC. 1869. Op. 6, no. 3. A Major. 4/4, Allegro vivo. For Middle Voice: b–a². Dedicated to **Aleksándra Kóchetova** (1833-1902), a soprano at the Bolshoy from 1865-77. In a period of the dominance of Italian opera, she was instrumental in getting the Bolshoy to stage Glinka's operas. She was also a concert artist and teacher. She was the first to sing this song in March 1870, and the first to sing Song 10 in March 1871 (*DG*, 74). Her grave, with a touching monument erected by her students, is at Donskoy Monastery in Moscow.

RECORDINGS. Dolukhanova, Krasnaya, Lemeshev, Obraztsova, Rautio, Shumskaya, Vayne.

Stanza 4, omitted from the song

Настанет разлука,	Separation will come,
И, холодно, гордо простясь,	And saying a cold, proud farewell,
Уйдёшь с своей тайной и мукой!..	You depart with your secret and torment!..
А в сердце истома и скука,	Your heart is heavy and dull,
И вечностью нам каждый час,	And each hour for us is an eternity,
И смерть нам разлука!..	And separation for us is death!..

7   *Слеза дрожит*
A tear trembles

Op. 6, No. 4

The source for this beautiful love song for baritone was one of Aleksey Tolstoy's philosophical love poems, consisting actually of five stanzas, not just two. In the poem, as elsewhere in his work, Tolstoy expresses the view that our life, however illuminated with glimpses of beauty in love, nature, and art, is sadly—no, *grievously*—small and confining compared to Love, to God, to life's source, into which all will ultimately merge. Yet when Tolstoy wants to describe these fleeting glimpses of beauty in love and nature, he can do it wonderfully well, with that particular zest of (seemingly) plain Russian speech which is a trademark of the Tolstoy name. If this sounds like the conflict of hedgehog and fox in one man which Isaiah Berlin saw in his more famous cousin, it has to be added that Aleksey Konstantinovich was a Russian traditionalist who never questioned his own birthright, his own class, his own beliefs or his own art in the name of universal morality. Still, like Lev Nikolayevich, he saw things on a big scale, and in this poem he takes these big issues up with his beloved. The result is a definition of love which shows it to be cosmic in scale, much vaster than the feeling of two people merely for each other; love as they know it turns out to be grief and earthly bondage. Tchaikovsky knew that to argue this philosophy in a love song would not work. As a result, he used only the first and last stanzas of the poem, discarding the middle three.

Shortened to two stanzas, it still presents problems as a lyric to a love song. *He* sees the big picture, his love is boundless, and he knows happiness lies ahead, while she does not. Yet it is *her* hurt, in the image of a jealous tear, which is the most genuine human feeling in the text. The song has to make his feelings genuine, too: he has to do more than reassure. Tchaikovsky did this by adding the words "my love" (мой друг) at the beginning of the second stanza, by ardent repetition in the last lines of both stanzas, and, most important, in the music. It has an interesting beginning, with the piano meandering pensively one note at a time for a few bars in A-flat minor before modulating into the major key, at which point the beautiful melody is handed over to the voice. This gives the voice part the soaring melodic power it needs, but it is also expressively slowed down, controlled and paused, which gives it the sincerity of feeling the words need. The song was popular early on and has remained so. Of the many good recordings, Dmitri Hvorostovsky's sensitive reading stands out, accompanied by the limpid pianism of Oleg Boshniakovich.

Слеза дрожит в твоём ревнивом взоре —
О, не грусти, ты всё мне дорога!
Но я любить могу лишь на просторе —
Мою любовь, широкую как море,
Вместить не могут, нет! вместить не могут
жизни берега.

О, не грусти, мой друг, земное минет горе,
Пожди ещё — неволя недолга —
В одну любовь мы все сольёмся вскоре,
В одну любовь, широкую как море,
Что не вместят, нет! что не вместят
земные берега.

Slezá drazhýt f tvajóm revnívam vzóre –
O, ne grustí, ty fsjo mne daragá!
No ja ljubít' magú lish na prastóre –
Majú lyubóf', shyrókuju kak móre,
Vmestít' ne mógut, nét!
vmestít' ne mógut zhýzni beregá.

A tear trembles in your jealous gaze –
Oh, don't be sad, you're dear to me as ever!
But I can only love in boundless freedom –
My love is wide as the sea,
Life's shores cannot, no!
cannot contain it all.

O, ne grustí, moj drúk, zemnóje
mínet góre,
Pazhdí jeshchó – nevólja nedalgá –
V adnú lyubóf' my fse sal'jómsa fskóre,
V adnú lyubóf', shyrókuju kak móre,
Shto ne vmestját, net!
shto ne vmestját zemnýje beregá.

Oh, don't be sad, my love, earthly grief
will pass,
Wait a little longer – this bondage is brief –
Soon we all will merge into love alone,
Into a love as wide as the sea,
That earthly shores never, no!
never could contain.

TEXT. **Alekséy Tolstóy**, 1858. Untitled. First set by Tchaikovsky; later by Felix Blumenfeld (1889).

METER. Binary. Iambic, 5-foot:
   A tear is trembling in your jealous gaze —
   Oh, don't be sad, you're dear to me as ever.

MUSIC. 1869. Op. 6, no. 4. G-flat Major. 4/4, Moderato assai. For Baritone: d flat–f¹ flat. Dedicated to Tchaikovsky's publisher and close business friend **Pyotr Jurgensón** (1836-1904). Their extensive correspondence is a primary source of information about Tchaikovsky's publications and financial affairs (*Jurgenson*).

RECORDINGS. Anders (in German), Baikov, Burchuladze, Eizen, Fischer-Dieskau, Ghiaurov, Hvorostovsky, Andrey Ivanov, Kozlovsky, Krasnaya, Larin, Leiferkus, Mazurok, Mkrtchyan, Ots, Pedrotti, Petrov, Politkovsky, Rebroff, Reizen, Vedernikov.

Stanzas 2, 3, and 4, omitted from the song

Когда Глагола творческая сила
Толпы миров воззвала из ночи,
Любовь их все, как солнце, озарила,
И лишь на землю к нам её светила
Нисходят порознь редкие лучи.

И, порознь их отыскивая жадно,
Мы ловим отблеск вечной красоты:
Нам вестью лес о ней шумит отрадной,
О ней поток гремит струёю хладной
И говорят, качаяся, цветы.

И любим мы любовью раздробленной
И тихий шёпот вербы над ручьём,
И милой девы взор, на нас склоненный,
И звёздный блеск, и все красы вселенной,
И ничего мы вместе не сольём.

When the creative power of the Word
Summoned out of night masses of worlds,
Love, like a sun, illuminated them all,
But beams from those bright worlds reach our earth rarely
And are scattered into separate rays.

And avidly seeking those separate rays,
We catch but a reflection of eternal beauty:
The rustling forest gives us joyous tidings of it,
The flood announces it in its cold surge,
And the flowers tell of it, swaying back and forth.

And the love we feel is scattered too,
And the soft whisper of willow above a stream,
And a dear girl's gaze turned in our direction,
And the blaze of stars, and all the beauties of the universe,
And none of this do we merge together.

8 *Отчего?*
Why?

Op. 6, No. 5

The theme here is "abandoned and forgotten," handled as romantic irony by the incomparable German lyric poet Heinrich Heine. The illusion of a wintry spring is abruptly broken in the last two lines by the outcry of the poet, which shows that it is his feelings which have made the world so desolate.

Tchaikovsky changed one word in Lev Mey's excellent translation: for земля сера, "the earth is *gray*," in stanza 3 (in German this is *grau*), he uses instead сыра, "raw, damp," an adjective linked in Russian folk poetry with "mother earth." It is a tiny emendation, but it turns the German original into something which could only be a Russian text—an impression driven home by Mey's last two lines, consisting entirely of ordinary conversational Russian words.

For musical expression of a powerful emotion which continually unfolds, Tchaikovsky never wrote a better song than this. He does it in a very short space with great economy of means. The tension is evident from the first nervously percussive notes of the piano accompaniment, so at odds with the calm melancholy of the vocal line. Yet the vocal part has a concentrated, incessant quality too. Every line in the first two stanzas ends in four repeated notes, each with a different time value—a dotted quarter note, a quarter note, an eighth note, and a dotted half note—that move in small intervals up and down to land finally on the tonic at the end of line 8. Then this pattern changes, bringing instability that culminates in the powerful outburst of the last two lines of the song. The song dies down with a few soft arpeggios: nothing remains but a fugitive echo of the lover's lost happiness. Singers, understandably, like this song, as the many fine recordings of it show.

> Отчего побледнела весной
> Пышноцветная роза сама?
> Отчего под зелёной травой
> Голубая фиалка нема?
>
> Отчего так печально звучит
> Песня птички, несясь в небеса?
> Отчего над лугами висит
> Погребальным покровом роса?
>
> Отчего в небе солнце с утра
> Холодно и темно как зимой?
> Отчего и земля вся сыра
> И угрюмей могилы самой?

Отчего я и сам всё грустней
И болезненней день ото дня?
Отчего, о скажи мне скорей,
Ты, покинув, забыла меня?

Atchevó pablednéla vesnój	Why has the radiant rose
Pyshnatsvétnaja róza samá?	Grown pale in the springtime?
Atchevó pad zeljónaj travój	Why does the blue violet lie
Galubája fijálka nemá?	Mute under the green grass?
Atchevó tak pechál'na zvuchít	Why is the bird's song so sad
Pésnja ptíchki, nesjás' v nebesá?	As it rises up to heaven?
Atchevó nad lugámi visít	Why does the dew on the meadows
Pagrebál'nym pakróvam rasá?	Hang like a mourning veil?
Atchevó v nébe sóntsa s utrá	Why is the sun in the sky this morning
Khaladnó i temnó kak zimój?	Cold and dark as in winter?
Atchevó i zemljá fsja syrá	Why is the earth all damp
I ugrjúmej magíly samój?	And gloomier than the grave?
Atchevó ja i sám fsjo grusnéj	Why do I feel sadder and sadder
I baléznennej dén' ata dnjá?	And sicker from day to day?
Atchevó, o skazhý mne skarjéj,	Why, oh tell me right now,
Ty, pakínuf, zabýla menjá?	Did you leave me and forget me?

TEXT. **Lev Mey**, 1858. A translation of "Warum sind denn die Rosen so blaß" (1822), by the German Romantic poet **Heinrich Heine** (1797-1856). First set (in Russian) by Tchaikovsky; set in German by Fanny Hensel (Mendelssohn's sister) and the Swiss composer Othmar Schoeck.

METER. Ternary. Anapest, 3-foot:

> *In a season of desolate spring*
> *Can the rose and the violet bloom?*

MUSIC. 1869. Op. 6, no. 5. D Major. 12/8, Moderato. For High Voice: d^1–a^2. Dedicated to Tchaikovsky's close friend **Iván Kliménko** (1841-1914). He wrote an excellent memoir about Tchaikovsky (*Klimenko*, republished in *Vaidman and Belonovich 1995*; partial English translation in *Poznansky 1999*).

RECORDINGS. Anders (in German), Borodina, Caruso (in French), Figner, Gedda, Gmyria, Jadlowker (in German), Kovalyova, Krasnaya, Kruglikova, Larin, Leiferkus, Lemeshev, Martynov, Maxwell, Mkrtchyan, Nesterenko, Obukhova, Ognivtsev, Page-Green, Rodgers, Rosing, Siniavskaya, Söderström, Solovianenko, Sterling, Varady, Vishnevskaya.

9 *Нет, только тот, кто знал*
 None but the lonely heart

Op. 6, No. 6

Tchaikovsky wrote this last song of Opus 6 to a Lev Mey translation of a famous Goethe lyric. As a song, it surpassed all the others in its immediate impact and staying power. "I've been swamped," he wrote his sister just a few days before starting these songs, "hurrying to finish the new overture, plus a lot of other deadlines besides. I intend to take a break and not do anything except teach my classes. When I can face the thought of music again, I want to write some romances to earn some money" (*MN*, 432). At the end of the week when the songs were finished he felt buoyant, and joked about them with his friend Ivan Klimenko in mock 18th-century Russian. Known in English as "None but the Lonely Heart," a title given to it by the best of its many translators Arthur Westbrook, it is the most famous song Tchaikovsky ever wrote.

First sung by Lavrovskaya in March 1870, and again by her a year later at a concert at which Turgenev was present (*DG*, 74) it made an immediate impression among the public, despite efforts by Cui and Balakirev to downplay it. Tchaikovsky wrote Klimenko in May 1870 that Balakirev had dissuaded Khvostova from singing the song dedicated to her, lest it "ruin" a concert made up of music by Musorgsky and others (*Klimenko*, 55). But records of concert programs during Tchaikovsky's lifetime show that it was a favorite in the two Russian capitals and in other cities with a prominent musical life like Tiflis (Tbilisi), Kiev, Kharkov, and Odessa. It was sung in Paris, too, by leading singers like the famous Polish bass Edouard De Reszke.

Pauline Viardot, one of the greatest 19th-century singers and Turgenev's lifelong love, sang it at a concert to raise money for the Russian library she and Turgenev founded in Paris in 1875 (*Turgenev*, XIII, 589). It was a staple in her repertoire. Turgenev would have known from Viardot exactly how it should be sung. The modulations of volume from *piano* to *forte* and back at certain points in the vocal part are a key feature of the song, and this is just what Turgenev focuses on in his spooky story of romantic obsession "Clara Milich (After Death)" (1882), in which he has his mysterious heroine sing it at an amateur concert in Moscow. The song is the defining moment in the story, from which everything else follows.

Its English title was so well known that Richard Llewellyn used it as the title for his novel about Cockneys in London's East End. This in turn was made into a film called "None but the Lonely Heart" (1944), with Cary Grant and Ethel Barrymore, who were nominated for Academy Awards, as was the musical score, a "symphonic entity" by Constantin Bakaleinikoff and Hanns

Eisler inspired by Tchaikovsky's music. A violin transcription of the song turned up in an even better score from an earlier film, David Selznick's "Intermezzo" (1939), in which Ingrid Bergman made her American debut.

It was very well known in England and America in the first half of the 20th century. An orchestral version of it was a favorite in Arthur Fiedler's Boston Pops concerts. It was recorded and sung in English on the radio by famous concert singers like Marian Anderson, John McCormack, and Richard Tauber. It was taken up in the 1940s by Frank Sinatra, who recorded it several times. For articulation of the lyric and its emotional impact, his last recording made at the peak of his vocal powers in 1959 is unmatched in English.

The song gets its staying power from a beautiful melody which has a recurring, endless quality. Tchaikovsky in his characteristic way goes back in the middle of the song to take up the words in the first stanza again, and after this repetition there is a pause which seems to announce that the song has ended. Only then, with the words "my heart's on fire" (in Westbrook, "my senses fail"), does the song proceed to its conclusion. David Jackson has described this well: "the masterstroke… is the moment near the end, when after the climactic pause the voice sings a new counter-melody while the piano reiterates the opening theme. No matter how often the song is heard, this moment never fails to make its effect" (*Jackson*, 162).

Нет, только тот, кто знал	Ах, только тот, кто знал
Свиданья жажду,	Свиданья жажду,
Поймёт, как я страдал	Поймёт, как я страдал
И как я стражду.	И как я стражду.
	Поймёт, как я страдал
Гляжу я вдаль… нет сил,	И как я стражду.
Тускнеет око…	
Ах, кто меня любил	Вся грудь горит… Кто знал
И знал — далёко!	Свиданья жажду,
	Поймёт, как я страдал
	И как я стражду.

Net, tól'ka tót, kto znál	No, only one who's known
Svidán'ja zházhdu,	Longing to be together,
Pajmjót, kak ja stradál	Can know what I've suffered
I kak ja strázhdu.	And how I'm suffering.
Gljazhú ja vdál'… net síl,	I gaze at the distance... faint,
Tusknéjet óka…	My eye grows dim...
Akh, kto menjá ljubíl	Ah, how far away's the one
I znál – daljóka!	Who loved me, knew me!

Akh, tól'ka tót, kto znál	Ah, only one who's known
Svidán'ja zházhdu,	Longing to be together
Pajmjót, kak ja stradál	Can know what I've suffered
I kak ja strázhdu.	And how I'm suffering.
Pajmjót, kak ja stradál	Can know what I've suffered
I kak ja strázhdu.	And how I'm suffering.

Fsja grud' garít... Kto znál	My heart's on fire... Whoever's known
Svidán'ja zházhdu,	Longing to be together,
Pajmjót, kak ja stradál	Knows what I've suffered
I kak ja strázhdu.	And how I'm suffering.

TEXT. **Lev Mey**, 1857. Title: "Песнь Арфиста" ("Song of the Harpist"). A translation of "Nur wer die Sehnsucht kennt" (1785), from Book 4, Chapter 11 of *Wilhelm Meisters Lehrjahre* by **Johann Wolfgang von Goethe** (1749-1832). In the scene from which the present text is taken, Mignon joins in the song the harpist is singing—hence Mey's title "Song of the Harpist." One of three of Mignon's songs set by Tchaikovsky (the other two are Songs 21, 70).

Goethe's famous lyric has been set by many composers, including Beethoven (4 versions, 1807-8), Schubert (5 versions, 1815-26), Robert Schumann (1849), and Hugo Wolf (1888). The Russian composer Nikolay Medtner also set the German text (1908-9). Mey's Russian text was first set by A. A. Derfeldt in 1862. Since Mey's translation preserves the Russian equivalent to Goethe's metrics, Tchaikovsky's music is perfectly suited to Goethe's text (including the lines which Tchaikovsky repeats), as can be seen by the frequent recordings of the song in German, some of which are listed below.

METER. Binary. Iambic, 3- and 2-foot lines:
Alone, and parted far
From joy and gladness.

MUSIC. 1869. Op. 6, no. 6. D-flat Major. 4/4, Andante non tanto. For Middle Voice: c^1-f^2. Numerous transcriptions for strings and other instruments, notably for cello by Gregor Piatigorsky.

Dedicated to **Alína Khvostóva** (1846-1904), a mezzo-soprano who studied at the Petersburg Conservatory in Tchaikovsky's class with the famous voice teacher Henriette Nissen-Saloman. Tchaikovsky knew her and her family before he entered the conservatory. She was close to the "mighty handful," which was fine with Tchaikovsky, but he was offended that she yielded to their demands not to sing the song he had dedicated to her (*Sokolov*).

RECORDINGS. Anders (in German), Anderson, Arkhipova, Atlantov, Borg, Borodina, Burchuladze, Choi, Christoff, DeGaetani, Descamps, Eddy (in English), Eizen, Ghiaurov, **Gmyria**, Homer (in German), Hvorostovsky, Koshetz, Kovalyova, Krasnaya, Kurenko, Kuuzik, Lanza (in English), Larin, Leiferkus,

Lemeshev, Lisitsian, Maxwell, Mishura, Mkrtchyan, Nelepp, Nesterenko, Obraztsova, Obukhova, Ognivtsev, Olszewska (in German), Ots, Pedrotti, Petina, Piatigorsky (cello transcription), Ponselle (in German), Price, Reizen, Rethberg (in German), Rodgers, Schumann-Heink (in German), Schwarzkopf (in German), Sinatra (in English), Siniavskaya, Slobodskaya, Söderström, Souzay (in French), Tauber (in English), Tear, Tourel, Vaughan (in English), Vishnevskaya, Zbruyeva, Zhadan, Zimmermann.

Goethe's Text	*Arthur Westbrook's Translation*
Nur wer die Sehnsucht kennt,	None but the lonely heart
Weiß, was ich leide!	Can know my sadness;
Allein und abgetrennt	Alone, and parted far
Von aller Freude,	From joy and gladness.
Seh ich ans Firmament	Heav'n's boundless arch I see
Nach jener Seite.	Spread out above me.
Ach! der mich liebt und kennt,	Ah! what a distance drear
Ist in der Weite.	To one who loves me!
Es schwindelt mir, es brennt	None but the lonely heart
Mein Eingeweide.	Can know my sadness;
Nur wer die Sehnsucht kennt,	Alone, and parted far
Weiß, was ich leide!	From joy and gladness,
	Alone, and parted far
	From joy and gladness.
	My senses fail,
	A burning fire devours me.
	None but the lonely heart
	Can know my sadness.

10 Забыть так скоро
To forget so soon

Outside Russia, except for singers—such fine artists as Elisabeth Söderström and Joan Rodgers have recorded it—this song has puzzled critics, who have ignored it, or, worse, dismissed it as "limp" (*Brown I*, 270), without making any attempt to understand what Tchaikovsky had in mind when he sat down to put these words by his friend Aleksey Apukhtin to music. In Russia, however, the song caught on right away and has never lost its popularity. Nicolas Slonimsky included it in his collection of fifty Russian songs as one of only four songs chosen to represent Tchaikovsky as a composer of romances (*Slonimsky 1949*).

It is clearly a new departure. A manuscript of a draft of the song shows Tchaikovsky worked on it over a period of time, and his conception evolved into its present form (for a discussion of the two versions of the song, see *Al'shvang 1951*). The changes in key and tempo in the score show the three-part structure, which readily becomes apparent when the song is heard. The opening Moderato section in F Major corresponds to stanzas 1 and 2 of the text. The middle Andante section, with a key shift to D-flat Major, is stanza 3 of the text. The final section, marked Allegro, is in F Minor. The voice part softens to triple *piano* at the end of the middle section, and grows to double *forte* in the final section. Through all this, the accompaniment shapes the three-part structure: there is a prominent crescendo transition from the middle to the final section, and a long piano postlude of thirteen bars.

Some emphasize its operatic quality, the way it unfolds dramatically (*Tumanina 1962*, 197-8). Arnold Alshvang sees it as "a new psychological type of song" that reveals "three different psychological states." In the first part, "the idea of disappointment and suffering emerges movingly and simply... the soul cannot comprehend its hurt"; this is followed in the middle section by "recollection of... the intimacy of completely reciprocal love" in "nocturne-like music... with its crystallised charm of remembrance," in which "the lips are still whispering words of resentment, but the imagination is drawing pictures full of undisturbed happiness"; then the restless, painful final section follows, where the "voice of passion overwhelms all other voices." He traces the origin of the song's structure to the classical aria, where the first part is "dramatic recitative," the second part is a "slow, lyrical episode, full of deep feeling," and the third part is a "final allegro" (*Al'shvang 1946*, 206-210). Vera Vasina-Grossman, recognizing the exceptional popularity of the song, points to its multiple, dramatic shifts in intonation, including the long piano coda (*Vasina-Grossman*, 272). Everyone agrees that this song is written in a new way.

As a lyric, however, it is not an aria, but an urban romance—so-called because songs to this kind of text were exceedingly popular among urban audiences in Russia from 1800 to 1900 and beyond. This text is as canonical a specimen of the genre as one could find. For this reason it is a misreading of the song to say that "the content of the music is immeasurably richer than the text" (*Al'shvang 1946*, 207). On the contrary, as an urban romance about romantic love, Apukhtin's poem is of exceptionally high quality: it includes so many of the best-loved banalities of the genre without being stylistically banal itself. The challenge was to write music that would not be banal either.

In two witty and original essays on the popularity of urban romance at the beginning of the 20th century, Miron Petrovsky writes about the poetics of their texts and the features they share (*Petrovsky 1984, 1997*). Apukhtin's lyric is made out of the two verbs essential to the urban romance, "remember" and "never forget," but with an unusual twist. The poem not only recalls a love affair, but comments on it too. As expected in this kind of song, one of the lovers addresses the other. Love here is neither more nor less than what it should be in an urban romance, an intimacy between two people, with absolutely no Turgenevian or Tolstoyan links to an outside world beyond the two of them. Any possibility that this relationship might be connected with marriage, much less child-bearing, is totally out of the picture; no Anna Kareninas are allowed here. Within these lyric boundaries, however, a story is told, from "mute conversations with the eyes" to trysts in the garden, to a memory of being together in a room by moonlight, and then to those fatal-sounding "vows" in the dead of night. The most original image is the rustling of the blinds, with the two of them alone in a room. This is that same 19th-century world inhabited by Bazarov and Odintsova in *Fathers & Sons*, but stripped of all the particularity of character that makes Turgenev's novel so fine. What is left is a song for everyone, in which every image evokes charged romantic associations: lovers' dreams, lovers' hopes, remembered intimacy, and—most striking here—total disenchantment. Apukhtin was very good at this sort of text; it was material Tchaikovsky liked; in this romance, he found a fresh approach to the genre, one in which the urban romance remains true to itself but at the same time takes on new dimensions as a song. The result is one of the most original songs he ever wrote.

When Cui first heard it, his comment was "Good God!"

> Забыть так скоро, Боже мой,
> Всё счастье жизни прожитой!
> Все наши встречи, разговоры,
> Забыть так скоро, забыть так скоро!

Забыть волненья первых дней,
Свиданья час в тени ветвей!
Очей немые разговоры,
Забыть так скоро, забыть так скоро!

Забыть, как полная луна
На нас глядела из окна,
Как колыхалась тихо штора,
Забыть так скоро, забыть так скоро, так скоро!

Забыть любовь, забыть мечты,
Забыть те клятвы, помнишь ты, помнишь ты, помнишь ты?
В ночную пасмурную пору, в ночную пасмурную пору,
Забыть так скоро, так скоро! Боже мой!

Zabýt' tak skóra, Bózhe mój,	To forget so soon, good God,
Fsjo shchást'je zhýzni prazhytój!	All the happiness we lived through!
Fse náshy fstréchi, razgavóry,	All the times we met, the conversations,
Zabýt' tak skóra, zabýt' tak skóra!	To forget so soon, forget so soon!
Zabýt' valnén'ja pérvykh dnéj,	Forget the emotions of those first days,
Svidán'ja chas	The hour of rendezvous
f tení vetvéj!	under shady branches!
Achéj nemýje razgavóry,	Mute conversations of the eyes,
Zabýt' tak skóra, zabýt' tak skóra!	To forget so soon, forget so soon!
Zabýt', kak pólnaja luná	To forget the full moon
Na nás gljadéla iz akná,	Gazing at us through the window,
Kak kalykhálas' tíkha shtóra,	The quiet rustle of the blinds,
Zabýt' tak skóra, zabýt' tak skóra,	To forget so soon, forget so soon,
tak skóra!	so soon!
Zabýt' ljubóf', zabýt' mechtý,	Forget love, forget dreams,
Zabýt' te kljátvy, pómnish ty,	Forget the vows, do you remember them,
pómnish ty, pómnish ty?	do you, do you?
V nachnúju pásmurnuju póru,	At night's bleakest hour,
v nachnúju pásmurnuju póru,	night's bleakest hour,
Zabýt' tak skóra, tak skóra! Bózhe mój!	To forget so soon, so soon! Good God!

TEXT. **Alekséy Apúkhtin**; date unknown, but no later than 1870. First published in 1870 with the score of this song. Not published by the poet nor found among his papers. First included in an edition of his works in 1991 (*Apukhtin*, 366).

Apukhtin (1840-1893) was Tchaikovsky's exact contemporary and classmate at the Law Academy in St. Petersburg (they graduated in 1859, but their friendship began in 1853 when they were both thirteen). Apukhtin was already aware of his own homosexuality and came to terms with it early, rather in the spirit of an Oscar Wilde, with wit, irony, and a melancholy fatalism. He was Tchaikovsky's first close friend who was gay and with whom Tchaikovsky could talk openly about his own homosexuality.

When Apukhtin was still in school, Turgenev and Fet welcomed him as a promising new talent. He sent Turgenev two poems and a gloomy letter in 1858, to which Turgenev replied "...don't surrender to the pleasures of melancholy: it's the same thing as onanism and just as harmful... What would you have done in 1838, when there really was no hope? Think less about yourself and your own sufferings and joys... You have a duty to your comrades not to sit back and do nothing" (*Turgenev, Pis'ma*, vol. 3, 29 September 1858). But Apukhtin did not take Turgenev's advice. He let himself grow fat, and he liked to say that work was the greatest curse of mankind. In this regard, he and Tchaikovsky were utterly different and their relations eventually cooled even though they remained old friends. His all-or-nothing lyrical intensity and his fondness for the sad summing-up were not qualities admired by the serious intellectuals (Nina Berberova in her memoirs dismisses him as "deservedly forgotten," *Berberova 1972, 635*), but they were "Russian." Hence his popularity among the public, and among composers, too: 90 of his poems were set to music before 1917 (*Ivanov*). Tchaikovsky's four romances to Apukhtin's own poems (Songs 10, 37, 50, 79) are among his most inspired and original songs.

METER. Binary. Iambic tetrameter:
>*Forgotten dreams, forgotten vows,*
>*Forgotten meetings in the moonlight,*
>*Mute conversations of the eyes!*

MUSIC. October 1870. Without opus number. F Major—F Minor. 2/4. Moderato; Andante; Allegro. For High Voice: e^1–a^2 flat. First published in *Muzykal'nyi vestnik* (Musical Herald), Moscow, no. 12, 1870. Published by Jurgenson in 1873. No dedication.

RECORDINGS. Borisenko, Davrath, Gorchakova, Kasrashvili, Kazarnovskaya, Korjus, Krasnaya, Kruglikova, Kurenko, Larin, Lemeshev, Maksakova, Martynov, Leokadiya Maslennikova, Milashkina, Mkrtchyan, **Nezhdanova**, Ognivtsev, Petrov, Preobrazhenskaya, Rautio, Rodgers, Siniavskaya, Slobodskaya, Söderström, Tear, Tourel, Vayne, Vinogradov, Vishnevskaya, Zhadan.

6 Romances, Opus 16 (1872)

In January 1870, when Mily Balakirev came for a second time to visit Tchaikovsky in Moscow, he brought Nikolay Rimsky-Korsakov along. Tchaikovsky had the feeling Balakirev was treating him with new respect. Rimsky told Tchaikovsky the first romance in his new set of songs Opus 8, a song called "Wherever you are, my thoughts are there too," was dedicated to him. Balakirev continued to try to turn him their way by feeding him themes he and Stasov considered suitable.

What Tchaikovsky himself wanted was to write another opera, and he did begin work on his third opera *The Oprichnik*, set in the reign of Ivan the Terrible (the title means a member of the Tsar's personal bodyguard). Meanwhile, Nikolay Rubinstein suggested Tchaikovsky write something for a small ensemble that could be premiered in a concert scheduled for March 1870 to be devoted entirely to works by him. He wrote a string quartet, Op. 11, which Rubinstein liked and so did the public. Its second movement, Andante cantabile, proved to be the single most frequently performed work of his in Russia in the 19th century (*Poznansky 1991*, 130). In 1876, when Tchaikovsky asked Rubinstein to arrange a concert for Lev Tolstoy who was visiting Moscow and whom Tchaikovsky had met for the first time, the concert included a performance of the quartet. Tolstoy shed some tears during the Andante cantabile as Tchaikovsky sat next to him (*DG*, 138). Ruminating much later on Tolstoy in his diary, Tchaikovsky wrote that this was possibly the most flattering moment in his life as a composer (*Dnevniki*, 1 July 1886).

In 1871 he moved at last into an apartment of his own. He published a textbook on harmony and began to write reviews for the papers, excited by recent concerts that included Beethoven's 8th Symphony, the Prelude to *Lohengrin*, and, at the Bolshoy, Adelina Patti singing in *The Barber of Seville*. He heard her again in 1872 in *La Traviata* and *La Sonnambula*—there was something so perfect in the beauty of her voice, the nightingale-like purity of her trills, the ease of her coloratura, that she was almost superhuman (*DG*, 77). He continued to write reviews and articles on music for the next several years, taking the job seriously, as a challenge, trying to enlighten the public, and producing some witty pieces along the way, such as the one poking fun at the Wagner cult at Bayreuth when he went there to hear the *Ring*.

When the "Romeo and Juliet" overture was published in Berlin, Balakirev chided him for rushing it into print before it was polished and ready. He reorchestrated it. He wrote Balakirev: "You asked me to make the introduction like one of those Lisztian religious passages from *Faust*. It didn't turn out that way. I tried to express a lonely soul striving in thought towards heaven. Whether I succeeded or not I don't know" (*DG*, 73).

In the summer of 1872, when Tchaikovsky finished *Oprichnik*, he began work on a new symphony, his second (Op. 17). He finished it that fall. He called it "The Crane" because the last movement was based on a Ukrainian folk song by that name. Other Ukrainian folk motifs were incorporated into the symphony too, and it has come to be called the "Little Russian" (i.e., Ukrainian) symphony. In a gesture of allegiance to all that Balakirev and the "Five" stood for in preaching the cause of "national" music, Tchaikovsky dedicated his new symphony to the Moscow branch of the Russian Musical Society. When Nikolay Rubinstein (who was head of the RMS in Moscow) conducted the premiere of the symphony a month later, it received an ovation.

Not unlike the desire he felt after finishing "Romeo and Juliet" in 1869, Tchaikovsky now wanted to write some romances. On 10 December 1872 he wrote his brother Modest that he was having difficulty finding texts he liked. The two most interesting texts he eventually chose were translations from Greek folk songs, and for one of the romances he ended up writing the text himself.

They were finished by Christmas, when he was summoned to St. Petersburg to discuss *Oprichnik* at the Imperial Theater. He had to play the whole of it through on the piano for the committee at the Mariinsky, but the opera was accepted. While he was there he was invited to a party at the Rimsky-Korsakovs (Tchaikovsky dedicated the first two romances in the new opus to his hostess and host). That evening at their apartment he played a piano transcription of "The Crane," the finale of his new symphony, to the enthusiastic reception of the assembled Five.

His success in Petersburg only made Tchaikovsky keener to get back to Moscow, which was now home. Before boarding the train, he gave the manuscript of the six new songs to his classmate from the conservatory Vasily Bessel, who had gone into music publishing. The songs of Opus 16 passed the censor in January and were published by Bessel in St. Petersburg in March 1873.

11 Колыбельная
Lullaby

Op. 16, No. 1

Lullabies are folk songs of ancient origin, but in modern times Schubert and other composers wrote them too. Russian lullabies sometimes use interesting texts which are not as bland as the "roses bedight and lilies bedecked" of the famous Brahms lullaby (1857). Examples include all three of Musorgsky's lullabies (1865-1875), Grechaninov's Cossack lullaby (1889) to words by Lermontov (with a dagger and a moon over the Caucasus), and the lullabies Stravinsky wrote to Russian folk texts about cats (1915). In American music, George Gershwin's "Summertime" from *Porgy and Bess* (1935) is a familiar example of another highly original lullaby text.

The text of this lullaby, with its animistic detail of a Homeric world, is unique in Russian. It comes from a set of Greek folk songs translated into Russian by Apollon Maikov (1821-1897), a St. Petersburg poet who was interested in Roman and Hellenic themes. Maikov made a naval cruise in 1858-59 to the Greek archipelago, for which he prepared himself by studying the history and culture of modern Greece and taking lessons in the language. When he published his translations in 1861, Maikov explained that the poems are not literal translations but free versions of modern folk songs, some of which he heard being sung. His aim was to be faithful to the spirit of the originals, especially the "Greek love of life and feeling for the natural world" (*Maikov 1977*, 826).

Tchaikovsky made minor adjustments to Maikov's text, lengthening the first line and repeating the entire first stanza as a reprise at the end. There is some confusion about the preposition in line 6: Maikov has the sun setting "under" the water, but Tchaikovsky has it setting "over" the water. Some singers (Galina Kovalyova, Boris Christoff) avoid this confusion by having the sun set "behind the mountain" (за горой, za garój).

It is one of the best-loved Russian lullabies. Tchaikovsky transcribed it for piano. Rachmaninoff's piano transcription of it was a favorite piece in the program of his final American concert tours. Other lullabies by Tchaikovsky include Song 61 and the lovely finale of his opera *Mazeppa* (1883), to a plainer, generic Russian lullaby text.

> Спи, дитя моё, спи, усни! спи, усни!
> Сладкий сон к себе мани:
> В няньки я тебе взяла
> Ветер, солнце и орла.

Улетел орёл домой;
Солнце скрылось над водой;
Ветер, после трёх ночей,
Мчится к матери своей.

Спрашивала ветра мать:
«Где изволил пропадать?
Али звёзды воевал?
Али волны всё гонял?»

«Не гонял я волн морских,
Звёзд не трогал золотых;
Я дитя оберегал,
Колыбелочку качал!»

Спи, дитя моё, спи, усни! спи, усни!
Сладкий сон к себе мани:
В няньки я тебе взяла
Ветер, солнце и орла.

Spí, ditjá majó, spí, usní! spí, usní!	Sleep, my baby, hushaby! sleep, hushaby!
Slátkij són k sebé maní:	Welcome sweet sleep:
V nján'ki ja tebé vzjalá	Nannies three watch over you –
Véter, sóntse i arlá.	Wind, sun, and eagle.
Uletél arjól damój;	The eagle flew home;
Sóntse skrýlas' nad vadój;	The sun hid over the water;
Véter, pósle trjókh nachéj,	The wind, after three nights,
Mchítsa k máteri svajéj.	Comes racing to his mother.
Spráshyvala vétra mát':	His mother asked the wind:
"Gdé izvólil prapadát'?	"Where have you been hiding all this time?
Ali zvjózdy vajevál?	Were you playing battle with the stars?
Ali vólny fsjo ganjál?"	Or just pushing waves around?"
"Ne ganjál ja vóln marskíkh,	"I wasn't pushing any sea waves around,
Zvjóst ne trógal zalatýkh;	I didn't touch the golden stars;
Ja ditjá aberegál,	I was keeping a baby safe from harm,
Kalybélachku kachál!"	I was rocking a little cradle!"
Spí, ditjá majó, spí, usní! spí, usní!	Sleep, my baby, hushaby! sleep, hushaby!
Slátkij són k sebjé maní:	Welcome sweet sleep:
V nján'ki ja tebé vzjalá	Nannies three watch over you –
Véter, sóntse i arlá.	Wind, sun, and eagle.

TEXT. **Apollón Máikov**, between 1858-1860; published 1861. From a cycle called "Motifs from the Folk Poetry of the Modern Greeks"; later just "Modern Greek Songs." In the 1861 publication there were 21 poems in the cycle, but in later editions of Maikov's works there are 33. After Tchaikovsky set two of them in this opus, these unusual texts attracted other Russian composers too (Ippolitov-Ivanov, Taneyev, Arensky, Nikolay Tcherepnin).

Set by over twenty composers; before Tchaikovsky, by three minor composers, including an 1870 setting by Tchaikovsky's classmate at the St. Petersburg Conservatory, Aleksandr Rubets (1838-1913), an important collector of folk songs, especially from his native Ukraine.

METER. Binary. Trochee, 4-foot:
> *Nannies three watch over you*
> *Wind and sun and eagle too.*

MUSIC. 1872. Op. 16, no. 1. A-flat Minor. 2/4, Andantino. For High Voice: d^1 sharp–a^2 flat. Transcribed for piano by Tchaikovsky (1873) and later by Rachmaninoff (1941).

Dedicated to **Nadézhda Rímskaya-Kórsakova** (1848-1919), pianist and wife of the composer, who was expecting her first child at the time.

RECORDINGS. Borisenko, Borodina, Christoff, Dolukhanova, Gorchakova, Igumnov (Tchaikovsky piano transcription), Kazarnovskaya, Koshetz, **Kovalyova**, Krasnaya, Lemeshev, Marsh, Milashkina, Mkrtchyan, Nezhdanova, Ognivtsev, Oleinichenko, Rachmaninoff (Rachmaninoff piano transcription), Rautio, Rodgers, Shpiller, Siniavskaya, Söderström, Stepanova, Sterling, Tear, Tourel, Vishnevskaya, Zimmermann.

12 *Погоди!*
Stay a while!

Op. 16, No. 2

Nikolay Grekov (1807-1866), a poet neglected by literary historians, but important for composers of Russian romances, translated *Romeo and Juliet* for Nekrasov's edition of Shakespeare published in 1866. The poem Tchaikovsky used for this song reads like a variation on Act III Scene V of the play, set in the Capulet orchard, where Juliet tries to prolong her night of love with Romeo as dawn is breaking. In addition, the first two lines of the second stanza are a paraphrase of Lorenzo's invitation to Jessica to look at the night sky in *The Merchant of Venice*, Act V. Though Shakespeare may be the inspiration, the poem is meant to stand on its own. By omitting the tragic foreshadowing in the last stanza of Grekov's poem, Tchaikovsky lifted the song entirely out of its Shakespearean context so that it really does stand on its own.

The song is a beautiful, continually changing elaboration of the musical material Tchaikovsky created for the charming text. The image of birches is a characteristically Russian touch.

Погоди! для чего торопиться!
Ведь и так жизнь несётся стрелой.
Погоди! Погоди! ты успеешь проститься,
Как лучами восток загорится,
Но дождёмся ль мы ночи такой?

Посмотри, посмотри, как чудесно
Убран звёздами купол небесный!
Как мечтательно смотрит луна!
Как темно в этой сени древесной,
И какая везде тишина!

Только слышно, как шепчут берёзы
Да стучит сердце в пылкой груди…
Воздух весь полон запахом розы…
Милый друг! Это жизнь, а не грёзы!
Жизнь летит… Погоди!
Жизнь летит… Погоди!

Pagadí! dlja chevó tarapítsa!	Stay a while! why hurry!
Vet' i ták zhyzn' nesjótsa strelój.	As it is life rushes by like an arrow.
Pagadí! Pagadí! ty uspéjesh prastítsa,	Stay! Stay! you'll have time to say goodbye,
Kak luchámi vastók zagarítsa,	When sunrise turns the east to fire,
No dazhdjómsa l' my nóchi takój?	But will we ever see another night like this?
Pasmatrí, pasmatrí, kak chudésna	Look, look, how wondrously
Úbran zvjózdami kúpal nebésnyj!	Is heaven's cupola inlaid with stars!
Kak mechtátel'na smótrit luná!	How the dreaming moon looks on!
Kak temnó v ètaj séni drevésnaj,	How dark it is here under the trees,
I kakája vezdé tishyná!	How quiet it is everywhere!
Tól'ka slýshna, kak shépchut berjózy	The only sound is the birches whispering
Da stuchít sérttse f pýlkaj grudí...	And a heart beating in an ardent breast...
Vózdukh ves' pólan zápakham rózy...	The scent of roses fills the air...
Mílyj drúk! Èta zhýzn', a ne grjózy!	Darling! This is life, not a daydream!
Zhýzn' letít... Pagadí!	Life flies... Stay a while!
Zhýzn' letít... Pagadí!	Life flies... Stay a while!

TEXT. **Nikoláy Grékov**, 1850s; published 1860. Untitled. Not set by any other composers.

METER. Ternary. Anapest, 3-foot:

> *For we know life's an arrow in flight—*
> *Will we ever see such a rare night?*

MUSIC. 1872. Op. 16, no. 2. A Minor—A Major. 9/8, Moderato assai. For High Voice: d^1 sharp–f^2 sharp.

Dedicated to the composer **Nikoláy Rímsky-Kórsakov** (1844-1908).

RECORDINGS. Fomina, Karolik, **Katulskaya**, Kazarnovskaya, Krasnaya, Kruglikova, Lemeshev, Martynov, Maxwell, Rautio, Tear, Tourel.

Stanza 4, omitted from the song

Пусть погаснут ночные светила.	Let the night stars burn out.
Жизнь летит... а за жизнью могила,	Life flies... and after life's the grave,
А до ней люди нас разлучат...	And before that people will keep us apart...
Погоди! — люди спят,	Wait a while! — people are sleeping,
ангел милый.	my darling angel.
Погоди! — ещё звёзды горят!	Wait a while! — the stars are still burning!

☙

13 *Пойми хотъ раз*
Understand just once

Op. 16, No. 3

Just as there was a love song for baritone in Opus 6, in this opus too Tchaikovsky writes a song for bass or baritone, evidently intended, like Song 7, to be an anthem of love on a rather elevated plane. The poem, by Afanasy Fet, was inspired by a Beethoven song cycle on the theme of the suffering felt by a lover who is parted from the woman he adores. Fet develops only one of the images in the German cycle, namely "Singen will ich, Lieder singen, die dir klagen meine Pein" (I will sing, sing songs to you, that bewail my pain). But this poem of Fet's lacks the tenderness and light grace of the poem Tchaikovsky used for Song 1. The woman he addresses here is like a statue: there is no conversation going on. Fet's eagerness to suffer in the service of this perfect but cold beauty leaves us cold too (none of this is present in the Beethoven cycle). Only Alexander Blok, nearly fifty years later, knew how to pull off a line like "I foresee the triumph of your beauty."

Tchaikovsky made a minor change of word order in line 9, and two other small changes to the text which bring it marginally closer to everyday Russian: in line 6, немею (I am speechless) for и млею (and I swoon); and in the last line of the poem, предвижу (I foresee) for Fet's more bookish провижу. The piano part is very prominent, as if to compensate for the heartfelt conviction missing in the words. Nevertheless, a passionate sincerity comes through.

Пойми хоть раз тоскливое признанье,
Хоть раз услышь души молящей стон!
Я пред тобой, прекрасное созданье,
Безвестных сил дыханьем окрылён.

Я образ твой ловлю перед разлукой,
Я, полон им, немею и дрожу, —
И без тебя, томясь предсмертной мукой,
Своей тоской как счастьем дорожу.

Пою её, во прах упасть готовый,
Ты предо мной стоишь как божество —
И я блажен; я в каждой муке новой
Твоей красы предвижу торжество.

Pajmí khat' rás tasklívaje priznán'je,
Khat' rás uslýsh dushý maljáshchej stón!
Ja pret tabój, prekrásnaje sazdán'je,
Bezvéstnykh síl dykhánjem akryljón.

Understand just once this sad confession,
Just once hear the moaning of a suppliant soul!
I stand before you, beautiful creature,
Elated by mysterious forces.

Ja óbras tvoj lavljú pered razlúkaj,
Ja, pólan im, nemjéju i drazhú, —
I bes tebjá, tamjás' pretsmértnaj múkaj,
Svajéj taskój kak shchást'jem darazhú.

I study your image before we part,
Filled with it, I tremble and stand mute, —
Without you I feel the torment of the dying,
And prize my longing as happiness itself.

Pajú jejó, va prákh upást' gatóvyj,
Ty preda mnój staísh kak bazhestvó —
I ja blazhén; ja f kázhdaj múke nóvaj
Tvajéj krasý predvízhu tarzhestvó.

I make a song of it, myself consigned to dust,
You stand before me like one divine —
And I am blessed; in each new torment
I foresee the triumph of your beauty.

TEXT. **Afanásy Fet**, 1857. Title: Anruf an die Geliebte Бетховена (Beethoven's Appeal to his Beloved). Fet's title is a reference to Beethoven's song cycle "An die ferne Geliebte" (To the Distant Beloved), Opus 98 (1816), six songs to poems by Aloys Jeitteles (1794-1858). In the manuscript and all editions of the song published during Tchaikovsky's lifetime, the author of the text is erroneously given as Maikov.

METER. Binary. Iambic, 5-foot:

> *Just once be mindful of this sad confession,*
> *And hear the moaning of a suppliant soul!*

MUSIC. 1872. Op. 16, no. 3. C Minor. 4/4, Allegro non tanto. For Low Voice: B–f^1.

Dedicated to Tchaikovsky's classmate from the St. Petersburg Conservatory, and close friend, the gifted music critic **Hermann Laroche** (1845-1904). His writings about Tchaikovsky's music (*Larosh*), and his reminiscences (partially translated into English in *Poznansky 1999*) are among the best things written about the composer by any of his contemporaries.

RECORDINGS. Fischer-Dieskau, Aleksey Ivanov, Krasnaya, Mazurok, Nesterenko, Petrov, Pirogov.

14 *О, спой же ту песню*
O, sing that song

Op. 16, No. 4

The text of this "domestic romance" can be traced back to the English poet Felicia Hemans (1793-1835). It is one of those poems which works better in Russian (or German) translation than in English. Aleksey Pleshcheyev did not even attempt to translate Mrs. Hemans's poem line for insipid line. Instead, he wrote a new poem, with longer, looser, strongly accented lines, humanizing the situation with pictorial detail that sets the scene in a cozy nook. The speaker is a woman, a daughter, now older and wiser. It is not just vague "songs" she asks her mother to sing: she has one particular song in mind. Moreover, this mother is Russian, the song she sang was sad, and it had some soul. Tchaikovsky kept the soulful song, but shortened the text by discarding four of the more pictorial stanzas; then he added a reprise at the end. Written for a good amateur singer, the song has warmth and charm.

О, спой же ту песню, родная,
Что пела ты в прежние дни,
В те дни, как ребёнком была я.

Ты песенку вдруг запевала,
И я на коленях твоих
Под звуки той песни дремала.

Ты пела, томима тоскою;
Из тёмных, задумчивых глаз
Катилась слеза за слезою…

Протяжно и грустно ты пела…
Любила напев я простой,
Хоть слов я понять не умела…

О, спой же ту песню, родная,
Как пела её в старину;
Давно её смысл поняла я!

И пусть под знакомые звуки,
Убитая горем, засну
Я сном, что врачует все муки.

О, спой же ту песню, родная,
Как пела её в старину!
О, спой же ту песнь! Спой же ту песнь!
Как пела её в старину!

O, spój zhe tu pésnju, radnája,
Shto péla ty f prézhnije dní,
F te dní, kak rebjónkam bylá ja.

O, sing that song then, mother dear,
The one you used to sing in days gone by,
In the days when I was a child.

Ty pésenku vdrúk zapevála,
I ja na kolénjakh tvajíkh
Pad zvúki toj pésni dremála.

You'd suddenly begin that song I love,
And, sitting in your lap,
I'd drowse to its lulling sounds.

Ty péla, tamíma taskóju;
Is tjómnykh, zadúmchivykh glás
Katílas' slezá za slezóju...

You sang, tormented by longing;
From your dark, pensive eyes
Tear after tear rolled down...

Pratjázhna i grúsna ty péla...
Ljubíla napév ja prastój,
Khat' slóf ja panját' ne uméla...

Sadly and oh so slowly you sang...
I loved the simple tune,
Though I couldn't understand the words...

O, spój zhe tu pésnju, radnája,
Kak péla jejó f starinú;
Davnó jejó smýsl panjalá ja!

O, sing that song then, mother dear,
As you sang it in the olden days;
I've long understood what it means!

I púst' pad znakómyje zvúki,
Ubítaja górem, zasnú
Ja snóm, shto vrachújet fse múki.

And to those familiar strains, let me
Fall asleep when troubles strike me down,
In a sleep that soothes all pains.

O, spój zhe tu pésnju, radnája,
Kak péla jejó f starinú!
O, spój zhe tu pésn'! Spój zhe tu pésn'!
Kak péla jejó f starinú!

O, sing that song then, mother dear,
As you sang it in the olden days!
O, sing that song then! Sing that song!
As you sang it in the olden days!

TEXT. **Alekséy Pleshchéyev**, 1871. Based on an English poem by **Felicia Hemans**. Out of a twelve-line English original, Pleshcheyev produced a "translation" of thirty lines (the full text is in *Pleshcheev 1905*).

The English original has not been identified, so I have included it below. Dubbed "A Canción," it is from a cycle called "Songs of Spain." What is Spanish about it is the arrangement of seven-syllable lines at the beginning and end of each quatrain, with the same masculine rhyme throughout.

This same poem, translated into German, was used by Robert Franz for his much-admired song "Mutter, o sing' mich zur Ruh!" (1860).

METER. Ternary. Amphibrach, 3-foot:

> *You sang me a song full of longing,*
> *Your eyes shedding tear upon tear...*

MUSIC. 1872. Op. 16, no. 4. G Major. 3/4, Allegro moderato. For High Voice: d^1–g^2. Transcribed by Tchaikovsky for piano (1873). A transcription for violin with piano (1873), supposedly by Tchaikovsky and published by Bessel, is of doubtful authenticity (*MN*, 437-8).

Dedicated to **Nikoláy Hubert** (Gúbert in Russian), 1840-1888, a classmate of Tchaikovsky's at the St. Petersburg Conservatory and, later, colleague at the Moscow Conservatory.

RECORDINGS. Anders (in German), Krasnaya, Shpiller, Söderström, Tugarinova.

Original English Poem by Felicia Hemans

"Mother! Oh, Sing me to Rest"
   A Canción

Mother! oh, sing me to rest
  As in my bright days departed:
  Sing to thy child, the sick-hearted,
Songs for a spirit oppress'd.

Lay this tired head on thy breast!
  Flowers from the night-dew are closing,
  Pilgrims and mourners reposing:
Mother! oh, sing me to rest!

Take back thy bird to its nest!
  Weary is young life when blighted,
  Heavy this love unrequited;
—Mother, oh! sing me to rest!

from "Songs of Spain," (*Hemans*, Vol. 1, p. 30)

15
Так что же?
So what more can I say?

Op. 16, No. 5

For an urban romance that could follow on the breakthrough made in Song 10, Tchaikovsky decided to write his own words for this song. He seems to have taken Fet's poem in Song 13 as his starting point—ideal beauty adored—and then tried to warm it up and give it some real passion. The combination is quite original. Reading the words without hearing the music, it looks like a "cruel romance," an offshoot of the kind of urban song the gypsy divas specialized in, a song of fatal passion, desperate extremes, "love me or kill me." But hearing it, we realize at once that we are not in a gypsy night club. There is something playful about it that gives the text as sung a sophisticated edge it lacks on the page. What the song does is to translate wild and desperate "gypsy" passions into the musical language of urban romance going back to the so-called "dilettantes" (a misnomer), the three Alexanders—Aliabiev (1787-1851), Varlamov (1801-1848), and Gurilyov (1803-1858)—who wrote excellent songs still sung today, songs at the very heart of the urban romance tradition. One Russian commentator goes so far as to say of this song that "its elegance makes it a model of exquisite *facture*; its harmonic language, in combination with its light, natural melodic line, shows a kind of perfection of musical logic present earlier only in Glinka's finest romances" (*Al'shvang 1951*, 38).

Tchaikovsky considered it one of the best songs in the new Opus 16, even his favorite. When Bessel sent him the freshly printed score of the new songs in March 1873, he wrote back horrified: "sequestrate all copies *immediately...* there are *appalling* misprints. I found several typos in the music, and one textual error which is enough to sink the whole song. In the best romance of the lot (in my opinion), No. 5, instead of коришь [you find fault, line 3 of the second stanza] is кутишь [you go on a drinking binge], which made me shudder... I was counting on the success of No. 5, but the word *binge* wrecks any chances it might have had." (*MN*, 437).

Твой образ светлый, ангельский
и денно и нощно со мной;
и слёзы, и грёзы,
и жуткие, страшные сны,
ты всё наполняешь собой!
Ты всё наполняешь собой!
Так что же? Что же? Что же?
Хоть мучь, да люби!

Я тайну страсти пагубной
глубоко хороню;
а ты коришь, стыдом язвишь!
Ты только терзаешь меня
безжалостной, грубой насмешкой,
безжалостной, грубой насмешкой!
Так что же? Что же? Что же?
Терзай, да люби!

Тебе до гроба верен я,
но ты каждый день, каждый час
изменою яд в сердце льёшь,
ты жизнь отравляешь мою!
Нет, я не снесу этой муки!

Нет жалости в сердце твоём!
Так что же? Что же? Что же?
Убей, но люби,
убей, но люби, убей, убей меня!
Убей! Но люби!

Tvoj óbras svétlyj, ángel'skij,	Your bright, angelic image
I dénna i nóshchna sa mnój;	Is with me day and night;
I sljózy, i grjózy,	My tears, my fantasies,
I zhútkije, stráshnyje sný,	My awful, frightening dreams,
Ty fsjo napalnjájesh sabój!	Are filled to overflowing with you!
Ty fsjo napalnjájesh sabój!	Are filled to overflowing with you!
Tak shtó zhe? Shtó zhe? Shtó zhe?	So what more can I say? Then what? What?
Khat' múch', da ljubí!	Torment me if you want, but love me!

Ja tájnu strásti págubnaj	I keep the secret of this fatal passion
Glubóka kharanjú;	Hidden deep within;
A ty karísh, stydóm jazvísh!	But you find fault, sting me with shame!
Ty tól'ka terzájesh menjá	You only cut me to the quick
Bezzhálastnaj, grúbaj nasméshkaj,	With harsh, cruel ridicule,
Bezzhálastnaj, grúbaj nasméshkaj!	With harsh, cruel ridicule!
Tak shtó zhe? Shtó zhe? Shtó zhe?	So what more can you ask? Then what? What?
Terzáj, da ljubí!	Cut away, but love me!

Tebé da gróba véren ja,	I'm yours to the grave,
No ty kázhdyj dén', kázhdyj chás	But every day, every hour,
Izménaju ját f sérttse ljósh,	Your treachery pours venom in my heart,
Ty zhýzn' atravljájesh majú!	You're poisoning my life!
Net, ja ne snesú ètaj múki!	No, I can't bear this torment!
Net zhálosti f sérttse tvajóm!	There's no mercy in your heart!
Tak shtó zhe? Shtó zhe? Shtó zhe?	So what more do you want? Then what? What?
Ubéj, no ljubí,	Kill me, but love me,
Ubéj, no ljubí, ubéj, ubéj menjá!	Kill me, but love me, kill me, kill me!
Ubéj! No ljubí!	Kill me! But love me!

TEXT. **N. N. [P. I. Tchaikovsky]**, 1872. One of three romances to words written by the composer (Songs 15, 38, 78).

METER. Mixed Ternary and Binary. Unrhymed lines of varying length, with the first downbeat on the second syllable.

MUSIC. 1872. Op. 16, no. 5. F-Sharp Minor—A Major. 3/8, Allegretto. For High Voice: e^1–a^2. Dedicated to **Nikoláy Rubinstéin** (1835-1881).

RECORDINGS. Anders (in German), Kasrashvili, Krasnaya, Kruglikova, Lemeshev, Lisovsky, Martynov, Shpiller, Tear.

16　Новогреческая песня (на тему "Dies irae")
Modern Greek song (to the "Dies irae" theme)

Op. 16, No. 6

The song begins with the eight-note sequence from the 13th-century Latin mass for the dead "Dies irae" ("day of wrath"). In modern times, use of the theme is common in requiem as well as secular music (Mozart, Berlioz, Verdi, Liszt, and many other composers). In Russian music, its use seems to originate with this song. Tchaikovsky used it again in his "Grand Sonata" for Piano in G-major, Op. 37 (1878), and in the "Manfred" Symphony, Op. 58 (1885). Later, it appears in works by Rachmaninoff, Glazunov, Shostakovich and others. What is unique here is its use in a Russian song, and, moreover, a song whose text comes out of the world of the Greek Christian tradition rather than the Latin. The song is striking in its picture of a Homeric world, side by side with Orthodox images of "gold icons" and "God's churches."

Like Song 11, it comes from Apollon Maikov's translations of Greek folk songs. Though the Greek songs are known to scholars in Greece and Russia (*Neishtadt*), the Greek text of this particular song has never been identified. I have therefore included it below (in Russian and English). It is contained in a collection of songs published in Athens in 1973, kindly given to me by a Greek friend who is a poet. The book itself is a reprint of an older volume originally published in a surprising (or perhaps not so surprising) place. In 1843, a Russian Greek named Georgy Evlampios published in St. Petersburg a collection of modern Greek songs called *Amarantos*, which contains the Greek text of this song with a parallel Russian translation. Did Maikov take the song from this collection, or did he hear it being sung when he was in Greece? He must have known the Evlampios book, but he could have heard it sung, too. According to Evlampios, these laments were learned (not improvised) by Greek women and sung in more or less the same way from generation to generation.

The commentators have paid more attention to it than singers and the public. Boris Asafiev included it in his short list of Tchaikovsky's greatest songs (*Asaf'ev*, 80); Alshvang wrote an extensive analysis of it (*Al'shvang 1946*, 210-214); Cui admired it, as did David Brown, with reservations (*Brown I*, 272-3). The challenge Tchaikovsky took on here was to turn this somber plainchant into a powerful requiem in the form of a song—a lament, but not a Russian lament. It is one of his rarest and most unusual songs.

Tchaikovsky made minor adjustments in lines 8 and 9 of Maikov's text; these and his characteristic use of repetition may be seen below. Maikov's text, which has not been published in more than a century, is hard to find, so I have included it in full.

Tchaikovsky's Text	*Maikov's Text*
В тёмном аде, под землёй,	В тёмном аде, под землёю,
Тени грешные томятся;	Тени грешные томятся;
Стонут девы, плачут жёны,	Стонут девы, плачут жёны,
И тоскуют, и крушатся…	И тоскуют, и крушатся…
Всё, всё о том, что не доходят	Всё о том, что не доходят
Вести в адские пределы — жёны	Вести в адские пределы —
плачут, стонут:	Есть ли небо голубое?
Есть ли небо голубое?	Есть ли свет ещё наш белый!
Есть ли свет ещё там белый!	И на свете — церкви Божьи,
Есть ли в свете церкви Божьи,	И иконы золотые,
И иконы золотые,	И как прежде, за станками
И, как прежде, за станками	Ткут ли девы молодые?
Ткут ли девы молодые?	
Ткут ли девы молодые?	— *Maikov 1884*, Vol. I, 531
В тёмном аде, под землёй,	
Тени грешные томятся;	
Стонут девы, плачут жёны,	
И тоскуют, и крушатся…	

F tjómnam áde, pad zemljój,	In dark Hades, under the earth,
Téni gréshnyje tamjátsa;	Sinful shades suffer torment;
Stónut dévy, pláchut zhóny,	Maidens moan, women weep,
I taskújut, i krushátsa…	Long for home, pine away…
Fsjo, fsjo a tóm, shto ne dakhódjat	Long, long, for tidings from beyond
Vésti v átskije predély — zhóny	Hades' confines — women
pláchut, stónut:	weep, moan:
Jést' li néba galubóje?	Is there a blue sky?
Jést' li svét jeshchó tam bélyj!	Is the wide world still there!
Jést' li f svéte tsérkvi Bozhi,	Are God's churches there,
I ikóny zalatýje,	And gold icons,
I, kak prézhde, za stankámi	And are young maidens still weaving
Tkút li dévy maladýje?	At their looms as they did before?
Tkút li dévy maladýje?	Are young maidens still weaving?
F tjómnam áde, pad zemljój,	In dark Hades, under the earth,
Téni gréshnyje tamjátsa;	Sinful shades suffer torment;
Stónut dévy, pláchut zhóny,	Maidens moan, women weep,
I taskújut, i krushátsa…	Long for home, pine away…

TEXT. **Apollón Máikov**, between 1858-1864; published 1864. Untitled. A translation of a Greek folk song from the cycle "Modern Greek Songs." The Greek song as Evlampios translated it into Russian is reproduced below. The word "Mirolog" in the title of the song is etymologically related to "Moira"

(Fate) and should perhaps be transcribed as "Moirolog." The spelling "Miriolog" in Evlampios's translation is not quite consistent, but I have left it as printed in his book.

METER. Binary. Trochee, 4-foot:

Maidens moan and women weep,
Long for home and pine away.

MUSIC. 1872. Op. 16, no. 6. E-Flat Minor. 4/4, Moderato lugubre. For High Voice: d¹ flat–f². Transcribed for voice and orchestra by Anatoly Liadov (1909).

Dedicated to Tchaikovsky's colleague, the cellist **Konstantín Álbrecht** (1836-1893). He helped Nikolay Rubinstein found the Moscow Conservatory; he later founded the Russian Choral Society (1878).

RECORDINGS. Fischer-Dieskau, Krasnaya, Mazurok.

Greek Folk Song (in Evlampios's Russian translation)

Миролог из Ада	Mirolog (Lament) from Hades
Внизу — в жилищах ада,	Below — in the dwelling places of Hades,
Поют свой Миріолог	Beautiful young women
Красавицы младые;	Sing their Miriolog;
Их песне со слезами	All the youths heed
Все юноши внимают.	Their song with tears.
Но что за Миріолог,	But what Miriolog is this,
При коем слёзы льются?	With tears being shed?
«Стоит ли твердь небесна?	"Does the firmament of heaven stand there?
Стоит ли верхний свет?	Does the upper world still stand?
Стоит ли ряд церквей,	Do churches stand in a row,
Икон святынею блистая?	Shining with holy icons?
И ткацкие станки,	And the weavers' looms,
Где наши ткут хозяйки,	Where our goodwives weave,
Стоят ли так, как прежде?»*	Do they stand too, as they did before?"*

*These last two lines recall Penelope, the wife of Ulysses, who did not consider weaving beneath her dignity and promised to choose a husband when her weaving was done. It is remarkable that thousands of years later this occupation remains a noble handicraft of Greek women. This is one of the many pieces of evidence that in the domestic life of today's Hellenes are preserved the ancient customs of the times of Homer. (Georgy Evlampios's note to the song, *Evlampios*, 13-14.)

2 Romances without opus (1873)

When Tchaikovsky returned to Moscow from Petersburg at the end of December 1872, he found a letter from Stasov giving him three ideas for musical compositions: Scott's *Ivanhoe*, Shakespeare's *Tempest* ("it would make a wonderful overture"), and Gogol's *Taras Bulba* ("a whole symphonic poem could be concocted out of this, with even more poetry, passion, and power than in your superb 'Romeo and Juliet' overture"). Having only a vague memory of what *Ivanhoe* was about, he reread *The Tempest* and, thanking Stasov, wrote back that he had decided to try that.

At a matinee chamber concert in January 1873, he heard Beethoven's last quartet (No. 16 in F Major, Op. 135) and, under the powerful impression it made on all present, he began an essay called "Beethoven and His Time," which came out in four long installments. Laroche wrote an inspired review of Tchaikovsky's Second Symphony, and Cui praised the edition Tchaikovsky was bringing out in two volumes of 65 Russian folk songs collected by a young musical ethnographer named Vasily Prokunin, who was one of his students. Cui's April review of the Opus 16 romances, however, was less kind: "Tchaikovsky's romances are the work of an artist who has no sense of self-criticism, but is entirely satisfied with what has worked in the past and what he already knows; he looks down on inspiration, if he believes in it at all, and is quite content with ordinary musical ideas that never go beyond the commonplace" (*DG*, 93). He was aware of the shortcomings of his compositions, but the way Cui put it made him sound like a complacent hack.

Tchaikovsky was teaching 27 hours a week, so he did not have a lot of time to brood over it. Besides, it was spring, his favorite season, and that year its arrival was early and spectacular. The Bolshoy commissioned him to write music for a new play by Ostrovsky on a theme from Russian folklore having to do with spring. It was called *Snegurochka* (The Snow Maiden). Inspired by the theme and the season, and drawing on some of Prokunin's folk motifs, he wrote the music, Opus 12, in only three weeks. Nikolay Rubinstein conducted it at the Bolshoy. The public liked it, at least the music, which was thought to be better than the play (Rimsky-Korsakov based his 1882 opera on the same play).

The fee Tchaikovsky earned of 350 rubles allowed him to spend July in Germany, Switzerland, Italy, and Paris. The extra money was welcome. His third opera, *The Oprichnik*, finished a year earlier, had won him a prize from the Russian Music Society of 300 R. (*DG*,105). His fourth opera, *Vakula the Smith*, written in the summer of 1874, won first prize in a contest being given by the Directorate of the Imperial Theaters: the monetary award was 1500 R. Though he told Rimsky-Korsakov he had not entered the contest for the money (*MN*, 32), it was a substantial sum, money that he needed if he wanted to travel to Europe regularly, which he did want to do. His annual salary at the Moscow Conservatory (2300 R. in 1873) was not enough.

Songs sold well and were another way of putting extra money in his pocket. In addition to his regular Moscow publisher Peter Jurgenson, Tchaikovsky sold songs during the mid-1870s to two other publishers, both in Petersburg, Vasily Bessel, who had published Opus 16, and Nikolay Bernard, heir to the publishing house of his father, Matvey Bernard. In the pages of Bernard's monthly magazine *Nouvelliste*, musical readers could find songs and short pieces by the likes of Chopin, Liszt, Schumann, and Glinka. All four of the songs without opus number which Tchaikovsky wrote between 1873-75 (Songs 17, 18, 25, 26) came out in *Nouvelliste*. Not a lot of money was involved. For the six songs of Opus 25, for example, Bessel paid him 150 rubles. He was not paid royalties, but he did want the songs to sell, and he wrote Bessel that everyone in Moscow "is swearing mercilessly at you for charging so much for my compositions. Wouldn't it be more profitable to lower the price? There would be more buyers" (*DG*, 108). Bessel's rapacity eventually offended Tchaikovsky when Bessel offered him only 100 rubles for his revised Second Symphony, and he broke with him (*Vol'man*, 117).

When he returned from Paris in the summer of 1873, he went to Usovo, the Ukrainian estate of his pupil Vladimir Shilovsky. He had the place to himself for two weeks, during which time he was in "bliss," taking afternoon walks in the woods, in the evening venturing out into the vast steppe, then coming home to sit by the window and listen to "the majestic silence, now and then broken by indefinable night sounds" (*DG*, 96). During those two weeks, he wrote a finished draft of the symphonic fantasy "The Tempest," Op. 18. A year later, on 13 November 1874, Stasov and Rimsky-Korsakov heard the work for the first time in rehearsal at the Russian Music Society in St. Petersburg. Stasov wrote him that the two of them "melted with ecstasy" as they listened to it. Its Petersburg premiere was three days later: Cui wrote a glowing review. Tchaikovsky dedicated the work to Stasov.

Exactly when he composed the two romances of 1873 is not known. Both were in the hands of the censor for *Nouvelliste* by September. Perhaps the first was inspired by those evening walks and the night sounds he heard in August at Usovo, and the second by the perfect spring earlier that year.

17 Уноси моё сердце
Carry my heart away

Afanasy Fet (1820-1892) did not make his living by writing, as Mey and Pleshcheyev did, but served in the army and then farmed his estate. What made his reputation early was a gift for lyric flights that seem to come out of nothing extraordinary. One of his best poems is about lying on a haystack at night, looking up (a poem Tchaikovsky wanted to set to music but never did). A line like "the nightingale's song scatters alarm and love in the air" caused Lev Tolstoy to wonder "how does a well-fed, good-natured army officer come up with this lyrical daring that only the greatest poets have?" (*Fet*, 30). In the 1860s, when prose and "civic" themes were all that mattered, the radical critics succeeded in "hooting him into silence" for what they saw as the uselessness of his poetry (*Mirsky*, 235). Friends like Turgenev and Tolstoy and others knew his worth, but only at the end of the century when he was discovered by the Symbolists was he widely read again. In the 20th century, his influence was very great on Boris Pasternak and others. Russian composers, however, always looked to Fet's poems for lyrics: he is second only to Pushkin among 19th-century Russian poets in number of lyrics set to music.

Tchaikovsky believed that some of Fet's poems attained the status of music. He mentioned this in one of his letters to Grand Duke Konstantin Romanov: "Fet at his best goes beyond poetry and boldly steps into *our sphere* [music]... He's not just a poet, but a poet-musician, who even avoids subject matter that can easily be expressed in words. This is why he's often not understood, and there are people who make fun of him or say that a poem like 'Carry my heart away' is mere nonsense" (*Romanov 1999*, 52).

In 1842, Fet translated a lyric by Heine which begins "I'll carry you far away on wings of song" ("Auf Flügeln des Gesanges" from the *Lyrical Inter- mezzo*). The present text might be seen to begin from that metaphor, but Fet takes it much further, expressing, in images of light and moving water, music's power to transport, calming as the emanation of a smile, overwhelming as a wave crashing on the shore. Though its essence is sorrow, there is love and sudden shimmering beauty in it. The poem is a statement of total surrender to music by the poet, his heart "a trembling shadow made by a wing," carried away into "distant harmony" along the "silvery path" of a woman's voice.

Tchaikovsky tries to express that in this song. The music is in restless motion, testing shifts of key and trying out unexpected repeated notes. The forward motion is impelled by the 6/8 time, so that the piano seems to step lightly ahead with the voice in thrilling pursuit. There is a sense of risk about it. It anticipates the exploratory quality of Rachmaninoff's Song 70, "Music" (Op. 34/8, 1912), which, interestingly, is dedicated to Tchaikovsky. The song

is not easy to sing well. Just to deliver all the notes perfectly is not enough—
the words do matter. When the singer pays attention to the words and delivers
them with warmth, as Elisabeth Söderström or Georgy Vinogradov do, it is a
hauntingly beautiful song unlike any other.

> Уноси моё сердце в звенящую даль,
>   Где, как месяц за рощей, печаль;
> В этих звуках на жаркие слёзы твои
>   Кротко светит улыбка любви.
>
> О дитя! как легко средь незримых зыбей
>   Доверяться мне песне твоей!
> Выше, выше плыву серебристым путём,
>   Будто шаткая тень за крылом.
>
> Вдалеке замирает твой голос, горя,
>   Словно за морем ночью заря,
> И откуда-то вдруг, я понять не могу,
>   Грянет звонкий прилив жемчугу.
>
> Уноси ж моё сердце в звенящую даль,
>   Где кротка, как улыбка, печаль,
> И всё выше помчусь серебристым путём
>   Я, как шаткая тень за крылом.

Unasí majó sérttse
  v zvenjáshchuju dál',
Gde, kak mésjats za róshchej,
  pechál';
V ètikh zvúkakh na zhárkije sljózy tvají
Krótka svétit ulýpka ljubví.

Carry my heart away
  into distant harmony,
Where sorrow dwells, like the moon
  behind a grove;
In these sounds there's a smile of love
Gently shining on your burning tears.

O ditjá! kak lekhkó sred' nezrímykh
  zybéj
Daverjátsa mne pésne tvajéj!
Výshe, výshe plyvú serebrístym
  putjóm,
Bútta shátkaja tén' za krylóm.

O child! Here in these invisible
  waves
How easily I surrender to your song!
Higher, higher I soar on a silvery
  path
Like a trembling shadow cast by a wing.

Vdaleké zamirájet tvoj gólas, garjá,
Slóvno zá marem nóch'ju zarjá,
I atkúda-ta vdrúk, ja panját'
  ne magú,
Grjánet zvónkij prilíf zhemchugú.

Your voice dies in the distance, fading
Like sunset at sea in the night.
And from somewhere suddenly,
  I know not how,
A ringing tide of pearl crashes down.

Unasí sh majó sérttse	Then carry my heart
v zvenjáshchuju dál',	into distant harmony,
Gde kratká, kak ulýpka, pechál',	Where sorrow is as gentle as a smile,
I fsjo výshe pamchús'	And I'll rise ever higher
serebrístym putjóm	on a silvery path
Ja, kak shátkaja tén' za krylóm.	Like the trembling shadow of a wing.

TEXT. **Afanásy Fet**, 1857. Title: Певице (To a female singer). First set by Tchaikovsky; later by Nikolay Tcherepnin (1905).

METER. Ternary. Anapest, alternating 4 and 3-foot lines:
As I soar on the silvery path of your voice
And surrender my heart to your song…

MUSIC. Date unknown, but probably 1873. Published November 1873 in *Nouvelliste*, No. 11, St. Petersburg; in separate editions by Bernard, 1875; by Jurgenson, 1885. Without opus number. A Minor. 6/8, Allegro moderato. For Middle Voice: d^1 sharp–f^2. No dedication.

RECORDINGS. Arkhipova, Borodina, DeGaetani, Dolukhanova, Kazarnovskaya, Krasnaya, Rautio, Söderström, Vinogradov.

18 *Глазки весны голубые*
Little blue eyes of spring

Everything about this song is admirable. The excellent translation from Heine is by Mikhail Mikhailov (1829-1865), who translated over 100 of Heine's poems into Russian. Alexander Blok considered them "pearls," though he criticized Mikhailov for not trying harder to capture in Russian the form (meter, rhymes) of the originals (*Etkind*, II, 391). Tchaikovsky made two minor changes to the Russian text, and repeated some last lines.

Only a handful of singers have recorded it, but they include outstanding performances by Galina Kovalyova and Konstantin Lisovsky. It cannot be sung in the original German, which is in a different meter.

Глазки весны голубые
Кротко глядят из травы.
Любы вы милой, фиялки, —
С полем расстанетесь вы.

Рву я цветы и мечтаю. . .
В роще поют соловьи. . .
Боже мой! кто рассказал им
И думы и грёзы мои?
И думы и грёзы мои?

Громко они распевают
Всё, что на сердце таю. . .
Целая роща узнала
Нежную тайну мою,
Целая роща узнала
Нежную тайну мою,
Нежную тайну мою.

Gláski vesný galubýje	Little blue eyes of spring
Krótka gljadját is travý.	Peer out meekly in the grass.
Ljúby vy mílaj, fijálki, —	My sweetheart loves you, violets, —
S pólem rasstánetes' vý.	You and the meadow must part.
Rvú ja tsvetý i mechtáju…	I dream as I pick the flowers…
V róshche pajút salav'jí…	Nightingales are singing in the grove…
Bózhe moj! któ rasskazál im	Good God! who was it that told them
I dúmy i grjózy mají?	My thoughts, and my dreams too?
I dúmy i grjózy mají?	My thoughts, and my dreams too?

Grómka aní raspevájut	Loudly they warble abroad
Fsjó, shto na sérttse tajú…	All that I hide in my heart…
Tsélaja róshcha uznála	The whole grove has discovered
Nézhnuju tájnu majú,	This tender secret of mine,
Tsélaja róshcha uznála	The whole grove has discovered
Nézhnuju tájnu majú,	This tender secret of mine,
Nézhnuju tájnu majú.	This tender secret of mine.

TEXT. **Mikhaíl Mikháilov**, 1857. A translation of "Die blauen Frühlings-augen" (1831) by **Heinrich Heine**. Set in German by several composers including Anton Rubinstein (1856) and Charles Ives (1896). Set in Russian by some minor composers, including Dubuque (1865).

METER. Ternary. Dactyl, 3-foot:
Violets, off to my sweetheart—
You and the meadow must part.

MUSIC. Date unknown, but probably 1873. Published January 1874 in *Nouvelliste*, No. 1, St. Petersburg; in separate editions by Bernard, 1875; by Jurgenson, 1885. Without opus number. A Major. 2/4, Allegro grazioso, ma non tanto. For Middle Voice: e^1–f^2 sharp. No dedication.

RECORDINGS. DeGaetani, Kovalyova, Krasnaya, Lisovsky, Orfyonov.

Romances of 1875
Opus 25, 2 Romances without opus, Opus 27, Opus 28

In the first half of the 1870s, Tchaikovsky, now in his early thirties, was writing good music in a variety of genres, for large and small groups of instruments, as well as vocal music, including theater music. But the fact that he was still agreeing to suggestions like Stasov's "Tempest"—which he abandoned with relief when he first attempted it in June 1873 (*DG*, 94)—shows that up to this time he was still looking for that degree of independence in musical thought that he wanted, and needed, to realize his full potential.

Reaching an audience was something that mattered greatly to him, whether it be the mass audience of opera that he always aimed for, or the coterie audience of his fellow musicians and musical friends. In October 1873 he wrote six charming and inventive piano pieces, Op. 19, which he dedicated to his friends, and six more piano pieces, Op. 21, which he dedicated to Anton Rubinstein, the most commanding authority of his early years and his most important teacher. If he looked for approval from his teacher, however, he was mistaken. When one of his best new works, the second string quartet, was played in February 1874 at a soirée at Nikolay Rubinstein's, Anton happened to be in Moscow. He sat listening with a "gloomy look of dissatisfaction," and when the music ended, he said, with ruthless candor, that this was not "chamber-music style" and he did not understand it, no, he did not understand it at all. For Tchaikovsky, it was a wound that was hard to forget. But it is characteristic of his fairness that he said shortly thereafter of one of Rubinstein's concerts: "he played much, long, and well, as only a virtuoso can, who possesses both a talent of genius and an inimitable mastery long since attained" (*DG*, 101).

It was Nikolay Rubinstein's turn next to deliver a stunning blow. Since October 1874 Tchaikovsky had been trying to write a piano concerto, and by mid-November he was totally engrossed in it; it was moving ahead, but with difficulty. Bessel was pestering him for a new set of romances, but he wrote back asking not to be rushed: he promised to write the songs that winter, but had a "big work" to finish first. On Christmas Eve, on their way to a party at the conservatory, he asked Rubinstein to listen to the piano part of his first concerto, which he had just finished. He needed Rubinstein's expert advice on technique: could it be played as written? did he have any comments to give him? Rubinstein sat through the first movement without uttering a single word. (This is the very same work of which Richard Rodgers wrote in his memoirs that, as a young man, he once bought a standing-room ticket at Carnegie Hall to hear the great pianist Josef Hofmann, and when Hofmann came in under the short first statement of the orchestra with the opening chords of Tchaikovsky's first piano concerto, Rodgers had to reach for a railing for support lest his legs give way under him.) Silence. Tchaikovsky played on to the end. Then Rubinstein exploded, saying it was bad, banal, with passages plagiarized or impossible to play; two or three pages might be kept but the rest would have to be rewritten! Tchaikovsky had wanted to ask him to be the first to play the concerto and to dedicate it to him. He was offended to the core; though Rubinstein tried to make peace by offering to play it if all the changes he wanted were made, Tchaikovsky told him he would not alter a single note. Eventually, he did make some changes in the score; he forgave Rubinstein, who eventually did play the concerto. But he dedicated it to another pianist (Hans von Bülow), who gave the work its premiere, not in Moscow, but in Boston. What offended him so deeply was that by now he was aware of his worth as a composer, and was outraged to be treated like a novice. At least that was how he saw it on reflection. He could be his own harshest critic, but never again would a cold, or furious, response to his music be painful to him in that way. These rebuffs were a salutary experience: the brothers Rubinstein forced him out of the nest once and for all.

In February 1875 when Tchaikovsky finished orchestrating his piano concerto, he gave his full attention to writing twenty new songs. In March he sent six romances, as promised, to Bessel. He numbered them Opus 25; four of them were dedicated to singers who had sung the leading roles in the premiere of *Oprichnik* in Petersburg in April 1874.

Jurgenson had also asked him for some new songs. A month later Tchaikovsky sent him the two sets of six songs that became Opus 27 and Opus 28. He dedicated the whole of Opus 27 to Elizabeth Lavrovskaya, writing all six songs for her voice (she sang contralto and mezzo roles). The songs of Opus 28 were dedicated to singers, too, in this case those who were rehearsing at that very time (April 1875) for the Moscow premiere of *Oprichnik*.

Finally, to keep all his publishers happy, he sent two songs without opus to Bernard for *Nouvelliste*. I have retained the 1940 *PSS* order of these two songs, where they are listed as Songs 25 and 26, even though Tchaikovsky sent them to the publisher a few days after sending Opus 28 (Songs 33-38). The exact order in which these twenty songs were written is uncertain: they all come out of the same short, productive period of late winter and early spring 1875.

19 *Примиренье*
Reconciliation

Op. 25, No. 1

This lyric by Nikolay Shcherbina (1821-1869) has the familiarity of a "litany" (*Ries*, 83): once you realize what is being said, you know where it is going, because the same sentiments are heard in dozens of other Russian songs. It sounds like this: "the past is gone now, and with it the joy you once knew; don't try to recall it, don't try to bring it back; it can't be done, and thinking about it will only cause you pain." A central 19th-century Russian theme both in poetry and song, it was carried over into the 20th century, radically reimagined in modern terms by Anna Akhmatova and Joseph Brodsky from starting points in urban romance and the philosophical elegy.

In the 19th century the line between folk songs and romances sometimes gets blurred. In a famous song of the 1840s by Alexander Varlamov, "Ах ты время, времячко" (Ah, time, dear old golden time, where have you gone), the text is a literary one by Nikolay Tsyganov written in 1832, but ever since it first appeared in popular song books it has been thought of simply as a "Russian folk song." Poets of the early 19th century like Zhukovsky, Pushkin, and Baratynsky took it up in their "elegies," which are not so much poems about death as poems about the passage of time and its attendant losses. Many literary elegies made their way into song before Tchaikovsky was born. Aliabiev set Zhukovsky's "Воспоминание" (Remembrance) in 1815—"Gone, gone are the days of enchantment"—which is one of his earliest songs. The second song Glinka wrote to a Russian text was his 1825 setting of Baratynsky's elegy "Не искушай меня без нужды" (Don't tempt me needlessly), where the theme, in the context of a love affair now over, is a defense against memories that still cause pain. Glinka's 1851 reworking of this song is one of the most famous Russian romances—quoted in literature (Ostrovsky, Chekhov), a song everyone in Russia knew, and knows to this day. The theme occurs in popular urban romances like Pyotr Bulakhov's "Don't awaken memories of days gone by," 1877, also well-known today. Variations on this theme were common in the early 20th century in the repertoire of the gypsy contralto Varvara Panina, a singer greatly admired by Lev Tolstoy, Anton Chekhov, and Alexander Blok.

Shcherbina's two-stanza poem distills and universalizes the theme. Like earlier elegies of disillusionment, it is a summarizing poem, which looks back on the whole of the past in order to state what it adds up to. Read on its own, it cannot (nor is it meant to) bear comparison with the best elegies of Pushkin or Baratynsky, where philosophical detachment and precise expression of emotion are inseparably combined, with no residue of mere melancholy left over.

But the melancholy is essential to the song. Tchaikovsky reinforces it in a characteristic reprise. It is a song where the words say one thing ("find peace in acceptance"), but the very powerful feelings expressed in the music say just the opposite: in every phrase of the song's conclusion there is resistance and regret. In the eloquent piano part (as played, for example, by Oleg Boshniakovich in the fine recording he made with Dmitri Hvorostovsky) the author of the first piano concerto can be heard. Deeply tied to the urban romance tradition, yet completely original and bearing his unique signature, the song is a quintessential Tchaikovsky romance and one of his best.

О, засни, моё сердце, глубоко!
Не буди—не пробудишь, что было,
Не зови, что умчалось далёко,
Не люби, что ты прежде любило...
    Пусть надеждой и лживой мечтой
    Не смутится твой сон и покой.

Для тебя невозвратно былое,
На грядущее нет упованья...
Ты не знало в блаженстве покоя,
Успокойся ж на ложе страданья,
    И старайся не помнить зимой,
    Как срывало ты розы весной!

О, засни, моё сердце, глубоко!
Не буди—не пробудишь, что было,
Не зови, что умчалось далёко,
Не люби, что ты прежде любило...
    Пусть надеждой и лживой мечтой
    Не смутится твой сон и покой,
    Не смутится твой сон и покой!
    И старайся не помнить зимой,
    Что срывало ты розы весной!

O, zasní, majo sérttse, glubóka!
Ne budí—ne prabúdish, shto býla,
Ne zaví, shto umchálas' daljóka,
Ne ljubí, shto ty prézhde ljubíla...
    Pust' nadézhdaj i lzhívaj mechtój
    Ne smutítsa tvoj són i pakój.

O, fall asleep deeply, my heart!
Don't try to waken the past—you can't do it,
Don't try to call back what's fled far away,
Don't keep on loving what you once loved...
    May hope and delusive dreams
    Not trouble your sleep and peace.

Dlja tebjá nevazvrátna bylóje,
Na grjadúshcheje nét upaván'ja...
Ty ne znála v blazhénstve pakója,
Uspakójsa sh na lózhe stradán'ja,
    I starájsa ne pómnit' zimój,
    Kak sryvála ty rózy vesnój!

You can't bring back what used to be,
The future is no bastion of hope...
You knew no peace in bliss,
Be at peace now on your couch of suffering,
    And try not to remember in winter,
    How you gathered roses in the spring!

O, zasní, majo sérttse, glubóka!
Ne budí—ne prabúdish, shto býla,

O, fall asleep deeply, my heart!
Don't try to waken the past—you can't do it,

Ne zaví, shto umchálas' daljóka,	Don't try to call back what's fled far away,
Ne ljubí, shto ty prézhde ljubíla...	Don't keep on loving what you once loved...
Pust' nadézhdaj i lzhívaj mechtój	May hope and delusive dreams
Ne smutítsa tvoj són i pakój.	Not trouble your sleep and peace,
Ne smutítsa tvoj són i pakój!	Not trouble your sleep and peace!
I starájsa ne pómnit' zimój,	And try not to remember in winter,
Shto sryvála ty rózy vesnój!	That you gathered roses in the spring!

TEXT. **Nikoláy Shcherbiná**, 1848; published 1857. Title: Примиренье (Reconciliation). Two now-forgotten composers are listed as having set this poem, one of them, A. M. Larme, a year or so before Tchaikovsky. But no serious composer has ever attempted it since Tchaikovsky's setting, which is so definitive that it is impossible to read the words without hearing his music.

METER. Ternary. Anapest, 3-foot:

> *Fall asleep, oh my heart, now it's winter,*
> *And forget you picked roses in springtime...*

MUSIC. Winter 1874-5; published April 1875. Op. 25, no. 1. G Minor. 4/4, Moderato quasi andantino. For Middle Voice: a–g^2.

Dedicated to **Aleksándra Krútikova** (1851-1919), a contralto who studied with Nissen-Saloman at the St. Petersburg Conservatory, 1866-72. Sang at the Mariinsky Theater in St. Petersburg from 1872-76; in the premiere of *Oprichnik* there in 1874 she sang the part of Boyarina Morozova, for which Tchaikovsky wrote some of the best music in the opera. Later, at the Bolshoy, she sang Lyubov in the premiere of *Mazeppa* (1884) and the Countess in the first Moscow *Queen of Spades* in November 1891, a performance which Tchaikovsky attended. Song 73 is also dedicated to her. Married to Gottfried Korsov (see Song 37).

RECORDINGS. Arkhipova, Borodina, Descamps, Gmyria, Hvorostovsky, Krasnaya, Leiferkus, Lemeshev, Levko, Lisitsian, Mishura, Mkrtchyan, Obraztsova, **Obukhova**, Reizen, Tear, Vishnevskaya.

∽

20 *Как над горячею золой*
As over darkly glowing embers

Op. 25, No. 2

It is surprising that Fyodor Tyutchev (1803-1873), one of the greatest Russian lyric poets, was not set by any of the major 19th-century composers except Tchaikovsky. A few of his poems were set early as popular romances, but the finest songs to poems by Tyutchev were written by Rachmaninoff and Medtner in the 20th century—in other words, after the Symbolists had rediscovered his greatness as a poet.

This poem is an interesting choice. What makes it typical of Tyutchev is its combination of slightly archaic language and perfect colloquial ease, the undeniable force of its idea, and the way the idea arises out of something physical, something as ordinary as watching a stoked fire burn down, something that the senses can weigh and assess and independently confirm. The comparison is exact, that certain lingering degree of heat that causes burning to be so slow it isn't noticed. This is what life comes down to, and death is there so inescapably it doesn't even have to be mentioned. The idea is as old as Shakespeare's image of burning out "on the ashes of his youth" (Sonnet 73). Walter Pater's idea of living for moments of ecstasy by burning with a "hard, gemlike flame" would be taken up in Russia later, during the Symbolist period, but it is striking how the last line of Tyutchev's poem anticipates it—with a difference, however.

Lev Tolstoy used to mark poems that he thought were profound with a special sign. This is one of the poems he marked. He did not say what made it profound for him. Was it the explosive force of the final stanza, the desperate wish that bursts out in it? If so, what is striking in Tchaikovsky's musical setting of the poem is not the last stanza, but the middle one, sung slowly with free expression (*ad libitum*). In the song, the last stanza does not stand out or build to a strong climax because it is in symmetry with the first, and these are preceded and followed by prominent piano parts (the conclusion of the song actually states a "fate" motif Tchaikovsky used later in his opera *Queen of Spades*). The first and third stanzas are declamatory, shaped dramatically rather like Rachmaninoff's declamatory songs. At the very heart of the song, surrounded by all this "allegro con spirito," is the middle stanza of the poem, which floats up to be sung with slow, lyrical melancholy.

The material, both for the singer and accompanist, is strong; it has compactness and contrasting intensity. Tchaikovsky's setting of the text throws a completely unexpected light on the poem. Perhaps because it is so original it has been overlooked: commentary on it is hard to find with the exception of a recent study (*Blagoi*, 563-68). Pavel Lisitsian's fine reading shows the song to good advantage.

Как над горячею золой	Так грустно тлится жизнь моя
Дымится свиток и сгорает,	И с каждым днём уходит дымом;
И огнь сокрытый и глухой	Так постепенно гасну я
Слова и строки пожирает:	В однообразьи нестерпимом...

О, небо, если бы хоть раз
Сей пламень развился по воле,
И, не томясь, не мучась доле,
Я просиял бы и погас!

Kak nad garjácheju zalój	As over darkly glowing embers
Dymítsa svítak i zgarájet,	A scroll will smoke and be consumed,
I ógn' sakrýty i glukhój	And fire, invisible and mute,
Slavá i stróki pazhyrájet:	Will swallow up the words and lines:

Tak grúsna tlítsa zhýzn' majá	So my life sadly smolders too,
I s kázhdym dnjóm ukhódit dýmam;	And day by day it drifts away in smoke;
Tak pastepénna gásnu já	So gradually I'm burning down
V adnaabráz'ji nesterpímam...	In unendurable monotony...

O, néba, jésli by khat' rás	O, heaven, if only once this fire
Sej plámen' razvilsá pa vóle,	Might burst into an open flame,
I, ne tamjás', ne múchas' dóle,	And, without further grief or torment,
Ja prasijál by i pagás!	I would flare up brightly and burn out!

TEXT. **Fyódor Tyútchev**, 1829. Set first by Tchaikovsky; later by some minor composers, all students of Rimsky-Korsakov (Antsev, Catoire, Yulia Veisberg).

METER. Binary. Iambic, 4-foot:

> *As over darkly glowing embers*
> *A scroll will smoke and be consumed...*

MUSIC. Winter 1874-75; published April 1875. Op. 25, no. 2. B Minor. 2/4, Allegro con spirito. For High Voice: f^1 sharp–g^2.

Dedicated to the tenor **Dmítry Orlóv** (1842-1919), who sang the role of Andrey in the premiere of *Oprichnik* in St. Petersburg, April 1874.

RECORDINGS. Descamps, Fischer-Dieskau, Kazarnovskaya, Krasnaya, Lemeshev, Lisitsian, Nelepp, Petrov, Söderström, Tear.

21 Песнь Миньоны
Mignon's song

Op. 25, No. 3

Goethe's lyric about making a journey together to a warm, blue-and-gold south, with treks through misty, magical mountains, was, in the Romantic Age, at least in Northern Europe, a poem everyone knew and quoted.

This version of the German original was only one of several translations into Russian, but in choosing it Tchaikovsky picked the most interesting one. Tyutchev's translation is unusual because it reverses the order of the second and third stanzas. It seems unlikely this was an accident: Tyutchev knew German and German literature as well as he knew Russian, and he spent time on this translation, revising it for publication, saying he considered it a true test of any poet's skill as a translator. His rearrangement of the stanzas has the effect of ending the poem not in the high mountain landscape of cliffs and raging torrents, but in the valley, in the domestic setting of a house—a rather grand house, to be sure, a marble-columned edifice with statues, which for Goethe was inspired by a palace he admired in Vicenza. In moving the two stanzas, however, Tyutchev did not move the word "father," but kept it in the concluding line of the poem. Tyutchev's version of the poem ends on a note of going home at last, after long wanderings.

Tchaikovsky repeated lines, sometimes with slight changes in wording. Here, his custom of reprising the first stanza at the end makes no sense in terms of the text, which is already in three parts and leads in a definite direction. It is a rarely performed song. A recent study suggests that it owes something to Robert Schumann, whose piano style Tchaikovsky paid homage to on more than one occasion (*Blagoi*, 571).

> Ты знаешь край, где мирт и лавр растёт,
> Глубок и чист лазурный неба свод,
> Цветёт лимон и апельсин златой,
> Как жар, горит под зеленью густой?..
>   Ты знаешь край? Ты знаешь край?
>   Туда, туда, туда с тобой
>   Хотела б я укрыться, милый мой!..
>   Ты знаешь край? Туда с тобой
>   Хотела б я укрыться, милый мой!

Ты знаешь высь, с стезёй по крутизнам,
Лошак бредёт в тумане по скалам,
В ущельях гор отродье змей живёт,
Гремит обвал и водопад ревёт?...
 Ты знаешь путь? Ты знаешь путь?
 Туда, туда и нам с тобой
 Проложен след: уйдём, властитель мой!
 Ты знаешь путь? Туда и нам
 След проложен: уйдём, властитель мой!

Ты знаешь дом на мраморных столбах,
Сияет зал и купол весь в лучах;
Глядят кумиры молча и грустя:
"Что, что с тобой, бедное дитя?"
 Ты знаешь дом? Ты знаешь дом?
 Туда с тобой уйдём, родитель мой!

(Reprise first stanza. Songs ends with a final "Милый мой!")

Ty znájesh kráj, gde mírt i lávr rastjót,	Know you the land where bay and myrtle grow,
Glubók i chíst lazúrnyj néba svót,	Where heaven's azure vault is deep and pure,
Tsvetjót limón i apel'sín zlatój,	Where lemon and the golden orange bloom
Kak zhár, garít pad zélen'ju gustój?	Like fire burning under dense green leaves?
Ty znájesh kráj? Ty znájesh kráj?	Know you that land? Know you that land?
Tudá, tudá, tudá s tabój,	There, there, there with you
Khatéla b ja ukrýtsa, mílyj mój!	I'd hide away, my darling!
Ty znájesh kráj? Tudá s tabój,	Know you that land? There with you
Khatéla b ja ukrýtsa, mílyj mój!	I'd hide away, my darling!
Ty znájesh výs', s stezjój pa krutiznám,	Know you the summit with the steep path,
Lashák bredjót f tumáne pa skalám,	Where a mule climbs by cliffs in mist,
V ushchél'jakh gór atród'je zméj zhivjót,	Where in mountain gorges a dragon-brood dwells,
Gremít abvál i vadapát revjót?	Where an avalanche booms and falling water roars?
Ty znájesh pút'? Ty znájesh pút'?	Know you the path? Know you the path?
Tudá, tudá, i nám s tabój	There, there for you and me
Pralózhen slét: ujdjóm, vlastítel' mój!	Lies the trail: let us go, my protector!
Ty znájesh pút'? Tudá i nám	Know you the path? For you and me
Slét pralazhón: ujdjóm, vlastítel' mój!	The trail lies there: let us go, my protector!

Ty znájesh dóm na mrámarnykh stalbákh,	Know you that house on marble columns,
Sijájet zál i kúpal ves' v luchákh;	Its hall shining, its dome in rays of light;
Gljadját kumíry mólcha i grustjá:	There gaze the idols silent and sad:
"Shtó, shtó s tabój, bédnaje ditjá?"	"What is it, what's happened, poor child?"
Ty znájesh dóm? Ty znájesh dóm?	Know you that house? Know you that house?
Tudá s tabój ujdjóm, radítel' mój!	Let us go there, father, you and I!

(Reprise first stanza. Songs ends with a final "My darling!")

TEXT. **Fyódor Tyútchev**, 1851. A translation of Mignon's song "Kennst du das Land, wo die Zitronen blühn," from Book 3 of *Wilhelm Meisters Lehrjahre* (1795) by **Goethe**. Second of three of Mignon's songs set by Tchaikovsky (the others are Songs 9 and 70). The German lyric is one of the most famous in European literature: set by many composers, including Beethoven, Schubert, Liszt, Schumann, Wolf, and Berg.

METER. Binary. Iambic, 5-foot, with shorter (inset) lines of 4 feet:

Know you the land where bay and myrtle grow,
Where heaven's azure vault is deep and pure?

Tyutchev's translation is in a Russian equivalent to Goethe's meter, so Tchaikovsky's song could be sung to the German text.

MUSIC. Winter 1874-75; published April 1875. Op. 25, no. 3. E-flat Major. 4/4, Allegro moderato. For High Voice: e^1 natural–g^2 flat.

Dedicated to the mezzo-soprano **Maria Kaménskaya** (1854-1925). At the time of the dedication, she was a young singer just out of the Petersburg Conservatory. In December 1873 she sang Songs 9 and 14 at a student concert reviewed by Cui, who wrote that the latter was "worthless musically," but Song 9 (None but the lonely heart) "in spots has a certain Italian charm" (*DG*, 99). This is the only dedication in Opus 25 not connected with *Oprichnik*: perhaps it was Tchaikovsky's way of saluting her for singing his songs on hostile territory. During her career at the Mariinsky and in Tiflis she sang major roles in nearly all of his operas.

RECORDINGS. Krasnaya, Tugarinova, Zelenina.

☙

22 Канарейка
The canary

Op. 25, No. 4

Romantic poems with oriental subjects became popular in Russia and the rest of Europe after the brilliant success of poems like Byron's *Giaour* and *Bride of Abydos* (both 1813). These tales and others like them are full of Turkish pashas and harems, with a cast of heroes rescuing heroines named Zuleika—"the young, the beautiful, the brave"—risking everything for love and *freedom*. For Russians, all this, including the word "freedom," had a special resonance because of Russia's own proximity to the edges of this exotic world. Pushkin, Lermontov, and Tolstoy wrote poems and stories that captured, better than anything in Byron, the color, the poetry, the values and outlook of the Eastern world, after they saw it with their own eyes in the Crimea and the Caucasus.

In Russian music, orientalism is usually traced back to the Georgian dance in Glinka's *Ruslan and Ludmila* (1842). Famous later examples of it are Rimsky-Korsakov's *Scheherazade*, a work whose "synthetic orientalism even influenced composers in Arab countries" (*Slonimsky 1989*, 424), and Borodin's opera *Prince Igor*, "the most gorgeous panoply of Russian orientalism" (*ibid.*, 384). Good songs in the oriental style were written by Anton Rubinstein, Balakirev, and Rimsky-Korsakov. Tchaikovsky knew Rubinstein's "Persian" songs well (Op. 34, 1854), because he translated their lyrics from German into Russian in 1869 and these are the versions which are sung in Russia to this day.

This is Tchaikovsky's only romance on an oriental theme. The music achieves its color from graceful triplets and devices like the interval of the augmented second, solidly established in the second line of the text.

Говорит султанша канарейке:
«Птичка! лучше в тереме высоком
Щебетать и песни петь Зюлейке,
Чем порхать на Западе далёком?
Спой же, спой же мне про заморе, певичка,
Спой же, спой же мне про Запад, непоседка!
Есть ли там такое небо, птичка,
Есть ли там такой гарем и клетка?
У кого там столько роз бывало?
У кого из шахов есть Зюлейка —
И поднять ли так ей покрывало?»

Ей в ответ щебечет канарейка:
«Не проси с меня заморских песен,
Не буди тоски моей без нужды:
Твой гарем по нашим песням тесен,
И слова их одалискам чужды…
Ты в ленивой дрёме расцветала,
Как и вся кругом тебя природа,
И не знаешь — даже не слыхала,
Что у песни есть сестра — свобода.»

Gavarít sultánsha kanaréjke:

"Ptíchka! lúchshe f téreme vysókam

Shchebetát' i pésni pet' Zjuléjke,

Chem parkhát' na Západe daljókam?

Spóy zhe, spóy zhe mne pra zámare,
    pevíchka,

Spóy zhe, spóy zhe mne pra Západ,
    nepasétka!

Jést' li tam takóje néba, ptíchka,

Jést' li tam takój garém i klétka?

U kavó tam stól'ka rós byvála?

U kavó is shákhaf jést' Zjuléjka —

I padnját' li tak jej pakryvála?"

Jej v atvét shchebéchet kanaréjka:

"Ne prasí s menjá zamórskikh pésen,

Ne budí taskí majéj bez núzhdy:

Tvoj garém pa náshim pésnjam tésen,

I slavá ikh adalískam
    chúzhdy...

Ty v lenívaj drjóme rastsvetála,

Kak i fsja krugóm tebjá priróda,

I ne znájesh, dázhe ne slykhála,

Shto u pésni jést' sestrá — svabóda."

Says the sultan's wife to her canary:

"Little bird! is it better in a palace tower

To chirp and sing Zuleika songs

Than to dart about in distant Western lands?

Sing for me, songbird, sing of lands across
    the sea,

Sing about the West to me, restless little
    thing!

Is there a sky there like ours,

Is there a harem, does it have a birdcage?

Who there ever had so many roses?

Do any of their Shahs have a Zuleika —

And can she lift her veil like this?"

Chirping her reply the canary answers:

"Don't ask for songs of distant lands from me,

I'm homesick as it is, don't make it worse:

Your harem's too confining for our songs,

And to your slave-girls' ears the words are
    strange...

You and all of nature here around you

Reached your lovely prime in lazy ease,

You couldn't know, no one ever even told you,

A song has a sister — her name is freedom."

Text. **Lev Mey**, 1859. Title: Канарейка (The Canary). First set by Tchaikovsky; later by several minor composers. Tchaikovsky set Mey's text as written, except for the repeated verb in lines 5 and 6 and two very minor changes in spelling and pronoun usage in the second stanza.

Meter. Binary. Trochee, 5-foot:

> *You and all of nature here around you*
> *Reached your lovely prime in lazy ease...*

The choice of this rather rare "Slavic" meter for a poem on an oriental theme is highly unusual. Mey's technical originality was not appreciated until the 20th century (*RP* III, 567-8).

Music. Winter of 1874-75; published April 1875. Op. 25, no. 4. G Minor. 4/4, Moderato. For High Voice: c^1–g^2. Dedicated to the soprano **Wilhelmina Raab** (1848-1917), who sang Natalia in the premiere of *Oprichnik* in 1874.

Recordings. Christoff, DeGaetani, Katulskaya, Krasnaya, Oleinichenko, Rautio, Rodgers, Sterling, Tugarinova.

23 *Я с нею никогда не говорил*
I never spoke to her

Op. 25, No. 5

The text of this song is actually two stanzas taken from a longer poem called "Octaves." Octaves are the Russian equivalent of *ottava rima*, a meter used in Italy by Boccacio, Ariosto, and Tasso, and adapted in England by Byron to brilliant comic effect in his *Beppo* (1818) and *Don Juan* (1819-24). In Russia, Pushkin used it in Byron's half-serious vein in "Little House in Kolomna" (1830), whence Stravinsky a century later took the subject of his opera *Mavra*.

Octaves give you room to tell a story, to ruminate, to digress. Lev Mey's poem of fifteen stanzas does that, though the comic possibilities are absent. It is a lyrical confession of a young man who, as a schoolboy, had fallen in love from a distance with one of the Empress's young maids of honor (Mey's school was the Lycée located next to the summer palace at Tsarskoe Selo, founded in 1811 by Alexander I for sons of the nobility, famous because Pushkin was a member of its first class).

In Tchaikovsky's two earlier sets of romances there was a love song for baritone (Songs 7 and 13), which is what we have here. In this case, though, the text is not problematical: the sentiments are completely believable as a literary expression of adolescent first love. Like Song 1, also written for low voice, this song is about idealized adoration strongly felt. It may be a coincidence, but Tchaikovsky, who brings much feeling to this theme, was himself a baritone. Dietrich Fischer-Dieskau's recording brings out the abundant beauty of the lyrical material in this song—a lyricism which does not yet have the strong melodic definition of *Eugene Onegin*, but points in that direction.

Я с нею никогда не говорил,
Но я искал повсюду с нею
    встречи,
Бледнея и дрожа, за ней следил.
Её движенья, взгляд, улыбку,
    речи
Я жадно, я внимательно ловил,
А после, я убегал от всех далече,
Её в мечтах себе я представлял,
Грустил, вздыхал, томился и
    ревновал.
Грустил, вздыхал, томился и
    ревновал!

Не рассказать—что делалось со мною.
Не описать волшебной красоты…
    волшебной красоты не описать!
С весенним солнцем, с розовой зарёю,
С слезой небес, упавшей на цветы,
С лучом луны, с вечернею звездою
В моих мечтах слились её черты…
В моих мечтах слились её черты…
Я помню только светлое виденье,
    светлое виденье,
Мой идеал, отраду и мученье,
Мой идеал, отраду и мученье!

Ja s néju nikagdá ne gavaríl,   I never spoke to her,
No ja iskál pafsjúdu s néju fstréchi,   But tried to meet her everywhere I could,
Blednéja i drazhá, za néj sledíl.   Pale and trembling I pursued her.
Jejó dvizhén'ja, vzgliát, ulýpku, réchi   The way she moved, her look, smile, voice,
Ja zhádna, ja vnimátel'na lavíl,   I eagerly drank in every detail,
A pósle, ja ubegál at fsékh daléche,   Then would go off by myself
Jejó v mechtákh sebé ja pretstavljál,   And imagine her in my dreams,
Grustíl, vzdykhál, tamílsa i revnavál.   I grieved, sighed, pined, was jealous.
Grustíl, vzdykhál, tamílsa i revnavál!   I grieved, sighed, pined, was jealous!

Ne rasskazát' — shto délalas' sa mnóju.   What I experienced is past all telling.
Ne apisát' valshébnaj krasatý...   Enchanting beauty cannot be described...
    valshébnaj krasatý ne apisát'!   beauty like that can't be described!
S vesénnim sóntsem, s rózavaj zarjóju,   The sun in spring, the rosy dawn,
S slezój nebés, upáfshej na tsvetý,   Heaven's tear falling on the flowers,
S luchóm luný, s vechérneju zvezdóju   Moonbeam and evening star,
V majíkh mechtákh slilís' jejó chertý...   It all blended in my dreams with her...
V majíkh mechtákh slilís' jejó chertý...   It blended in my dreams with her...
Ja pómnju tól'ka svétlaje vidén'je,   I remember only the bright vision,
    svétlaje vidén'je,   the bright vision,
Moj ideál, atrádu i muchén'je,   My ideal, my joy and torment,
Moj ideál, atrádu i muchén'je!   My ideal, my joy and torment!

TEXT. **Lev Mey**, 1844. Stanzas 10 and 11 of verses entitled "Октавы" (Octaves). First set by Tchaikovsky; later by a minor composer.

METER. Binary. Iambic, 5-foot:

What I experienced is past all telling,
Enchanting beauty cannot be described!

In the song, the two stanzas have more than the canonical eight lines of *ottava rima*, owing to Tchaikovsky's repetition of some lines and phrases. He also inserted a hypermetrical one-syllable word in lines 6, 8, and 9.

MUSIC. Winter 1874-75; published April 1875. Op. 25, no. 5. A Major. 3/4, Andante semplice. For Low Voice: A–e¹.

Dedicated to the baritone **Iván Mélnikov** (1832-1906), who sang the role of Prince Vyazminsky in the premiere of *Oprichnik* in 1874.

RECORDINGS. Descamps, Fischer-Dieskau, Krasnaya, Mazurok, Migay.

24   *Как наладили: «Дурак*   As they harped their tune: "You fool

Op. 25, No. 6

Lev Mey (1822-1862) is remembered in Russian music as the author of both original lyrics and good translations set by Musorgsky, Rimsky-Korsakov, Rachmaninoff, Grechaninov, and others, as well as two historical plays used by Rimsky-Korsakov as the basis for his operas *The Maid of Pskov* (1891) and *The Tsar's Bride* (1899). Tchaikovsky set four of Mey's own lyrics (Songs 22, 23, 24, and 35), and seven of his translations (Songs 8, 9, 25, 30, 31, 32, 34).

Mey's interest in Russian lore, especially his knowledge of the beliefs and superstitions of the Russian people, was something Tyutchev noticed and remarked on in a letter to Vyazemsky (*Tiutchev 1957*, 9 July 1857). He was not interested in writing the kind of imitation folksongs which Aleksey Koltsov made popular with the urban audience, and which were taken up by composers great and small as texts for "Russian songs" in the 19th century. Mey tried to get closer to the village source, both in terms of peasant psychology and the authentic language used to express it. His literary folksongs are few in number, but include extraordinary texts like the one Musorgsky used for his song "Hunting for mushrooms" ("Po griby," 1867). The poem Tchaikovsky chose for this monologue by a fool who is a chronic drunkard is equally unusual.

In Russia the mention of drunkenness is liable to evoke sighs about "our national *woe*"—as, indeed, it is. Mey knew what it felt like to be the *durák*, the "fool" in this poem: he was dead at 40, in fact, as a result of the drinking binges he never could give up once he and his friends, the poet and critic Apollon Grigoriev and the dramatist Alexander Ostrovsky, began carousing in the Moscow taverns when the three of them were starting out as young writers.

What is one to make of this text? On the one hand, the poem laughs at the fool—anyone who thinks that bowing down to the river to learn how water can cure a man from vodka surely is a fool. But on the other hand the problem is real, the need to drown that "serpent sorrow," which is a Russian equivalent of the blues and just as serious. The fool has a conscience, too, a sense of shame before other people. Maybe there is hope for him after all.

Tchaikovsky's reading of the text combines all this into a song of comic realism, to be sung "Allegro giocoso." He brings out the good-natured simplicity of the fool, who, in his innocence, rashly appeals to the river to cure his drunkenness. But Tchaikovsky also makes his shame prominent, building up to it with a sudden shift to 3/2 time in the penultimate line of the second stanza, giving an urgency to that line about shame, then making it emphatic by repeating it in the original 4/4 meter. The song has been criticized (*Vasina-*

Grossman, 273) for not bringing out the "tragic irony" in Mey's text (more about this presently), but Tchaikovsky's treatment is a valid reading of the poem—a comic reading which implies a happy outcome. He was no doubt drawn to it because it was in the spirit of his comic opera *Vakula the Smith* (1874), which he found exhilarating to work on and wrote quickly. Nevertheless, it is unique among Tchaikovsky's songs, an experiment in a kind of song he did not attempt again—something more in Musorgsky's line, perhaps. Oddly, it is the only song in Opus 25 without a dedication.

The irony missing in Tchaikovsky's song is that in folk tradition, as in life, drunken fools are not very likely to be cured. On the contrary, in the old songs they are more likely to be drowned (literally) as a result of going to the tavern in the first place. Addressing a river, as the fool is advised to do in Mey's poem, can be quite dangerous: the more forceful the words, the greater the danger, all the way to boasting, which is a guarantee of being drowned (*Sobolevskii*, I, nos. 280-290). There are sly allusions to drowning in Mey's poem.

It is striking that it begins with antiquated language from a famous cycle of folk songs and tales about a drunkard who is pursued by a figure named "Woe." Songs on this theme begin with warnings from parents sending their son into the world:

Не ходи, мой сын, во царёв кабак,   Don't go, my son, to the Tsar's kabak,
Ты не пей, мой сын, зелена вина…   Don't drink, my son, any green wine…

These odd expressions go back to the sixteenth century, when vodka began to be distilled in Russia. The *kabák* is a tavern, a Tatar word first attested in Russian in 1563, a few years after Ivan the Terrible laid siege to Kazan. Though the Tatar Khans did not allow drinking in the city, strong drink was sold outside the city gates in stalls called "kabaks." Tsar Ivan was impressed. He declared a monopoly on the vodka trade in Russia and ordered that it be distilled and sold in an institution to be called the *kabák*—inside the city gates, however, and eventually in the villages, too. Hence a place to get a drink of vodka came to be known popularly in Russia as a "Tsar's kabak." As for the vodka itself, it was popularly called "green wine" owing to the greenish tinge it acquired from the copper in vessels used to distill it (*Christian*, 27). In the fourth line of Mey's poem, then, "wine" is understood to mean vodka.

Mey clearly took as his starting point lines like those above from the oral songs about Woe (*Гope*), who is a nemesis figure. From the outset, then, a possibility of nemesis haunts this text. Even the verb in the first line, *naládili*, has a double meaning: to harp on one and the same thing, but also to cast a spell, to direct evil (*pórcha*) on someone, a usage which is still current in some Russian villages today (*Paxson*). The whole force of the figure of Woe in these old folk songs that go back to the reign of Ivan the Terrible is that once encountered in the tavern, the "fool" can never be rid of him: as a gray wolf, he runs across a field, but Woe is a dog chasing him down; he is a falcon in flight, but Woe is a raven in pursuit; he dives into the "swift river," but Woe is a fisherman waiting for him; he floats out to sea, but Woe sits on his "white breast" and he drowns (*Sobolevskii*, I, nos. 438-446).

There is a postscript to Tchaikovsky's song. In 1895, long after Musorgsky was dead, and two years after Tchaikovsky himself had died, Mily Balakirev sat down to make a song out of this same text. The old, stubborn leader of the "national" school must have wanted to have the last word one more time. He undoubtedly knew, as Mey knew, that "Woe" is present in this text even though he is never mentioned by name. The fool in Balakirev's song is a corrective to Tchaikovsky's in the direction of realism, with a comic swagger to be sure, but altogether more driven, impulsive, out of control, and very likely destined to end up in a ditch.

Both songs may be heard on Boris Christoff's splendid "Mélodies russes," in strong, vivid performances which, however, take some small liberties with the lyrics.

Как наладили: «Дурак,
Брось ходить в царёв кабак!»
Так и ладят все одно:
«Пей ты воду, не вино;
Вон хошь речке поклонись,
Хошь у быстрой поучись».

Уж я к реченьке пойду,
С речкой речи поведу:
«Говорят мне — ты умна,
Поклонюсь тебе до дна;
Научи ты, как мне быть,
Пьянством люда не срамить?
Пьянством люда не срамить?

Как в тебя, мою реку,
Утопить змею–тоску?
А научишь — век тогда
Исполать тебе, вода,
Что отбила дурака
От царёва кабака!»

Kak naládili: "Durák,	As they harped their tune: "*Durák*,
Brós' khadít' f tsarjóf kabák!"	Give up going to the Tsar's *kabák*!"
Tak i ládjat fsjó adnó:	So they harp still that old line:
"Péj ty vódu, ne vinó;	"Drink the water, not the wine;
Vón khosh réchke paklanís',	Bow down to the river now,
Khosh u býstraj pauchís'."	Let the swift stream teach you how."
Ush ja k réchenke pajdú,	To the river then I'll go,
S réchkaj réchi pavedú:	Water and I will have a word:
"Gavarját mne — ty umná,	"You're a clever girl, I've heard, —
Paklanjús' tebé da dná;	I'll bow down to your depths below;
Nauchí ty, kák mne být',	Can you teach me truer aim,
P'jánstvam ljúda ne sramít'?	Sparing folks my drunken shame?
P'jánstvam ljúda ne sramít'?	Sparing folks my drunken shame?
Kak f tebjá, majú rekú,	Water, if I drink you down,
Utapít' zmejú-taskú?	Will the serpent sorrow drown?
A naúchish — vék tagdá	If you teach me — then forever
Ispalát' tebé, vadá,	Hallelujah to you, river,
Shto adbíla duraká	That you rescued this *durák*
At tsarjóva kabaká!"	From going to the Tsar's *kabák*!"

TEXT. **Lev Mey**, date unknown, first published 1860. Title: Песня (Song). First set by Tchaikovsky; later by Balakirev (1895-6).

METER. Binary. Trochee, 4-foot:

> *Water, if I drink you down,*
> *Will the serpent sorrow drown?*

MUSIC. Winter 1874-75; published April 1875. Op. 25, no. 6. G Minor. 4/4, Allegro giocoso. For Middle Voice: f–f¹. No dedication.

RECORDINGS. Anders (in German), Christoff, Descamps, Fischer-Dieskau, Krasnaya, Mazurok, Tear.

Balakirev: Christoff.

⌣⌐

25 Хотел бы в единое слово
I wish I could pour into a single word

The dichotomy between waking and dreaming is basic to the psychology of Romanticism. It is put to original use by Heine in this poem translated by Lev Mey. The song is straightforward, eminently singable, one of Tchaikovsky's shortest and best known. Instead of a piano introduction, there are just two chords that state the dichotomy as a dissonance. The vocal part has a simple, quite modern design. The form is AABA, with one melody for the A sections, and a different melody for the B section (the third stanza of the poem). The singer's part is like the refrain of a 32-bar American standard song, with four sections of eight bars each; the release, or "bridge," which is the B section, is a new melody in a different key, just as we might expect in a song written by George Gershwin or Richard Rodgers. Musically, the A and B sections bring out different emotions. There is longing and ardent determination in the A stanzas, but the release, sung a little more slowly, is intimate, with subconscious hints of the erotic, as the singer's "word" violates the sleep of his beloved and enters secretly into her dream life.

A very different setting of the same poem, focused more on the inner, morbid side of Heine, was composed earlier by Musorgsky, though his song was not published until 1911.

> Хотел бы в единое слово
> Я слить мою грусть и печаль
> И бросить то слово на ветер,
> Чтоб ветер унёс его вдаль.
>
> И пусть бы то слово печали
> По ветру к тебе донеслось,
> И пусть бы всегда и повсюду
> Оно тебе в сердце лилось!
>
> И если б усталые очи
> Сомкнулись под грёзой ночной,
> О пусть бы то слово печали
> Звучало во сне над тобой!
>
> Хотел бы в единое слово
> Я слить мою грусть и печаль
> И бросить то слово на ветер,
> Чтоб ветер унёс его вдаль.
> Чтоб ветер унёс, унёс его вдаль.

Khatél by v jedínaje slóva	I wish I could pour into a single word
Ja slít' maju grúst' i pechál'	All my sorrow and sadness
I brósit' to slóva na véter,	And throw that word to the wind,
Shtob véter unjós jevo vdál'.	So the wind would carry it far away.
I púzd' by to slóva pecháli	And I wish that word of sadness
Pa vétru k tebé daneslós',	Would be brought to you on the wind,
I púzd' by fsegdá i pafsjúdu	So that always and everywhere
Anó tebé f sérttse lilós'!	It would flow into your heart!
I jésli b ustályje óchi	And if your tired eyes
Samknúlis' pad grjózaj nachnój,	Should close in reverie at night,
O púzd' by to slóva pecháli	O may that word of sadness
Zvuchala va sné nat tabój!	Resound above you in your dreams!
Khatél by v jedínaje slóva	I wish I could pour into a single word
Ja slít' maju grúst' i pechál'	All my sorrow and sadness
I brósit' to slóva na véter,	And throw that word to the wind,
Shtob véter unjós jevo vdál'.	So the wind would carry it far away.
Shtob véter unjós, unjós jevo vdál'.	So the wind would carry it away, carry it far away.

TEXT. **Lev Mey**, 1859. A translation of "Ich wollt, meine Schmerzen ergössen," no. 61 in "Die Heimkehr" (The Homecoming, 1823-24), by **Heinrich Heine**. Published in *Russkoe Slovo* (Russian Word), no. 3, 1859, with an essay by Apollon Grigoriev on Heine. First set by Musorgsky in 1866 with the title Желание (Wish), published in 1911. Settings in German by Alexander Fesca (1844) and Ignaz Brüll (1860s).

METER. Ternary. Amphibrach, 3-foot:
A word on the wind I would send you,
With all of my sadness and grief...

MUSIC. 1875 (by 3 May). Without opus number. D Minor. 6/8, Allegro moderato. For High Voice: e^1–g^2. First published by Bernard in *Nouvelliste*, no. 9 (September), 1875, and in a separate edition in 1876. Republished by Jurgenson in 1885. No dedication.

RECORDINGS. Gmyria, Guliayev, Hvorostovsky, Khromchenko, Kovalyova, Krasnaya, Larin, Leiferkus, Lemeshev, Magomayev, Martynov, Mazurok, Mkrtchyan, Morozov, Nesterenko, Pechkovsky, Petina, Petrov, Serkebayev, Varady, Vladimirov, Zhadan, Zimmermann.

Musorgsky: Christoff.

26 *Не долго нам гулять*
We haven't long to stroll

Like the text of Song 12, also by Nikolay Grekov, this is a variation on the *carpe diem* theme. Again, two lovers are together under the stars: "let's enjoy it while we can, we haven't long to make the most of it." Hence the title of the song (sometimes mistranslated as "we have not far to walk").

In the earlier poem Grekov drew his idea from *Romeo and Juliet*, adding a birch tree as a Russian touch. But in this poem, all the imagery is thoroughly Russian. To *stroll* (to take a walk purely for pleasure without trying to get somewhere at a certain time) in an *orchard* or *garden*—the same word in Russian—is a tradition observed by all classes of Russians, as the folklore of wedding songs shows, with their "strolling" in the garden or the orchard (*Spitz*, 17). The *linden alleys* are long shady paths lined with black-trunked linden trees, like the path leading to the pond at Turgenev's estate at Spasskoye-Lutovinovo, near Mtsensk: they are an almost obligatory feature on the grounds of Russian country estates. Russian literature from Pushkin to Chekhov is full of these scenes and variations on them. It is the *soul*, not the mind or heart, that knows the poetry of these moments, and responds so intensely to it. The word occurs twice in the song, and in the second stanza Tchaikovsky repeats it to emphasize it.

All this appealed to Tchaikovsky, as it would have appealed to Tatyana, the heroine of Pushkin's *Eugene Onegin*. When he wrote the song, he did not yet know that his next opera would be based on that novel. But he is already close to the world of the novel here. Grekov, who feels his romanticism intensely and trusts it completely, is rather like a real-life Lensky, the poet in Pushkin's novel. There is a clear musical parallel between line 4 of the second stanza of the song, "dreaming of what we can't put into words," and the line "always, everywhere the same dream" in Lensky's long aria in Scene 1 of the opera (*Al'shvang 1951*, 50). The song is a foretaste of the musical world of the opera, a rare song, unknown to most singers. It deserves to be rediscovered.

Не долго нам гулять рука с рукой
В саду густом, по липовым аллеям,
При блеске звёзд, вечернею порой,
    И жизнь, и жизнь разнеженной душой
Благодарить за всё, за всё, за всё, что мы имеем.

Не долго нам под обаяньем снов,
Как молодость, игривых и летучих,
Следя луну в изгибах облаков,
    Мечтать о том, чему нет слов,
Но что живёт в душах, в душах у нас кипучих.

О, милый друг! цвести не долго нам
Блаженством чувств! за то мы долго будем
За них судьбе страданьем дань нести
И слова, слова страшного: прости!
Мы никогда с тобой, с тобой, с тобой не позабудем.

Ne dólga nam guliát' ruká s rukój
F sadú gustóm, pa lípovym alléjam,
Pri bléske zvjóst, vechérneju parój,
I zhýzn', i zhýzn' raznézhennaj
  dushój
Blagadarít' za fsjó, za fsjó, za fsjó,
  shto my iméjem.

We haven't long to stroll together arm in arm
Through the lush orchard, down linden alleys,
By starlight, in an evening hour,
And say to life, to life, with tender
  souls,
Thank you for all this, for all, for all
  that we possess.

Ne dólga nam pad abajánjem snóf,
Kak móladast', igrívykh i letúchikh,
Sledjá lunú v yzgíbakh ablakóf,
Mechtát' a tóm, chemú net slóf,
No shto zhyvjót v dushákh,
  v dushákh u nas kipúchikh.

We haven't long to be allured by dreams,
As full of play and flight as youth itself,
Watching the moon scud between the clouds,
Dreaming of what we can't put into words,
Though it lives in our souls,
  our souls so full of life.

O, mílyj drúk! tsvestí ne dólga nám
Blazhénstvam chústf! za tó
  my dólga búdem
Za níkh sud'bé stradánjem dán' nestí
I slóva, slóva stráshnava: prastí!
My nikagdá s tabój, s tabój, s tabój
  ne pazabúdem.

Oh, darling! we haven't long to flower
In the happiness of all we're feeling now!
  but there'll be time
To pay back fate for it with suffering,
And the word, the awful word: farewell!
Is one we two, we two, we two
  never will forget.

TEXT. **Nikoláy Grékov**, date unknown, published 1860. Untitled. Tchaikovsky's song is the only setting of this poem. The repetitions in lines 4, 5, 10, 14, and 15 were added by Tchaikovsky. He also changed the word order in line 11, and made the verb in the last line more colloquial by adding a prefix.

METER. Binary. Iambic, 5-foot (the fourth line in each stanza is 4-foot):
> *So brief our time for strolling arm in arm*
> *Through orchard dense, down linden alleys long…*

MUSIC. 1875 (by 3 May). Without opus number. E Major. 4/4, Moderato. For Middle Voice: c¹ sharp–f² sharp. Published by Bernard in *Nouvelliste*, no. 11 (November), 1875, and in a separate edition in 1876. Republished by Jurgenson in 1885. No dedication.

RECORDINGS. Borisenko, Isakova, Obraztsova.

27 *На сон грядущий*
Prayer at bedtime

Op. 27, No. 1

When the leaders of the revolt of December 1825 were hanged by order of Nicholas I the following summer, two boys, still in their early teens but already fast friends and destined to remain closest comrades the rest of their lives, stood on the Sparrow Hills overlooking Moscow and made a solemn vow. They swore to avenge the "Decembrists"—who had fallen in their attempt to wrest from the Romanovs a constitution for Russia—and to devote their lives to the struggle for "the rights of man." One of the boys was Alexander Herzen, who would become one of Russia's most important writers and thinkers; the other was his friend and ally, the poet Nikolay Ogaryov, author of the "prayer" that serves as text to the present song. When in their late teens they entered Moscow University, it was, in Herzen's words, with "the thought that here our dreams would be accomplished, that here we should sow the seeds and lay the foundation of a league ... which would follow in the Decembrists' footsteps, and that we should be in it" (*Herzen*, 90). But under the eye of Nicholas's secret police, their dreams were not to be accomplished at the university; and after university, first Ogaryov and then Herzen were arrested and banished from Moscow—undefeated, to be sure, but knowing that their dreams would have to be rethought.

This text is not about that, but it comes out of that. In its final irony, "may you have dreams, even if it means you are deceived," there is something characteristic of the post-Decembrist sensibility of Ogaryov, and characteristic, too, of the greatest poet of their generation, Mikhail Lermontov, who also wrote poems called "prayers" that sometimes have the force of accusations.

Tchaikovsky knew this poem earlier, as a student at the Petersburg Conservatory, when he first set it to be sung *a cappella* by a mixed choir in 1863. That he returned to it twelve years later shows that it had a compelling power for him. It was not the accusatory irony that drew him to it, but rather its compassion for a suffering world and the somber meaning of its final benediction.

The music he wrote for it is arresting and powerful. The song is in two distinct parts. The first stanza is a slow, quiet recitative, that moves trance-like from one state (waking) to the threshold of another (sleeping); this section is marked by the unusual phrase Adagio misterioso. The rest of the song is in a different meter and is marked Andante sostenuto. This part, the prayer, moves forward with conviction to become dramatic, even impassioned, a mood the strong piano part reinforces. As the notes to the score show, Tchaikovsky revised it more elaborately than usual when proofreading it for publication (*PSS,* vol. 44, 145-148). The song is not well known. Owing to its religious language, it was rarely performed in the Soviet period. The 1996 recording by Nina Rautio, who sings it in the original tonality written for Lavrovskaya, brings out well the song's remarkable power.

> Ночная тьма безмолвие приносит
> И к отдыху зовёт меня.
> Пора, пора! покоя тело просит,
> Душа устала в вихре дня.
>
> Молю Тебя, пред сном грядущим, Боже:
> Дай людям мир; благослови
> Младенца сон, и нищенское ложе,
> И слёзы тихие любви!
>
> Прости греху, на жгучее страданье
> Успокоительно дохни,
> И все Твои печальные созданья
> Хоть сновиденьем обмани!
>
> И все Твои печальные созданья
> Хоть сновиденьем обмани,
> Хоть сновиденьем обмани!

Nachnája t'má bezmólvije prinósit
　I k óddykhu zavjót menjá.
Pará, pará! pakója téla prósit,
　Dushá ustála v víkhre dnjá.

Maljú Tebjá, pred snóm grjadúshchim,
Bózhe:
　Daj ljúdjam mír; blagaslaví
Mladéntsa són, i níshchenskaje lózhe,
　I sljózy tíkhije ljubví!

Prastí grekhú, na zhgúcheje stradán'je
　Uspakaítel'na dakhní,
I fsé Tvají pechál'nyje sazdán'ja
　Khot' snavidén'jem abmaní!

I fsé Tvají pechál'nyje sazdán'ja
　Khot' snavidén'jem abmaní,
　Khot' snavidén'jem abmaní!

Night's darkness brings an end to talk
　And summons me to rest.
It's time, it's time! the body wants peace,
　The soul is weary after busy day.

I pray, before I go to sleep,
O God:
　Give peace to people; bless
Infant's sleep, and pauper's bed,
　And quiet tears of love!

Forgive sins, soothe burning suffering
　With a breath of relief,
And give Thy sad creatures all
　At least a dream to be deceived by!

And give Thy sad creatures all
　At least a dream to be deceived by,
　At least a dream to be deceived by!

TEXT. **Nikoláy Ogaryóv.** Early 1840s; pub. 1856. Title: "На сон грядущий" (Prayer at Bedtime). Line 3 is a paraphrase of the opening line of a lyric by Pushkin, "Пора, мой друг, пора! покоя сердце просит," ("It's time, my friend, it's time! the heart asks for peace," 1834).

First set by Tchaikovsky, later by half a dozen minor composers. Originally used by Tchaikovsky at the St. Petersburg Conservatory in 1863-4 in unpublished settings for mixed choir, first unaccompanied and then with orchestra.

METER. Binary. Iambic, alternating lines of 5 and 4 feet:

As now I lay me down to sleep, O God,
Give peace to men, and bless the child,
And all who rest in lowly pauper's bed,
And those whose loving tears are mild.

MUSIC. March-April 1875. Op. 27, no. 1. B-flat Minor. 4/4, Adagio misterioso (first stanza); 6/8, Andante sostenuto (remainder of song). For Middle Voice: b flat-f². Published by Jurgenson in May 1875, and again in 1890-91.

Opus 27 is dedicated to the contralto **Yelizavéta Andréyevna Lavróvskaya** (1845-1919). She studied at the Petersburg Conservatory with Henriette Nissen-Saloman from 1865-68 and also took lessons in Baden-Baden and Paris with Pauline Viardot. Tchaikovsky knew her throughout his professional life. She was on the faculty of the Moscow Conservatory from 1888 until her death. The songs in this opus are all written for the range of her voice. The third one (Song 29) is known to have been sung by her in concert during Tchaikovsky's lifetime (*DG*, 142, 462).

RECORDINGS. Christoff, DeGaetani, Isakova, Rautio.

Version of 1863 for unaccompanied choir: Polyansky, Sveshnikov.

28 *Смотри: вон облако*
Look: that cloud there

Op. 27, No. 2

Heine could be the inspiration behind this attractive lyric by Nikolay Grekov. But Grekov's sensibility is Slavic in its dualism and its fatalism.

Heine's thinking is active rather than passive: he looks for a link, maybe metaphysical, maybe only a wish or even an accusation, but whatever it is, it has the force of binding the two lovers together in an intimate way despite the fact that they are separated. But Grekov simply reads fate and accepts it: "that is who you are and that is the path fate gave you, and this is the path fate has given me; wishing it were different will not make it so; if it's dark, so be it— that's how it is." And he's gentler than Heine: there's no fury lurking at the edges of Grekov's poem, no explosive potential waiting to break out.

In Tchaikovsky's hands Grekov's lyric acquires the power to delight and move us as a song. The musical phrases are beautifully crafted to express the very Slavic text, but never in a routine way. The long iambic lines are sung in declamatory style, but there is drama, passion, melancholy and tender lyricism in them. Dualism is built into the song, with changes of key, meter, and tempo in the middle of each stanza, but with an asymmetry that has the power to surprise. The piano part is attractive throughout, with haunting reminiscences of what might be Chopin in the concluding solo.

In short, this is a very good song which has been overlooked and is almost unknown. The excellent Zara Dolukhanova makes a strong case for it.

> Смотри: вон облако несётся серебристое;
> Везде вокруг него сияет небо чистое,
>   Как молодость прекрасная твоя.
> И утра блеск на нём так ярко отражается;
> И так оно светло, как будто улыбается —
>   Оно похоже на тебя.
>   Оно похоже на тебя.
>
> Смотри: вон туча там выходит одинокая;
> Она темна, как ночь, как грусть души глубокая —
>   Не просветлит её сиянье дня…
> Быть может оттого она мрачна так грозная,
> Что с светлым облаком дана стезя ей розная, —
>   Она похожа на меня.
>   Она похожа на меня.

Smatrí: von óblaka nesjótsa
serebrístaje;
Vezdé vakrúk nevó sijájet néba
chístaje,
Kak móladast' prekrásnaja tvajá.
I útra blésk na njóm tak járka
atrazhájetsa;
I tak anó svetló, kak bútta
ulybájetsa —
    Anó pakhózhe na tebjá.
    Anó pakhózhe na tebjá.

Look: that cloud there moving by, the
silver one;
There's clear sky shining all
around it,
Like your young age in all its loveliness.
And it reflects so vividly the morning's
brilliance;
And it's so bright, as if it's
smiling —
    It matches you.
    It matches you.

Smatrí: von túcha tam vykhódit
adinókaja;
Aná temná, kak nóch, kak grúst' dushý
glubókaja —
Ne prasvetlít jejó siján'je dnjá...
Byt' mózhet attavó aná mrachná
tak gróznaja,
Shto s svétlym óblakam daná stezjá
jej róznaja, —
    Aná pakhózha na menjá.
    Aná pakhózha na menjá.

Look: that rain cloud moving
solitary there;
It's dark as night, as soul's deep
sadness —
Shining day itself can't make it bright...
Maybe what makes the thundercloud
so gloomy
Is that the bright cloud's course and his
are always separate —
    It matches me.
    It matches me.

TEXT. **Nikoláy Grékov.** Date unknown, published 1860. Title: Стансы (M. Ф. К.) (Stanzas, to M. F. K.). Tchaikovsky kept Grekov's text exactly, but repeats the last line of each stanza. Set first by Tchaikovsky, later by a minor composer.

METER. Binary. Iambic, 6-foot (with shorter lines of 5 and 4 feet inset):
> *Look there: you see that silver cloud that's moving by,*
> *Around it everywhere there's purest shining sky,*
> *Like your young age in all its lovely brightness...*

MUSIC. March-April 1875. Op. 27, no. 2. C Minor. 9/8, Andante semplice, with sections in 3/4 time marked Moderato. For Low Voice: g-f². Dedicated to **Yelizavéta Lavróvskaya.**

RECORDINGS. Borisenko, Dolukhanova, Isakova.

29   *Не отходи от меня*
Don't leave me

Op. 27, No. 3

This short poem written by Afanasy Fet when he was twenty-two seems designed expressly as a lyric for a Russian romance. Its basic theme, which is "don't leave—stay here with me," is one of the most common themes in urban romance, especially the "cruel" romances involving "fatal passions" that Russian gypsy singers made into a specialty.

But Fet's poem is a completely original variation on the theme, one that excludes cruelty and fatal passion, and provides instead true delicacy of feeling and psychological realism. It has an ambiguity that is not typical of cruel romance, where the terms are "either-or" and "all or nothing." The verb "to leave" used by Fet here, reiterated three times in the poem, and four times in Tchaikovsky's song, does not mean "go away for good," but simply to step out of the room, to turn your attention elsewhere for a moment. Even if she leaves, she will be back soon, so what is all the fuss? Yet there is vulnerability here on both sides, and for some reason she is "sad." The scene pictures lovers' happiness, but their happiness is less than perfect. All of this implies a relationship which has its own particular story. The story remains a mystery, but the feelings are clear—and that is just what Tchaikovsky was looking for when he set words to music.

As a rule, he preferred to choose texts which no one else had used, but in this case he made an exception. An earlier setting of Fet's poem was made in the 1840s by Alexander Varlamov. Without taking anything away from Varlamov as a popular composer—his romances include classics still sung today—one has only to start from Varlamov's song and then listen to what Tchaikovsky does with it, to realize the extent to which he was able to breathe original musical life into the beloved old tradition. Varlamov's song is strophic (each of the three stanzas is sung to the same melody), and the song as a whole conveys not so much a feeling as a mood of melancholy against the background of a pleasant waltz. Once the pattern is established, it does not change. But Tchaikovsky's song is full of changes. It is also a waltz, but an ardent one, charged with feeling and, moreover, a whole range of feelings, now tender, now pleading. The very last line of the song introduces a note of passion, almost sultry, written at the low end of the range of the contralto to whom it was dedicated, and heard in the exemplary recording by Zara Dolukhanova.

The song shows how Tchaikovsky's habit of repeating lines is far from mechanical repetition. On the contrary, his aim is to vary and elaborate the feelings that can be imparted by different music to the same words.

Не отходи от меня,
Друг мой, останься со мной!
Не отходи от меня:
Мне так отрадно с тобой...
Мне так отрадно с тобой!

Ближе друг к другу, чем мы,
Ближе нельзя нам и быть;
Чище, живее, сильней
Мы не умеем любить.

Если же — ты предо мной,
Грустно головку склоня —
Мне так отрадно с тобой...
Не отходи от меня!

Мне так отрадно с тобой...
Не отходи от меня!
Мне так отрадно с тобой,
Мне так отрадно с тобой!

Ne atkhadí at menjá,
Drúk moj, astán'sa sa mnój!
Ne atkhadí at menjá:
Mné tak atrádna s tabój...
Mné tak atrádna s tabój!

Don't go, don't leave me
Darling, stay here with me!
Don't go, don't leave me:
I'm so happy with you...
I'm so happy with you!

Blízhe drug g drúgu, chem mý,
Blízhe nel'zjá nam y být';
Chíshche, zhyvéje, sil'néj
Mý ne uméjem ljubít'.

We couldn't be closer than this,
Closer than we are to each other;
Purer or stronger or more full of life
We couldn't imagine our love.

Jésli zhe — tý preda mnój,
Grúsna galófku sklanja'—
Mné tak atrádna s tabój:
Ne atkhadí at menjá!

If, then — with you here before me,
Your dear head sadly inclined —
I'm so happy with you...
Don't go, don't leave me!

Mné tak atrádna s tabój...
Ne atkhadí at menjá!
Mné tak atrádna s tabój,
Mné tak atrádna s tabój!

I'm so happy with you...
Don't go, don't leave me!
I'm so happy with you...
I'm so happy with you!

TEXT. **Afanásy Fet**, 1842. Untitled. This lyric turned up often in popular songbooks, sometimes with the subtitle "Song of the Moscow Gypsies" (*PRP*, II, 439). Set earlier by Varlamov (1849) and Rubets (1868). Tchaikovsky left Fet's text as is, but he added all the repeated lines.

METER. Ternary. Dactyl, 3-foot:
> *No one could possibly be*
> *Closer together than we...*

MUSIC. March-April 1875. Op. 27, no. 3. F Major. 3/4, Andante amoroso. For Middle Voice: a-f². Dedicated to **Yelizavéta Lavróvskaya**. Orchestrated by Sergey Taneyev in 1887.

RECORDINGS. Descamps, Dolukhanova, Fischer-Dieskau, Isakova, Kazarnovskaya, Legostayeva, Milashkina, Rautio, Tear.

Varlamov: Borisenko.

30 *Вечер*
Evening

Op. 27, No. 4

When he was twenty-five, Tchaikovsky spent a happy summer with his sister Aleksandra (Sasha) and her husband Lev Davydov on their estate in the Ukrainian village of Kamenka. He wrote down a song he heard women singing while they were working in an orchard, and used the melody in two of his early works (*DG*, 36). The image in this poem by Taras Shevchenko of women singing as they come home from the fields must have reminded Tchaikovsky of that summer as he sat down to write this song. A singularly beautiful moment in the vocal part of the song coincides exactly with the words in line 4 "singing as they go." The whole song is one of Tchaikovsky's loveliest and shows that Shevchenko's text stirred deep lyrical associations in him.

For Shevchenko, who was born a peasant and who grew up in a Ukrainian village, there are images here that could have gone back to his earliest memories, when he was brought up by an older sister while his mother worked in the fields. It is not an autobiographical poem, however, but an idyll showing a peasant family gathering for supper at day's end. The time is early summer, in May or June, when the nightingales are still singing—a golden time, when everyday life and poetry overlap, when women talking and birds singing make two kinds of natural music competing and blending with each other against the background stillness of the Ukrainian night.

The lyric is highly pictorial: Shevchenko was a trained artist who liked sketching scenes from Ukrainian life. The song is "pictorial" too, with each descriptive vocal phrase laid down like a separate brush stroke; between the lines the piano elaborates on the lyric mood. Unlike songs in which the singer expresses a strong emotion, this song sketches in a declamatory style a scene for the mind's eye and ear. As the song ends, the last echoes of the women's voices and the trill of the nightingale are heard in the concluding piano postlude.

Вишнёвый садик возле хаты;	А мать сказала бы ей слово,
Жуки над вишнями гудят;	Да соловейко не даёт.
Плуг с нивы пахари тащат;	
И, распеваючи, девчаты	Мать уложила возле хаты
Домой на вечерю спешат.	Малюток–деточек своих;
	Сама заснула возле них…
Семья их ждёт, и всё готово;	Затихло всё… одни девчаты,
Звезда вечерняя встаёт,	Да соловейко не затих.
И дочка ужин подаёт.	

Vishnjóvyj sádik vózle kháty;	A little cherry orchard by a peasant house;
Zhukí nad víshnjami gudját;	Above the cherries June bugs hum away;
Pluk s nívy pákhari tashchát;	Plowmen haul the plow off the field;
I, raspevájuchi, defcháty	And, singing as they go, the young women
Damój na vécherju speshát.	Hasten home to the evening meal.
Sem'já ikh zhdjót, i fsjó gatóva;	The family's waiting for them, all's in readiness;
Zvezdá vechérnjaja fstajót,	The evening star is coming up,
I dóchka úzhyn padajót.	And daughter passes supper round to all.
A mát' skazála by jej slóva,	Mother has something to tell her,
Da salavéjka ne dajót.	But the nightingale won't let her speak.
Mat' ulazhýla vózle kháty	By the house mother tucks in
Maljútak-détachek svajíkh;	Her little ones all;
Samá zasnúla vózle níkh...	She's beside them now asleep herself...
Zatíkhla fsjó... adní defcháty,	It's quiet all around... only the young women
Da salavéjka ne zatíkh.	And the nightingale haven't yet quieted down.

TEXT. **Lev Mey**, 1858-59. Title: Вечер (Evening). Translation of "Садок вишневий коло хати," a Ukrainian poem by **Taras Shevchenko** (1814-1861). Tchaikovsky is the only composer who has used this text.

When Shevchenko wrote the poem he was far from the place depicted in it, though the season was the same. It is one of thirteen poems he wrote in prison in St. Petersburg, after he was arrested in Kiev in April 1847 and brought to the Russian capital for interrogation. Charged with membership in the "Brotherhood of Sts. Cyril and Methodius," a Ukrainian organization similar to the Decembrists, he was sentenced to be banished to a remote fort on the frontier to do military service for an indefinite period. Nicholas I added his own particularly cruel note to the sentence, stipulating that he be forbidden to write and paint. After the death of Nicholas, Shevchenko was finally freed (in 1857). In 1860 a volume of his poems translated into Russian was published in St. Petersburg under the title *Kobzar'* (The Bard). It included Mey's translation of this poem.

METER. Binary. Iambic tetrameter:
> *Some cherry trees beside a hut;*
> *The hum of June bugs in the air...*

MUSIC. March-April 1875. Op. 27, no. 4. B-flat Major. 4/4, Moderato assai. For Middle Voice: c^1-f^2. Dedicated to **Yelizavéta Lavróvskaya**.

RECORDINGS. Isakova, Lemeshev, Preobrazhenskaya, Rautio, Söderström.

31   *Али мать меня рожала*
Did mother give me life

Op. 27, No. 5

For Opus 27 Tchaikovsky chose only lyrics which are unmistakably Slavic. The first three are Russian, the fourth is a translation from Ukrainian, and the last two are translations from Polish, attributed (by Tchaikovsky and all his editors since) to Adam Mickiewicz, the greatest of the Polish Romantic poets. Song 32 is indeed by Mickiewicz, but the present text is by his younger contemporary, Teofil Lenartowicz (1822-1893). Lenartowicz was admired in Russia as a poet seen to be doing in Polish something similar to what the very popular Aleksey Koltsov had done in Russian in the 1830s, writing imitation folk songs that conveyed "village" feelings in a poetical "folk" style, that is, using language, imagery, poetic formulas and rhythmic devices found in real folk songs and popular lore.

This song is a ballad, a lament of a village girl whose sweetheart has ridden off with the army and has vanished or been killed. Like Barbara Allen in the English folk song, she imagines that she and her true love can only be together again in death. She feels alone and doomed. Her mother has called in the village matchmakers to marry her off. When she lights a candle in church for her sweetheart's safe return, it burns out; other omens, too, point darkly to her early death from grief.

What appealed to Tchaikovsky in this text was the young woman's helpless and disconsolate sadness, rather than the notion that she feels doomed to die of grief (he omitted the last two lines of Mey's translation which speak of her death). The theme here is the "sadness" of a girl left alone after her true love has gone away. One of the best of all the "Russian songs" ("русская песня," a composed song meant to sound like a folk song) is actually called "Грусть девушки" (A girl's sadness), written by Alexander Gurilyov to a Koltsov text. Tchaikovsky undoubtedly knew Gurilyov's song and might have been aware of it when he chose this text. The song shows Tchaikovsky taking as his starting point a "Russian song," but bringing his own original musical material to it by writing a stately mazurka, yet with its own peculiar melancholy, unlike any of his other songs. It has never caught on and is almost unknown. Maybe the music is too "Polish" to convey the classic theme, at least to Russian ears.

Али мать меня рожала   Напролёт и дни и ночи
На горе большое?   Плачу, как ребёнок;
Али ведьма зачурала   Сваты придут — нет мне мочи
Мне гнездо родное?   Выстоять смотрёнок.

Ох, уехал да и сгинул
Милый за дружиной;
Не сберёг — одну покинул
Панночку с кручиной.

У подружек в церкви ясно
Свечка догорает;
У меня одной, несчастной,
Сразу погасает.

В поле осень; лист валится;
Пёс наш землю роет,
Сыч на крышу к нам садится:
«Что ж ты скоро?» — воет.

Скоро я с тобою, значит,
Свижуся, мой милый!

Али мать меня рожала
На горе большое?
Али ведьма зачурала
Мне гнездо родное?
Али ведьма зачурала
Мне гнездо родное?

Ali mát' menjá razhála
Ná gore bal'shóje?
Ali véd'ma zachurála
Mne gnezdó radnóje?

Did mother give me life
That this great sorrow be my destiny?
Or was it wished upon me by a witch
Who cursed the nest where I was born?

Napraljót i dní i nóchi
Pláchu kak rebjónak;
Sváty prídut — nét mne móchi
Výstajat' smatrjónak.

I spend the days and nights
Crying like a child;
Matchmakers come, but I've no strength
To stand and be looked over.

Okh, ujékhal da i zgínul
Míly za druzhínaj;
Ne zberjók — adnú pakínul
Pánnachku s kruchínaj.

Oh, he rode away, my dear lad did,
And vanished with the army;
He left his lass here all alone,
Abandoned with her sorrow.

U padrúzhek f tsérkvi jásna
Svéchka dagarájet;
U menjá adnój, neshchástnaj,
Srázu pagasájet.

Candles all my girlfriends light
Burn brightly in the church;
Mine alone, unlucky me,
Burns out when I light it.

F póle ósen'; líst valítsa;
Pjós nash zémlju rójet,
Sých na krýshu k nam sadítsa:
"Shtó sh ty skóra?" — vójet.

Fall's in the field; the leaf drops down;
Our dog digs in the ground,
An owl perches on our roof:
"Why you so soon?" he screeches.

Skóra ja s tabóju, znáchit,
Svízhusa, moj mílyj!

Soon, my sweetheart, you and I
Will meet, will be together!

Ali mát' menjá razhála
Ná gore bal'shóje?
Ali véd'ma zachurála
Mne gnezdó radnóje?
Ali véd'ma zachurála
Mne gnezdó radnóje?

When mother gave me life
Was great sorrow in my destiny?
Or was it wished upon me by a witch
Who cursed the nest where I was born?
Or was it wished upon me by a witch
Who cursed the nest where I was born?

TEXT. **Lev Mey**, 1857. Title Песня (Song). Translation of a ballad by **Teofil Lenartowicz** entitled Tęsknota (Longing), 1843. Mey certainly knew that it was written by Lenartowicz, but after Mey's death his editors evidently found it among his papers with other translations of poems by Mickiewicz. Editions of Mey's poems (and all editions of Tchaikovsky's songs) erroneously indicate Mickiewicz as the author. Set only by Tchaikovsky.

The original Polish poem has never been identified, so I have included it below, but only the stanzas Mey used for his translation. The entire ballad is in *Zgorzelski*, 397-99 (Lenartowicz wrote a different version in 1872 which has no relation to Mey's translation or Tchaikovsky's song). In the song, Tchaikovsky omitted the last two lines of Mey's translation, "soon mother will be weeping over my grave," and repeated the first stanza at the end.

METER. Binary. Trochee, 4-foot alternating with 3-foot lines:
Soon, my sweetheart, you and I,
Soon, we'll be together.

MUSIC. March-April 1875. Op. 27, no. 5. E-flat Minor. 3/8, Allegro non troppo. Tempo di mazurka. For Middle Voice: b-g^2 flat. Dedicated to **Yelizavéta Lavróvskaya**.

RECORDINGS. DeGaetani, Fomina, Postavnicheva, Preobrazhenskaya.

Mey's Polish Source by Lenartowicz (abbreviated)

Tęsknota

Czy mnie matka porodziła
Pod nieszczęsną gwiazdą?
Czy mi wiedźma określiła
Rodzicielskie gniazdo?

Całe noce, dnie i lata
Płaczę bez ustanka,
Przyszły swaty – nie chcę swata,
Męża ni kochanka.

Oj! pojechał, oj! pogonił
Maciek na wojenkę;
Ni zasłonił, ni obronił,
A rzucił panienkę.

W dzień Najświętszej Matki Boskiej
Siła gromnic jaśnie;
Z wszystkich świeczek całej wioski
Moja pierwsza gaśnie.

Zima idzie, liść opada,
W polu pies skowyczy;
Nocą pućka na dach siada:
»Pójdź, Marychno!« – krzyczy.

Pewno, zanim ja zobaczę,
Kochaneczku, ciebie,
Pierwej mateńka zapłacze
Na moim pogrzebie!

32 Моя баловница
My darling girl

Op. 27, No. 6

This charming poem by Adam Mickiewicz (1798-1855) was a nineteenth-century favorite, judging by the many composers who set it to music: first Chopin and Moniuszko, who used the original Polish lyric; then the Russians, using two different translations—Glinka, Dubuque, Tchaikovsky, Nápravník, Cui, and Rimsky-Korsakov. Of the Russian versions, the one by Glinka is the earliest and also the best known.

It comes from a series of amorous lyrics Mickiewicz wrote when he spent a year in Odessa and the Crimea in 1825. The woman it is addressed to cannot be identified with certainty—the initials in the title are a reference to Dante's *Vita Nuova* (*Weintraub*, 89)—but it does not matter. The poet had a lively schedule that year in Odessa society with its numerous Polish, Ukrainian, and Russian grandees, and in that milieu there was more than one beautiful woman whom he might have considered both muse and mistress.

The poem is in two stanzas, with each stanza a single, long sentence: "when my girl friend (my spoiled pet) chirps away like a happy bird, I want nothing more than to listen to her forever" (stanza 1), "but when she speaks with feeling, and her eyes flash and her cheeks flush, all I can think of is kissing those lips" (stanza 2). For Glinka—who, in addition to being fond of amorous play with pretty women, liked to keep songbirds in his apartment, in and out of cages, trilling away at all hours—the poem must have had an immediate appeal. The song he wrote is a mazurka. The young Dostoyevsky actually heard Glinka sing it in 1849 at a soirée in the company of friends. For Glinka this was just a late-night bachelor party of the kind he liked, a literary-musical evening where in the general merriment he might sing a song, but for Dostoyevsky it took on an entirely different significance, being the last meeting of the Palm-Durov circle before they were all arrested. The song made a charming impression on Dostoyevsky that night, obliterated for a long time by his arrest and exile, but recalled years later in his short novel "The Eternal Husband" (1871). There his protagonist sings Glinka's song to a pretty young woman at a party. Dostoyevsky describes what appealed to him in Glinka's performance of it years ago: its subject is mounting passion, but it is delivered with utter simplicity, without risqué hints or knowing overtones, and without any of the false mannerisms of a professional salon singer. Passion (страсть) and naive sincerity (простодушие) *together*—this is what gives the song its charm.

Like Glinka, Tchaikovsky set his song in 3/4 time, marked "Tempo di mazurka," in tribute to its Polish provenance. Compared to Glinka's mischievous Italianate setting, Tchaikovsky's version has more heart, more warmth. This is the only one of his songs published in two different versions. His revision is thought to have been prompted by Cui's criticism that Tchaikovsky had "compromised the poetic form of a poet of such genius as Mickiewicz" (*MN*, 441). But by this time Tchaikovsky was used to Cui's continual pedantic carping, and he would not have revised it unless he had his own reason for doing so. What is wrong with the original version is that the song ends by returning to the first stanza, so that the final words are "listen" instead of "kiss." He understood that the song has to end on those repeated kisses. He corrected this in the second version of the song, and it is that newer version—moderated slightly from Allegro to Allegretto—which is sung today.

> Моя баловница, отдавшись веселью,
> Зальётся, как птичка, серебряной трелью,
> Как птичка, начнёт щебетать, лепетать,
> Так мило начнёт лепетать, щебетать,
> Что даже дыханьем боюсь я нарушить
> Гармонию сдалкую девственных слов,
> И целые дни, и всю жизнь я готов
> Красавицу слушать, и слушать, и слушать,
> и слушать, слушать!
>
> Когда ж живость речи ей глазки зажжёт
> И щёки сильнее румянить начнёт,
> Когда при улыбке, сквозь алые губы,
> Как перлы в кораллах, блеснут её зубы,
> О, в эти минуты я смело опять
> Гляжуся ей в очи и жду поцелуя,
> И более слушать её не хочу я,
> А всё целовать, целовать, целовать,
> целовать!
>
> Мою баловницу всю жизнь я готов
> целовать, целовать, целовать.

Majá balavnítsa, addáfshys' vesél'ju,	My heart's delight, the darling girl,
Zal'jótsa, kak ptíchka, serébrjanaj trél'ju,	When she's in a merry mood,
Kak ptíchka, nachnjót shchebetát', lepetát',	Can chatter and babble sweet as a bird,
Tak míla nachnjót lepetát', shchebetát',	Break out in such silvery trills and chirps,
Shto dázhe dykhán'jem bajús' ja narúshyt'	I dare not breathe to miss a single word
Garmóniju slátkuju défstvennykh slóf,	Or interrupt such artless harmony,
I tsélyje dní, i fsju zhýzn' ja gatóf	And I'd be glad my whole life long
Krasávitsu slúshat', i slúshat', i slúshat', i slúshat', slúshat'!	Just to listen to the pretty girl, and listen, and listen, and listen, listen!

Kagdá zh zhývast' réchi jej gláski	But when her talk is full of
zazhzhót	feeling,
I shchóki sil'néje rumjánit' nachnjót,	Her eyes flash and her cheeks flush red,
Kagdá pri ulýpke, skvos'	When she smiles, and through her
ályje gúby,	scarlet lips,
Kak pérly f karállakh, blesnút jejo zúby,	Her teeth sparkle like pearls in coral,
O, v èti minúty ja sméla	Oh, in moments like these, my boldness
apját'	returns,
Gljazhúsa jej v óchi i zhdú patselúja,	I look in her eyes and wait for a kiss,
I bóleje slúshat' jejo ne khachú ja,	And what I crave now is not to listen to her,
A fsjó tselavát', tselavát', tselavát',	But to kiss her and keep on kissing, kissing,
tselavát'!	kissing!
Majú balavnítsu fsju zhýzn' ya gatóf	With my darling girl I'd spend my life
tselavát', tselavát', tselavát'.	kissing, kissing, kissing.

TEXT. **Lev Mey**, 1849. Translation of a poem by **Adam Mickiewicz**, "Moja pieszczotka" (My darling pet), titled "Do D. D." (To D. D.), 1825. After Tchaikovsky, set by Cui (Op. 11/2, 1877) and Rimsky-Korsakov (Op. 42/4, 1897). Cui, not satisfied with Mey's translation, made his own revisions.

Set by Glinka (1843), Dubuque (1863), and Nápravník (1877), using an earlier translation by S. G. Golitsyn (1834).

Set in the original Polish by Chopin, Op. 74, no. 12 (composed 1837, published posthumously in 1857), and by Stanisław Moniuszko (1838).

METER. Ternary. Amphibrach, 4-foot:

> *In moments like these all my boldness returns,*
> *I look in her eyes and crave nothing but kisses...*

MUSIC. March-April 1875. Op. 27, no. 6. Two versions. A Major. 3/4, Allegretto con spirito (version 1 is Allegro con spirito). Tempo di mazurka. For Middle Voice: a-f^2 sharp. Dedicated to **Yelizavéta Lavróvskaya**.

RECORDINGS. Descamps, Fischer-Dieskau, Mazurok, Shaposhnikov, Tear.

Chopin: Celine, Kurenko, Tear, Verhaeghe.

Glinka: Arkhipova, Gerasimova, Vishnevskaya.

Cui: Sharonova.

Rimsky-Korsakov: Khromchenko, Martynov.

33 *Нет, никогда не назову*
No, never will I name her

Op. 28, No. 1

Love, in particular the vulnerability of the lover, is the theme of the six songs of Opus 28. Of course, most Russian urban romances are about love and vulnerability. But in this set of songs Tchaikovsky was aiming less at the poetry of romantic love and more at expressing feelings stirred by ambiguity, frustration, obsession, and other aspects of the psychology of love. In these songs the fact of love mostly gives rise to questions.

The first of them is a translation by Nikolay Grekov of a French lyric by Alfred de Musset. Tchaikovsky read and liked Musset, but that was later. He may not have known that this lyric is a song sung by the character Fortunio in Musset's early play "The Candlestick." The title refers to a French expression "to hold the candle," meaning "to assist another man in an amorous tryst" (*Sices*, 116). It is a comedy of adultery in which the innocent young Fortunio is used as a decoy by the heroine in order to conceal the identity of her actual lover from her stupid and cuckolded husband. In the play, the song is a moment of genuine feeling in a context of otherwise wholly cynical manipulation.

Not a hint of this context appears in the song Tchaikovsky composed. His is a song of innocence, ardent and adoring. The theme of "gallant discretion" is foreign to the Russian romance, but the theme of "undeclared love" is not uncommon. This song is a variation on that theme, a theme to which Tchaikovsky was clearly drawn (Songs 6, 23, 70, 75, 98). The counter-theme, to admit love openly, to *declare* it, underlies one of his most original songs (the last song in this opus, Song 38), as well as Tatyana's letter scene in *Eugene Onegin*, his starting point when he began composing the opera in 1877.

Нет, никогда вам не узнать,
　Кого люблю я.
За всю вселенную её
　Не назову я.

Давайте петь! и будет вам
　Мой вторить голос,
Что белокурая она,
　Как зрелый колос;

Что воли ни за что её
　Я не нарушу,
И, коль захочет, ей отдам
　Всю жизнь и душу.

Я муки пламенной любви
　От ней скрываю:
Они не сносны, и от них
　Я умираю.

Но кто она… но кто она…

Нет, я люблю её, люблю с такою
　силой,
Что пусть умру, что пусть умру,
　но не скажу
　Я имя милой.
Пусть умру, пусть умру, но не скажу
　Я имя милой.

Net, nikagdá vam ne uznát',	No, never will you learn
Kavó ljubljú ja.	Whom I'm in love with.
Za fsju fselénnuju jejó	For all the world
Ne nazavú ja.	I'd not reveal her name.
Davájte pet'! i búdet vám	Let's sing! and may your voices
Moj ftórit' gólas,	Echo mine,
Shto belakúraja aná,	She is fair and flaxen-haired
Kak zrélyj kólas;	As ripened wheat;
Shto vóli ni za shtó jejó	Whatever she desired
Ja ne narúshu,	I'd not refuse her,
I, kol' zakhóchet, jej addám	And, if she asked, I'd give her
Fsju zhyzn' i dúshu.	All my life and soul.
Ja múki plámennaj ljubví	I hide from her the torments
At nej skryváju:	Of my burning love:
Aní ne snósny, i at níkh	They are unbearable,
Ja umiráju.	I'm dying from them.
No któ aná... no któ aná...	But who she is... but who she is...
Nét, ja ljubljú jejó, ljubljú	No, I love her, I love her
s takóju sílaj,	with such force,
Shto pust' umrú, shto pust' umrú,	That I would die, I'd rather die,
no ne skazhú	than tell
Ja ímja mílaj.	My darling's name,
Pust' umrú, pust' umrú, no ne skazhú	I'd rather die, I'd rather die, than tell
Ja ímja mílaj.	My darling's name.

TEXT. **Nikoláy Grékov**, published 1860. Title: Песня (из Альфреда Мюссе) (Song: from Alfred Musset). Translation of a poem by **Alfred de Musset**, "Chanson de Fortunio" (Fortunio's Song), from his comedy *Le Chandelier* (The Candlestick), 1835. Set only by Tchaikovsky. There is a comic opera based on this play (*Fortunio*, 1907) by André Messager.

METER. Binary. Iambic, alternating lines of 4 feet and 2 feet:
> *No, never will you learn from me*
> *My lady's name.*

MUSIC. April 1875. Op. 28, no. 1. E-flat Major. 4/4, Moderato quasi andantino (*dolce e molto espr*). For High Voice: e^1 flat–a^2 flat.

Dedicated to **Antón Nikoláyev** (1836-1904), Russian lyric tenor. After 1874 he left the stage and became an admired concert singer, famous for performances of romances of the Russian composers, including Tchaikovsky.

RECORDINGS. Lemeshev, Lisovsky, Martynov, Migay.

34 *Корольки*
Coral beads

Op. 28, No. 2

Tchaikovsky found this unique text among Lev Mey's translations from Polish. The original poem is what is called in Poland a "gawęda," a tale or ballad, but narrated by a hero from the common folk who tells his story in his own colorful style. These were a specialty of the 19th-century Polish poet Ludwik Kondratowicz (1823-1862), better known to his contemporaries by his pseudonym "Władysław Syrokomla." Syrokomla was admired as a poet who was sensitive to peasant themes (like most Russian and Polish writers of the time, he was not a peasant himself but a member of the gentry of poor to average means). He imagined episodes from village life as seen through peasant eyes and told in their words. He called this poem "Korale: Dumka kozacka" (Corals: A Cossack ballad), a reference to the necklaces of coral beads that were a favorite form of jewelry worn by Polish and Ukrainian women (Shevchenko has a poem which begins "O mother, if I only had a string/Of corals, I would take my fling in town," *Shevchenko*, 409). In the song, a young Cossack tells his story. Before he leaves his village to take part in a raid against the Tatars, his sweetheart Hannah prays for his safe return; assured that God will protect him, she asks in return that he bring her a string of coral beads when they raid the Khan's town. With God's help, he keeps his promise and races home to give her the coral beads, but when he arrives the whole village is returning from the cemetery where they have just buried her. His heart broken, he leaves the coral beads on a holy icon in the church.

The song is remarkable, very far from the urban romance tradition so central to Tchaikovsky's popularity as a songwriter. Like some other unusual experiments among his songs (Songs 16 and 24, for example), it has not been frequently sung and is not widely known. But critics both Russian and Western have admired it. Boris Asafiev includes it among Tchaikovsky's greatest songs because, like all his best songs, in Asafiev's view, its strong "melody-idea," stated immediately, provides the basis of the entire work, by means of elaboration and recapitulation (*Asaf'ev*, 80). Arnold Alshvang sees everything in it from a polonaise to symphonic form (*Al'shvang 1951*, 73-78, and, in English, *Al'shvang 1946*, 217-222). David Brown also admires it, though he argues that what makes it good is that Tchaikovsky aligns himself here with the "heroic strand" of Glinka rather than the "soft pleasantries of the drawing-room"; it is a "powerful rejoinder to any who would assert that Tchaikovsky was incapable of music that was truly masculine" (*Brown II*, 38-40).

To appreciate this song it is not necessary to understand symphonic form or to be able to tell which music is sufficiently "masculine" to pass muster. Like all of Tchaikovsky's songs, it is written to be immediately comprehensible when performed well and listened to with ears that can hear. The dramatic episodes in the narrative are paced and clearly marked by differences in tempo, which I have indicated in the text below. The result is a continual revelation of character and of a whole range of changing feelings communicated in the music (how this works is variously understood, but that this is what Tchaikovsky tried to do in his music was asserted by him many times). The song is a striking example of what Gerard McBurney points to in his comments on Tchaikovsky, that he is "among the most centrifugal of composers," that "a single genre could be the vehicle for a multitude of different intentions," and that successive works, rather than following a "single line of development," seem instead to suggest a "new beginning" (quoted in *Bartlett*, 301).

[Moderato assai]
Как пошёл я с казаками,
   Ганна говорила:
[Moderato]
«За тебя я со слезами
   Бога умолила:
Ты вернёшься с первой битвы
   Весел и здоров —
Привези ж мне за молитвы
   Нитку корольков!»

[Allegro con spirito]
Бог послал нам атамана:
   Сразу мы разбили
В пух и прах всё войско хана,
   Город полонили,
Сбили крепкие ворота —
   Пир, пир для казаков!
[tempo I]
У меня одна забота:
   Нитка корольков!

[Allegro non tanto]
Вдруг сама в глаза блеснула —
   Знать, знать помог
Всевышний —
И сама мне в горсть юркнула
   Алой, крупной вишней.

[Allegro con fuoco]
Я добычу крепко стиснул,
   Да и был таков:
Прямо к Ганне степью свистнул
   С ниткой корольков,
И не спрашивал я брода
   Гати или моста...
Звон у нашего прихода;
   Люд валит с погоста —
И кричит мне вся громада
   Сотней голосов:
[meno mosso]
«Ганна там — и ей не надо
   Нитки корольков!»

[Andante]
Сердце сжалось, замирая,
   В груди раздроблённой,
И упал с коня, рыдая,
   Я пред иконой! о пощаде
Я молил без слов
И повесил на окладе
   Нитку корольков.

[Moderato assai]
Kak pashól ja s kazakámi,
    Gánna gavaríla:
[Moderato]
"Za tebjá ja sa slezámi
    Bóga umalíla:
Ty vernjóshsa s pérvaj bítvy
    Vésel i zdaróf —
Privezí zh mne za malítvy
    Nítku karal'kóf!"

[Allegro con spirito]
Bokh paslál nam atamána:
    Srázu my razbíli
F púkh i prákh fsjo vójska khána,
    Górat palaníli,
Zbíli krépkije varóta —
    Pir, pir dlja kazakóf!
[Tempo I]
U menjá adná zabóta:
    Nítka karal'kóf!

[Allegro non tanto]
Vdruk samá v glazá blesnúla —
    Znat', znat' pamók Fsevýshnij —
I samá mne v gorst' jurknúla
    Álaj, krúpnaj víshnej.

[Allegro con fuoco]
Ja dabýchu krépka stísnul,
    Da i být takóf:
Prjáma g Gánne stép'ju svísnul
    S nítkaj karal'kóf,
I ne spráshival ja bróda
    Gáti ili mósta…
Zvon u násheva prikhóda;
    Ljut valít s pagósta —
I krichít mne fsja gramáda
    Sótnej galasóf:
[meno mosso]
"Gánna tam — i jej ne náda
    Nítki karal'kóf!"

[Moderato assai]
When I rode off with the Cossacks
    Hannah said to me:
[Moderato]
"With tears I prayed to God
    And moved Him to help you:
You'll return from the first battle
    Happy and hale —
Bring me then, for my prayers,
    A string of coral beads!"

[Allegro con spirito]
God sent us a [good] ataman:
    Right away we beat
To smithereens the khan's men,
    Took the city prisoner,
Knocked down the strong gates —
    A feast it was, a feast for Cossacks!
[Tempo I]
There's only one thing on my mind:
    A string of coral beads!

[Allegro non tanto]
Suddenly I saw it flashing there —
    See, see, the Almighty came to my aid—
And it jumped right into my hands
    Like a string of big red cherries.

[Allegro con fuoco]
I clenched my prize with a strong grip,
    For that's the kind of fellow I am:
Straight across the steppe I flew to Hannah
    With the string of coral beads,
I didn't stop to ask for bridge or ford,
    Or where to cross the marshes…
Bells ring in our parish,
    Folk stream from the graveyard —
And the whole crowd is shouting at me,
    A hundred voices strong:
[meno mosso]
"Hannah's there — and doesn't need
    The string of coral beads!"

[Andante]	[Andante]
Sérttse zzhálas', zamirája,	My heart sank, nearly stopped
V grudí razdrabljónnaj	In my shattered breast,
I upál s kanjá, rydája,	I fell from my horse, sobbing,
Ja pred ikónaj! a pashcháde	Before an icon! without a word
Ja malíl bes slóf	I begged for mercy
I pavésil na akláde	And on the holy icon hung
Nítku karal'kóf.	The string of coral beads.

TEXT. **Lev Mey**, 1861. Title: Корольки. Песня (The Corals. A Song). Translated from a Polish ballad written by **Władysław Syrokomla**. The Syrokomla ballad was first published in 1854 in "Pieśni do muzyki," a group of poems set to music by the Polish composer Wiktor Każyński (*Kondratowicz*, 225-6, and note, 228). First set in Russian in 1861 by Matvey Ivanovich Bernard (1794-1871).

METER. Binary. Trochaic, alternating lines of 4 and 3 feet:
And it jumped into my hands,
Like a string of cherries.

MUSIC. April 1875. Op. 28, no. 2. F-sharp Minor. 3/4, with 2/4 in the second stanza. Moderato assai (initially, with subsequent changes indicated in the text). For High Voice: f^1 sharp–a^2.

Dedicated to **Aleksándr Dodónov** (1837-1914), a tenor at the Bolshoy who sang Andrey in the Moscow premiere of *The Oprichnik* on 4 May 1875. Dodonov's voice teacher was Manuel Garcia (Viardot's brother), whose vocal technique and teaching style were instrumental in forming the "Russian school" of singing in the 19th century (see pp. 297-8 in SINGERS & RECORDINGS). Like many others, Dodonov later became a teacher himself, passing this tradition on to the next generation. One of his pupils was the famous tenor Leonid Sobinov.

RECORDINGS. Golovin, Karolik, **Lemeshev**, Lisovsky, Nelepp.

Dmitry Golovin's recording of the song (made in 1956) uses a bowdlerized text purged of religious references: see Song 61 for a discussion of this practice.

35 *Зачем?*
Why?

Op. 28, No. 3

Tchaikovsky was the first composer to see the possibilities in this lyric by Lev Mey. In its odd use of language, and in the way an entire intimate relationship is implied in the images of her hair and lips and his hot pillow, it has that combination of something at once archaic and modern found in a Renaissance poet like Thomas Wyatt. The meter is strange (Mey was an experimenter with meter)—iambic lines with dactylic endings. Tchaikovsky found a perfect melodic phrase to contain this unusual meter, so that once you have heard the song, you cannot read the lines without hearing the melody.

Though the poem is arranged in four stanzas of four lines each, its content naturally divides it differently, into three parts: lines 1-5 (the sudden occurrence of the dream and his wish to banish it); lines 6-12 (the dream's vivid detail and its powerful emotional force); and the final quatrain, the recurring question about the dream and what it means. Tchaikovsky's song is written to reflect these three parts, and that is how the lines are arranged below.

It is easy to confuse the title of this song with Song 8, also called "Why?" But in Russian the two words are different. The "why" of Song 8 (отчего) means "what is the cause?", but this "why" (зачем) means "for what purpose, to what end?" The recurring melodic phrase building to a climax recalls the earlier Heine song, but there the final question is an angry explosion, an accusation, while here it is an unanswered question that will not go away.

Зачем же ты приснилася,
Красавица далёкая,
И вспыхнула, что в полыме,
Подушка одинокая?
Ох, сгинь ты, сгинь ты,
полуночница!

Глаза твои ленивые,
И пепел кос рассыпчатый,
И губы горделивые, —
Всё наяву мне снилося,
И всё, что грёза вешняя,
Умчалося, — и на сердце
Легла потьма кромешная!

Зачем же ты приснилася,
Красавица далёкая,
Коль стынет вместе с грёзою
Подушка одинокая?
Зачем же, зачем же ты приснилася!

Zachém zhe ty prisnílasa,	So why then did I dream of you,
Krasávitsa daljókaja,	Oh lady fair so far away,
I fspýkhnula, shto f pólyme,	To light a fire instantly
Padúshka adinókaja?	On my lonely pillow here?
Okh, zgín' ty, zgín' ty,	Oh midnight visitor, begone,
palunóshnitsa!	begone!
Glazá tvají lenívyje	Your eyes that look so languorous,
I pépel kos rassýpchatyj,	Your braids shot through with ashen gray,
I gúby gardelívyje, —	Your lips in all their haughtiness, —
Fsjo najavú mne snílasa,	All this I dreamed as clear as day,
I fsjo, shto grjóza véshnjaja,	Then, like a vision in spring,
Umchálasa, — i ná serttse	It flew away, and left my heart
Leglá pat'má kraméshnaja...	In impenetrable darkness...
Zachém zhe ty prisnílasa,	So why then did I dream of you,
Krasávitsa daljókaja,	Oh lady fair so far away,
Kol' stýnet vméste z grjózaju	Only to have this fading vision of you
Padúshka adinókaja?	Grow cool like my lonely pillow?
Zachém zhe, zachém zhe	So why then, why then did
ty prisnílasa!	I dream of you?

TEXT. **Lev Mey**, 1861. Title: Зачем? (Why?). First set by Tchaikovsky, later by some minor composers.

METER. Binary. Iambic, lines of 3 feet, with dactylic endings throughout:
> *Your eyes that look so languourous,*
> *Your lips in all their haughtiness...*

MUSIC. April 1875. Op. 28, no. 3. D Minor. 3/4, Moderato assai. For High Voice: d^1-a^2.

Dedicated to **Márya Ivánovna Iliná**, born Dundukova-Korsakova, mezzo-soprano, dates unknown. She sang Boyarina Morozova in the premiere of *The Oprichnik* in Kiev.

RECORDINGS. Arkhipova, Andrey Ivanov, Kasrashvili, Kruglikova, Larin, Lemeshev, Levinsky, Martynov, Mishura, Nelepp, Pishchayev, Rodgers, Söderström, Varady, Vinogradov, Vishnevskaya.

36 *Он так меня любил*
He loved me so

Op. 28, No. 4

Delphine Gay (1804-55), wife of the journalist Emile de Girardin, famed for her beauty and queen of the Romantic salons in Paris, published this "Romance" as the last poem in her collected poems in 1846. Aleksey Apukhtin translated it and presumably gave it to Tchaikovsky to use in this song. The theme is unrequited love, but seen from an unusual angle—in retrospect, with regret, as love unfulfilled.

Нет, не любила я! но странная забота
Теснила грудь мою, когда он приходил;
То вся краснела я, боялася чего-то, —
Он так меня любил, он так меня любил!

Чтоб нравиться ему тогда, цветы и те наряды
Я берегла, что он по сердцу находил;
С ним говорила я, его ловила взгляды, —
Он так меня любил, он так меня любил!

Но раз он мне сказал: «В ту рощу, в час заката
Придёшь ли?» «Да, приду!» Но не хватило сил;
Я в рощу не пошла, он ждал меня напрасно!

Тогда уехал он, сердясь на неудачу;
Несчастный, как меня проклясть он должен был!
Я не увижусь с ним, мне тяжело, я плачу…
Он так меня любил! Он так меня любил!
Он так меня любил! Он так меня любил!

Nét, ne ljubíla ja! no stránnaja zabóta
Tesníla grút' majú, kagdá on prikhadíl;
To fsja krasnéla ja, bajálasja chevó-ta, —
On ták menjá ljubíl, on ták menjá ljubíl!

Shtob nrávitsa jemú tagdá, tsvetý i te narjády
Ja bereglá, shto on pa sérttsu nakhadíl;

No, I didn't love him! but felt a strange alarm
Within my breast, when he would come to call;
His presence made me blush, or feel afraid of something —
He loved me so, he loved me so!

To please him then, I put on flowers
And wore the dresses he was fond of;

S nim gavaríla ja, jevó lavíla	The two of us would talk, I'd catch
vzgljády, —	his every glance, —
On ták menjá ljubíl, on ták menjá ljubíl!	He loved me so, he loved me so!
No ras on mne skazál: "F tu róshchu,	But once he said to me: "To the grove,
v chás zakáta	at sunset,
Pridjósh li?" "Dá, pridú!"	Will you come?" "Yes, I'll come!"
No ne khvatíla síl;	But I was too weak;
Ja v róshchu ne pashlá, on zhdál menjá	I didn't go to the grove, he waited for me
naprásna!	in vain!
Tagdá ujékhal on, serdjás' na neudáchu;	Then he went away, angry at his failure;
Neshchástnyj, kák menjá prakljást'	Unlucky man, how he must have
on dólzhen byl!	cursed me!
Ja ne uvízhus' s nim, mné tjazheló,	I'll never see him, heavy is my heart,
ja pláchu...	I weep...
On ták menjá ljubíl! On ták menjá ljubíl!	He loved me so! He loved me so!
On ták menjá ljubíl! On ták menjá ljubíl!	He loved me so! He loved me so!

TEXT. **Alekséy Apúkhtin**, date unknown but no later than 1875. Translation of a French poem by **Delphine de Girardin** (Delphine Gay), entitled "Il m'aimait tant! Romance," date unknown (*Girardin*, 388-9). Set only by Tchaikovsky. The translation was first published with Apukhtin's poems in 1991 (*Apukhtin*, 352), where the poem is arranged into four quatrains, each ending with the line "He loved me so, he loved me so!"

METER. Binary. Iambic hexameter:

I didn't love him, no, but felt a strange alarm
Within my breast when he would come to call on us...

MUSIC. April 1875. Op. 28, no. 4. D Minor. 4/4, Moderato. For High Voice: d^1-a^2.

Dedicated to **Yekaterína Massíni** (1840-1912), Russian soprano. Studied at La Scala where she took Massini as her stage name (her real name was Vedeniapina). She sang Natalia in the Kiev premiere of *Oprichnik* on 9 December 1874, a performance Tchaikovsky attended and particularly liked. She went on to sing at the Bolshoy from 1876-1881.

RECORDINGS. Fomina, Gorchakova, Kazarnovskaya, Kudriavtseva, Lavrova, Levko, Maksakova, Irina Maslennikova, Rautio, Vishnevskaya.

37 *Ни отзыва, ни слова, ни привета*
No response, no word, no greeting

Op. 28, No. 5

This poem by Aleksey Apukhtin is one of his best and most characteristic. The theme of a love now over, seen across a desert barren of feelings, goes back to the theme of disillusionment in Song 10, also by Apukhtin. But here the consequences are an emptiness, in which the past is not just forgotten but obliterated. The text speaks of anger, but the song is tender and wounded, with melancholy in the piano part, and hope as well as pain in the free rising and falling melodic phrases of the voice part—laconic, and very fine.

Ни отзыва, ни слова, ни привета,
Пустынею меж нами мир лежит,
И мысль моя с вопросом без ответа
Испуганно над сердцем тяготит!

Ужель среди часов тоски и гнева
Прошедшее исчезнет без следа,
Как лёгкий звук забытого напева,
Как в мрак ночной упавшая звезда?

Как лёгкий звук забытого напева,
Как в мрак ночной упавшая звезда?

Ni ódzyva, ni slóva, ni privéta,
Pustýneju mezh námi mir lezhýt,
I mýsl' majá s vaprósam bez atvéta
Ispúganna nat sérttsem tjagotít!

No response, no word, no greeting,
A desert is the world that lies between us,
And a fearful thought weighs on my heart,
A question with no answer!

Uzhél' sredí chasóf taskí i gnéva
Prashétsheje ishchéznet bes sledá,
Kak ljókhkij zvúk zabýtava napéva,
Kak v mrák nachnój upáfshaja zvezdá?

In hours of longing and anger
Can the past disappear without a trace,
Like the dying sound of a forgotten tune,
Like a falling star swallowed by the night?

Kak ljókhkij zvúk zabýtava napéva,
Kak v mrák nachnój upáfshaja zvezdá?

Like the dying sound of a forgotten tune,
Like a falling star swallowed by the night?

TEXT. **Akseséy Apúkhtin**, 1867. Words mistakenly attributed to Aleksey Tolstoy in editions prior to 1940. First set by Tchaikovsky; later by several other composers including Donaurov (1876) and Cui (1881).

METER. Binary. Iambic pentameter:
> *In hours like these of anger and of longing*
> *The past can disappear without a trace,*
> *A falling star that vanished in the night...*

MUSIC. April 1875. Op. 28, no. 5. C Minor. 4/4, Andante sostenuto. For Middle Voice: c–f¹.

Dedicated to **Bogomír Kórsov** (1845-1920), Russian baritone. His real name was Gottfried Gering. He studied singing with Piccioli as a boy and met Tchaikovsky in Piccioli's house. Trained in Milan and Paris, he sang in Petersburg 1869-81 and Moscow 1882-1905. He was a major singer, who was the first to sing many leading roles in Russian operas. Tchaikovsky admired him both for his singing and acting; he also dedicated Song 69 to him. Married to Aleksandra Krutikova (see Song 19).

RECORDINGS. Descamps, Fischer-Dieskau, Jadlowker (in German), Leiferkus, Lemeshev, Mazurok, Migay, Tear.

38 Страшная минута
The fearful minute

Op. 28, No. 6

This song about the moment of suspense after making a declaration of love is a variation on the theme with which Opus 28 began (Song 33). Tchaikovsky himself wrote the text. The song takes as its starting point urban romance of the "cruel" variety, where passion means "torment," where a single word can mean "paradise" or "a knife to the heart." But musically it is an original approach to the genre. The vulnerability is refined, expressed as it is in a song to be sung "con tenerezza," with tenderness, and to be accompanied "dolce," sweetly. Galina Vishnevskaya recalls a performance of it in England with Benjamin Britten accompanying her on the piano: "The song 'A Fearful Minute' concludes with but a few bars on the piano, which seemingly offer little to reflect upon. Yet after Britten played them, one wanted to hear nothing more and let the unearthly purity of that brief ending live on in one's soul" (*Vishnevskaya*, 309). A finely written psychological study in the form of a short story by Alexander Kuprin ("The Fearful Minute," 1895) offers insight into how Tchaikovsky's contemporaries saw the song. It was one of his best known songs during his lifetime.

Ты внимаешь, вниз склонив головку,
очи опустив и тихо вздыхая!
Ты не знаешь, как мгновенья эти
страшны для меня и полны значенья,
как меня смущает это молчанье.
Я приговор твой жду, я жду решенья —
иль нож ты мне в сердце вонзишь,
иль рай мне откроешь.
Ах, не терзай меня, скажи лишь слово!

Отчего же робкое признанье
в сердце так тебе запало глубоко?
Ты вздыхаешь, ты дрожишь и плачешь —
иль слова любви в устах твоих немеют,
или ты меня жалеешь, не любишь?
Я приговор твой жду, я жду решенья —
иль нож ты мне в сердце вонзишь,
иль рай мне откроешь!
Ах, внемли же мольбе моей,
отвечай, отвечай скорей!
Я приговор твой жду, я жду решенья.

Ty vnimájesh, vnis sklaníf galófku,
óchi apustíf i tíkha vzdykhája!
Ty ne znájesh, kak mgnavén'ja èti
stráshny dlja menjá i pólny znachén'ja,
kak menjá smushchájet èta malchán'je.
Ja prigavór tvoj zhdú, ja zhdú reshén'ja —
il' nósh ty mne f sérttse vanzísh,
il' ráj mne atkrójesh.
Akh, ne terzáj menjá, skazhý lish slóva!

Atchevó zhe rópkaje priznán'je
f sérttse tak tebé zapála glubóka?
Ty vzdykhájesh, ty drazhýsh i pláchesh —
il' slavá ljubví v ustákh tvajíkh neméjut,
ili ty menjá zhaléjesh, ne ljúbish?
Ja prigavór tvoj zhdú, ja zhdú reshén'ja —
il' nósh ty mne f sérttse vanzísh,
il' ráj mne atkrójesh!
Akh, vnemlí zhe mal'bé majéj,
atvecháj, atvecháj skaréj!
Ja prigavór tvoj zhdú, ja zhdú reshén'ja.

You listen, your dear head inclined,
your eyes lowered, quietly sighing!
You don't know how these moments
frighten me, how full of meaning they are,
how this silence upsets me.
I await your verdict, your decision —
you'll either stab me in the heart
or show me heaven.
Oh, don't torture me, say just one word!

How could my shy confession
sink so deeply in your heart?
You sigh, you tremble and weep —
are you holding back words of love,
or do you pity me, not love me?
I await your verdict, your decision —
you'll either stab me in the heart
or show me heaven!
Oh then, hear my plea,
answer me, answer now!
I await your verdict, your decision.

TEXT. **N. N. [P. I. Tchaikovsky]**, 1875. One of three song texts written by the composer (the others are Songs 15 and 78).

METER. Accentual rather than syllabo-tonic, but arranged in definite patterns in contrasting sections of the song; there are no rhymes to mark the ends of the lines, but the final word (with two deliberate exceptions) is always trochaic:

> *As you listen, downward head inclining,*
> *Lowering your eyes and sighing so softly…*

MUSIC. The manuscript is dated 11 April 1875. Op. 28, no. 6. F-sharp Minor. 4/4, Andante non troppo (con tenerezza). For High Voice: c^1 sharp-g^2 sharp. One of four songs Tchaikovsky singled out in 1881 as his best known, Songs 6, 9, and 40 being the others (*Jurgenson*, I, 207). Orchestrated by Taneyev in 1891.

Dedicated to **Yevláliya Kádmina** (1853-1881), Russian contralto. Discovered by Nikolay Rubinstein, she studied at the Moscow Conservatory with Aleksandrova-Kochetova; she sang in "The Snow Maiden" in 1873. Turgenev later used her suicide as the basis for his story "Clara Milich" (see Song 9).

RECORDINGS. Baikov, Borodina, Eizen, Figner, Gmyria, Hvorostovsky, Andrey Ivanov, Kasrashvili, Kurenko, Lemeshev, Lisitsian, Lisovsky, Nelepp, Nesterenko, Obukhova, Ognivtsev, Pechkovsky, Petrov, Rautio, Reizen, Rodgers, Söderström, Vedernikov, Vishnevskaya.

6 Romances, Opus 38 (1878)

In the three years between the 1875 songs and the songs of Opus 38, Tchaikovsky wrote some of his best-loved music, including the ballet *Swan Lake*, the opera *Eugene Onegin*, his Fourth Symphony, and his Violin Concerto. But during this same period, through his own folly, he also brought on a personal crisis which nearly destroyed him. The events that so decisively altered his life in the summer of 1877 can be traced back to three seemingly inconsequential entries in *Days and Years* (*DG*), the day-by-day chronicle of his life—minor moments that had far-reaching consequences he could not have foreseen. Chance played a crucial role in them and in his mind he saw connections between them, reinforcing his natural Russian tendency to see the hand of fate in everything of permanent consequence.

One of these moments occurred on 13 May 1877. He was visiting Elizabeth Lavrovskaya, the singer to whom he had dedicated the Opus 27 songs. Tchaikovsky was always looking for good subjects for an opera, and she told him he ought to try *Eugene Onegin*, the long poem Pushkin had called his "novel in verse." The idea seemed "wild" to him when she suggested it and he did not know what to say. But the next day dining alone in a tavern he remembered her idea, was quickly taken by it, and ran out to a bookshop to find the poem. He read into the night, becoming more and more excited by the "mine of poetry" he found in Pushkin's story (*DG*, 146), and went to his friend Konstantin Shilovsky to ask him to collaborate with him on a libretto. The resulting opera, sketched out quickly in the summer and completed that winter, turned out to be the breakthrough he had been seeking in operatic form. He found in it a creative freedom he had not known in his other operas, calling it not an opera but "lyrical scenes," and writing it, in fact, to be performed by students at the conservatory rather than in the Imperial theaters where his operas, despite the good music they contained, had been such disappointing flops. He doubted *Onegin* would ever be popular with the public (he was wrong), but he never doubted its musical worth.

The earliest of the three moments, one that signals the disaster to come, is the curious entry of 20 September 1876, from a letter to his sister: "I continue to think about marriage." If any idea should have seemed "wild" to him, it was this one. He was thirty-six and his sexual identity had long since been formed and confirmed in his circle of gay friends like Apukhtin and the Shilovsky brothers; he had many good friends who were women, but he never had a mature romantic relationship with a woman or any real interest in seeking one. Yet though the romantic side of his sexuality—his tendency to fall in love with younger men—remained a constant throughout his life, the sexual escapades of his youth had lost some of their allure for him by this time. There

were numerous instances of gay men he knew who were marrying and estab-
lishing a seemly family life, at least outwardly. It seemed to solve the problem
of one's position in society; besides, he was lonely. Maybe he should try it too?
The opportunity came at the end of April 1877, when he received a love letter
from a young woman named Antonina Milyukova (1849-1917), a former student at the Moscow Conservatory. Less than a month later, after a few more
letters (in one of them, she hinted at suicide) and after very few meetings, he
asked her to be his wife. If there was dishonesty in his proposal, it was above all
dishonesty with himself. He promised to love her not as a husband but as a
friend—terms to which she readily agreed, not that either of them understood
their implications. He felt he was acting in a moral and upright manner; the
reassuring thing was that she loved him "like a kitten," as he wrote to his
younger brother Anatoly on 23 June (Anatoly Ilyich was the twin brother of
Modest, but unlike Modest, he was not gay). These fateful days coincided with
the early days of inspiration over *Eugene Onegin*. He had begun composing the
opera with the famous letter scene, when Tatyana, who has fallen in love with
Onegin, stays up all night writing him a letter, confessing her love, and setting
herself up to be rejected. What Onegin did to Tatyana in coldly dismissing her
love, he himself could never be accused of doing to Antonina.

Both were cruelly punished for his self-deception. The wedding was held
in July, without announcement and without any friends being present except
his former pupil, a violinist named Joseph Kotek, and his brother Anatoly.
The couple went directly to Petersburg to visit Tchaikovsky's father. Then
they lived together in Moscow for two excruciating weeks, during which time
Tchaikovsky realized that he could not give her the conjugal relations she
wanted, and that she could never give him the musical and intellectual companionship he wanted. He fled to his sister's at Kamenka for the summer, telling
his wife he needed to be alone to compose. In August he finally was able to get
some work done on *Onegin* and the Fourth Symphony. He delayed his return
to Moscow as long as he could, arriving on 11 September, late for the beginning of classes. Jurgenson hosted a supper to introduce Tchaikovsky's wife to
his friends; it was awkward though amiable, but it must have shown Tchaikovsky that he had arrived at a dead end. A few days later, he walked into the
Moscow River and stood up to his chest in its cold water as long as he could
stand it in the hope that he would catch a deathly chill and die. But it did not
work. (The evidence for this story has been questioned: Berberova accepts it,
but Poznansky does not; see *Poznansky 1999*, 111-2.) In any case, no option
remained but a nervous breakdown, which is what happened. On 23 September he telegraphed Anatoly, asking him to send a fake telegram from Nápravník
(conductor at the Mariinsky Theater) requesting his immediate presence in
Petersburg. When he got to Petersburg, he collapsed, dispatching Anatoly to

Moscow to tell his wife that they must separate. He wanted to run away, and that is what he did. Anatoly accompanied him to Berlin. He spent the entire winter and spring in Europe, not returning to Moscow until June 1878, and then only for a few days. He never lived with Antonina again, dealing with her through intermediaries and trying to furnish her with the necessary support. But her refusal to let go of him was a torment to him the rest of his life, nor could he blame anyone for it but himself.

A few months before these events began, on 18 December 1876, Tchaikovsky received a letter from another woman, also a complete stranger. This missive out of the blue was the first of the three cards fate handed him that year, and it turned out to be the luckiest thing that ever happened to him. The woman was Nadezhda Filaretovna von Meck (1831-1894). She was a rich widow who sojourned in Europe and lived in Russia in her several grand town houses and country estates. She had many children, and kept her own household musicians to teach them, one of whom was that same Joseph Kotek who had been a witness at Tchaikovsky's wedding. She was a serious music lover, well informed and acquainted with many in the musical world, including Nikolay Rubinstein. Whether Rubinstein suggested to her that she might write Tchaikovsky and help him in discreet ways, or whether her own love of his music prompted her to do it, she asked for his help in some small musical matters, offering to pay him handsomely for his troubles. It seemed almost too handsome a sum at first, but he needed the money and agreed. The correspondence quickly assumed a level of platonic friendship between a composer of genius just then entering into his full artistic maturity, and an enlightened, generous patron, a forgiving woman who agreed to be his "friend" and only that (though she might have wished for more), interested in and able to understand the artistic issues that mattered to him, even if they did not always agree on a particular poet or painter or composer. She was also sensitive enough to understand that their friendship was viable only if conducted at a safe distance. They corresponded for the next fourteen years, but never met face to face; he was invited to live in her houses as her guest, but never when she herself was in residence. Their relationship is one of the most extraordinary in the history of artistic patronage.

In December 1877 he dedicated his Fourth Symphony to her—"To My Best Friend." She helped him out with "loans," and even more important for his own sanity, she lent a sympathetic ear to his written accounts of what he was going through. When he arrived in Europe in October she sent him 3000 francs and thereupon began a regular monthly stipend to him of 1500 francs. The letters they exchanged, especially in the first few years of their correspondence, are a conversation between Tchaikovsky and a friend, present in his life every day, but unseen, a companion of the spirit, not the flesh. We hear him expressing his views on music, literature, and art, on philosophy and religion, and on places and persons, including himself and the contemporaries who mattered most to him. He needed to be engaged in that conversation, and he wrote her nearly every day.

When Tchaikovsky fled Russia in the fall of 1877, he and Anatoly travelled together to Switzerland, Paris, Florence, Rome, Venice, and Vienna. In Vienna, in December, Anatoly left him and went home. Tchaikovsky returned to Italy. He gradually recovered; he completed the orchestration of the symphony and the opera; he sent the symphony to Rubinstein at the end of the year, and finished *Onegin* in San Remo in February. From there he wrote Anatoly that the months of "madness" he had been through were behind him. He went on to Florence, where one morning between breakfast and lunch he wrote an extraordinary song to a poem Mrs. von Meck had mentioned in one of her letters to illustrate a point about poetry and music (Song 43). He asked her to look in Fet, Aleksey Tolstoy, Mey, and Tyutchev for more poems that he might set to music. Of those she sent, he especially liked four of the Tolstoy poems which he chose.

He returned at last to Russia in April 1878. In May he spent two weeks at the von Meck estate at Brailov in the Ukraine (the whole staff, the splendid house and grounds were all at his disposal, but she was absent). There he wrote the four Tolstoy songs. One night at the end of his stay he sat alone at one of her pianos and played through nearly the whole score of *Eugene Onegin*—no one was present to hear the music except the man who had written it, but it moved him to tears. On the following day, 17 May 1878, he began making clean copies of the six romances of Opus 38, finishing them later that summer. He dedicated them all to Anatoly.

39   *Серенада Дон-Жуана*
Don Juan's Serenade

Op. 38, No. 1

The text comes from a play Aleksey Tolstoy wrote about Don Juan. In the play, this serenade is sung as a joke under the balcony of Nisetta, a loose woman of the town. Don Juan, who has rashly promised the Commendatore he will marry Donna Anna, hopes this insolent act will show the old man he is not son-in-law material (the duel and scene with the statue follow, but Tolstoy has mercy on his sinner, who ends up in a monastery). Having written it as a plot device, Tolstoy himself evidently did not consider it very important. When it was pointed out to him that it is a good lyric in its own right (Tyutchev reportedly committed it to memory as soon as he read it), he seemed surprised (*Tolstoi*, II, 669).

It is a deliberate piece of seductive serenading by an expert and determined Don Juan. That is how Tchaikovsky saw it and rendered it musically. There was added inspiration in the fact that, for him, of all the works of music ever written, Mozart's *Don Giovanni* was at the top of the list. The song has always been popular, sung by tenors as well as baritones and basses. It is marked "allegro," but "non tanto," not too fast. In performance, the insolence should not turn into shouting; a lightened, "fleet" approach works best (*Jackson*, 165).

Гаснут дальней Альпухарры	От Севильи до Гранады,
Золотистые края,	В тихом сумраке ночей,
На призывный звон гитары	Раздаются серенады,
Выйди, милая моя!	Раздаётся стук мечей;
Всех, кто скажет, что другая	Много крови, много песней
Здесь равняется с тобой,	Для прелестных льётся дам, —
Всех, любовию сгорая,	Я же той, кто всех прелестней,
Всех, всех, всех зову на	всё, всё,
смертный бой!	Песнь и кровь мою отдам!
От лунного света	От лунного света
Зардел небосклон,	Зардел небосклон,
О, выйди, Нисета,	О, выйди, Нисета,
О, выйди, Нисета,	О, выйди, Нисета,
Скорей на балкон!	Скорей на балкон.
Gásnut dál'nej Al'pukhárry	Nightfall comes to the golden lands
Zalatístyje krajá,	Of distant Alpujarras,
Na prizývnyj zvon gitáry	To the call of my guitar
Výjdi, mílaja majá!	Come out, my darling!
Fsekh, kto skázhet, shto drugája	If any dare say another
Zdes' ravnjájetsa s tabój,	Can compare with you,

Fsekh, ljubóviju zgarája, Fsekh, fsekh, fsekh zavú na smértnyj boj!	If any burn with love for you, All, all, all I'll fight to the death!
At lúnnava svéta Zardél nebasklón, O, výjdi, Niséta, o, výjdi, Niséta, Skaréj na balkón!	Red in the moonlight The sky's all aglow, O, come out, Nisetta, O, come out, Nisetta, Come out on your balcony now!
At Sevíl'ji da Granády, F tíkham súmrake nachéj, Razdajútsa serenády, Razdajótsa stuk mechéj; Mnóga króvi, mnóga pésnej Dlja preléstnykh l'jótsa dam, — Ja zhe toj, kto fsekh preléstnej, 　fsjo, fsjo, Pesn' i krof' majú addám!	From Seville to Granada, At quiet dusk as night comes on, Serenades are sung, The clatter of swords is heard; A lot of blood and many songs Pour out for lovely women's sake, — For her who's loveliest, 　I'll give it all, All my song and all my blood!
At lúnnava svéta Zardél nebasklón, O, výjdi, Niséta, o, výjdi, Niséta, Skaréj na balkón.	Red in the moonlight The sky's all aglow, O, come out, Nisetta, O, come out, Nisetta, Come out on your balcony now.

TEXT. **Alekséy Tolstóy**. From Дон Жуан (Don Juan), a dramatic poem, written 1859-60. First set by Tchaikovsky; later by several minor composers. In *PSS*, Granada is spelled "Grenada", and in older performances it was sung that way. In my text I have restored the correct spelling, which is also the spelling used by Tolstoy's modern editors.

METER. Binary. Trochaic tetrameter:

> *Nightfall comes to Alpujarras,*
> *Heed the call of my guitar...*

The short lines at the end of each stanza are two-foot amphibrachs:

> *And red in the moonlight*
> *The sky's all aglow...*

MUSIC. May 1878. Op. 38, no. 1. B Minor. 3/4, Allegro non tanto. For Baritone: B–f¹ sharp. Dedicated to **Anatóly Ilyích Tchaikóvsky** (1850-1915).

RECORDINGS. Atlantov, Baikov, Borg, Caruso (in French), Christoff, Edouard De Reszke (in French), Descamps, Eizen, Fischer-Dieskau, Gedda, Ghiaurov, Gmyria, Hvorostovsky, Jadlowker (in German), Larin, Leiferkus, Lemeshev, Lisitsian, Magomayev, Martynov, Nesterenko, Nortsov, Pedrotti, Petrov, Politkovsky, Rebroff, Reizen, Rosing, Savenko, Serkebayev, Souzay, Tartakov, Tear, Zakharov.

40 *То было раннею весной*
It was in early spring

Op. 38, No. 2

Aleksey Tolstoy took the idea for this poem from Goethe's "Mailied" (May Song, 1771), with its jubilant exclamations "O Erd', o Sonne! O Glück, o Lust! O Lieb', o Liebe!" (*Tolstoi*, I, 544). In Tolstoy's hands, however, a new and altogether Russian poem was made out of images commonly associated with the Russian spring: the tightly curled fiddlehead tops of the ferns breaking through the ground in a stand of evergreens, and the image of birches, repeated three times, including the "fresh smell of the birch tree," which is the culminating image in the poem and the song.

The poem reverses the attitude to the past that was expressed in Song 19—"don't try to recall the past, it will only cause you pain"—by remembering it with all the fresh excitement it originally held, so that in reimagining it, it regains its sacral power, a power associated with the rebirth of nature, with youth and the "morning" of life, and with awakening love. Here, opposites are reconciled, the bright sun and the shade of the birch tree; tears and happiness go together, everything is possible, and life is at its point of fullest potential. It is a little Russian rite of spring, very nineteenth-century, but just as valid in the present, too, for that matter, in its evocation of the thrill felt with the first tender arrival of spring.

David Brown finds this romance does not have "any notable mark of character or quality to lift it above the general run of Tchaikovsky's romances" (*Brown II*, 281). If that is so, then it must follow that the general run of Tchaikovsky's romances is at a very high level indeed. Certainly no Russian, nor any singer of Russian songs, would agree that this song is somehow flat and uninspired. It was one of Tchaikovsky's best-known songs in his own lifetime, and one of the songs Slonimsky picked to represent Tchaikovsky the songwriter at his most poignant (*Slonimsky 1949*). It is interesting to compare it with Rimsky-Korsakov's romance written years later to the same text, all poetic reverie and calm recollection. In contrast, the Tchaikovsky song fully surrenders to the past moment in order to relive it. As a result the emotions are felt as if they were happening again in the present, here and now, an impression underscored in the *ad libitum* section marked double *forte* beginning with the words "Oh happiness! Oh tears!" The rising intonation that drives the song—an indicator of strong affirmation—is unmistakable in both the vocal and piano parts.

То было раннею весной,
Трава едва всходила,
Ручьи текли, не парил зной,
И зелень рощ сквозила;

Труба пастушья поутру
Ещё не пела звонко,
И в завитках ещё в бору
Был папоротник тонкий;

То было раннею весной,
В тени берёз то было,
Когда с улыбкой предо мной
Ты очи опустила...

То на любовь мою в ответ
Ты опустила вежды —
О жизнь! О лес! О солнца свет!
О юность! О надежды!

И плакал я перед тобой,
На лик твой глядя милый, —
То было раннею весной,
В тени берёз то было!

То было в утро наших лет —
О счастье! О слёзы!
О лес! О жизнь! О солнца свет!
О свежий дух берёзы!

To býla ránneju vesnój,
Travá jedvá fskhadíla
Ruchjí teklí, ne páril znój,
I zélen' róshch skvazíla;

It was in early spring,
The grass was just appearing,
The streams were flowing, the air was warm,
In the groves there was a thin veil of green;

Trubá pastúshja pautrú
Jeshchó ne péla zvónka,
I v zavitkákh jeshchó v barú
Byl páparatnik tónkaj;

Too early to hear the shepherd's horn
Ring out in the morning,
And in the grove of conifers, still twisted tight,
Stood the first slender ferns;

To býla ránneju vesnój,
F tení berjós to býla,
Kagdá s ulýpkaj preda mnój
Ty óchi apustíla...

It was in early spring,
It was in the shade of birches,
When, standing before me, smiling,
You lowered your eyes...

To na ljubóf' majú v atvét
Ty apustíla vézhdy —
O zhýzn'! O lés! O sólntsa svét!
O júnast'! O nadézhdy!

It was an answer to my love,
Your lowered glance —
O life! O woods! O sunlight!
O youth! O hopes!

I plákal ja peret tabój,
Na lík tvoj gljádja mílyj, —
To býla ránneju vesnój,
F tení berjós to býla!

And I wept before you,
Gazing at your dear face, —
It was in early spring,
In the shade of birches!

To býla v útra náshikh lét —
O shchást'je! O sljózy!
O lés! O zhýzn'! O sólntsa svét!
O svézhyj dúkh berjózy!

It was in the morning of our days —
O happiness! O tears!
O woods! O life! O sunlight!
O fresh smell of the birch tree!

TEXT. **Alekséy Tolstóy**, May, 1871. Inspired by Goethe's "Mailied" (set by Beethoven, 1796, Op. 52/4). First set by Tchaikovsky; later by Rimsky-Korsakov (1897, Op. 43/4).

METER. Binary. Iambic, alternating lines of 4 and 3 feet:

> *It was the morning of our days—*
> *Oh happiness! Oh tears!*
> *Oh woods! Oh life! Oh sun-filled sky!*
> *Oh springtime scent of birches!*

MUSIC. May 1878. Op. 38, no. 2. E-flat Major. 6/8, Allegro moderato. For High Voice: e¹ flat–g². Dedicated to **Anatóly Ilyích Tchaikóvsky**.

RECORDINGS. Arkhipova, Borodina, DeGaetani, Dolukhanova, Ghiaurov, Gorchakova, Hvorostovsky, Kasrashvili, Krasnaya, Larin, Leiferkus, Lemeshev, Magomayev, Martynov, Mkrtchyan, Obraztsova, Obukhova, Petina, Reizen, Rodgers, Söderström, Solovianenko, Sterling, Tourel, Vedernikov, **Vishnevskaya**.

Rimsky-Korsakov: Borisenko, Gedda, Lemeshev, Martynov.

41 Средъ шумного бала
Amid the din of the ball

Op. 38, No. 3

The words for this famous song were written by Aleksey Tolstoy in 1851, the year he first saw his future wife at a masquerade ball which he and Turgenev attended in Petersburg during the Christmas season (*Tolstoi*, I, 532). The song Tchaikovsky made of Tolstoy's poem is so widely known in Russia that from the first notes everyone knows the words. In a 1975 film (a classic romantic comedy shown on TV every New Year's Eve called "The Irony of Fate, or Fresh from the Bathhouse"), there is a scene in which the hero first realizes he has found the woman he is going to marry and starts dancing around the room alone singing this song to himself. In the Soviet context it is funny, but we laugh at the hero, not the song, which instantly evokes a romantic charm that has never faded. The song is about falling in love with a stranger at a ball and recalling it later. Tchaikovsky made it into a waltz-reverie in slowed-down 3/8 time.

Tolstoy's poem has two literary antecedents. One is Pushkin's famous "Я помню чудное мгновенье" (I remember a wonderful moment, 1825), about seeing a woman of ideal beauty by chance and recalling it later. Tolstoy clearly had Pushkin's poem in mind, and even took his second line from it, changing the wording and the meter. The other is a poem by Lermontov about seeing a beautiful stranger at a masquerade ball, "Из-под таинственной, холодной полумаски" (Behind a mysterious, cold half-mask, 1841). Taking Pushkin as his starting point, Lermontov creates out of this chance encounter a dream he carries with him ever after to cherish and love. It is an original and utterly Lermontovian poem, with his special combination of idealism, cynical realism, and steely resolve. It was pointed out to Tolstoy's famous cousin the novelist that Aleksey Tolstoy's poem resembled the one by Lermontov, to which Lev Nikolayevich replied "Good for him—only Lermontov did it much better" *(Tolstoi, I, 532).*

But there is a difference between a great poem and a great song lyric. As a lyric for a song, Tolstoy and Tchaikovsky did it better. What makes Lermontov's poem so good is the way it reveals him perfectly—but only him. The Tolstoy-Tchaikovsky song takes the experience out of literature and hands it to everyone, so even the hero of "Irony of Fate" can sing it to himself, about himself. There is unanimity of opinion about this song: the public, the singers—both men and women—and even the critics agree that it is one of Tchaikovsky's best.

Средь шумного бала, случайно,
В тревоге мирской суеты,
Тебя я увидел, но тайна
Твои покрывала черты.

Лишь очи печально глядели,
А голос так дивно звучал,
Как звон отдалённой свирели,
Как моря играющий вал.

Мне стан твой понравился тонкий
И весь твой задумчивый вид,
А смех твой, и грустный и звонкий,
С тех пор в моём сердце звучит.

В часы одинокие ночи
Люблю я, усталый, прилечь,
Я вижу печальные очи,
Я слышу весёлую речь.

И грустно я, грустно так засыпаю
И в грёзах неведомых сплю…
Люблю ли тебя, я не знаю,
Но кажется мне, что люблю!

Sret' shúmnava bála, sluchájna,	Amid the din of the ball, by chance,
F trevóge mirskój sujetý,	In all of vain society's alarms,
Tebjá ja uvídel, no tájna	I caught sight of you, but a mystery
Tvají pakryvála chertý.	Hid your features from me.
Lish óchi pechál'na gljadéli,	Your eyes were gazing sadly,
A gólas tak dívna zvuchál,	But your voice had a wonderful sound,
Kak zvón addaljónnaj viréli,	Like notes played on a distant flute,
Kak mórja igrájushchij vál.	Like waves swelling playfully in the sea.
Mne stán tvoj panrávilsa tónkij	I liked your slim figure
I ves' tvoj zadúmchivyj vít,	And your pensive look;
A smékh tvoj, i grúsnyj i zvónkij,	Your laughter, sad and musical,
S tekh pór v majóm sérttse zvuchít.	Rings in my heart ever since.
F chasý adinókije nóchi	At night in solitary hours,
Ljubljú ja, ustályj, priléch,	Tired, I like to lie back,
Ja vízhu pechál'nyje óchi,	I see your sad eyes,
Ja slýshu vesjóluju réch.	I hear your gay speech.

I grúsna ja, grúsna tak zasypáju   And, melancholy, I fall asleep
I v grjózakh nevédamykh spljú...   And dream mysterious dreams...
Ljubljú li tebjá, ja ne znáju,   I don't know if this means I love you,
No kázhetsa mne, shto ljubljú!   But it seems to me I'm in love!

TEXT. **Alekséy Tolstóy**, 1851. Untitled; first published 1856. According to *Ivanov*, it was set before Tchaikovsky by Aleksandrova-Kochetova (1865). Set by some other composers after Tchaikovsky, but only his version is still sung. After Song 9, this is his most frequently recorded song.

The Pushkin and Lermontov poems have also been set to music: Pushkin's poem in a famous setting by Glinka (1840), and Lermontov's by Balakirev (1903-4) and Vissarion Shebalin (Op. 48/1, 1952).

METER. Ternary. Amphibrachs, 3 feet:
    Your voice had a wonderful music,
    Like notes on a flute far away...

MUSIC. May 1878. Op. 38, no. 3. B Minor. 3/8, Moderato. For Middle Voice: b–e². Dedicated to **Anatóly Ilyích Tchaikóvsky**.

RECORDINGS. Anders (in German), Baikov, Borg, Burchuladze, Descamps, Dolukhanova, Eizen, Fischer-Dieskau, Frijsh (in French), Gedda, Ghiaurov, Gmyria, Guliayev, Hvorostovsky, Andrey Ivanov, Kasrashvili, Kastorsky, Kazarnovskaya, Koshetz, Kozlovsky, Kurenko, Larin, Leiferkus, Lemeshev, Levko, Magomayev, Martynov, Mazurok, Mei-Figner, Migay, Mishura, Mkrtchyan, Nesterenko, Obraztsova, Ots, Petina, Petrov, Price, Rebroff, Reizen, Resnik, Rodgers, Rosing, Savenko, Schock, Serkebayev, Slobodskaya, **Sobinov**, Söderström, Solovianenko, Souzay, Sterling, Tartakov, Tear, Tourel, Vedernikov, Vinogradov, Vishnevskaya, Zakharov.

42 *О, если б ты могла*
O, if you could

Op. 38, No. 4

Here is another poem by Aleksey Tolstoy built around a tear in the eye of his beloved, but this is a different tear, brought on not by jealousy as it was in Song 7, but by "troubles and grief." And again, as in the earlier poem, he would banish it if he could, but now he does not claim to know some higher philosophical truth that contains the remedy to the grief she knows. Instead, there are only the beautiful images of passing clouds in the second quatrain. It is altogether a better poem, short but powerful, with each iambic hexameter line taking a long breath. The music is equally strong. For some reason the song never caught on, though the few recordings of it are very fine.

О, если б ты могла, хоть на единый миг,
Забыть свою печаль, забыть свои невзгоды,
О, если бы, хоть раз, я твой увидел лик,
Каким я знал его в счастливейшие годы!

Когда в глазах твоих засветится слеза,
О, если б эта грусть могла пройти порывом,
Как в тёплую весну пролётная гроза,
Как тень от облаков, бегущая по нивам!

О, если б ты могла, хоть на единый миг,
Забыть свою печаль, забыть свои невзгоды,
О, если бы, хоть раз, я твой увидел лик,
Каким я знал его в счастливейшие годы!

O, jésli p ty maglá, khot' na jedínyj mík,
Zabýt' svajú pechál', zabýt' svají nevzgódy,
O, jésli by, khot' rás, ja tvoj uvídel lík,
Kakím ja znál jevó f shchastlívejshije
    gódy!

Kagdá v glazákh tvajíkh zasvétitsa slezá,
O, jésli b èta grúst' maglá prajtí parývam,
Kak f tjópluju vesnú praljótnaja
    grazá,
Kak tén' at ablakóf, begúshchaja
    pa nívam!

O, if you could, just for a single moment,
Forget your sadness, forget your troubles,
O, if only once to see the look you wore
As I knew it in our years of highest
    happiness!

When in your eyes a tear glistens,
O, if that grief could pass in a flash,
Like a warm spring thunderstorm that
    flies through and is gone,
Like cloud shadows running across
    fields of grain!

O, jésli p ty maglá, khot' na jedínyj mík,   O, if you could, just for a single moment,
Zabýt' svajú pechál', zabýt' svají nevzgódy,   Forget your sadness, forget your troubles,
O, jésli by, khot' rás, ja tvoj uvídel lík,   O, if only once to see the look you wore
Kakím ja znál jevó f shchastlívejshije   As I knew it in our years of highest
    gódy!   happiness!

TEXT. **Aleks-éy Tolstóy**, 1859. Untitled. First set by Tchaikovsky; later by more than twenty composers, including Ippolitov-Ivanov (Op. 5/3, 1886) and Rimsky-Korsakov (Op. 39/1, 1897). Tchaikovsky made one small change in the text: in line 5, where Tolstoy has "в твоих глазах" (in your eyes), Tchaikovsky reversed the order of the words to "в глазах твоих," no doubt for reasons of euphony as that line begins; he also repeated the first stanza as a reprise.

METER. Binary. Iambic hexameter, caesura after third foot:
> *Like thunderstorms in spring that fly through and are gone,*
> *Like shadows made by clouds that run across a field...*

MUSIC. May 1878. Op. 38, no. 4. D Major. 4/4, Allegro agitato. For Baritone: c sharp–e¹ flat. Dedicated to **Anatóly Ilyích Tchaikóvsky**.

RECORDINGS. Fischer-Dieskau, Hvorostovsky, Petrov, Pirogov.
Rimsky-Korsakov: Borisenko, Petrov.

43 Любовъ мертвеца
A dead man's love

Op. 38, No. 5

This is a very unusual song which has received almost no comment, except the observation that the music in the second stanza anticipates Liza's final aria in *Queen of Spades* and is written in the same key (*Vasina-Grossman*, 281). It is far from urban romance, much closer to an aria than a song. Only singers have paid attention to it. It is a "big" song, challenging to sing, but impressive in a good performance such as those by Dmitri Hvorostovsky or Sergei Leiferkus. Its strange power is only partly explained by the macabre text.

It is the first song Tchaikovsky wrote after the crisis of the previous winter. He had just finished *Onegin*, and was back in Florence, where he felt himself completely recovered and restored to life again. Maybe his fresh awareness of being alive and feeling more vigorous than ever entered into the powerful feeling expressed in the song. On Mrs. von Meck's recommendation he was reading Schopenhauer, whose pessimistic view of life he rejected. She sent him this poem by Mikhail Lermontov (1814-1841), and another Lermontov poem, much better known, called "Fatherland," which they discussed. He was at pains to explain to her that his love for Russia, which he felt very strongly, being away so long, and his experience of "non-Platonic" love, too, was not the result of being won over by attractive qualities, but was simply in his nature—he could not help but love (letter to von Meck, 9/21 February 1878). More than anything, this was what he tried to express in music.

Two days later, between breakfast and dinner, he wrote the song. Despite its somber beginning, its theme is love as an undying force that binds two souls forever. One wonders if he would have chosen this text for a song had it not come to him by chance at just this time in his life. That Florence was the city of Dante might have crossed his mind when he came to Lermontov's line "your words flow like scorching fire all over me": this is the climax of the song before the final reprise, coming at the end of a crescendo passage and marked double *forte*. Perhaps he saw in Lermontov's theme of a love which defies natural law a second, personal meaning for him, about homosexual love, which is also in defiance of "natural law" but which he never doubted had the same permanent meaning as all love. Whatever his thinking was about this text, it evoked very powerful music in him.

Пускай холодною землёю
    Засыпан я,
О, друг! всегда, всегда, везде с
тобою
    Душа моя,
    Душа моя всегда, везде с
тобой!

Любви безумного томленья,
    Жилец могил,
В стране покоя и забвенья
    Я не забыл.
Без страха в час последней муки
    Покинув свет,
Отрады ждал я от разлуки —
    Разлуки нет!

Что мне сиянье Божьей власти
    И рай святой?
Я перенёс земные страсти
    Туда с собой.

Ласкаю я мечту родную,
    Везде одну;
Желаю, плачу и ревную,
    Как в старину.

Коснётся ль чуждое дыханье
    Твоих ланит, —
Моя душа в немом страданьи
    Вся задрожит;
Случится ль, шепчешь, засыпая,
    Ты о другом —
Твои слова текут, пылая,
    По мне огнём!

Пускай холодною землёю
    Засыпан я,
О, друг! всегда, всегда, везде с тобою
    Душа моя,
    Душа моя всегда, всегда, везде с
тобой!

Puskáj khalódnaju zemljóju
    Zasýpan já,
O, drúk! fsegdá, fsegdá, vezdé s tabóju
    Dushá majá,
    Dushá majá fsegdá, vezdé s tabój!

Ljubví bezúmnava tamlén'ja,
    Zhyléts magíl,
F strané pakója i zabvén'ja
    Ja ne zabýl.
Bes strákha f chas paslédnej múki
    Pakínuf svét,
Atrády zhdál ja at razlúki —
    Razlúki nét!

Shtó mne siján'je Bózhej vlásti
    I ráj svjatój?
Ja perenjós zemnýje strásti
    Tudá s sabój.
Laskáju ja mechtú radnúju,
    Vezdé adnú;
Zheláju, pláchu i revnúju,
    Kak f starinú.

Though I lie covered over
    By cold ground,
O love! always, always, wherever you are
    My soul is with you,
    My soul is always, everywhere with you!

Love's mad and anguished longing,
    Though I dwell in a grave,
In the land of peace and oblivion
    I cannot forget.
Fearless in the hour of final agony
    I left this world,
Hoping absence would bring comfort —
    There is no absence!

What to me is God's bright kingdom,
    And blessed paradise?
I took my earthly passions
    With me there.
I cherish a precious dream,
    Ever the same;
I desire, weep, am jealous,
    As in the past.

Kasnjótsa l' chúzhdaje dykhán'je	If someone else's breath
Tvajíkh laním, —	Touches your hair, —
Majá dushá v nemóm stradán'ji	My soul shudders
Fsja zadrazhýt;	In mute torment;
Sluchítsa l', shépchesh, zasypája,	Whenever, waking up, you whisper
Ty a drugóm —	Another's name —
Tvají slavá tekút, pylája,	Your words flow like scorching fire
Po mné agnjóm!	All over me!
Puskáj khalódnaju zemljóju	Though I lie covered over
Zasýpan já,	By cold ground,
O, drúk! fsegdá, fsegdá, vezdé s tabóju	O love! always, always, wherever you are
Dushá majá,	My soul is with you,
Dushá majá fsegdá, fsegdá,	My soul is always, always,
vezdé s tabój!	everywhere with you!

TEXT. **Mikhaíl Lérmontov**, 1841. Title: Любовь мертвеца (A dead man's love). A free imitation of "Le mort amoureux" by **Alphonse Karr** (1808-1890), a journalist remembered for his epigram "plus ça change, plus c'est la même chose." Lermontov came across the French poem in a lady's album (*Lermontov*, II, 691). The Lermontov poem has five stanzas of eight lines each. Tchaikovsky omitted the second half of stanza 2 and all of stanza 5; the repetitions are his. There are earlier settings by A. M. Stanyukovich (1853), Cui (1859), and V. I. Glavach (1873).

METER. Binary. Iambic, alternating 4-foot and 2-foot lines:
> *If ever someone else's breath*
> *Should touch your hair, —*
> *My soul in painful torment mute*
> *Would tremble there...*

MUSIC. 11 (23) February 1878. Op. 38, no. 5. F Major. 2/4, Andante non tanto. For Middle Voice: c–f¹. Dedicated to **Anatóly Ilyích Tchaikóvsky**.

RECORDINGS. Burchuladze, Fischer-Dieskau, Hvorostovsky, Leiferkus, Mazurok, Ots, Petrov, Pirogov.

§

44 *Pimpinella–Флорентинская песня*
Pimpinella–Florentine song

Op. 38, No. 6

Still in Florence, during carnival week in March 1878, he heard a boy
street singer named Vittorio singing this song. He wrote down the words and
music, harmonized it, and provided his own quite different text in Russian
alongside the Italian. Most singers sing it in Italian, sometimes in abbreviated
form. Caruso's fine recording is of textual interest: in the last line of the second
verse, he sings "potermi amar" (to be able to love me) instead of "portarmi
amor" (to bring me love).

(1) Non contrastar cogl' uomini,
fallo per carità.
Non sono tutti gli uomini
della mia qualità!

(refrain)
Io ti voglio bene assai, Pimpinella,
quanto per te penai solo il cuor lo sa,
io ti voglio bene assai, Pimpinella,
quanto per te penai solo il cuor lo sa!

(2) Ti prego i dì di festa, Pimpinella,
non ti vestir confusa,
non ti mostrar chiassosa, Pimpinella
se vuoi portarmi amor!
(repeat refrain)

(3) Dalla tua stessa bocca, Pimpinella,
attendo la risposta,
non far soffrir, o bella Pimpinella,
e non mi dir di no! no!
e non mi dir di no!
(repeat refrain)

(4) Ora che siamo soli, Pimpinella,
vorrei svelare il mio cuore,
languisco per amore, Pimpinella,
solo il mio cuore lo sa!

(final refrain)
Io ti voglio bene assai, Pimpinella,
quanto per te penai solo il
cuor lo sa,

(1) Don't be contrary with men,
for charity's sake don't.
Not all men are
of my quality!

(refrain)
I love you very much, Pimpinella,
How I've suffered for you only the
heart knows. (twice)

(2) I beg you, on feast days, Pimpinella,
not to dress gaudily,
not to be in loud clothes
If you want to bring me love!
(repeat refrain)

(3) From your own mouth, Pimpinella,
I'm waiting for a reply,
don't make me suffer, oh pretty
Pimpinella, and don't tell me no! no!
and don't tell me no!
(repeat refrain)

(4) Now that we are alone, Pimpinella,
I would like to disclose my heart,
I'm languishing with love, Pimpinella,
only my heart knows!

(final refrain)
I love you very much, Pimpinella,
How I've suffered for you only the
heart knows,

io ti voglio bene assai, Pimpinella,	I love you very much, Pimpinella,
quanto per te penai, quanto	How I've suffered for you, how I've suf-
per te penai,	fered for you,
solo il mio cuor lo sa, Pimpinella,	Only my heart knows, Pimpinella,
solo il mio cuor, solo il mio cuor lo sa,	Only my heart knows, only my heart knows,
Pimpinella, solo il mio cuor lo sa!	Pimpinella, only my heart knows!

TEXT. Florentine song, written down by Tchaikovsky in March 1878. Russian text by Tchaikovsky.

MUSIC. March 1878. Op. 38, no. 6. G Major. 3/4, Allegretto molto moderato, grazioso. For Middle Voice: a–f² natural. Dedicated to **Anatóly Ilyích Tchaikóvsky**.

RECORDINGS. Arkhipova, Bogachova, Caruso, Kozlovsky (in Russian), Kudriavchenko, Lemeshev, Lisovsky, Magomayev, Obukhova, Ots, Schock, Schwarzkopf, Sterling, Tauber (in English), Vinogradov (in Russian).

Russian Text by Tchaikovsky

(1) Если ты хочешь, желанная,
знать, что я в сердце таю;
ревность какая-то странная
душу терзает мою!

(1) If, darling, you want to know,
what's hidden in my heart,
a strange kind of jealousy
is tearing my soul!

(refrain)
Я молю тебя: и взглядом и улыбкой
радуй меня одного, одного меня,
я молю тебя: и взглядом и улыбкой
радуй меня одного, одного меня!

(refrain)
I beg you: with both your glance and smile
gladden me alone, me alone,
I beg you: with both your glance and smile
gladden me alone, me alone!

(2) Чары, тебе Богом данные,
лишь для меня расточай,
и на признанья нежданные
гневно, мой друг, отвечай! (repeat refrain)

(2) All the charms God gave you
lavish only on me,
and to other uninvited advances
reply angrily, my dear! (repeat refrain)

(3) Очи твои так светлы, так прекрасны,
краше здесь нет лица,
речи твои пленительны, опасны,
губишь ты все сердца! ах!
губишь ты все сердца! (repeat refrain)

(3) Your eyes are so bright, so fair,
there's no face more beautiful,
your words are captivating, dangerous,
you destroy all hearts! ah!
you destroy all hearts! (repeat refrain)

(4) Будь же довольна, желанная,
сердцем покорным одним,
чтоб не страдал непрестанно я,
будь недоступна другим!
(Song ends with modified refrain)

(4) Then be content, darling
with one vanquished heart,
so I don't suffer constantly,
be unattainable to others!
(Song ends with modified refrain)

7 Romances, Opus 47 (1880)

The crisis of 1877 brought defining changes to Tchaikovsky's life. The "misanthropy" he felt during the "madness" that followed his marriage receded to the back of his mind, but it left an indelible mark on his thinking. He began reading more seriously: first history, especially the 18th century, then Rousseau, philosophical essays by Vladimir Solovyov, and novels by Tolstoy and Dostoyevsky and Dickens, seeing the world around him more objectively than before. In Tolstoy's "Confession" he recognized aspects of his own past errors, fears, and doubts. The crisis made his limits, above all his mortality, real to him. If he was to write the music he had within him—and most of his greatest music came during and after the crisis—he had to go on working, harder than ever before. This meant being willing to give up anything that stood in the way of that.

As the summer of 1878 was drawing to a close, he resolved to give up his teaching duties at the Moscow Conservatory. Though he had pangs of conscience about deserting his colleagues before a worthy successor could be found, he never regretted the decision. He found his successor in the person of the young Sergey Taneyev (1856-1915), who had finished the conservatory with a gold medal in 1875. He was very fond of Taneyev, who studied harmony and composition with him for six years and to whom he had dedicated his symphonic fantasia "Francesca da Rimini" in 1876. Taneyev proved worthy of his confidence, going on to become an exceptional pianist and an admired composer and teacher. On 6 October 1878 Tchaikovsky taught his last class. Jurgenson, Kashkin, Albrecht, and Taneyev were present at a farewell dinner given for him by Nikolay Rubinstein, fresh from Paris, where he had played the piano concerto at last in a series of "Russian concerts" held at the Trocadéro. Stasov, who was reviewing these concerts for a Petersburg newspaper and who did not like Rubinstein, dismissed the concerto as one of Tchaikovsky's less good works, saying the pianist should have stopped after the first movement, but could not resist playing the whole work through in order to impress the public with his brilliance at the keyboard (DG, 186).

Tchaikovsky's decision to leave the conservatory together with the patronage of Nadezhda Filaretovna von Meck made it possible for him to devote himself exclusively to composition. As was his habit, he wrote significant major works over the next two years, and only when they were finished did he turn to another set of songs. In August 1878 he started his First Suite, Op. 43, which he finished in December and dedicated (as a secret between them) to Nadezhda Filaretovna. He had been in Florence a week by that time, where she set him up in a villa not far away from hers. There the two exchanged letters by messenger, with Nadezhda Filaretovna sending fresh Russian newspapers for him to read every day. It was luxurious and charming, but it was all a little too close. It was piquant to spy her once or twice from a distance, but the "ideal" nature of their friendship, which for him was the essence and strength of the bond he felt between them, could not be sustained if the ideal kept threatening to materialize in the flesh. As soon as the suite was finished he began composing a new opera about Joan of Arc, *The Maid of Orleans*, a major effort which took him until March to compose in draft form. By that time he was in Switzerland at a more comfortable distance from his patron. He went back to Moscow for the premiere of *Eugene Onegin* on 17 March 1879, performed, as he had originally envisioned it, by students from the conservatory. Present were Modest and Anatoly, and Anton Rubinstein, who did not say a single word indicating whether he liked the music or not.

Also present was Aleksandra Panayeva (1853-1942), a soprano and beautiful new favorite of Apukhtin and the Petersburg mélomanes, with whom Anatoly had been hopelessly in love all year (the subject was a matter of some concern to Tchaikovsky and Mrs. von Meck in their letters). She had studied with the best teachers (Nissen-Saloman and Viardot), but because she belonged to higher society she could not appear on the stage for money and hence never had a professional career. But she sang in charity concerts and private productions: Dostoyevsky, Turgenev, and Flaubert are said to have admired her. To the generation of Sergey Levik (1883-1967), she was famous as the "first Tatyana" (*Levik*, 432), which is true enough, because two weeks before the Moscow premiere of *Eugene Onegin*, a concert performance of the opera was given at a Petersburg salon: Panayeva sang Tatyana, with Lavrovskaya as Olga (*MN*, 46). Tchaikovsky was still in Europe and could not attend that performance, but he invited her to come to the Moscow premiere. Before the performance, Nikolay Rubinstein, who conducted it and who told Tchaikovsky he was *in love with the music*, called him on stage before the assembled company and presented him with a crown of laurel (*DG*, 211).

The success of *Eugene Onegin* confirmed Tchaikovsky's growing reputation at home and abroad. While he summered at his sister's in Kamenka finishing the instrumentation of *Maid of Orleans*, Rubinstein arranged a special performance of *Onegin* at the conservatory for Grand Duke Konstantin Nikolayevich (1827-92), the brother of Alexander II. Word of the opera had long been spreading. Back in October, Lev Tolstoy wrote Turgenev from Yasnaya Polyana asking if he knew anything about it, saying he had not heard it but was very interested in it. Turgenev wrote back from Paris that Viardot had the piano score and had given her opinion that the music was "without a doubt remarkable," but that he found the liberties taken with Pushkin's text quite astonishing. He added that a professor of music at Cambridge had recently told him that "Tchaikovsky is the most remarkable musical personality of our time: I dropped my jaw" (*DG*, 191-2).

In Simaki in August, as a guest of Nadezhda Filaretovna in a cottage on her Brailov estate, he went for a walk in the woods at a time when he knew she would be at dinner in her house. But she was not in her house; she was leading an expedition to those same woods for a picnic, followed by two carriages filled with her children. They met face-to-face for the only time in their lives; he tipped his hat and retreated in embarrassment.

That fall and winter he wrote his Second Piano Concerto, Op. 44, and the "Capriccio Italien," Op. 45; the concerto was dedicated to Nikolay Rubinstein and given its first performance by Taneyev. He worked steadily and carried on his correspondence in Paris and Rome, where one day he sat for a long time admiring the Sistine Chapel, experiencing for the first time in his life "real *artistic* ecstasy from a painting" (*DG*, 228). When he returned to Petersburg in March 1880, there were several concerts at which his works were performed. One was devoted entirely to works by him, including a scene from *Onegin* and some of his romances sung by Panayeva (*DG*, 230). When he got an offer the next month from the Russian Musical Society in Kiev to be head of the conservatory and director of concerts, a post analogous to Nikolay Rubinstein's position in Moscow, he instantly and unhesitatingly turned it down.

In July at Brailov Nadezhda Filaretovna sent him a gold watch, engraved with Joan of Arc, Apollo, and the muses. He finished correcting the final proofs of the opera a few days later, writing her that *Maid of Orleans* might not be his best composition, but it might be the one that would make him popular. He always wanted that. The distinction between his private life and his public life as a composer had never been clearer to him. When Taneyev chided him that summer for his unwillingness to be sociable and make new acquaintances, he wrote back saying he wanted more than anything that people would be interested in his music, would praise and like it, but never that they would take an interest in him personally, in what he looked like and talked about; he wanted his name to be a *trademark*, identifying his product from others, a trademark to be prized, known, and in demand in the market (*Taneev*, 57).

That summer he wrote the six duets, Op. 46, at Jurgenson's request (duets were a marketable product). When they were finished, he turned to the songs of Opus 47, finishing them on 29 July 1880 at Simaki. Both the duets and the new set of songs drew heavily on poems by Aleksey Tolstoy, of whom he said in a letter to his patron in May that "he is an inexhaustible source of texts for music; I find him one of the most attractive of all poets." The Tolstoy texts plus three other poems chosen for Opus 47 are all admirable. These songs show a new mastery of the romance genre, with remarkable piano parts that figure prominently in the composition as a whole. When Jurgenson published them on 25 March 1881, all seven songs were dedicated to Aleksandra Panayeva.

45 *Кабы знала я*
If only I had known

Op. 47, No. 1

Among Russian folk songs there are many examples of the kind of song Aleksey Tolstoy used as a model for this text. They are songs about unhappy love, sung by a young woman who gave her heart to a man who rode away and has not come back. They are songs of experience, not innocence. They express regret, but also usually the wish to go find him if she could. Like the Ira Gershwin–Harold Arlen variation on this old theme, these are songs about "the man that got away" (1954). They typically begin like this one, found in the collection of folk songs compiled by Aleksey Sobolevsky in the second half of the 19th century (*Sobolevskii*, vol. 5, no. 59):

Как бы я знала, млада, ведала,	If I'd known, being young, if I'd realized,
Неприятство друга милого,	It wasn't friendship my darling felt,
Нелюбовь друга сердечного —	It wasn't love my sweetheart felt —
Не сидела бы поздо вечером,	I'd not be sitting up late in the evening,
Я не жгла б свечи воску ярого,	I'd not be burning a candle's bright wax,
Не ждала бы я друга милого…	I'd not be waiting for him, my darling friend…

Songs like this were sung in villages in the 19th century but they go back at least a century earlier. Ivan Dmitriev (1760-1837) wrote a literary folk lyric called "Ах, когда б я прежде знала" (Oh, if I'd known beforehand, 1792) which was set by Aliabiev in 1832 and sung by the gypsy singer Steshka, a singer much admired by Pushkin, Glinka, and Gurilyov. When Glinka set the song to his own music in 1855, he subtitled it "old gypsy song sung by the famous Steshka," apparently unaware that the words were by Dmitriev. Glinka's song is one of his most famous, a classic still sung today. A modern authority re-marks of Glinka's song that it cannot be thought of as a stylization of folklore because Dmitriev's poem "has nothing in common with the oldest folk songs" (*Vasina-Grossman*, 24). But the numerous examples in Sobolevsky show that Dmitriev took his imagery and phrasing directly from songs like these, only he changed the meter drastically, giving his song a very different rhythm.

Aleksey Tolstoy's poem goes back to the old meter, restoring the lilt of the original folk verse. With that as his starting point, Tolstoy reimagines the theme in contemporary terms, using his own vivid images which are completely origi-nal: the "dun" horse, light gray with black tail, one of the most beautiful of typical Russian horses, and the jaunty rider wearing his "murmolka," a type of fur or velvet cap which the Slavophiles revived and made fashionable. The image of gold in the old songs (an image of treasure squandered on the untrue lover) is here, too, but woven on the scarlet ribbon plaited into her long braid.

Tchaikovsky's song expresses a range of feelings that trace the course from innocence to experience, from love to heartbreak, through passion, anger, and frustration, culminating in the wail of pain at the end. The piano part supports this in a dramatic way. The piano also frames the whole song in a light-stepping allegro theme which contrasts with the sorrow in the young woman's song. It portrays, perhaps, the handsome rider who is still the object of her desire, reminding her of the ease with which she fell in love so heedlessly.

Кабы знала я, кабы ведала,
Не смотрела бы из окошечка
Я на молодца разудалого,
Как он ехал по нашей улице,
Набекрень заломивши мурмолку,
Как лихого коня буланого,
Звонконогого, долгогривого
Супротив окон на дыбы вздымал!

Кабы знала я, кабы ведала,
Для него бы я не рядилася,
С золотой каймой ленту алую
В косу длинную не вплетала бы,
Рано до свету не вставала бы,
За околицу не спешила бы,
В росе ноженьки не мочила бы,
На просёлок тот не глядела бы,
Не проедет ли тем просёлком он,
На руке держа пёстра сокола?
Кабы знала я, кабы ведала!

Кабы знала я, кабы ведала,
Не сидела бы поздним вечером,
Прогорюнившись на завалине,
На завалине, близ колодезя,
Поджидаючи, да гадаючи,
Не придёт ли он, ненаглядный мой,
Не придёт ли он, ненаглядный мой!
Ах, ах!
Не придёт ли он, ненаглядный мой,
Напоить коня студеной водой!

Кабы знала я, кабы ведала!
Кабы знала я! Кабы ведала!
Ах!

Kaby znála ja, kaby védala,
Ne smatréla by iz akóshechka
Ja na mólattsa razudálava,
Kak on jékhal pa nashej úlitse,
Nabekrén' zalómifshy múrmalku,
Kak likhóva kanjá bulánava,
Zvankanógava, dalgagrívava
Supratív akón na dybý vzdymál!

Kaby znála ja, kaby védala,
Dlja nevó by ja ne rjadílasa,
Z zalatój kajmój léntu áluju
F kósu dlínnuju ne fpletála by,
Rána dó svetu ne fstavála by,

If I'd known, if I'd realized,
I'd not have looked out the window
At the dashing young man,
Riding down our street,
His fur cap at a jaunty angle,
On his swift dun horse,
Hoofs ringing loud, long-maned,
Rearing up outside my windows!

If I'd known, if I'd realized,
I wouldn't have dressed up for him,
Wouldn't have plaited in my long braid
A scarlet ribbon with a gold border,
Wouldn't have risen early before light,

Za akólitsu ne speshýla by,	Wouldn't have hurried to the edge of town,
V rose nózhen'ki ne machíla by,	Got my feet wet in the dew,
Na prasjólak tot ne gljadéla by,	Watching the road,
Ne prajédet li tem prasjólkam on,	Will he come this way,
Na ruké derzhá pjóstra sókala?	A speckled falcon riding on his arm?
Kaby znála ja, kaby védala!	If I'd known, if I'd realized!

Kaby znála ja, kaby védala,	If I'd known, if I'd realized,
Ne sidéla by póznim vécheram,	I'd not be sitting up late in the evening,
Pragarjúnifshys' na zaváline,	Grieving on the knoll by the house,
Na zaváline, blis kalódezja,	On the knoll, near the well,
Padzhydájuchi, da gadájuchi,	Watching and waiting and wondering,
Ne pridjót li on nenagljádnyj moj,	Will he come, my handsome one,
Ne pridjót li on nenagljádnyj moj!	Will he come, my handsome one!
Akh, akh!	Oh, oh!
Ne pridjót li on nenagljádnyj moj,	Will he come, my handsome one,
Napaít' kanjá studenój vadój!	To water his horse at the cold well!

Kaby znála ja, kaby védala!	If I'd known, if I'd realized!
Kaby znála ja! Kaby védala!	If I'd known, if I'd realized!
Akh!	Oh!

TEXT. **Alekséy Tolstóy,** 1858. Before Tchaikovsky, set by Baron Boris A. Vietinghoff-Schell in 1867, and Anton Rubinstein in 1877 (Op. 101/10). The Baron, a minor composer (in Russian his name is spelled Fitinghof-Shel', 1829-1901), knew Tchaikovsky and wrote an interesting brief memoir about him (*Poznansky 1999,* 173-5).

METER. Imitation folk line of ten syllables, with obligatory strong downbeats on syllables 3 and 8. The line is perceived as being two half-lines of five syllables each, with a stress in the middle of each 5-syllable cluster. The end of the line is always a dactylic clausula. This rhythmic pattern is easy to sustain in Russian, with its long words where only one syllable is stressed, but it is practically impossible in English:

> Had I knówn it then, / had I réalized,
> I should nót have looked / through the wíndow there
> At the stálwart lad, / at the hórseman fair...

MUSIC. July 1880. Op. 47, no. 1. C Minor. 3/8, Allegro moderato. For High Voice: e¹flat–a² flat. Dedicated to **Aleksándra Panáyeva.**

RECORDINGS. Arkhipova, Belmas, Kasrashvili, Katulskaya, Kazarnovskaya, Maksakova, Mkrtchyan, Obraztsova, Podleś, Rautio, Rodgers, Sharubina, Slobodskaya, Söderström, Tugarinova, Varady, Vishnevskaya.

☙

46 *Горними тихо летела душа небесами*
A soul flew quietly in the heavenly heights
Op. 47, No. 2

Both the poet and the composer found their inspiration for this song in earlier works of art.

Aleksey Tolstoy wrote his poem as a variation on Lermontov's famous poem "Angel" (1831), written in long ternary lines, alternating 4- and 3-foot amphibrachs, but really 7-foot intervals between the intonational pauses:

> По небу полуночи ангел летел
> И тихую песню он пел;
> И месяц, и звёзды, и тучи толпой
> Внимали той песне святой.

"An angel flew through the midnight sky, singing a song softly; and the moon, and stars, and clouds in a throng hearkened to that holy song." The angel carries a young soul down to earth, to "the world of sorrow and tears," where the sound of the angel's song remains, filling the young soul with wondrous longing; "and never for her could earth's tedious songs take the place of the sounds of heaven." Lermontov's poem is about an innocent soul encountering earthly sorrow for the first time. Tolstoy's poem, written to a similar music of long 5-foot dactyls, is experience's answer to innocence, where the soul longs to return to earth to comfort those who sorrow there.

Tchaikovsky's song was inspired by a melody he found in a work of the French composer Jules Massenet (1842-1912). It was his custom to study the scores of all the new music he could get hold of, and in July 1880 he read through Massenet's oratorio "Marie-Magdeleine" (1873). He was especially moved by the duet between Christ and Mary Magdalen, where he found a powerful expression of Christ's "благость" (goodness, charity). After writing the song on 19 July, he realized the melody had been suggested to him by Massenet's duet (*DG*, 237-8).

> Горними тихо летела душа небесами,
> Грустные долу она опускала ресницы;
> Слёзы, в пространство от них упадая звездами,
> Светлой и длинной вилися за ней вереницей.
>
> Встречные тихо её вопрошали светила:
> «Что ты грустна? и о чём эти слёзы во взоре?»
> Им отвечала она: «Я земли не забыла,
> Много оставила там я страданья и горя.

Много, много страданья,
Ах, много оставила я там страданья и горя.

Здесь я лишь ликам блаженства и радости внемлю,
Праведных души не знают ни скорби, ни злобы, —
О, отпусти меня снова, Создатель, на землю
Было б о ком пожалеть и утешить кого бы.
О, отпусти меня снова, Создатель, на землю,
Было б о ком пожалеть и утешить кого бы!»

Górnimi tíkha letéla dushá nebesámi,
Grúsnyje dólu aná apuskála resnítsy;
Sljózy, f prastránstva at níkh upadája zvezdámi,
Svétlaj i dlínnaj vilísja za néj verenítsej.

> A soul flew quietly in the heavenly heights,
> She lowered her eyes sadly looking downward;
> Her tears were like stars falling in space,
> Trailing behind her in a long bright row.

Fstréchnyje tíkha jejó vaprasháli svetíla:
"Shtó ty grusná? i a chóm eti sljózy va vzóre?"
Im atvechála aná: "Ja zemlí ne zabýla,
Mnóga astávila tam ja stradán'ja i górja.
Mnóga, mnóga stradán'ja,
Akh, mnóga astávila ja tam stradán'ja i górja.

> Heavenly objects she met quietly asked her:
> "Why are you sad? and what brings these tears to your eyes?"
> This was her answer to them: "I have not forgotten the earth,
> I left there behind me so much suffering and woe.
> Much, much suffering,
> Oh, I left there much suffering and woe.

Zdés' ja lish líkam blazhénstva i rádosti vnémlju,
Právednykh dúshy ne znájut ni skórbi, ni zlóby, —
O, atpustí menja snóva, Sazdátel', na zémlju,
Býla b a kóm pazhalét' i utéshyt' kavó by.
O, atpustí menja snóva, Sazdátel', na zémlju,
Býla b a kóm pazhalét' i utéshyt' kavó by!"

> Here I only hear songs of bliss and gladness,
> Souls of the just know neither grief nor anger, —
> Oh, Creator, release me to go there again, to the earth,
> There would I have someone to grieve for and comfort.

Oh, Creator, release me to go there again, to the earth,
There would I have someone to grieve for and comfort!"

Text. **Alekséy Tolstóy**, 1858. First set by Musorgsky (1877). After Tchaikovsky, by Rimsky-Korsakov (Op. 27/1, 1883), Keneman (Op. 6/4, 1899), Cui (Op. 67/2, 1903), Arensky (Op. 64/3, 1903), and Pavel Chesnokov (for women's or children's choir, 1910). Also set by K. R. in 1880 (see *Romanov 1999*, 33).

Meter. Ternary. Long lines of five-foot dactyls:
Quietly flying with souls in the heavenly heights,
Here do we hearken to songs of our bliss and our gladness...

Music. July 1880. Op. 47, no. 2. E Major. 6/8, Andantino con moto. For High Voice: e^1–g^2 sharp. Dedicated to **Aleksándra Panáyeva**.

Recordings. Kazarnovskaya, Kozlovsky, Kudriavchenko, Lisovsky, Martynov, Varady.

Musorgsky: Christoff, Vishnevskaya.

Rimsky-Korsakov: Gerasimova.

47   *На землю сумрак пал*
Dusk fell on the earth

Op. 47, No. 3

The lyric to this song comes from Adam Mickiewicz's cycle of Petrarchan sonnets written during the poet's Odessa period in 1825 (see Song 32). Very different from the playful text of "My darling girl," this is a serious love poem. The title of the sonnet, number VI in the cycle, is "Ranek i wieczór" (Morning and evening). In the morning after sunrise the poet (the lover) comes to stand by the window of his beloved Laura (the name comes from Petrarch), and like the waning moon and the drooping morning violet, he has a sad look; in the evening when he comes to see her, the moon is full and red, the violet has raised its petals, and Laura stands beautiful and cheerful at her window, but he has the same sad look in his eyes he had in the morning. What is implied in this self-portrait of a sad-eyed lover is the power of the intense love he feels, including feelings of passionate and unfulfilled desire.

The poem Tchaikovsky found in Russian translation is quite different. The translator, Nikolay Vasilievich Berg (1823-1884), knew Polish well, had a Polish wife, lived in Warsaw, edited a Warsaw newspaper, and taught Russian literature at Warsaw University. He had earlier been a war correspondent in Sevastopol, and then in Serbia; his translations from both South Slavic and West Slavic poetry, including the whole of Mickiewicz's masterpiece *Pan Tadeusz*, amounted to well over half of all the translations of Slavic poetry into Russian (*RP*, I, 243-4). But though he was an expert translator, known for carrying over original patterns of rhyme and meter into Russian, his "translation" in this case amounts to a new poem based on Mickiewicz. He evidently wanted to write his own variation on the theme. He published it without any reference to the Petrarchan cycle it comes from, and it is not in sonnet form; the fact that it occurs in a context of an intense love affair is completely absent. In his poem, the sequence is evening first, followed by the next morning (his title is "Вечер и утро," Evening and morning). Berg is more conscious of being in an actual landscape on the ground. He gets rid of the sun and the moon altogether, and adds a lake, which is not in Mickiewicz at all: the lake also has its own mood swings. The duality of nature and mood, and the way the two can be harmonious at one moment, and out of harmony at another—all this is much more pronounced in Berg's poem than in the Mickiewicz original. The mood, not the love affair, is the main theme.

This duality is very Russian, like the duality in the Grekov lyric Tchaikovsky used in Song 28. In this case we know the composer's reaction to the words: he found them "wonderful" (чудные), saying he was "inordinately fond of the song" after he wrote it, and could not play it through without a "liberal out-pouring of tears" (*DG*, 238). Some object that Tchaikovsky's songs are too often about "sadness," but listening to how he uses the piano chords in this song as a harmonic platform for the line "I'm sad" is enough to show how good a sad mood can be. The tears the composer shed here were undoubtedly sweet: in the song he expresses the melancholy mood in the Berg-Mickiewicz text in music of exceptional beauty.

> На землю сумрак пал; не шелохнут кусты;
> Свернулись лилии поблекшие листы,
>   И тихо озеро почило.
> Под обаянием волшебной красоты,
> Стою задумавшись: «Что грустен нынче ты,
>   И всё кругом тебя уныло?»
>
> Поутру прихожу: оживлена росой,
> Проснулась лилия, блистая красотой,
>   И милая, в блистающей одежде,
> С улыбкою привет на небо шлёт она.
> И плещет в озере весёлая волна…
>   А я? я… Мне грустно!
>   Мне грустно, как и прежде!…

Na zémlju súmrak pál;
  ne shelakhnút kustý;
Svernúlis' lílii pablékshyje listý,
  I tíkha ózera pachíla.
Pad abajánijem valshébnaj krasatý,
Stajú zadúmafshys': "Shto grústen
  nýnche tý,
    I fsjó krugóm tebjá unýla?"

Paútru prikhazhú: azhyvlená
  rasój,
Prasnúlas' lílija, blistája krasatój,
  I mílaja, v blistájushchej adézhde,
S ulýpkaju privét na néba shljót aná.
I pléshchet v ózere vesjólaja valná…
    A já? Já… Mné grústna!
  Mné grústna, kak i prézhde!…

Twilight's fallen on the earth;
  the bushes aren't stirring;
The lily's faded leaves are folded closed,
  And the lake's in quiet slumber.
In the spell of this magic beauty,
I stand and ponder: "Why are you so sad
  today,
    Why's everything around you melancholy?"

In the morning I come back: refreshed
  by the dew,
The lily's awake again, blazing with beauty,
  And my sweetheart, in a splendid dress,
Sends a smiling greeting to the sky.
And a merry wave splashes in the lake…
    And I? I… I'm sad!
  I'm sad as before!…

TEXT. **Nikoláy Berg**, early 1860s; published in 1865 in Warsaw (*Berg*, 220). Title: Вечер и утро (Evening and morning). Paraphrase of a Polish sonnet by **Adam Mickiewicz** entitled "Ranek i wieczór" (Morning and evening, 1825). Set only by Tchaikovsky. He added a repetition at the end and made significant changes in wording, including different rhymes in the second stanza; he discarded entirely Mickiewicz's image of the "window" at which his sweetheart is standing.

METER. Binary. Iambic, long lines are hexameters, shorter ones tetrameters:

I stand and ponder: "why are you so sad today,
And why this melancholy mood?"

MUSIC. July 1880. Op. 47, no. 3. F Major. 2/4, Allegro moderato. For High Voice: e¹–f². Dedicated to **Aleksándra Panáyeva**.

RECORDINGS. Dolukhanova, Kazarnovskaya, Leiferkus, Lisovsky, Martynov, Ognivtsev, Petrov, Pirogov, Reizen.

ֆֆ֍

48 *Усни, печальный друг*
Sleep, sad friend

Op. 47, No. 4

This is a love poem which comes out of the same group of intimate love lyrics addressed to or prompted by the woman Aleksey Tolstoy fell in love with when he was 34, Sofia Andreyevna Miller, whom he had first glimpsed "amid the din of the ball" (Song 41), and with whom he lived (though they were not yet married, because it was many years before she was able to secure a divorce from her first husband) when he wrote the lyrics to Songs 4, 7, and 42. That latter lyric spoke of her "sadness" and his wish that he could do something to make it pass. In another lyric from this same period (most of them were written in the late 1850s) he speaks of her extraordinary sensitivity to the sorrows of all those around her, but her absence of pity for herself. In the poem which is lyric to the present song, he addresses this theme and wishes "the angel of sleep" to give her a night's rest and comfort after sorrows have accumulated again. The use of the word "child" here should not be taken to mean that he is addressing a child, but rather the "child" in her, the vulnerable and innocent soul which is in everyone.

So in Tchaikovsky's song, despite the mournful theme, it is the burden of the music to convey love and tender caring, not some sort of lugubrious benediction. The love evoked by this music is felt in hearing the song well sung. Such a song has its usefulness at a time of sadness, as I witnessed in May 1998. The occasion was a memorial service held in the Great Hall of the Moscow Conservatory for the soprano Nina Dorliak (1908-1998), an admired concert singer and widow of Svyatoslav Richter, who had taught singing to many generations of students at the conservatory. The first half of the service was Baroque instrumental music played by a string ensemble. Students and colleagues wandered in, sat with friends, whispered among themselves. Then a soprano who had been one of Dorliak's students walked onto the stage with her accompanist and sang Song 11, a lullaby, followed by this song. From the first notes, Tchaikovsky's music was a reminder that at this moment, feelings were appropriate: suddenly, unfocused sorrow became something clear, simple, and true.

> Усни, печальный друг, уже с грядущей тьмой
> Вечерний алый свет сливается всё боле;
> Блеящие стада вернулися домой,
> И улеглася пыль на опустелом поле.

Да снидет ангел сна, прекрасен и крылат,
И да перенесёт тебя он в жизнь иную!
Издавна был он мне в печали друг и брат,
Усни, моё дитя, к нему я не ревную.

На раны сердца он забвение прольёт,
Пытливую тоску от разума отнимет,
И с горестной души на ней лежащий гнёт
До нового утра незримо приподнимет.

Томимая весь день душевною борьбой,
От взоров и речей враждебных ты устала;
Усни, моё дитя, меж ними и тобой
Он благостной рукой опустит покрывало.

Усни, моё дитя! Усни, моё дитя, усни, дитя, усни!...

Usní, pechál'nyj drúk, uzhe
   z grjadúshchej t'mój
Vechérnij ályj svét slivájetsa fsjo bóle;
Blejáshchije stadá vernúlisa damój,
I uleglása pýl' na apustélam póle.

Da snídet ángel sná, prekrásen
   i krylát,
I da perenesjót tebjá on v zhýzn' inúju!
Izdávna býl on mné f pecháli drúk
   i brát,
Usní, majó ditjá, k nemú ja ne
   revnúju.

Na rány sérttse on zabvénije pral'jót,
Pytlívuju taskú at rázuma
   atnímet,
I z górestnaj dushý na néj lezháshchij
   gnjót
Da nóvava utrá nezríma
   pripadnímet.

Tamímaja ves' dén' dushévnaju
   bar'bój,
At vzóraf i rechéj vrazhdébnykh
   ty ustála;
Usní, majó ditjá, mezhními i tabój
On blágostnaj rukój apústit pakryvála.

Usní, majó ditjá! Usní, majó ditja,
   usní, ditjá, usní!...

Sleep, sad friend, darkness will be
   coming soon,
Evening's crimson light grows ever deeper;
The bleating herds have returned home,
The dust has settled on the now deserted field.

May the angel of sleep descend, fair
   and winged,
And may he bring you to a different life!
Long in sadness has he been my friend
   and brother,
Sleep, my child, I feel no jealousy toward
   him.

He will pour oblivion on your heart's wounds,
Will take away tormenting longing from your
   mind,
And from your grieving soul, the burden
   lying there,
Before next morning, invisibly,
   he will lift away.

You've struggled all day with anguish
   in your soul,
Angry looks and words have
   worn you out;
Sleep, my child, between you and them
With merciful hand he will lower his veil.

Sleep, my child! Sleep, my child,
   sleep, child, sleep!...

TEXT. **Alekséy Tolstóy**, August 1856. Untitled. First set by Anton Rubinstein (Op. 101/9, 1877); after Tchaikovsky by Rimsky-Korsakov (Op. 39/4, 1897). Tchaikovsky modernized two verb endings in the third stanza and added the repeated line at the end.

METER. Binary. Iambic hexameter:
> *And may he pour relief on all that wounds your heart,*
> *And lift away unseen the anguish from your mind.*

MUSIC. July 1880. Op. 47, no. 4. G Flat Major. 3/4, Andante non tanto. For Middle Voice: d^1 flat–e^2 natural. Dedicated to **Aleksándra Panáyeva**.

RECORDINGS. DeGaetani, Dolukhanova, Isakova, Leiferkus, Maksakova, Vishnevskaya.

49 *Благословляю вас, леса*
I bless you, forests

Op. 47, No. 5

The last three songs in this opus, Songs 49, 50, and 51, are among Tchaikovsky's most famous songs. Critics and historians of music tend to favor Song 51, because it has ties with folk songs: it shows the downward, or "falling intonation" of Russian folk melody, especially typical of laments. The popular preference, however, by which I mean the choice of singers and the public, would probably lean the other way, to Songs 49 and 50, because they are not a conscious offshoot of folk music, but are completely original songs that work on their own terms without reference to anything else.

Of course these two songs do assume that tradition and come out of it in their own way. If melodic intonation moving in a descending direction expresses grief, loss, sorrow, trouble and woe, then rising intonation can express the opposite—love, dedication, commitment, affirmation, praise. The present song, a perfect match of words to music, with its steady rise to soaring heights (but never losing sight of the ground beneath), is an outstanding example.

The text by Aleksey Tolstoy is an excerpt from his long narrative poem about the theologian and church father Saint John Damascene, as told in the Russian book of saints' lives known as the Menologion. John, giving up the comforts of court life, sets out from Damascus on a pilgrim's path. Sometimes called in English "The Pilgrim's Song," this hymn to nature and all of creation is given a thoroughly Russianized landscape by Tolstoy. Tolstoy's own philosophy of "merging with the whole" discussed in connection with Song 7 is expressed powerfully here in the last lines of the text, to which Tchaikovsky gives a final rising affirmation on the word "заключить" (embrace). No one has sung it better than Mark Reizen, who recorded it four times.

Благословляю вас, леса,
Долины, нивы, горы, воды,
Благословляю я свободу
И голубые небеса!
И посох мой благословляю,
И эту бедную суму,
И степь от краю и до краю,
И солнца свет, и ночи тьму,
И одинокую тропинку,

По коей, нищий, я иду,
И в поле каждую былинку,
И в небе каждую звезду!
О, если б мог всю жизнь смешать я,
Всю душу вместе с вами слить,
О, если б мог в мои объятья
Я вас, враги, друзья и братья,
и всю природу, и всю природу
в мои объятья заключить!

Blagaslavljáju vás, lesá,
Dalíny, nívy, góry, vódy,

I bless you, forests,
Valleys, fields of grain, mountains, waters,

Blagaslavljáju já svabódu	I bless freedom
I galubýje nebesá!	And blue skies!
I pósakh mój blagaslavljáju	And my pilgrim's staff I bless,
I ètu bédnuju sumú,	And this poor knapsack,
I stép' at kráju i da kráju,	And the steppe from edge to edge,
I sóntsa svét, i nóchi t'mú,	And the sun's light, and night's darkness,
I adinókuju trapínku,	And the solitary path,
Pa kójej, níshchij, ja idú	Along which I, a poor man, walk,
I f póle kázhduju bylínku,	And every blade of grass in the field,
I v nébe kázhduju zvezdú!	And every star in the sky!
O, jésli b mók fsju zhýzn' smeshát' ja,	Oh, if only I could merge all of life,
Fsju dúshu vméste s vámi slít',	With my soul and all of you,
O, jésli b mok v mají abját'ja	Oh, if I could gather in my embrace
Ja vas, vragí, druz'já i brát'ja,	You, foes, friends, and brothers,
i fsju priródu, i fsju priródu	and all of nature, and all of nature,
v mají abját'ja zakljuchít'!	and hold you all in my embrace!

Text. **Alekséy Tolstóy**, 1858; published 1859. Title: Иоанн Дамаскин (John of Damascus), a narrative poem in twelve parts; this excerpt is the opening of Part Two. In line 7 of the text, Tolstoy uses an old-fashioned genitive form in the phrase "от краю и до краю" (from edge to edge), necessary for his rhyme; Tchaikovsky retains it. In performance, however, singers usually use the standard form "от края и до края," losing the rhyme. The repetitions in the last lines are Tchaikovsky's own. Set only by Tchaikovsky. After him, several composers used parts of Tolstoy's poem for musical settings, including Sergey Taneyev, who composed a Cantata for chorus and orchestra based on the poem (Op. 1, 1884).

Meter. Binary. Iambic tetrameter:

> *A blessing on you, woods and fields,*
> *On valleys, mountains, lakes and rivers...*

Music. July 1880. Op. 47, no. 5. F Major. 4/4, Andante sostenuto. For Baritone: c–f¹. Dedicated to **Aleksándra Panáyeva**. Orchestrated by Sergey Taneyev (not mentioned in *MN*, but there are two recordings of it below).

Recordings. Baikov, Borg, Chaliapin, Daunoras, Descamps, Eddy (in English), Eizen, Fischer-Dieskau, Ghiaurov, Ghiuzelev, Gmyria, Hvorostovsky, Andrey Ivanov, Kastorsky, Kuuzik, Leiferkus, Magomayev, Maxwell, Mazurok, Mkrtchyan, Nesterenko, Pedrotti, Petrov, Pirogov (Taneyev's orchestral version), **Reizen**, Savenko, Serkebayev, Tartakov, Tibbett (in English), Vedernikov (both piano and Taneyev's orchestral version).

Due to time constraints of the 78 rpm format, some early recordings omit or shorten the piano prelude or postlude or both.

50 *Денъ ли царит*
Whether day reigns

Op. 47, No. 6

The story that has come down about the origin of this lyric by Aleksey Apukhtin just waiting to be turned into a song is as follows: in March 1880 in Petersburg, after a rehearsal for a concert of Tchaikovsky's works in which Alexandra Panayeva was to sing some of his romances (this concert took place on 25 March), the composer, knowing that Apukhtin (like his own brother Anatoly) was an adoring fan of Panayeva, asked him how it could be that he had not yet dedicated a poem to her. Without a word, Apukhtin handed him a sheet of paper lying on his desk on which a draft of this poem was written out in pencil. Tchaikovsky read it through and, not saying a word himself, walked out with the poem and came back a day or two later with the finished song.

However it happened, it is one of Tchaikovsky's best songs. It takes the idea of a strong "yes" in the form of rising intonation to its maximum point. The piano supports this in a dramatic way, starting out deceptively in an easygoing "Andantino," then picking up the tempo to "Allegro agitato." The song ends with an ecstatic coda that elaborates the total commitment expressed in the marvelous final phrase of the voice part, prolonging it, underlining it, repeating it in its own pianistic language in order to reinforce it.

This outburst seems to irritate the English critics Gerald Abraham, and, after him, David Brown, who dismisses many of Tchaikovsky's songs as "fodder for domestic consumption" (*Brown IV*, 89). As Abraham puts it, Tchaikovsky was "defective" in having no "sense of the miniature... far too many of his songs are marred by over-long piano preludes and postludes which make no particular point and are often rather clumsily written," this song being a "classic instance" (*Abraham 1982*, 365-6). At the other end of the spectrum, in a characteristic Russian reaction to the song, Gina Levinson, a pianist from Leningrad, mentioning the song at a recent conference on Tchaikovsky, admires precisely the fact that the song has "a very hard piano part," adding "the music is absolutely gorgeous" (*Mihailovic*, 286). Like it or not, the song is unthinkable without the piano part as Tchaikovsky wrote it.

Apukhtin's lyric works so well because it is a fresh take on an old idea. The formula "you're my life, you're my happiness, you're my everything" was, and is, common in popular songs. Konstantin Shilovsky, that same friend to whom Tchaikovsky turned for help with the libretto of *Eugene Onegin*, wrote the words to such a song, called Для меня ты все (For me you're everything, 1870, with music by A. F. Titov), which never lost its popularity (Nadezhda Obukhova recorded it). Rearranging the terms of this formula, Apukhtin came up with "day or night, wherever I am and whatever I do, I think of you, you, you." In American song, one of Cole Porter's greatest songs, "Night and Day" (1932), elaborates the very same idea. Porter could have found the kernel of his lyric anywhere, but there can be little doubt that he knew this song. When he was taking music lessons in Paris in the 1920s, his teacher made him play many of Tchaikovsky's romances: surely this one—one of Tchaikovsky's most famous songs (with a hard piano part)—was among them. Whether or not this song jogged Porter's imagination when he came to write "Night and Day," it has been argued by the American composer Leo Smit that Cole Porter learned something about songwriting from his study of Tchaikovsky's songs: "From Tchaikovsky, a great and neglected songwriter, Porter adopted an expressive declamatory style, halfway between operatic recitative and aria, so appropriate for the verses that prepare the listener for the refrains. The verse of 'You'd Be So Easy to Love' is a perfect example of the Porter-Tchaikovsky arioso style, and the transfigured ending of 'So In Love' carries Slav *hommage* to exalted heights stirred by the ecstasy of 'None But the Lonely Heart'" (*Smit*).

Like Cole Porter's "Night and Day," the Tchaikovsky-Apukhtin "Day and Night" shows its composer at the top of his form.

День ли царит, тишина ли ночная,
В снах ли бессвязных, в житейской борьбе,
Всюду со мной, мою жизнь наполняя,
Дума всё та же, одна, роковая, —
    Всё о тебе! всё о тебе!
    всё, всё, всё, всё о тебе!

С нею не страшен мне призрак былого,
Сердце воспрянуло, снова любя...
Вера, мечты, вдохновенное слово,
Всё что в душе дорогого, святого, —
    Всё от тебя! всё, всё от тебя,
    всё от тебя!

Будут ли дни мои ясны, унылы,
Скоро ли сгину я, жизнь загубя, —
Знаю одно: что до самой могилы
Помыслы, чувства, и песни, и силы,
    Всё для тебя! всё для тебя,
Помыслы, чувства, и песни, и силы,
    Всё, всё, всё, всё для тебя!

Dén' li tsarít, tishiná li nachnája,
F snákh li bessvjáznykh, v zhytéjskaj
   bar'bé,
Fsjúdu sa mnój, majú zhýzn' napalnjája,
Dúma fsjo tá zhe, adná, rakavája, —
   Fsjó a tebé! fsjó a tebé!
   Fsjó, fsjó, fsjó, fsjó a tebé!

Whether day reigns, or stillness of night,
In dreams incoherent, or everyday struggle,
Wherever I am, to make my life whole,
Is one and the same thought, unchanging,
predestined —
   Always of you! always of you!
   Always, always, always, always of you!

S néju ne stráshen mne prízrak bylóva,
Sérttse vasprjánula, snóva ljubjá...
Véra, mechtý, vdakhnavénnaje slóva,
Fsjó shto v dushé daragóva, svjatóva, —
   Fsjó at tebjá! fsjó, fsjó at tebjá,
   fsjó at tebjá!

With it I don't fear ghosts from the past,
My heart can take wing, loving again...
Faith, dreams, an inspired word,
All in my soul that's dear, sacred —
   All of it comes from you! all, all of it
   from you, all from you!

Búdut li dní maji jásny, unýly,
Skóra li zgínu ja, zhýzn' zagubjá, —
Znáju adnó: shto da sámaj magíly
Pómysly, chústva, i pésni,
   i síly,
   Fsjó dlja tebjá! fsjó dlja tebjá,
Pómysly, chústva, i pésni, i síly,
   Fsjó, fsjó, fsjó, fsjó dlja tebjá!

Whether my days be bright or bleak,
If I burn out quickly, destroy my life, —
One thing I know: to the grave itself
All my hopes and feelings, all my songs
   and strength,
   All are for you! all for you,
Hopes, feelings, songs and strength,
   All, all, all, all—are for you!

TEXT. **Alekséy Apúkhtin**, 1880. The evidence for the story that the poem was dedicated to Panayeva comes from interviews conducted by F. N. Malinin before 1940 with people still alive who had known Apukhtin (*Apukhtin*, 372; *MN*, 447). In Panayeva's reminiscences of Tchaikovsky, including her meeting him in March 1880, she makes no mention of this story (*Bortnikova*, 140-161).
   METER. Ternary. Dactyls, 4-foot:
      Whether it's day or the still of the night,
      Lost in my dreams or in life's daily fight...
The last line in each stanza of the poem is a single two-foot dactyl, repeated by Tchaikovsky numerous times at the end of each stanza.
   MUSIC. March (?) 1880; finished that summer. Op. 47, no. 6. E Major. 9/8, Andantino (initially, piano introduction), then Allegro agitato. For High Voice: d^1 sharp–a^2. Dedicated to **Aleksándra Panáyeva.**
   Transcribed for voice with orchestra by Tchaikovsky in 1888 for Maria Benardaki, a salon singer who was a friend going back to their student days at the conservatory in St. Petersburg. Benardaki performed it in Paris (where she lived) at a concert of his works on 28 February 1888 which he conducted; the orchestration was not published, and the score is now lost. Gerald Abraham (*op. cit.*) supposes the orchestration must have been much better than the poor

piano version, and David Brown follows this lead, writing that even though the song is "one of the least distinguished in the set," Tchaikovsky "thought well enough of it" to score it for performance with orchestra (*Brown III*, 111). But Tchaikovsky did not orchestrate his songs because he "thought well" of them. In fact, he orchestrated his songs only two other times, both at the request of singers (Songs 51 and 56), and it is unlikely he would have considered orchestrating this song if Benardaki had not asked him to do it. When, three years later, Jurgenson wanted to know which of his songs had been transcribed for voice with orchestra and which others he would like to see transcribed, Tchaikovsky replied bluntly: "A romance is written for piano accompaniment and has no need for an orchestra" (*MN*, 449).

RECORDINGS. Arkhipova, Atlantov, Davrath, **Dolukhanova**, Hvorostovsky, Kasrashvili, Kazarnovskaya, Krasnaya, Kudriavchenko, Larin, Lemeshev, Levko, Magomayev, Leokadiya Maslennikova, Mishura, Mkrtchyan, Nesterenko, Obraztsova, Petina, Podleś, Rautio, Resnik, Rodgers, Schock, Sharubina, Shumskaya, Siniavskaya, Söderström, Solovianenko, Vishnevskaya, Voigt.

51 *Я ли в поле да не травушка была*
Was I not a blade of grass

Op. 47, No. 7

Tchaikovsky found the text for this lament among poems published in the 1870s by Ivan Zakharovich Surikov (1841-1880). From Surikov, he also took the texts for three of the duets, Opus 46, which he wrote just before the present song, and one of the songs for children in Opus 54. The two men were exact contemporaries, but from totally different backgrounds. Surikov was born a peasant in a village in Yaroslavl province, and came to Moscow as a boy. Aleksey Pleshcheyev recognized his talent and helped him get his poetry published; Tchaikovsky could have learned of him through Pleshcheyev. A few weeks before writing this song, he wrote Mrs. von Meck: "Is the name of the Moscow poet Surikov, who just died this spring of consumption, familiar to you? He was self-taught; his real profession was sitting in a wretched iron kiosk selling nails and horseshoes. He was a stall-keeper to the end of his life, but he had serious talent and his poems are imbued with authentic feelings. I want to use some of them for my own future works" (letter to von Meck, 5 June 1880).

Surikov thought of his poems as "songs," which he "sang" rather than recited. When he first published this poem, he gave it the title "Малороссийская мелодия" (Little-Russian Melody, *Surikov 1871*, 116-7). Though Surikov's poem does resemble the words of an actual Ukrainian folk song (one of those collected by Rubets, *MN*, 449), laments of a girl forced to marry against her will are common in Russian songs too. An example among earlier romances is Aleksey Koltsov's poem Без ума, без разума / Меня замуж выдали (For no good reason I was married off), set by Dargomyzhsky in 1856. Among Russian folk songs, a well-known one is "Матушка, матушка, что во поле пыльно" (Mother, mother, what's that cloud of dust in the field), where a girl sees riders approaching through a field: her mother assures her it is not a wedding party and she will not be married against her will, but by the end of the song that is what it turns out to be. The theme of a mother calling in the matchmakers to marry her daughter against her will came up earlier in Song 31.

In this song, a girl's parents have married her to an old man. The first two parts of the song use metaphor—the grass cut down for straw, the bush cut down for thatch—but the third, concluding section speaks directly of the cause for her grief in the line stating what has been done to her, which is then strongly repeated with falling intonation like a blow of fate. This passage—crescendo and double *forte* in the voice followed by emphatic piano chords—is the most dramatic moment in the song, powerfully brought out by Yelena Obraztsova in her recording. The long fluttering, falling intonation of the voice at the end of each refrain is the most striking feature of the song. The inspiration for it is the folk lament, or плач, sung in the "drawn-out," or "melismatic" style. An apt metaphor to describe it is the "falling leaf" (*Vasina-Grossman*, 58). Think of a leaf that flutters down and turns and may be caught up and rise, but then falls again: the tones in the singing are like that.

Я ли в поле да не травушка была,
Я ли в поле не зеленая росла;
Взяли меня, травушку, скосили,
На солнышке в поле иссушили.

   Ох, ты, горе моё, горюшко!
   Ох, ты, горе моё, горюшко!
   Знать, знать такая моя долюшка!

Я ли в поле не калинушка была,
Я ли в поле да не красная росла;
Взяли калинушку, сломали,
Да в жгутики меня посвязали!

   Ох, ты, горе моё, горюшко!
   Ох, ты, горе моё, горюшко!
   Знать, знать такая моя долюшка!

Я ль у батюшки не доченька была,
У родимой не цветочек я росла;
Неволей меня, бедную, взяли,
Да с немилым, седым повенчали,
С немилым, да с седым повенчали!

   Ох, ты, горе моё, горюшко!
   Ох, ты, горе моё, горюшко!
   Знать, знать такая моя долюшка!

Ja li f póle da ne trávushka bylá,	Wasn't I a blade of grass in the field,
Ja li f póle ne zeljónaja raslá,	Wasn't I growing green in the field?
Vzjáli menja, trávushku, skasíli,	I was taken, blade of grass, and cut down,
Na sólnyshke f póle issushíli.	Left in the field to dry in the sun.
Okh, ty, góre majo górjushka!	Oh, you, woe, heavy woe of mine!
Okh, ty, góre majo górjushka!	Oh, you, woe, heavy woe of mine!
Znat', znat' takája maja dóljushka!	So that's what fate had in store for me!
Ja li f póle ne kalínushka bylá,	Wasn't I a bush of guelder rose,
Ja li f póle da ne krásnaja raslá;	With berries red, growing in the field?
Vzjáli kalínushku, slamáli,	The bush was taken, cut down,
Da v zhgútiki menjá pasvjazáli!	And tied up into a bundle of twigs!

Okh, ty, góre majo górjushka!
Okh, ty, góre majo górjushka!
Znat', znat' takája maja dóljushka!

Oh, you, woe, heavy woe of mine!
Oh, you, woe, heavy woe of mine!
So that's what fate had in store for me!

Ja l' u bátjushki ne dóchen'ka bylá,
U radímaj ne tsvetóchek ja raslá;
Nevólej menja, bédnuju, vzjáli,
Da s nemílym, s sedým pavencháli,
S nemílym, da s sedým pavencháli!

Wasn't I my father's little daughter,
Wasn't I my mother's little flower?
By force they took me, poor girl,
And married me to a graybeard I don't love,
To a graybeard I don't love they married me!

Okh, ty, góre majo górjushka!
Okh, ty, góre majo górjushka!
Znat', znat' takája maja dóljushka!

Oh, you, woe, heavy woe of mine!
Oh, you, woe, heavy woe of mine!
So that's what fate had in store for me!

TEXT. **Iván Súrikov**, 1870. Title: Малороссийская мелодия (Little-Russian, i.e. Ukrainian, Melody). Tchaikovsky discarded the title and one stanza of the poem. Not set by any other composers.

METER. Binary. Loosely trochaic lines with two or three strong downbeats, similar to the folk meter used in North Russian laments (*Unbegaun*, 35):

> Wàsn't I my fáther's little dáughter dèar,
> Wàsn't I the flówer of my móther's èye?

The refrain has two strong downbeats and a dactylic clausula.

MUSIC. 1880. Op. 47, no. 7. F-sharp Minor. Mixed 3/2, 4/4, Moderato. For High Voice: d^1–a^2. Dedicated to **Aleksándra Panáyeva.** Transcribed for voice and orchestra by Tchaikovsky at Lavrovskaya's request (1884).

RECORDINGS. Belmas, Davrath, DeGaetani, Kasrashvili, Katulskaya, Kazarnovskaya, Kudriavchenko, Kurenko, Levko, Maxwell, Milashkina, Mkrtchyan, Obraztsova, Obukhova, Petina, Podleś, Rautio, Resnik, Rodgers, Siniavskaya, Slobodskaya, Söderström, Verrett, Vishnevskaya, Zimmermann.

Due to time constraints, older recordings of the song sometimes omit the second stanza.

16 Songs for Children, Opus 54 (1883)

Tchaikovsky distinguished between music written on commission, and works undertaken solely on his own inner prompting in his constant quest for new forms of musical expression. When Nikolay Rubinstein asked him to write an overture for an Exhibition of Arts and Industry to be held in August 1882, he wrote "1812," Op. 49, telling Mrs. von Meck "it will be loud and noisy, but I wrote it without any warm feeling of love and it will probably not have much artistic merit" (*DG*, 242; this work was a favorite with the public, however, and Tchaikovsky later enjoyed conducting it). At this same time he was writing a work that did stir him, the Serenade in C Major for String Orchestra, Op. 48, which he dedicated to his old friend Konstantin Albrecht, to whom he had earlier dedicated Song 16. The "Serenade for Strings" finally evoked a word of approval from Anton Rubinstein, who conducted it at the exhibition in Moscow and pronounced it the best thing Tchaikovsky had written (*DG*, 271). He took a serious interest in church music and derived satisfaction from hearing splendid performances of the music he wrote for unaccompanied choir, the Liturgy of St. John Chrysostom, Op. 41 (1878), and the Vesper Service, Op. 52 (1882); but when Jurgenson asked him to edit the sacred choral works of Dmitry Bortniansky (1751-1825) in ten volumes, he did it only on condition he be given a handsome fee, and even so, he regretted the onerous task: "O, this Bortniansky! Why did he write so much!" (*DG*, 258). When his patron asked him why he had never essayed a trio for piano, violin, and cello, he answered that he did not like the trio form and doubted he could write music for that sound combination that would be "warmed by genuine feeling" (*DG*, 243). Then he undertook precisely that challenge when Nikolay Rubinstein died unexpectedly in Paris in 1881, writing his beautiful Trio in A Minor, Op. 50. The dedication read "To the Memory of a Great Artist."

In his romances he almost always found the "warmth" he sought when he composed, even though they were slight pieces by comparison with the symphonies and concertos, suites and theater scores to which he gave most of his energy and time. So it was with the Songs for Children, Opus 54, written in two weeks at the end of October and beginning of November 1883. There were fifteen in all, to which he added Song 67, written two years earlier. He looked for ideas in Albrecht's children's songs, but found his texts in a little book of poems for children by Aleksey Pleshcheyev called Подснежник (*Snowdrop*), which the poet had given him in St. Petersburg in 1881, inscribed "To Pyotr Ilyich Tchaikovsky with respect and gratitude for his beautiful music to my poor words," a reference to Songs 5 and 14. In Opus 54, all but two of the songs are to words by Pleshcheyev, some of them translations but most of them original poems written for children.

Aleksey Pleshcheyev (1825-1893) was another "good" poet, not as good as Aleksey Tolstoy, but one of the most appealing and respected figures in Russian literary life in the second half of the 19th century. As a young poet in the late 1840s, he was full of enthusiasm for reformist ideas then being discussed in Petersburg with much passion but little alertness to the possibility of eavesdropping by the secret police of Nicholas I. It was he who introduced Dostoyevsky to Petrashevsky, and he who actually gave Dostoyevsky the copy of Belinsky's famous reply to Gogol that incriminated the two of them in the Petrashevsky affair after police spies turned them in. At their mock execution in December 1849, a day which changed their lives forever, Pleshcheyev and Dostoyevsky embraced and said "forgive, and farewell" to each other in those final moments before they thought they were to be shot. This scene, as an existential moment, became an unforgettable episode in Dostoyevsky's novel *The Idiot*, and the entire affair is recounted in detail in the first two volumes of Joseph Frank's remarkable study of the novelist (*Frank*). Pleshcheyev, like Dostoyevsky, was shackled and sent off to exile, but his rehabilitation took place differently, through service in the army, where, volunteering for a rescue mission, he distinguished himself and was promoted out of the ranks of private. In this act of doing the right thing without thought of the cost or possible risk to himself we have the key to his personality, both as a friend to Dostoyevsky after their return from exile, and as an editor of various journals of that time, some of them very important ones. He published Chekhov's first serious story over the ideological objections of some of his colleagues; their correspondence elicited Chekhov's most important statement about his beliefs as a writer (*Chekhov 1973*, Letter 23). Pleshcheyev was attracted to younger talent, without any thought to how this might or might not serve his own interests. So it was that late in his life he befriended the young Symbolist couple Dmitry Merezhkovsky and Zinaida Gippius, for whom he was an irresistible combination of literary legend from the past and kind-hearted simplicity, and on whom he bestowed such lavish generosity as he had at his disposal, while he had it. Quite unexpectedly in 1891, he inherited two million rubles from a distant relative, whereupon he retired forthwith from his job as poetry editor of *Severnyi vestnik* (*The Northern Herald*) and set himself up in grand style in one of the best Paris hotels. There he entertained everyone he could persuade to visit him from Russia, including the Merezhkovskys. For the next two years he was able to devote himself wholeheartedly to a "good-natured epicureanism" (*Gippius*, 137) which had evidently been latent within him but had never even remotely been within his means. On the eve of his death in Paris, he learned that it had all been a mistake and the real heir was someone else—but he had his fling in time to enjoy it.

His place in literary history is as a "civic" poet who suffered under the brutal hand of Nicholas I. He did suffer, and the times were brutal, but he came through it with his civility intact. He was a man of Tchaikovsky's class, but a generation older, with a social conscience and a belief in the power of poetry to enlighten and educate. His poems are more wide-ranging than the slogan "forward without fear or doubt," the line for which he was most famous and which became a call to the barricades, chanted by demonstrating students in St. Petersburg. He had other interests, music and children's literature among them (his first published poem was a lyric inspired by Pauline Viardot, whom he heard singing Desdemona in Rossini's *Otello* in St. Petersburg in 1843). He had his own three small children for whom he had to care after his young wife died unexpectedly. The children's poems were written for them. When his friend the novelist Aleksey Pisemsky first heard them, he copied out "Spring" (Song 60), saying Pleshcheyev was writing the best children's poems in Russia (*Kuzin*, 222). In 1878 Pleshcheyev collected them in *Snowdrop*, a title he took from the home journal the Maikov brothers wrote when they were all in their teens growing up in St. Petersburg.

When Tchaikovsky finished his Second Suite, Op. 53 in October 1883, he began the fifteen songs that became Opus 54, writing one song per day. These attractive songs, all for high voice, have the simplicity of easy pieces distinguished by Tchaikovsky's melodic inventiveness and harmonic mastery. Unlike the texts in Musorgsky's cycle "The Nursery" (1868-72), Pleshcheyev's poems do not really try to render the world as a child sees it. Rather, they are poems meant to give a child *understanding* of the world. Of all Tchaikovsky's songs, they are the least well known in the West, with the exception of a few that had an immediate success like Songs 56, 61, and 67. They are better known in Russia, where they are sung in music schools and conservatories. Songs 53, 56, 58, and 66 were not recorded at all in the Stalin period (official atheism ruled them out, and in some spots their protest against injustice was too close to home); three others that were recorded, Songs 61, 63, and 64, had to have the word "God" censored out of them (see Song 61). Recordings of most of them are rare, though some fine ones have been made. None are better than the complete set recorded in 1978 by Gennady Pishchayev, who sings them exactly as written with every word perfectly articulated.

Tchaikovsky sent them to Jurgenson on 3 November 1883, saying he could add Song 67, written in 1881, to the set, which was done. The edition came out in March 1884, without a dedication, and with a prefatory note by the composer begging the poet's indulgence for the few liberties taken and cuts made in the texts. He added that some of the songs, for example Songs 56 and 59, could be sung by a children's choir in unison. Tchaikovsky readily agreed with Taneyev's critique of two of the songs (*Taneev*, 105-8), but in subsequent editions he made no changes in the music as he originally wrote it.

52 Бабушка и внучек
Granny and grandson

Op. 54, No. 1

Tchaikovsky started with the very first poem in *Snowdrop*, which was on a subject close to the hearts of enlightened Russians in the latter half of the 19th century, after Alexander II ended serfdom in 1861. Set in a peasant house in a village, "Granny and Grandson" is a scene of some 30 stanzas in dialogue that tells the story of a boy who wants to go to school. Even one-room schools were by no means available everywhere yet. Among the peasants there was no tradition of attending school (gentry in the country who could afford it taught their children at home with private teachers who lived in the house). In this attractive little story in verse aimed at parents as well as children, Pleshcheyev wants to show his reader that school can be fun as well as enlightening. The boy tells his grandmother he happened to pass the school one day and listened through the window to what the teacher was talking about. He heard such interesting stories there! — about the world beyond the village, other lands, other climates, and how things were long ago when Russians still had pagan gods. The children draw and sing; the teacher even invited him to come in and sing with them in chorus. Seeing that the boy is eager to learn more, the teacher tells him to ask his family to let him attend school.

Tchaikovsky drastically shortened the text, using only 6 of the 30 stanzas, making small changes as needed and writing his own punch line at the end. As David Brown has pointed out, the music is simple, but cunningly contrived: the grandmother's music is in A minor, while the grandson's replies are in C or G major, making the song a "thoughtful little sketch, which Tchaikovsky treats with charmingly ironic seriousness" (*Brown III*, 236).

Soon after this, when Tchaikovsky moved to a rented house in Maidanovo (near Klin) where the nearest school was several miles away, he was depressed to see the peasant children cooped up all winter at home "in stifling darkness" with nothing to do (*DG*, 353). He persuaded the local authorities to open a school on the basis of an annual subsidy which he agreed to provide. He wrote Mrs. von Meck: "I feel proud that the initiative to accomplish this truly good work came from me" (*DG*, 360).

Под окном чулок старушка
Вяжет в комнате уютной,
И в очки свои большие
Смотрит в угол поминутно.

А в углу кудрявый мальчик
Молча к стенке прислонился.
На лице его забота,
Взгляд на что-то устремился.

«Что сидишь всё дома, внучек?
Шёл бы в сад, копал бы грядки,
Или кликнул бы сестрёнку,
Поиграл бы с ней в лошадки.»

Подошёл к старушке внучек
И головкою курчавой
К ней припал.
Он молчит, глаза большие
На неё глядят лукаво...

«Знать, гостинцу захотелось?»
Говорит ему старушка
«Винных ягод, винограду,
Иль тебе нужна игрушка?»

«Нет, гостинцев мне не надо!
У меня игрушек много.
Сумку ты купи, да в школу
Покажи-ка мне дорогу.»

Pad aknóm chulók starúshka	Granny sits and knits a stocking
Vjázhet f kómnate ujútnaj,	Beneath a window in the cozy room,
I v achkí svají bal'shíje	And looking up through large glasses
Smótrit v úgal paminútna.	Glances now and then at the corner.
A v uglú kudrjávyj mál'chik	There in the corner a curly-haired boy
Mólcha k sténke prislanílsa.	Leans in silence against the wall.
Na litsé jevó zabóta,	Some care or other shows on his face,
Vzglját na shtó-ta ustremílsa.	His gaze is fixed on something.
"Shtó sidísh fsjo dóma, vnúchek?	"Why sit home all day, my boy?
Shól by f sát, kapál by grjátki,	Go to the garden, play at digging rows,
Ili klíknul by sestrjónku,	Or find your little sister
Paigrál by s nej v lashátki."	And play a game of horses."

Padashól k starúshke vnúchek	Grandson came up to the old woman
I galófkaju kurchávaj	And his curly head
K nej pripál.	Fell on her lap.
On malchít, glazá bal'shíje	He doesn't say a word, his big eyes
Na nejó gljadját lukáva...	Look at her in a sly way...
"Znát', gastíntsu zakhatélas'?"	"So it's a treat you're after?"
Gavarít jemú starúshka,	Says the old woman to him,
"Vínnykh jágat, vinagrádu,	"Some grapes from the grapevine,
Il' tebé nuzhná igrúshka?"	Or do you want a toy?"
"Nét, gastíntsef mne ne náda!	"No, I don't need any treats!
U menjá igrúshek mnóga.	I have a lot of toys.
Súmku ty kupí, da f shkólu,	Buy me a satchel for school
Pakazhí-ka mne darógu."	And show me how to get there."

TEXT. **Alekséy Pleshchéyev**, 1878. Title: Бабушка и внучек (Granny and Grandson). First published in Pleshcheyev's anthology of poems entitled *Подснежник, Стихи для детей и юношества* (Snowdrop, Poems for children and teenagers, St. Petersburg, 1878), where it is the first poem in the volume. Not set by any other composers.

METER. Binary. Trochaic, 4-foot:

> *Granny sits and knits a stocking,*
> *'Neath a window in her room,*
> *Glancing over at the corner*
> *At her grandson standing there.*

MUSIC. 1883. Op. 54, no. 1. A Minor. 3/4, Moderato. For High Voice: d¹–e².

RECORDINGS. Lemeshev, Levinsky, Pishchayev.

53 *Птичка*
   Little bird

Op. 54, No. 2

Pleshcheyev had produced this translated text much earlier, before the emancipation of the serfs, but he included it in *Snowdrop* where Tchaikovsky found it. It comes from a Polish original by Władysław Syrokomla, author of "The Coral Beads" (Song 34). It is a free translation of the second half of a two-part poem called "Oracz do skowronka" (Plowman to the Lark) written in 1851. There is an irony in the Polish original missing from the translation. The first line, "You, lark, are at your song, and I am at my plowing", is a quote from an idyllic 17th-century poem of Jan Gawiński, a gentleman landowner who sees man in harmony with the lark and the natural world. In contrast, Syrokomla's poem is meant to bring out the injustice of a life of indentured labor as led under the serf system still in effect in Poland and Russia in the 1850s. At the time of *Snowdrop*, even though emancipation had taken place, things were not much better. The poem is meant to teach compassion for the peasant. Taneyev considered the song a small masterpiece (*Taneev*, 106).

Птичка Божия проснулася с зарёю,
А уж пахаря застала за сохою.

Полетит она к лазурным небесам
И, что видит в сёлах, всё расскажет там.

Скажет птичка Богу, что бедняк страдает,
Что кровавым потом ниву орошает.

Не мила, как птичке, пахарю весна,
Не несёт с собою радостей она…

Встретил бы он солнце песенкой весёлой,
Да молчать заставит гнёт нужды тяжёлый.

На сердце заботы, как свинец, лежат,
Поневоле песня не пойдёт на лад.

Скажет птичка Богу, чтоб Его рука
Поддержала в горькой доле бедняка.

Чтоб ему нести свой крест достало силы,
Чтоб без ропота добрёл он до могилы,
Чтоб без ропота добрёл он до могилы…

Ptíchka Bózhija prasnúlasa z zarjóju,	God's little bird woke with the dawn,
A ush pákharja zastála za sakhóju.	And found the plowman already at his plow.
Paletít aná k lazúrnym nebesám	She will fly to heaven's azure blue
I, shto vídit f sjólakh, fsjó rasskázhet tám.	And there tell all she sees in the villages.
Skázhet ptíchka Bógu, shto	The little bird will tell God that
bednják stradájet,	the poor man suffers,
Shto kravávym pótam nívu arashájet.	He waters the field with his blood and sweat.
Ne milá, kak ptíchke, pákharju	Spring is sweet to the bird, but not the
vesná,	plowman,
Ne nesjót s sabóju rádastej aná…	It brings no gladness when it comes…
Fstrétil by on sóntse pésenkaj vesjólaj,	He would greet the sun with a joyful song,
Da malchát' zastávit gnjót nuzhdý	But hard oppression weighs him down and
tjazhólaj.	makes him silent.
Ná serttse zabóty, kak svinéts, lezhát,	Cares, like lead, weigh on his heart,
Panevóle pésnja ne pajdjót na lát.	Keeping harmony from his song.
Skázhet ptíchka Bógu, shtop Jevó ruká	The little bird will ask God to lend a hand
Padderzhála v gór'kaj dóle bednjaká.	To help the poor man bear his bitter lot.
Shtop jemú nestí svoj krést dastála síly,	To have the strength to carry his cross,
Shtob bez rópata dabrjól on da magíly,	To make it to the grave without complaint,
Shtob bez rópata dabrjól on da magíly.	To make it to the grave without complaint.

TEXT. **Alekséy Pleshchéyev**, 1856. First published in 1857 with the title "Подражание польскому" (Imitation of the Polish) and a dedication to his friend, the translator Mikhail Mikhailov (see Song 18). In *Snowdrop* it has the title "С польского: Птичка" (From the Polish: Little Bird). A free translation of the second half of the two-part poem "Oracz do skowronka" (Plowman to the Lark) by **Władysław Syrokomla**, 1851. Tchaikovsky rewrote line 8 to make it more definite (from "spring brings few joys" to "spring brings no joys"); he left out one couplet ("no joyful gazing at a moonlit night for him, the farmer's eyes are dimmed with tears"); and he repeated the last line of the poem. After Tchaikovsky, set by Vladimir Rebikov for school choir (1902).

METER. Binary. Trochaic, 6-foot:
If he could, he'd greet the sun with joyful song,
Heavy need oppresses him and makes him silent.

MUSIC. 1883. Op. 54, no. 2. G Major. 4/4, Andante con moto. For High Voice: d¹ sharp–f² natural.

RECORDINGS. Levinsky, Pishchayev.

54   *Весна (Травка зеленеет)*
Spring (Grass is greening)

Op. 54, No. 3

One of three songs on the theme of spring (the others are Songs 60 and 64), this bright allegro song in 3/4 time goes back to an unknown Polish original. Pleshcheyev's translation is a very popular text which has been set by many Russian composers.

Травка зеленеет,	Травка зеленеет,
Солнышко блестит,	Солнышко блестит,
Ласточка с весною	Ласточка с весною
В сени к нам летит.	В сени к нам летит.
С нею солнце ярче	С нею солнце ярче
И весна милей…	И весна милей…
Прощебечь с дороги	Прощебечь с дороги
Нам привет скорей,	Нам привет скорей,
Прощебечь с дороги	Прощебечь с дороги
Нам привет скорей.	Нам привет скорей.
Дам тебе я зёрен	
А ты песню спой,	
Что из стран далёких	
Принесла с собой…	
Дам тебе я зёрен	
А ты песню спой…	

Tráfka zelenéjet,	Grass is greening,
Sólnyshka blestít,	Sun is shining,
Lástachka s vesnóju	With spring the swallow
F séni k nám letít.	Flies to our porch.
S néju sóntse járche	She makes the sun brighter
I vesná miléj…	And the spring nicer…
Prashchebéch z darógi	Chirp us a greeting
Nam privét skaréj,	As you fly our way,
Prashchebéch z darógi	Chirp us a greeting
Nam privét skaréj.	As you fly our way.
Dam tebé ja zjóren	Here's seed for you,
A ty pésnju spój,	Sing us a song,

Shto is strán daljókikh	A song you've brought
Prineslá s sabój…	From a distant land…
Dam tebé ja zjóren	Here's seed for you,
A ty pésnju spój…	Sing us a song…
Tráfka zelenéjet,	Grass is greening,
Sólnyshka blestít,	Sun is shining,
Lástachka s vesnóju	With spring the swallow
F séni k nám letít.	Flies to our porch.
S néju sóntse járche	She makes the sun brighter
I vesná miléj…	And the spring nicer…
Prashchebéch z darógi	Chirp us a greeting
Nam privét skaréj,	As you fly our way,
Prashchebéch z darógi	Chirp us a greeting
Nam privét skaréj.	As you fly our way.

TEXT. **Alekséy Pleshchéyev**, 1858. First published in *Russkii vestnik* (The Russian Herald), May-June 1858, no. 15, p. 618. Untitled, but identified as translated from the Polish. In subsequent editions of the poet's works, published as part of a cycle called Сельские песни (Rural Songs), from an unknown Polish poet. Tchaikovsky omitted the last five stanzas of the translation, which take up a different theme, a parent's lonesome thoughts about a daughter who married a soldier and moved far away. He changed the adjective describing the sun in the first line of the second stanza from краше (prettier) to ярче (brighter). All the repetitions are his.

First set by the publisher and composer Matvey Ivanovich Bernard (1794-1871, a student of John Field), published posthumously in 1872 with the title Ласточка (Swallow). After Tchaikovsky, by over fifteen composers, including Ippolitov-Ivanov (1884), V. I. Rebikov (1900, for children's choir), and Glière (1908).

METER. Binary. Trochaic, 3-foot:

> *Green so green the grass now,*
> *Bright so bright the sun,*
> *Swallow comes a-flying,*
> *Swallow in the spring.*

MUSIC. 1883. Op. 54, no. 3. G Major. 3/4, Allegro con spirito (punctuated with expressive *ritenuto* and *ritardando* passages). For High Voice: d^1–g^2.

RECORDINGS. Lemeshev, Levinsky, Pishchayev, Vinogradov.

ℰᴓ

55 *Мой садик*
My garden

Op. 54, No. 4

With characteristic insight, the critic Yuly Eichenwald (1872-1928) uses this poem about a garden that lacks fancy flowers as a metaphor for Pleshcheyev's modest attitude to his poetry in general (*Aikhenval'd*, 278). Pictured here is the kind of garden Russians typically prefer, informal and unpretentious, with a variety of flowers and blossoming trees in motley profusion. It seems an unlikely subject for a song, but it is thoroughly charming and continually interesting, with a little break between the third and fourth stanzas. To the "Allegro" marking is added "commodo", at a leisurely, easy pace; the piano is to be played "grazioso", gracefully, and "dolce", sweetly.

Как мой садик свеж и зелен!
Распустилась в нём сирень;
От черёмухи душистой
И от лип кудрявых тень...

Правда, нет в нём бледных лилий,
Горделивых георгин,
И лишь пёстрые головки
Возвышает мак один.

Да подсолнечник у входа,
Словно верный часовой,
Сторожит себе дорожку,
Всю поросшую травой...

Но люблю я садик скромный:
Он душе моей милей
Городских садов унылых,
С сетью правильных аллей.

И весь день, в траве высокой
Лёжа, слушать бы я рад,
Как заботливые пчёлы
Вкруг черёмухи жужжат.

Kak moj sádik svésh i zélen!	How fresh and green my garden is!
Raspustílas' v njóm sirén';	The lilac is in full bloom;
At cherjómukhi dushístaj	Fragrant bird-cherry
I at líp kudrjávykh tén'...	And curly lindens give it shade...

Právda, nét v njom blédnykh lílij,	True, it has no pale lilies
Gardelívykh geargín,	Or imposing dahlias,
I lish pjóstryje galófki	And motley are the flowers
Vazvyshájet mák adín.	Atop the single poppy.
Da patsólnechnik u fkhóda	And a plain sunflower at the entrance,
Slóvna vérnyj chasavój,	Like a faithful sentry,
Starazhýt sebé daróshku,	Stands guarding the path
Fsju parósshuju travój…	Overgrown with grass…
No ljubljú ja sádik skrómnyj:	But I love my humble garden:
On dushé majéj miléj	It's dearer to my soul
Garatskíkh sadóf unýlykh	Than gloomy urban parks
S sét'ju právil'nykh alléj.	With their network of straight paths.
I ves' dén', f travé vysókaj	And all day long in the tall grass
Ljózha, slúshat' by ja rát,	I could gladly lie and listen
Kak zabótlivyje pchóly	To the bees busy at their work,
Fkruk cherjómukhi zhuzhzhát.	Buzzing around the cherry blossoms.

TEXT. **Alekséy Pleshchéyev**, 1858. Title: Мой садик (My little garden). First set by Tchaikovsky; several other settings, including one for children's choir by Rebikov (1900).

The poem had six more stanzas, but Tchaikovsky probably did not know them, since they were cut by the censor in the edition of *Snowdrop* he used for the song. These stanzas speak of the garden in moonlight bringing thoughts of a better world of peace, truth, and brotherhood.

METER. Binary. Trochaic, 4-foot:

Fresh and green my garden small,
Curly lindens spreading shade…

MUSIC. 1883. Op. 54, no. 4. G Major. 4/4, Allegro commodo. For High Voice: e^1–f^2 sharp.

RECORDINGS. Barsova, Lemeshev, Levinsky, Pishchayev, Shpiller, Söderström, Vinogradov.

56 *Легенда*
Legend

Op. 54, No. 5

This is a unique song because in its meter and in the story it tells about the boyhood of Jesus it is a carol, and therefore not a Russian song. There is no evidence that Tchaikovsky knew the medieval European or English carols, though he probably did, but he captured their essence perfectly in the music he wrote to this text.

The source of the text has always been a mystery. When Pleshcheyev published the poem, he indicated that he had translated it "from English," but since that time no English source has been identified. My own search led me to the "Oxford Book of Carols," a standard compilation from medieval times forward, where the last carol in the volume, No. 197, is in fact this very song. It is called "The Crown of Roses," with music by Tchaikovsky, and a note which reads "Plechtcheev (*sic*) wrote the words, which were translated into German by Hans Schmidt" (*Oxford Book of Carols*, 439). Thus my search led in a circle back to Tchaikovsky and Pleshcheyev.

When I shared these inconclusive results with colleagues, one of them, an expert on songs from Eastern Europe, Robert A. Rothstein of the University of Massachusetts, provided the answer. He had found it earlier in a completely unexpected source. A Yiddish version of this same text was sung in the repertoire of a chorus in Wilno: "A yingl hot gehat a sod" (A boy had a garden). The song was discussed in January 1990 in the poetry column of the New York Yiddish weekly *Forverts*, where the editors' suspicions that the text was more Christian than Jewish eventually led them to Tchaikovsky's song. With the help of an early edition of Bartlett's "Quotations," Rothstein tracked down the English original to Richard Henry Stoddard (1825-1903), an American poet. Stoddard's poem, called "Roses and Thorns," will be found below.

Tchaikovsky's song has always been considered a minor masterpiece. He brought a transcription of the song for mixed choir, *a cappella*, with him to New York for the opening of Carnegie Hall, where it "made a great hit," according to the *New York Times* of 9 May 1891: "It is characteristic Russian music and the color is delightful. Tchaikovsky was called out twice after it with great enthusiasm..." (*Yoffe*, 101). He also made a transcription for tenor with orchestra. All versions have been recorded. In English, famous singers like John McCormack and Peter Pears have sung it, but always to a text retranslated back from Russian or German.

Был у Христа младенца сад,　　　　　«Как ты сплетёшь теперь венок?
И много роз взрастил он в нём.　　　　В твоём саду нет больше роз!»
Он трижды в день их поливал,　　　　«Вы позабыли, что шипы
Чтоб сплесть венок себе потом.　　　Остались мне,» сказал Христос.

Когда же розы расцвели,　　　　　　И из шипов они сплели
Детей еврейских созвал он;　　　　　Венок колючий для него, —
Они сорвали по цветку　　　　　　　И капли крови, вместо роз,
И сад был весь опустошён.　　　　　Чело украсили его.

Byl u Khristá mladéntsa sát,　　　　　The Christ-child had a garden,
I mnóga rós vzrastíl on v njóm.　　　　And he grew many roses there.
On trízhdy v dén' ikh palivál,　　　　Thrice a day he watered them
Shtop splést' venók sebé patóm.　　　To weave himself a crown later on.

Kagdá zhe rózy rastsveli,　　　　　　Then when the roses bloomed,
Detéj jevréjskikh sózval ón;　　　　　He summoned the Jewish children;
Aní sarváli pa tsvetkú　　　　　　　They picked one flower each
I sát byl vés' apustashón.　　　　　And the whole garden was left bare.

"Kák ty spletjósh tepér' venók?　　　　"Now how will you weave a crown?
F tvajóm sadú net ból'she rós!"　　　There are no more roses in your garden!"
"Vy pazabýli, shto shypý　　　　　　"You forget, the thorns
Astális' mné," skazál Khristós.　　　Remain for me," said Christ.

I is shypóf aní splelí　　　　　　　And from the thorns they wove
Venók kaljúchij dlja njevó, —　　　　A prickly crown for him, —
I kápli króvi, vmésta rós,　　　　　And drops of blood, instead of roses,
Cheló ukrásili jevó.　　　　　　　Adorned his head.

Text. **Alekséy Pleshchéyev**, by 1877; first published in the journal *Sem'ia i shkola* (Family and School), 1877, no. 4. Title: Легенда (Legend), subtitled "С английского" (From the English). Translated from a poem by the American poet **Richard Henry Stoddard** entitled "Roses and Thorns" (1857); in later editions of his work, Stoddard changed the title to "Legend." Tchaikovsky found the text in *Snowdrop*. Set by a few other composers after Tchaikovsky, including a version for school chorus by Rebikov.

Meter. Binary. Iambic, 4-foot:

> *They took the thorns, and made a crown,*
> *And placed it on his shining head;*
> *And where the roses should have shone*
> *Were little drops of blood instead!*

Pleshcheyev's translation is in the same meter as Stoddard's original poem, but uses exclusively masculine rhymes.

MUSIC. 1883. Op. 54, no. 5. E Minor. 2/4, Moderato. For High Voice: d^1-e^2. Tchaikovsky transcribed the song twice. The first transcription is for voice and orchestra, made in 1884 at the request of the tenor Dmitry Usatov, who sang it at the Bolshoy Theater. The second transcription, for mixed choir, *a cappella*, was done in 1889. A later work based on this song, "Variations for Orchestra" by Anton Arensky, Op. 35 (1894), is one of that composer's most famous works.

RECORDINGS. Christoff, Gedda, Levinsky, McCormack, Pears (orchestral version, with Benjamin Britten), **Pishchayev**, Polyansky Choir (choral version), Vayne.

Roses and Thorns (Richard Henry Stoddard)

The young child Jesus had a garden,
    Full of roses, rare and red:
And thrice a day he watered them,
    To make a garland for his head.

When they were full-blown in the garden,
    He called the Jewish children there,
And each did pluck himself a rose,
    Until they stripped the garden bare.

"And now how will you make your garland?
    For not a rose your path adorns."
"But you forget," he answered them,
    "That you have left me still the thorns."

They took the thorns, and made a garland,
    And placed it on his shining head;
And where the roses should have shone
    Were little drops of blood instead!

Songs of Summer, Boston, Ticknor and Fields, 1857,
page 43.

57 *На берегу*
On the riverbank

Op. 54, No. 6

Here is a long bedtime story for the children. Tchaikovsky set Pleshcheyev's entire text.

Домик над рекою,
В окнах огонёк,
Светлой полосою
На воду он лёг.

В доме не дождутся
С ловли рыбака:
Обещал вернуться
Через два денька.

Но прошёл и третий,
А его всё нет.
Ждут напрасно дети,
Ждёт и старый дед.

Всех нетерпеливей
Ждёт его жена, —
Ночи молчаливей
И как холст бледна…

Вот за ужин сели,
Ей не до еды:
«Как бы в самом деле
Не было беды.»

Вдоль реки несется
Лодочка; на ней
Песня раздаётся
Всё слышней, слышней.

Звуки той знакомой
Песни услыхав,
Дети вон из дому
Бросились стремглав.

Весело вскочила
Из-за прялки мать,
И у деда силы
Вдруг нашлось бежать.

Песню заглушает
Звонкий крик ребят,
Тщетно унимает
Старый дед внучат.

Вот и воротился
Весел и здоров!
В росказни пустился
Тотчас про улов.

В морды он и в сети
Наловил всего;
С любопытством дети
Слушают его.

Смотрит дед на щуку —
«Больно велика!»
Мать сынишке в руку
Сует окунька.

Девочка присела
Около сетей
И взяла несмело
Парочку ершей.

Прыгают, смеются
Детки, если вдруг
Рыбки встрепенутся,
Выскользнут из рук.

Долго раздавался
Смех их над рекой,
Ими любовался
Месяц золотой.

Ласково мерцали
Звёзды с вышины;
Детям обещали
Радостные сны.

Dómik nad rekóju,	A little house at river's edge,
V óknakh aganjók,	A light from the windows,
Svétlaj palasóju	It falls on the water
Ná vadu on ljók.	In a bright stripe.
V dóme ne dazhdútsa	Excited, all are waiting
S lóvli rybaká:	For the fisherman's return:
Abeshchál vernútsa	He promised to be back home
Cherez dvá den'ká.	In two short days.
No prashól i trétij,	But the third day has passed,
A jevó fsjo nét.	And he's still not back.
Zhdút naprásna déti,	The children find it hard to wait,
Zhdjót i stáryj dét.	And old granddad does too.
Fsékh neterpelívej	But most of all his wife
Zhdjót jevó zhená,	Waits impatiently for him,
Nóchi malchalívej	As silent as the night she is
I kak khólst bledná…	And pale as a sheet…
Vót za úzhin séli,	They sit down to supper,
Jéj ne da jedý:	But she can hardly eat:
"Kak by f sámam déle	"If only it be true
Né byla bedý."	That nothing bad has happened."
Vdol' rekí nesjótsa	Now a little boat comes
Lódachka; na néj	Sailing down the stream;
Pésnja razdajótsa	And as it does, a song is heard,
Fsjo slyshnéy, slyshnéy.	Loud, and louder still.
Zvúki tój znakómaj	The children know the song,
Pésni uslykháf,	And when they hear its sounds,
Déti von iz dómu	Headlong they dash
Brósilis' stremgláf.	Running from the house.
Vésela fskachíla	Mother jumps up gaily
Iz-za prjálki mát',	From her spinning wheel,
I u déda síly	And suddenly old granddad
Vdruk nashlós' bezhát'.	Has strength to run too.
Pésnju zaglushájet	The song is drowned out
Zvónkij krík rebját,	By the shouting of the children,
Chshchétna unimájet	In vain old granddad
Stáryj dét vnuchát.	Tries to make them quiet.
Vót i varatílsa	Here's Dad home again
Vésel i zdaróf!	Merry and hale as ever!
V róskazni pustílsa	Right away his stories start
Tótchas pra ulóf.	How he got his catch.

V mórdy on i f séti	In willow-traps and nets
Nalavíl fsevó;	He caught all the fish;
S ljubapýtstvam déti	With eager curiosity
Slúshajut jevó.	The children listen to him.
Smótrjat dét na shchúku —	Granddad eyes the pike —
"Ból'na veliká!"	"Mighty big he is!"
Mát' syníshke v rúku	Mother puts a perch
Sújet akun'ká.	In her sonny's hand.
Dévachka priséla	Little sister sits down
Ókala setéj	Next to the nets,
I vzjalá nesméla	And, hesitating, picks up
Párochku jershéj.	A pair of spiny ruffs.
Prýgajut, smejútsa	The kids are jumping, laughing,
Détki, jesli vdrúk	When without a warning
Rýpki fstrepenútsa,	Suddenly the fish flip,
Výskal'znut iz rúk.	Sliding out of their hands.
Dólga razdaválsa	Long was heard their laughter
Smékh ikh nad rekój,	At the river's edge,
Imi ljubaválsa	Admiring the scene
Mésjats zalatój.	The golden moon looked on.
Láskava mertsáli	The stars on high
Zvjózdy s vyshyný;	Twinkled tenderly,
Détjam abeshcháli	Promising the children
Rádasnyje sný.	Sweet dreams.

Text. **Alekséy Pleshchéyev**, 1874; first published in the journal *Sem'ia i shkola* (Family and School), 1874, no. 11. Title: На берегу: Картинка (On the Riverbank: A Picture). Set only by Tchaikovsky, who used all sixteen stanzas of the poem. He made minor changes in punctuation and a small change in wording in stanza 8.

Meter. Binary. Trochaic, 3-foot:

> *Long was heard their laughter*
> *At the river's edge...*

Music. 1883. Op. 54, no. 6. C Major. 2/4, Allegro non troppo. For High Voice: e^1 flat–e^2.

Recordings. Lemeshev, Levinsky, Pishchayev.

58 Зимний вечер
Winter evening

Op. 54, No. 7

This is a picture of happy children in a cozy house which is not "dark and stifling"—but not every child is so fortunate! The pathos is nicely expressed in the music, though Taneyev objected that it is heard too early (*Taneev*, 106-7).

Хорошо вам, детки,
Зимним вечерком
В комнате уютной
Сели вы рядком,

Пламя от камина,
Освещает вас...
Слушаете жадно
Мамы вы рассказ.

Радость, любопытство
На лице у всех,
Часто прерывает
Маму звонкий смех.

Вот рассказ окончен,
Все пустились в зал...
«Поиграй нам, мама,»
Кто-то пропищал.

«Хоть уж девять било,
Отказать вам жаль...»
И послушно села
Мама за рояль.

И пошло веселье!
Началась возня,
Пляска, песни, хохот,
Визг и беготня.

Пусть гудит сердито
Вьюга под окном —
Хорошо вам, детки,
В гнёздышке своём!

Но не всем такое
Счастье Бог даёт.
Есть на свете много
Бедных и сирот.

У одних могила
Рано мать взяла;
У других нет в зиму
Теплого угла.

Если приведётся
Встретить вам таких,
Вы, как братьев, детки,
Приголубьте их.

Kharashó vam, détki,
Zímnim vecherkóm
F kómnate ujútnaj
Séli by rjatkóm,

It's so nice for you, children,
On a winter evening
In the cozy room
Sitting side by side,

Plámja at kamína,
Asveshchájet vás...
Slúshajete zhádna
Mámy vy rasskás.

Lit by a flame
In the fireplace...
Eagerly you listen
To a story mama's telling.

Rádast', ljubapýtstva
Na litsé u fsékh,
Chásta preryvájet
Mámu zvónkij smékh.

Gladness and curiosity
Are on every face,
And mama often has to stop
When ringing laughter interrupts.

Vot rasskás akónchen,	Now the story's over,
Vse pustílis' v zál...	All go into the ballroom...
"Paigráj nam, máma,"	"Play something for us, mama,"
Któ-ta prapishchál.	Pipes a little voice.
"Khat' ush dévjat' bíla,	"Though it's after nine,
Atkazát' vam zhál'..."	It's a shame to say no..."
I paslúshna séla	And obediently mama
Máma za rajál'.	Sits down at the piano.
I pashló vesél'je!	Then the merriment begins!
Nachalás' vaznjá,	A whole array of fun starts,
Pljáska, pésni, khókhat,	Dancing, songs, laughter,
Vísk i begatnjá.	Squeals and running all about.
Púzd' gudít serdíta	However angry 'neath the window
V'júga pad aknóm —	The snowy blizzard blows —
Kharashó vam, détki,	You're all just fine, kids,
V gnjózdyshke svajóm!	In your cozy little nest!
No ne fsém takóje	But God does not give everyone
Shchást'je Bóg dajót.	Such good fortune.
Jést' na svéte mnóga	The world is full of children
Bédnykh i sirót.	Who are poor and orphaned.
U adníkh magíla	Some lost their mother
Rána mát' vzjalá;	To an early grave;
U drugíkh net v zímu	Others in the wintertime
Tjóplava uglá.	Have no nice warm corner.
Jésli privedjótsa	If you should ever happen
Fstrétit' vám takíkh,	On those who are in need,
Vý, kak brát'jef, détki,	Treat them like brothers, kids,
Prigalúp'te íkh.	Give them love and comfort.

TEXT. **Alekséy Pleshchéyev**, 1872; first published in the journal *Sem'ia i shkola* (Family and School), 1872, no. 2. Title: Зимний вечер (Winter Evening). Set first by Tchaikovsky, who made minor changes in punctuation. Later settings include one for children's choir by Rebikov.

METER. Binary. Trochaic, 3-foot:

> *If you ever happen*
> *On such kids in need,*
> *Be like brothers to them,*
> *Give them love and aid.*

MUSIC. 1883. Op. 54, no. 7. C minor. 3/4, Moderato. For High Voice: d^1–g^2.

RECORDINGS. Levinsky, Pishchayev.

59 *Кукушка*
Cuckoo

Op. 54, No. 8

Best song of all, according to Taneyev, who especially liked the grace notes in the piano part that represent the birds (*Taneev*, 106-7).

«Ты прилетел из города, — какие,
Скажи, там слухи носятся о нас?»
(Скворца кукушка спрашивала раз).
«Что́ жители толкуют городские,
Хоть, например, о песнях соловья?
Интересуюсь этим очень я.»

— «Весь город он приводит в восхищенье,
Когда в саду его раздастся трель.»
— «А жавронок?» —
                    — «И жаворонка пенье
Пленяет очень многих.» —
                    — «Неужель?
Ну, а каков их отзыв о дрозде?»
— «Да хвалят и его, хоть не везде.»

«Еще хочу спросить я, — может статься,
И обо мне ты слышал кое-что?»
«Вот про тебя, сестрица, так признаться,
Не говорит решительно никто!»
«А! Если так, — кукушка возопила, —
То о себе, чтоб людям отомстить,
Сама весь век, покуда хватит силы,
Не перестану я твердить:
    ку-ку, ку-ку, ку-ку, ку-ку,
    ку-ку, ку-ку, ку-ку, ку-ку,
    ку-ку, ку-ку, ку-ку, ку-ку,
    ку-ку, ку-ку, ку-ку, ку-ку,
        ку-ку, ку-ку!»

"Ty priletél iz górada, — kakíje
Skazhý, tam slúkhi nósjatsa a nás?"
(Skvartsá kukúshka spráshyvala rás).
"Shtó zhýteli talkújut garatskíje,
Khot', naprimér, a pésnjakh salav'já?
Interesújus' ètim óchen' já."

"You flew here from the town, — what,
Pray tell, are people saying of us there?"
(One day the cuckoo asked the starling).
"What do the townsfolk have to say,
For instance, of the nightingale's songs?
This interests me a lot."

— "Ves' górat on privódit v
vaskhishchén'je,
Kagdá f sadú jevó razdástsa trél'."
— "A zhávranak?" —
            — "I zhávaranka pén'je
Plenjájet óchen' mnógikh." —
            — "Neuzhél'?
Nu, a kakóf ikh ódzyf a drazdé?"
— "Da khváljat i jevó, khot' ne vezdé."

— "The whole town raves of nothing else,
When his trills are heard resounding in the
orchard."
— "And the lark?" —
            — "Many find the singing
Of the lark to be enchanting too." —
            — "You don't say!
Well, what is their opinion of the thrush?"
— "They praise him too, although not
everywhere."

"Jeshchó khachú sprasít' ja, —
mózhet státsa,
I aba mné ty slýshal kóje-shtó?"
"Vot pra tebjá, sestrítsa, tak priznátsa,
Ne gavarít reshýtel'na niktó!"
"Á! Jésli tak, — kukúshka vazapíla, —
To a sebé, shtop ljúdjam atamstít',
Samá ves' vék, pakúda khvátit síly,
Ne perestánu ja tverdít':
    ku–ku, ku–ku, ku–ku, ku–ku,
    ku–ku, ku–ku, ku–ku, ku–ku,
    ku–ku, ku–ku, ku–ku, ku–ku,
    ku–ku, ku–ku, ku–ku, ku–ku,
        ku–ku, ku–ku!"

"I also want to ask, — did you perchance
Hear anyone say anything of me?"
"About you, sister, I must confess,
No one has a single word to say!"
"Ah! If that's the case, — exclaimed the
cuckoo, —
I'll take revenge on folk then,
While I have the strength, and all my life
Remind them who I am:
cuckoo, cuckoo, cuckoo, cuckoo,
cuckoo, cuckoo, cuckoo, cuckoo,
cuckoo, cuckoo, cuckoo, cuckoo,
cuckoo, cuckoo, cuckoo, cuckoo,
cuckoo, cuckoo!"

TEXT. **Alekséy Pleshchéyev**, 1872, in *Snowdrop*. Translation of "Der Kuckuck", a fable by **Christian Gellert** (1715-1769), from Book I of his "Fabeln" (Fables, published in Leipzig 1769-74). Title: Кукушка (Басня Геллерта) (Cuckoo: A Fable of Gellert). Set only by Tchaikovsky, who added the cries of "cuckoo" at the end.

METER. Binary. Iambic, 5-foot:
        "I also want to ask, — did you perchance
        Hear anyone say anything of me?"
MUSIC. 1883. Op. 54, no. 8. G Major. 2/4, Moderato. For High Voice: b–g².
RECORDINGS. Lemeshev, Levinsky, Pishchayev, Rodgers, Söderström.

৵

60 Весна (Уж тает снег)
Spring (Snow's melting)

Op. 54, No. 9

A favorite. The high point is in the middle, in the third stanza, with a
dramatic *ritenuto ad libitum* on the words "Happiness seems just ahead."

Уж тает снег, бегут ручьи,
В окно повеяло весною...
Засвищут скоро соловьи,
И лес оденется листвою!

Чиста небесная лазурь.
Теплей и ярче солнце стало;
Пора метелей злых и бурь
Опять надолго миновала.

И сердце сильно так в груди
Стучит, как будто ждёт чего–то;
Как будто счастье впереди,
И унесла зима заботы!

Все лица весело глядят.
«Весна!» — читаешь в каждом взоре.
И тот, как празднику, ей рад,
Чья жизнь — лишь тяжкий труд и горе.

Но резвых деток звонкий смех
И беззаботных птичек пенье
Мне говорят — кто больше всех
Природы любит обновленье!
Мне говорят — кто больше всех
Природы любит обновленье!

Ush tájet snék, begút ruchjí,	Snow's melting now and streams are running,
V aknó pavéjala vesnóju...	You can smell spring through the window...
Zasvíshchut skóra salav'jí,	Soon the nightingales will start to trill,
I lés adénetsa listvóju!	And the woods will be dressed in leaves!
Chistá nebésnaja lazúr'.	The sky is pure azure-blue.
Tepléj i járche sóntse stála;	The sun's warmer and brighter;
Pará metélej zlýkh i búr'	The season of snowstorms and blizzards fierce
Apját' nadólga minavála.	Has gone away again for a long time.

I sérttse síl'na tak v grudí	And your heart beats strongly
Stuchít, kak bútta zhdjót chevó-ta;	As if waiting for something;
Kak bútta shchást'je fperedí,	Happiness seems just ahead,
I uneslá zimá zabóty!	Winter's gone, so are cares!

Fse lítsa vésela gljadját.	Faces have a happy look.
"Vesná!"— chitájesh f kázhdam vzóre.	"It's spring!" you read in every gaze.
I tót, kak prázniku, jej rát,	And folk whose life is toil and grief
Chja zhýzn'— lish tjáshkij trút y góre.	Are glad as on a holiday.

No rézvykh détak zvónkij smékh	But the ringing laughter of kids at play
I bezzabótnykh ptíchek pén'je	And the singing of the carefree birds
Mne gavarját — kto ból'she fsékh	Tell me who, more than anyone
Priródy ljúbit abnavlén'je!	Loves nature's new beginning!
Mne gavarját — kto ból'she fsékh	Tell me who, more than anyone
Priródy ljúbit abnavlén'je!	Loves nature's new beginning!

TEXT. **Alekséy Pleshchéyev**, 1872. Title Весна (Spring). First published in the journal *Sem'ia i shkola* (Family and School), 1872, no. 3. Tchaikovsky took the text from *Snowdrop*. First set by Tchaikovsky; several other settings, including one for children's choir by Rebikov. The only change in Pleshcheyev's text is the repetition of the last two lines.

METER. Binary. Iambic, 4-foot:
> *Now melting snow and running streams,*
> *The smell of spring in open windows...*

MUSIC. 1883. Op. 54, no. 9. F Major. 2/4, Allegro animato. For High Voice: e^1–f^2.

RECORDINGS. Barsova, Lemeshev, Levinsky, Pishchayev, Rodgers, Rozhdestvenskaya, Shpiller, Söderström, Vinogradov.

61 Колыбельная песнь в бурю
Lullaby in a storm

Op. 54, No. 10

This lullaby, an early favorite, is a song that singers have particularly liked. All the recordings listed below are outstanding.

Earlier Soviet recordings of it, however, are a reminder of how pervasive censorship was in the period of militant atheism initiated under Stalin and continued under Khrushchev. Wherever music was performed, in every school, conservatory, theater, concert hall, and especially in radio stations and recording studios, the smallest allusions to religious faith had to be expurgated even from songs by Tchaikovsky. For the singers, it was a case of self-preservation: a teacher in a music school could lose her job for assigning "Ave Maria" to a student.

Written instructions were not handed out (what people now say is that Stalin did not like to commit such things to paper), nor was there a committee of censors who provided safe texts. Singers were expected to come up with a suitable substitute *themselves*. In this song, the problem word is "Господня" (the Lord's) in the second stanza. Sergey Lemeshev's solution in his 1955 recording was to sing instead "Ах, уймися, буря", a variation on the first line of the song. In Georgy Vinogradov's recording of the song, he makes a different substitution, singing "Ты, гроза, утихни" (You, thunderstorm, quiet down).

Other songs in this opus that required more elaborate emendation are Songs 63 and 64.

Ах! уймись ты, буря!
Не шумите, ели!
Мой малютка дремлет
Сладко в колыбели.

Ты, гроза Господня,
Не буди ребёнка!
Пронеситесь, тучи
Чёрные, сторонкой!

Бурь ещё немало
Впереди, быть может,
И не раз забота
Сон его встревожит.

Спи, дитя, спокойно...
Вот гроза стихает;
Матери молитва
Сон твой охраняет.

Завтра, как проснёшься
И откроешь глазки,
Снова встретишь солнце,
И любовь, и ласки!

Ákh! ujmís' ty búrja!	Oh! calm down, storm!
Ne shumíte, jéli!	Stop howling, fir trees!
Moj maljútka drémlet	My baby's dreaming
Slátka f kalybéli.	Sweetly in his cradle.
Ty, grazá Gaspódnja,	You, thunderstorm of the Lord,
Ne budí rebjónka!	Don't wake the child!
Pranesítes', túchi	Pass by, black clouds,
Chórnyje, starónkaj!	Be on your way!
Búr' jeshchó nemála	There'll be many storms
Fperedí, byt' mózhet,	Ahead, maybe,
I ne rás zabóta	And more than once
Són jevó fstrevózhyt.	Worry will disturb his sleep.
Spí, ditjá, spakójna...	Sleep, child, peacefully...
Vót grazá stikhájet;	The storm is dying down now;
Máteri malítva	A mother's prayer
Són tvoj akhranjájet.	Protects your sleep.
Záftra, kak prasnjóshsa	Tomorrow, when you wake
I atkrójesh gláski,	And open your little eyes,
Snóva fstrétish sóntse,	Again you'll meet the sun,
I ljubóf', i láski!	And love, and caresses!

TEXT. **Alekséy Pleshchéyev**, 1872. First published in *Detskoe chtenie* (Reading for Children), 1872, no. 12. Title В бурю (In a storm). Tchaikovsky took the text from *Snowdrop*; he omitted the first five stanzas of the poem. First set by Tchaikovsky; later for children's choir by Rebikov.

METER. Binary. Trochaic, 3-foot:
> *Now the storm grows quiet,*
> *Mother's prayer protects you...*

MUSIC. 1883. Op. 54, no. 10. F Minor. 3/4, Moderato. For High Voice: e¹natural–f².

RECORDINGS. Katulskaya, Lemeshev, Levinsky, Martynov, Pishchayev, Rodgers, Slobodskaya, Vinogradov, Vishnevskaya.

62 Цветок
Flower

Op. 54, No. 11

This poem on the theme of *fraternité* with a prisoner far from home is one Pleshcheyev wanted his children to understand. In the attractive music Tchaikovsky tried to make it accessible.

Весело цветики в поле пестреют;
Их по ночам освежает роса;
Днём их лучи благодатные греют,
Ласково смотрят на них небеса.

С бабочкой пёстрой, с гудящей пчелою,
С ветром им любо вести разговор;
Весело цветикам в поле весною,
Мил им родимого поля простор!

Вот они видят: в окне, за решёткой,
Тихо качается бледный цветок…
Солнца не зная, печальный и кроткий,
Вырос он в мрачных стенах одинок.

Цветикам жаль его бедного стало,
Хором они к себе брата зовут:
«Солнце тебя никогда не ласкало,
Брось эти стены, зачахнешь ты тут!»

«Нет!», отвечал он, «хоть весело в поле,
И наряжает вас ярко весна,
Но не завидую вашей я доле
И не покину сырого окна.

Пышно цветите! Своей красотою
Радуйте, братья, счастливых людей.
Я буду цвесть для того, кто судьбою
Солнца лишён и полей.

Я буду цвесть для того, кто страдает.
Узника я утешаю один.
Пусть он, взглянув на меня, вспоминает
Зелень родимых долин!»

Vésela tsvétiki f póle pestréjut;	So gay and colorful the flowers in the field;
Ikh pa nachám asvezhájet rasá;	At night the dew refreshes them;
Dnjóm ikh luchí blagadátnyje gréjut,	They bask all day in life-giving sunbeams,
Láskava smótrjat na níkh nebesá.	The skies look down on them with tender love.

Z bábachkaj pjóstraj, z gudjáshchej
  pchelóju,
S vétram im ljúba vestí razgavór;
Vésela tsvétikam f póle vesnóju,
Míl im radímava pólja prastór!

They love conversing with the
  wind,
With humming bee and painted butterfly;
Spring makes them happy in the open field,
They love the ground on which they grow!

Vót ani vídjat: v akné, za reshótkaj,
Tíkha kachájetsa blédnyj tsvetók...
Sóntsa ne znája, pechál'nyj i krótkaj
Výras on v mráchnykh stenákh adinók.

Here's what they see: by the barred window,
A pale flower sways quietly inside...
Hidden from the sun, sad and meek
He grew up alone within dark walls.

Tsvétikam zhál' jevo bédnava stála,
Khóram oni k sebe bráta zavút:
"Sóntse tebjá nikagdá ne laskála,
Brós' eti stény, zachákhnesh ty tút!"

The flowers in the field feel sorry for him,
They call in chorus to their brother:
"Never have you felt the sun's caressing rays,
Leave those walls, you'll only languish there!"

"Nét!", atvechál on, "khot' vésela
  f póle,
I narjazhájet vas járka vesná,
No ne zavíduju vashej ja dóle
I ne pakínu syróva akná.

"No!", he replied, "it's jolly in the field, I
  know,
And spring dresses you in bright array,
But still I don't envy your lot in life
And never will I leave my dark damp window.

Pýshna tsvetíte! Svajéj krasatóju
Rádujte, brát'ja, shchastlívykh ljudéj.
Ja budu tsvést' dlja tavó, kto sud'bóju
Sóntsa lishón i paléj.

May you flower lushly! May your beauty
Gladden happy folk, brothers.
My flower's not for them, but for someone
Barred from sun and open fields.

Ja budu tsvést' dlja tavó, kto stradájet.
Úznika ja utesháju adín.
Pust' on, vzgljanúf na menjá,
  vspaminájet
Zélen' radímykh dalín!"

Let my flower be for him who suffers.
I am the only comfort a prisoner has.
And when he looks at me, may he
  remember
How green it was, the valley of his birth!"

TEXT. **Alekséy Pleshchéyev**, 1871; pub. 1872, later in *Snowdrop*. Title: Цветок: на мотив из Ратисбонна (Flower: on a motif from Ratisbonne). Based on an unknown poem by **Louis Ratisbonne** (1827-1900), a French children's writer. After Tchaikovsky, set by Rebikov (1902, for a school songbook) and Glière (Op. 24/5, 1906, for children's choir).

METER. Ternary. Dactyls, 4-foot (except two last lines of 3 feet):
  Here's what they see — in the window, secluded
  Silently swaying, a flower so pale...

MUSIC. 1883. Op. 54, no. 11. F Major. 6/8, Moderato con moto. For High Voice: e^1–f^2.

RECORDINGS. Levinsky, Pishchayev, Vinogradov.

63 Зима
Winter

Ор. 54, No. 12

This attractive scene "from life" pictures at length a grandfather's joy, sledding with the children after the first big snowfall. Tchaikovsky used only a few stanzas of the text, showing the children's excitement as Christmas approaches.

Дед, поднявшись спозаранку,
К внучкам в комнату спешит.
«Доброй весточкой утешить
Вас пришёл я,» говорит.

«Всё зимы вы ждали, детки,
Надоела вам давно
Осень хмурая с дождями;
Посмотрите-ка в окно!

За ночь выпал снег глубокий,
И мороз, как в декабре.
Уж впрягли в салазки Жучку
Ребятишки на дворе.»

И тормошит дед раскрывших
Глазки сонные внучат;
Но на старого плутишки
Недоверчиво глядят.

Поднял штору дед, — и точно!
Снег под солнечным лучом
Бриллиантами сверкает,
Отливает серебром.

«Слава Богу! Слава Богу!»,
Детки весело кричат,
И в уме их возникает
Уж картин знакомых ряд:

На салазках с гор катанье,
И катанье на коньках...
И Рождественская ёлка,
Сверху донизу в огнях!

Dét, padnjáfshys' spazaránku,	Granddad, up at crack of dawn,
K vnúchkam f kómnatu speshýt.	Hurries to his grandchildren's room.
"Dóbraj véstachkaj utéshyt'	"I've come to surprise you
Vas prishól ja," gavarít.	With good news," he says.

"Fsjó zimý vy zhdáli, détki,	"Waiting for winter, are you, kids,
Nadajéla vam davnó	All this time, so sick of autumn,
Ósen' khmúraja z dazhdjámi;	Gloomy fall and rainy days;
Pasmatríte-ka v aknó!	Just take a look out the window!
Zá nach výpal snék glubókij,	Overnight a deep snow fell,
I marós, kak v dekabré.	Outside there's a December frost.
Ush fprjaglí f saláski Zhúchku	The boys in the yard already have
Rebjatíshki na dvaré."	Zhuchka the mutt hitched to a sled."
I tarmóshyt dét raskrýfshykh	And granddad pesters them to get up,
Gláski sónnyje vnuchát;	Their sleepy eyes now open wide;
No na stárava plutíshki	But they just look at the old rascal,
Nedavérchiva gljadját.	Staring at him in disbelief.
Pódnjal shtóru dét, — i tóchna!	Granddad raises the shade — and it's true!
Snék pat sólnechnym luchóm	Everywhere there's sun and snow,
Brilliántami sverkájet,	It sparkles like diamonds
Atlivájet serebróm.	And shines like silver.
"Sláva Bógu! Sláva Bógu!",	"God be praised! God be praised!",
Détki vésela krichát,	The children shout in joy,
I v umé ikh vaznikájet	And picture in their minds
Ush kartín znakómykh rját:	Scenes they know so well:
Na saláskakh z gór katán'je,	Sledding down the hill,
I katán'je na kan'kákh...	Gliding on skates...
I Razhdéstvenskaja jólka,	And a Christmas tree,
Svérkhu dónizu v agnjákh!	In lights from top to bottom!

Text. **Alekséy Pleshchéyev**, 1873. Part 2 of a longer poem called "Из жизни" (From Life). First published in *Detskii sad* (Kindergarten), 1873, vol. 1. The title is Tchaikovsky's own. He omitted the first part of the poem, which is about the children coming home from school, and shortened the second part, keeping only 7 of the original 24 stanzas.

Meter. Binary. Trochaic, 4-foot:

> *Granddad, up at crack of dawn,*
> *Hurries to the children's room...*

Music. 1883. Op. 54, no. 12. D Major. 4/4, Moderato. For High Voice: d^1–e^2.

Recordings. Lemeshev, Levinsky, Pishchayev.

For "God be praised!" Lemeshev substitutes "Вот как славно!" (See how fine!), and the "Christmas tree" is a "trimmed tree" (украшенная ёлка).

✸

64 *Весенняя песня*
Spring song

Op. 54, No. 13

This poem takes the idea "greet the coming of spring with reverence—it is a miracle from God," and tries to convey that feeling to the reader. It was an article of faith with Pleshcheyev, just as his basic democratic outlook was. This attitude of reverence for nature is rather like the attitude in Boris Pasternak's late, "simplified" nature poetry, though Pleshcheyev is explicit where Pasternak, a much better poet, prefers to let direct description imply the awe he feels.

Tchaikovsky's music expresses this reverence. The song is a model of attractive simplicity. The anapests fall naturally into a slow waltz, and the words into a melody in A major which begs to be sung. The last line had to be censored (details below).

В старый сад выхожу я. Росинки,
Как алмазы, на листьях блестят.
И цветы мне головкой кивают,
Разливая кругом аромат.

Всё влечёт, веселит мои взоры:
Золотая пчела на цветке,
Разноцветные бабочки крылья
И синеющий лес вдалеке.

Как ярка эта зелень деревьев,
Купол неба как чист и глубок!
И брожу я, восторгом объятый,
И слеза застилает зрачок.

Как любовью и радостью дышит
Вся природа под вешним лучом,
И душа благодарная чует
Здесь присутствие Бога во всём!

F stáryj sát vykhazhú ja. Rasínki,   I walk out into the old garden. Drops of dew,
Kak almázy, na lístjakh blestját.   Like diamonds, glitter on the leaves.
I tsvetý mne galófkaj kivájut,   And flowers nod their heads at me,
Razlivája krugóm aramát.   Spreading their aroma all around.

Fsjo vlechót, veselít maji vzóry:	Everything attracts, delights my gaze:
Zalatája pchelá na tsvetké,	A golden bee on a flower,
Raznatsvétnyje bábachki krýl'ja	Many-colored wings of butterflies
I sinéjushchij lés vdaleké.	The dark blue forest in the distance.
Kak jarká eta zélen' derév'jef,	How clearly etched this green of trees,
Kúpal néba kak chíst i glubók!	How pure and deep the dome of sky!
I brazhú ja, vastórgam objátyj,	I wander, filled with ecstasy,
I slezá zastilájet zrachók.	And a tear blurs my eye.
Kak ljubóv'ju i rádast'ju dýshyt	How all of nature breathes love and joy
Fsja priróda pad véshnim luchóm,	In this vernal light,
I dushá blagadárnaja chújet	And a grateful soul senses
Zdes' prisútstvije Bóga va fsjóm!	Here the presence of God in everything!

Text. **Alekséy Pleshchéyev**, 1853. Title: Весна (Spring), with an epigraph from Goethe's "Mailied" (*Pleshcheev 1964*, 95-6). Tchaikovsky omitted one stanza, and changed the last line of the second stanza from "a sparrow hopping on the sand" to "a dark-blue forest in the distance." The title is his own.

First set by Tchaikovsky; later by Rebikov (1902, for a school songbook).

Meter. Ternary. Anapest, 3-foot:

> As I wálk through the gáte to the gárden,
> Drops of déw on the léaves are like díamonds…

Music. 1883. Op. 54, no. 13. A Major. 3/4, Allegro moderato (*dolce, molto espressivo*). For High Voice: e^1–e$^{2.}$

Recordings. Lemeshev, Levinsky, Pishchayev, Vinogradov.

In the last line, Vinogradov substituted the word "life" (жизни) for the word "God." Lemeshev changed the "garden" to a communal "park"; the final line is changed to "the breath of a new life in everything" (жизни новой дыханье во всём), a sentiment to which even the most orthodox Stalinist could not object.

ℬ

65 Осень
Autumn

Op. 54, No. 14

The mood is melancholy, but this beautifully composed song is very lovely.
It has three identical parts, each broken in two: declamatory then melodic.

Скучная картина!
Тучи без конца,
Дождик так и льётся,
Лужи у крыльца…
Чахлая рябина
Мокнет под окном;
Смотрит деревушка
Серьеньким пятном.

Что ты рано в гости,
Осень к нам пришла?
Еще просит сердце
Света и тепла!
Еще просит сердце
Света и тепла!

Все тебе не рады!
Твой унылый вид
Горе да невзгоды
Бедному сулит.
Слышит он заране
Крик и плач ребят;
Видит — как от стужи
Ночь они не спят.

Нет одежды тёплой,
Нету в печке дров…
Ты на чей же, осень,
Поспешила зов?
Ты на чей же, осень,
Поспешила зов?

Вон — и худ и бледен
Сгорбился больной…
Как он рад был солнцу —
Как был бодр весной!
А теперь — наводит
Жёлтых листьев шум
На душу больную
Рой зловещих дум!

Рано, рано, осень
В гости к нам пришла…
Многим — не дождаться
Света и тепла!
Многим — не дождаться
Света и тепла!

Skúshnaja kartína!
Túchi bes kantsá,
Dózhdik tak i ljótsa,
Lúzhy u kryl'tsá…
Chákhlaja rjabína
Móknet pad aknóm;
Smótrit derevúshka
Séren'kim pjatnóm.

Shtó ty rána v gósti,
Ósen' k nam prishlá?
Jeshcho prósit sérttse
Svéta i teplá!

Dreary picture!
Endless clouds,
Pouring rain,
Puddles by the porch…
The scrubby rowan tree
Under the window is soaked;
The village looks like
A gray smudge.

Autumn, early guest,
Why have you come so soon?
The heart craves its fill
Of light and warmth!

Jeshcho prósit sérttse	The heart craves its fill
Svéta i teplá!	Of light and warmth!
Fsé tebé ne rády!	No one's glad to see you!
Tvoj unýlyj vít	Your dismal look
Góre da nevzgódy	Promises a poor fellow
Bédnamu sulít.	Woe and bad luck.
Slýshyt on zaráne	Already he can hear
Krík i plách rebját;	The crying of the children;
Vídit — kak at stúzhy	He sees them in the freezing cold
Nóch aní ne spját.	Unable to sleep at night.
Nét adézhdy tjóplaj,	There's no warm clothing,
Nétu f péchke dróf...	There's no wood in the stove...
Ty na chéj zhe, ósen',	Whose invitation, autumn,
Paspeshýla zóf?	Do you hasten so to answer?
Ty na chéj zhe, ósen',	Whose invitation, autumn,
Paspeshýla zóf?	Do you hasten so to answer?
Vón — i khút i bléden	That ailing man there, thin and pale,
Zgórbilsa bal'nój...	See him, all bent over...
Kak on rát byl sóntsu —	How he welcomed the sun —
Kak byl bódr vesnój!	How sprightly he stepped in spring!
A tepér'— navódit	But now the swirling
Zhóltykh líst'jef shúm	Sound of yellow leaves
Ná dushu bal'núju	Brings to an ailing soul
Rój zlavéshchikh dúm!	A swarm of ominous thoughts!
Rána, rána, ósen'	Too soon, too soon, autumn
V gósti k nam prishlá...	Has come to visit us...
Mnógim — ne dazhdátsa	Many won't live to see again
Svéta i teplá!	Days of light and warmth!
Mnógim — ne dazhdátsa	Many won't live to see again
Svéta i teplá!	Days of light and warmth!

TEXT. **Alekséy Pleshchéyev**, date unknown, first published in 1860 in *Narodnoe chtenie* (Popular reading), no. 4. Untitled. Included in *Snowdrop* with the present title. First set by Tchaikovsky; also by Rebikov, for a school songbook. The repetitions are Tchaikovsky's.

METER. Binary. Trochaic, 3-foot:
> *Why so early, autumn —*
> *No one's glad to see you!*

MUSIC. 1883. Op. 54, no. 14. F-sharp Minor. 3/4, Moderato assai. For High Voice: f^1 sharp–e^2. Transcribed for voice with orchestra by Taneyev (1891).

RECORDINGS. Gmyria, Lemeshev, Levinsky, Pishchayev, Reizen, Vinogradov.

66 Ласточка
Swallow

Op. 54, No. 15

Like Song 62, this text evokes pity for a man in prison far from home, but Ivan Surikov gives it the feel of a Russian folk lyric. The poem is a translation from Polish of "Jaskółka" (Swallow) by Teofil Lenartowicz. The translation is close to the original, but there is a difference. In the Polish, the girl is free of cares and the prettiest lass in the village. But Surikov makes her an "orphan," an image signalling abandonment or isolation or separation from closest kin, in this case her brother. When Taneyev wrote Tchaikovsky about the Opus 54 songs, he included this one in his list of "small masterpieces," referring to it simply as "Сиротка" (Orphan girl, *Taneev*, 106). Surikov also omits the brother's question in the Polish original, "does she still wear a white rose in her fair hair?", an image quite foreign to the system of flower imagery in Russian folk poetry.

Идет девочка–сиротка,
　　Тяжело вздыхает,
А над нею, горемычной,
　　Ласточка летает.

И летает и щебечет,
　　Над головкой вьётся,
Вьётся крошка и крылами
　　В косу чуть не бьётся.

«Что ты вьёшься надо мною,
　　Над сироткой, пташка?
Ах, оставь меня, — и так мне
　　Жить на свете тяжко!»

— Не оставлю, не оставлю!
　　Буду я кружиться, —
Щебетать тебе про брата,
　　Что в тюрьме томится.

Он просил меня: «Слетай-ка,
　　Пташка, в край родимый, —
Поклонись моей сестрице,
　　Горячо любимой.

Всё ль меня она, голубка,
　　Добром вспоминает?
Всё ль она ещё о брате
　　Слёзы проливает?»

Idjot dévachka–sirótka,
　　Tjazheló vzdykhájet,
A nad néju, garemýchnaj,
　　Lástachka letájet.

I letájet i shchebéchet,
　　Nad galófkaj v'jótsa,
V'jotsa króshka i krylámi
　　F kósu chut' ne b'jótsa.

A little orphan girl is walking,
　　Breathing heavy sighs,
And over her unlucky head
　　A little swallow flies.

It flies and chirps,
　　And circles overhead,
With such a flutter of its little wings
　　It almost hits her braid.

"Shtó ty v'jóshsa nada mnóju,	"Birdie, why do you pester me,
Nad sirótkaj, ptáshka?	Me, an orphan girl?
Akh, astáf' menja, — i ták mne	Leave me alone — as it is
Zhýt' na svéte tjáshka!"	My life is hard enough!"
— Ne astávlju, ne astávlju!	— I won't leave, I won't leave!
Búdu ja kruzhýtsa, —	I'll keep circling, —
Shchebetát' tebe pra bráta,	Chirping to you about your brother,
Shto f tjur'mé tamítsa.	Who pines away in prison.
Ón prasíl menjá: "Sletáj-ka,	He sent me to you: "Fly home,
Ptáshka, f kráj radímaj, —	Birdie, to my native land, —
Paklanís' majej sestrítse,	Greet my little sister for me,
Garjachó ljubímaj.	Warmly do I love her.
Fsjó l' menjá, aná, galúpka,	Does she still, dear little dove,
Dobróm fspaminájet?	Think of me with kindness?
Fsjó l' aná jeshchó a bráte	Does she still shed some tears
Sljózy pralivájet?"	For her brother?"

Text. **Iván Súrikov**, 1872. Title: Ласточка (Из Т. Ленартовича) (Swallow, From T. Lenartowicz). Published in the anthology *Rassvet* (Dawn), 1872, no. 1; republished in subsequent editions of Surikov's poems in 1875, 1877, 1884. For other song texts by Surikov, see Song 51.

The poem is a translation of "Jaskółka" (Swallow) by **Teofil Lenartowicz**, 1853 (see Song 31). Surikov found it in an 1863 edition of Lenartowicz's poems published in Poznań (*Surikov 1951*, 330).

Tchaikovsky changed two words in Surikov's poem: in line 1, he substituted девочка (little girl) for девица (maiden), and he changed the form добрым in the last stanza to добром.

Meter. Binary. Trochaic, alternating 4- and 3-foot lines:
> *Birdie, to my native land,*
> *Fly and greet my sister...*

Music. 1883. Op. 54, no. 15. G Major—G Minor. 2/4, Allegro moderato. For High Voice: d¹ sharp–e².

Recordings. Levinsky, Pishchayev.

❧

67   *Детская песенка (Мой Лизочек)*
 Nursery song (My Lizzie-lad)

Op. 54, No. 16

This charming favorite was written in 1881 and added to the fifteen 1883 songs. The text by Konstantin Aksakov (1817-1860) is called "An Mariechen." Aksakov never published it, but it was well known from the time it was written in 1836. It first saw print in 1881 when Jurgenson published this song in a separate edition.

Aksakov's poem is addressed to "Mariechen," a German diminutive of Marie. By changing the little girl's name to "Lizochek," a Russian diminutive of Yelizaveta, Tchaikovsky makes the song solidly Russian in one stroke. "Lizochek" is a form of the name which brings in an element of play because it puts a masculine suffix onto a girl's name, and henceforth all the verbs and pronouns in the song have to be masculine too (this play with gender is already there in the Aksakov poem). Using a diminutive this way in Russian is common in the family and is taken to be playful and affectionate. My translation is a compromise: "Lizzie-lad" for the girl whose name sounds like a boy's, but "she" for the pronouns rather than "he."

> Мой Лизочек так уж мал, так уж мал,
> Что из крыльев комаришки
> Сделал две себе манишки,
>   И — в крахмал, и в крахмал!
>
> Мой Лизочек так уж мал, так уж мал,
> Что из грецкого ореха
> Сделал стул, чтоб слушать эхо,
>   И кричал, и кричал!
>
> Мой Лизочек так уж мал, так уж мал,
> Что из скорлупы яичной
> Фаетон себе отличный
>   Заказал, заказал!
>
> Мой Лизочек так уж мал, так уж мал,
> Что из скорлупы рачонка
> Сшил четыре башмачонка
>   И — на бал, и — на бал!

Мой Лизочек так уж мал, так уж мал,
Что из листика сирени
Сделал зонтик он для тени
　　И гулял, и гулял!

Мой Лизочек так уж мал, так уж мал,
Что, надувши одуванчик,
Заказал себе диванчик,
　　Тут и спал, тут и спал!

Мой Лизочек так уж мал, так уж мал,
Что наткать себе холстины
Пауку из паутины
　　Заказал, заказал,
Он наткать себе холстины
Пауку из паутины
　　Заказал, заказал!

Moj Lizóchek tak ush mál, tak ush mál,
Shto is krýl'ev kamaríshki
Zdélal dvé sebé maníshki,
I — f krakhmál, i f krakhmál!

My Lizzie-lad's so small, she's so small,
That from the wings of a mosquito
She made herself a pair of collars,
And — off to be starched, off to be
starched!

Moj Lizóchek tak ush mál, tak ush mál,
Shto iz grétskava arékha
Zdélal stúl, shtop slúshat' ékha,
I krichál, i krichál!

My Lizzie-lad's so small, she's so small,
That from a nice round walnut
She made a chair with built-in echo,
And shouted loud, shouted loud!

Moj Lizóchek tak ush mál, tak ush mál,
Shto is skarlupý jaíchnaj
Faetón sebé atlíchnyj
Zakazál, zakazál!

My Lizzie-lad's so small, she's so small,
From the shell of just one egg
She had a fancy fine new phaeton
Commanded to be made, to be made!

Moj Lizóchek tak ush mál, tak ush mál,
Shto is skarlupý rachónka
Sshil chetýre bashmachónka
I — na bál, i — na bál!

My Lizzie-lad's so small, she's so small,
From the shell of just one crayfish
She sewed herself four slippers
And — off to the ball, off to the ball!

Moj Lizóchek tak ush mál, tak ush mál,
Shto iz lístika siréni
Zdélal zóntik on dlja téni
I guljál, i guljál!

My Lizzie-lad's so small, she's so small,
That from a little leaf of lilac
She made a parasol to shade her
And strolled around, strolled around!

Moj Lizóchek tak ush mál, tak ush mál,
Shto, nadúfshy aduvánchik,
Zakazál sebé divánchik,
Tut y spál, tut y spál!

My Lizzie-lad's so small, she's so small,
That, just by puffing at a puffball,
She had enough to stuff a sofa,
And there she slept, there she slept!

Moj Lizóchek tak ush mál, tak ush mál,
Shto natkát' sebé khalstíny
Paukú is pautíny
Zakazál, zakazál,
On natkát' sebé khalstíny
Paukú is pautíny
Zakazál, zakazál!

My Lizzie-lad's so small, she's so small,
To spin a piece of gingham
She found a spider in its web
And put him to work, put him to work,
To spin a piece of gingham
She found a spider in its web
And put him to work, put him to work!

Text. **Konstantín Aksákov**, 1836. Title: An Mariechen (To Little Marie). First published in 1881 with the Tchaikovsky song. Aksakov's poem was popular and there were copies of it in circulation, which is presumably how Tchaikovsky found it (see *Mashinskii*, 1964). In Tchaikovsky's song, the order of two of the stanzas is different and there is a small difference in wording in the sixth stanza. Tchaikovsky repeated the punch line each time, and added a short reprise at the end.

Meter. Binary. Trochaic, 4-foot, but made asymmetrical by the repetition of "так уж мал" in the first line of each stanza, and by the truncated short lines which end each stanza, ingeniously all on the same masculine rhyme:

> *Lizzie-lad's so very small, very small,*
> *From the shell of just one crayfish*
> *Did she sew her dancing slippers —*
> *Off to the ball! Off to the ball!*

Music. 1881. Written two years before the other fifteen songs of Op. 54, and included with them as no. 16. A Minor. 2/4, Allegro moderato. For High Voice: e^1–e^2.

Recordings. Christoff, Kurenko, Lemeshev, Levinsky, Pishchayev, Slobodskaya.

6 Romances, Opus 57 (1884)

In March 1884 Tchaikovsky was summoned to St. Petersburg to be presented to the Tsar. At Gatchina palace outside the city Alexander III and his wife Maria Fyodorovna received him with notable kindness and affection. He walked away wearing the order of St. Vladimir, but more important than that, the reception given him by the Emperor and Empress symbolized recognition at the highest level of his achievement as a Russian composer. It was based above all on the genuine success his music had had with the Russian public. When he returned to Petersburg later that year, three of his operas were being performed in the city—*The Maid of Orleans*, *Mazeppa*, and *Eugene Onegin*, this latter to full houses every night. He had achieved fame at home and abroad. Yet at the very time this was happening, the critics were saying he had written himself out. Nearly every recent review spoke of "a decline in his creative powers," as Cui had put it in his review of *Mazeppa* (*DG*, 309). Every time he had a dry spell, or felt frustrated getting some section of a work in progress right, he thought of this, and wondered with some anxiety whether it might not be true.

Staying with his sister Sasha and her husband Lev Davydov on their Ukrainian estate at Kamenka, he wrote in his diary on the night before his birthday (25 April/7 May) in 1884: "Eleven o'clock. I am about to turn 44. How much has been lived, and, in truth, without false modesty, how little accomplished! Even in my real *work*: in all honesty, none of it is *perfect*, *exemplary*. I'm still searching, hesitating, wandering. And for the rest? I read nothing, I know nothing. All I do is waste precious time on vint [a Russian card-game resembling bridge]. But I know it isn't *helping* my *health*. I lost my temper today, got so angry, it seemed any moment I would make an ugly scene full of hatred and spite. In general I was irritable all day, and the period of calm, untroubled, quiet life has passed. Too much fuss, aggravation, everything a maniac my age can no longer take with indifference. No, it's time to live *in my own place* and *in my own way*" (*Dnevniki*, 14-15). But by the end of May, he realized he would have to put off buying his own place until he had sufficient funds (*DG*, 318).

Nevertheless, a day or two after his birthday, he started a serious new work, his Third Suite, Op. 55. He finished it at the end of July (when it was first performed in the two capitals in January 1885, the audiences were so moved by the music that no one could remember such applause for a new Russian orchestral work). His attempts to learn English were paying off: he was reading *David Copperfield* almost without a dictionary, even though he still could not understand a single sentence Miss Eastwood, the English governess at Kamenka, said at the dinner table. Aside from listening to Aleksandra Davydova reminisce about Pushkin's visits to Kamenka in the 1820s (she was the mother of Lev, and widow of the Decembrist Vasily Davydov), and playing the piano with his thirteen-year-old nephew Bob Davydov, there was little at his sister's house that gave him pleasure any more.

He spent September on one of Mrs. von Meck's estates at Pleshcheyevo near Moscow. There he wrote the second and third songs of Opus 57. In Paris in November he wrote the last three. Four of them were dedicated to singers who had taken part in the premiere of *Mazeppa* in Moscow earlier in the year. He had worked closely with them during rehearsals, accompanying them at the piano.

The Opus 57 songs have been called "a kind of intermezzo," situated between the "heights" already achieved in earlier romances, and the "heights" still ahead (*Vasina-Grossman*, 288). But they are really more than that, because they have a focus of their own. They come at the end of a period of taking stock. One of the themes is death (Songs 71 and 72), treated as something to be accepted as an inevitable and even welcome part of life. The other songs are about love as the primary force in life, whether given or not. Each of the songs has a summarizing force. In their inevitability and finality they confirm the mature acceptance of the tragic which is an essential dimension of Tchaikovsky's music.

68 Скажи, о чём в тени ветвей
Say of what, in the shade of branches

Op. 57, No. 1

Tchaikovsky knew this text as a young man in Petersburg. It comes from a one-act "comedy-vaudeville" by Count Vladimir Sollogub (1813-1882) called "Trouble from a Tender Heart," in which the young heroine sings this lyric. Tchaikovsky acted in an amateur production of the play in 1860 or 1861 (*DG*, 28). Much later, at his sister's estate in Kamenka in the Ukraine, he wrote music for a home production of the play, evidently a favorite of his. This setting of the song may go back to that, although the music for the entertainment at Kamenka is lost. The song is a beautiful concert showpiece for soprano.

Скажи, о чём в тени ветвей,
Когда природа отдыхает,
Поёт весенний соловей,
И что он песней выражает?
Что тайно всем волнует кровь?
Скажи, скажи, скажи, какое слово
Знакомо всем и вечно ново?
Любовь! любовь, любовь!

Скажи, о чём наедине,
В раздумьи, девушка гадает,
Что тайным трепетом во сне
Ей страх и радость обещает?
Недуг тот странный назови,

В котором светлая отрада,
Чего ей ждать, чего ей надо:
Любви! любви!

Скажи! когда от жизненной тоски
Ты утомлённый изнываешь,
И злой печали вопреки
Хоть призрак счастья призываешь,
Что услаждает грудь твою?
Не те ли звуки неземные,
Когда услышал ты впервые
Слова, слова любви!
Когда услышал ты впервые
Слова, слова любви!

Skazhý, a chóm f tení vetvéj,
Kagdá priróda addykhájet,
Pajót vesénnij salavéj,
I shtó on pésnej vyrazhájet?
Shtó tájna fsém valnújet króf'?
Skazhý, skazhý, skazhý, kakóje slóva
Znakóma fsém i véchna nóva?
Ljubóf', ljubóf', ljubóf'!

Skazhý, a chóm najediné,
V razdúm'ji, dévushka gadájet,
Shtó tájnym trépetam va sné
Jej strákh i rádast' abeshchájet?

Say of what, in the shade of branches,
When all of nature is at rest,
Is the nightingale singing in the spring,
What does his song express?
Why does it strangely stir our blood?
Say, say, say, what is that word
Known to all and always new?
Love, love, love!

What does a girl, in solitary thought,
Guess and wonder about,
What secret tremor in her sleep
Promises fear and gladness?

Nedúk tot stránnyj nazaví,	Name the strange affliction
F katóram svétlaja atráda,	Which is the bright joy
Chevó jej zhdát', chevó jej náda:	She wants and waits for:
Ljubví! ljubví!	Love! love!

Skazhý! kagdá ad zhýznennaj taskí	When life brings yearning,
Ty utamljónnyj iznyvájesh,	When you languish and pine away,
I zlój pecháli vaprekí	And, despite dejection,
Khat' prízrak shchást'ja prizyvájesh,	Wish for a ghost of happiness,
Shtó uslazhdájet grút' tvajú?	What can make your heart glad?
Ne té li zvúki nezemnýje,	Is it not those heavenly sounds,
Kagdá uslýshal ty fpervýje	When you heard for the first time
Slavá, slavá ljubví!	The words, words of love!
Kagdá uslýshal ty fpervýje	When you heard for the first time
Slavá, slavá ljubví!	The words, words of love!

TEXT. **Vladímir Sollogúb**, c. 1850. From "Беда от нежного сердца" (Trouble from a tender heart), a "comedy-vaudeville" in one act, published in St. Petersburg in 1850 (republished in 1945 in *Russkie klassicheskie vodevili*). The text is very similar to an 1827 poem entitled "Любовь" (Love), which begins "О чём, о чём в тени ветвей" (Of what, of what, in the shade of branches), written by the Decembrist Pavel Katenin (1792-1853). It has been suggested by D. G. Daragan that they both go back to an unknown original in a foreign language (note in the Index of Vocal Works seen at Klin in May 1998). Set earlier by some minor composers.

METER. Binary. Iambic tetrameter:
> *What secret tremor in her sleep*
> *Brings promises of fear and joy?*

MUSIC. Op. 57, no. 1. E Major. 4/4, Andante sostenuto. For High Voice: d^1 sharp–a^2. Written at an unknown date before the other songs in this opus. When Tchaikovsky learned that F. P. Komissarzhevsky had a copy of it, he included it in the set, and dedicated the song to him. **Fyódor Petróvich Komissarzhévsky**, Russian tenor, 1838-1905, created the role of Vakula in the 1876 premiere of *Vakula the Smith*. He taught opera classes, both singing and acting, at the Moscow Conservatory from 1883-88 (Stanislavsky took lessons from him); father of the famous actress Vera Komissarzhevskaya.

RECORDINGS. Dolukhanova, Kasrashvili, Kovalyova, Larin, Lemeshev, Irina Maslennikova, Leokadiya Maslennikova, Milashkina, Ognivtsev, Podleś, Rautio, Shpiller, Shumskaya, Sterling, Vishnevskaya.

69 *На нивы жёлтые*
On yellow fields of grain

Op. 57, No. 2

The love poems by Aleksey Tolstoy which Tchaikovsky used earlier as romance lyrics (Songs 4, 7, 40, 41, 42, and 48) form a cycle of occasional poems loosely connected in theme and prompted by Tolstoy's sometimes troubled relationship with his wife. The present text, written in 1872, is the last in this cycle. Like Song 42 and another poem related to it which Tchaikovsky did not set, "К страданиям чужим, ты горести полна" (For others' sufferings you are full of sorrow), it consists of two quatrains in long iambic hexameter lines:

> На нивы жёлтые нисходит тишина,
> В остывшем воздухе от меркнущих селений,
> Дрожа, несётся звон... Душа моя полна
> Разлукою с тобой и горьких сожалений.
>
> И каждый мой упрёк я вспоминаю вновь,
> И каждое твержу приветливое слово,
> Что мог бы я сказать тебе, моя любовь,
> Но что внутри себя я схоронил сурово.

> On yellow fields of grain silence descends,
> In the cool evening air from darkening villages,
> Trembling, a gong resounds... My soul is filled
> With your absence and with bitter regrets.

> And I recall anew each cold reproach I uttered,
> And I repeat each loving word of welcome
> I might have said to you, my love,
> But which within myself I kept guarded sternly.

The theme is remorse—the poet's realization at last that he, too, is to blame for her unhappiness, because of his own failure to love fully. Something stoic in him held him back. The pain he feels is one of desolation, his soul "filled with her absence," but the theme of separation, so common in lyric poetry, is accompanied here by "bitter regrets." Tolstoy always brings to these love poems a sense of ready understanding of the unhappiness of the woman he loves, but it is unique that he should admit, as he does here, his own large share of the blame for it. This same theme of remorse occurs in his cousin's epic novel *War and Peace*, when Prince Andrey tells Pierre that "remorse and illness are the only two real evils in life, and their absence is the only good." But the remorse Andrey becomes conscious of after his wife dies in childbirth, when he realizes his inability to undo the coldness with which he treated her when she was alive, is expressed in French—in the middle of a conversation entirely in Russian—in the form of a philosophical aphorism, elegantly put, universally true, and therefore absolving everyone from particular blame. There is stoicism in it, and even passion of a cold, intellectual kind, but not that desolation of soul expressed in Aleksey Tolstoy's poem.

After Tchaikovsky, other composers were drawn to several of these same poems, especially Rimsky-Korsakov, who set four of them (the texts to Songs 4, 40, 42, and the present text). Rimsky-Korsakov's beautiful word-for-word setting of this poem is in F major, at first idyllic and reflective, then, with rising intonation, warm and ardent in its affirmation of love; there are hints of "bitter regrets" in notes that stray from the major key, but if they acknowledge loss, it is not a loss that is irrevocable. Rather than remorse, his song conveys a memory of pain that has been overcome.

What Tchaikovsky wished to express was the tragic finality he found in the poem. He broke up key lines, repeated phrases, made emphatic additions, and changed one telling phrase in the last line from "внутри себя" (within myself) to "на дне души" (at the bottom of my soul). The deep sound of the bell is a call to reflection, brought out with arpeggio chords. The first line is shaped by falling intonation on the phrase "silence descends"; this is echoed in the third line, and again on the words "guarded sternly." This stanza is a new section of the song, with a rising intonation that denotes anxious struggle. Between these two sections is the refrain, created by Tchaikovsky for the song by repeating the lines "my soul is filled with your absence and with bitter regrets." The conclusion of the song is a reprise of this refrain. After this emphatic restatement, there can be no doubt of the irrevocable nature of this pain and the remorse it brings.

> На нивы жёлтые нисходит тишина,
> В остывшем воздухе от меркнущих селений,
> Дрожа, несётся звон...
>
> Душа моя полна
> разлукою с тобой,
> душа моя полна
> разлукою с тобой
> и горьких сожалений.
>
> И каждый мой упрёк я вспоминаю вновь,
> И каждое твержу приветливое слово,
> Что мог бы я сказать тебе, моя любовь, моя любовь,
> Но что на дне души я схоронил сурово.
>
> Душа моя полна
> разлукою с тобой!

Душа моя полна
разлукою с тобой
и горьких сожалений.

Na nívy zhóltyje niskhódit tishyná,	On yellow fields of grain silence descends,
V astýfshem vózdukhe	In the cool evening air
at mérknushchikh selénij,	from darkening villages,
Drazhá, nesjótsa zvón...	Trembling, resounds a gong...
Dushá majá palná	My soul is filled
razlúkaju s tabój,	with your absence,
dushá majá palná	my soul is filled
razlúkaju s tabój	with your absence
i gór'kikh sazhalénij.	and with bitter regrets.
I kázhdyj moj uprjók ja vspamináju	And I recall anew each cold reproach
vnóf',	I uttered,
I kázhdaje tverzhú privétlivaje slóva,	And I repeat each loving word of welcome
Shto móg by ja skazát' tebé, majá	I might have said to you, my love,
ljubóf', majá ljubóf',	my love,
No shto na dné dushý ja skharaníl	But at the bottom of my soul kept guarded
suróva.	sternly.
Dushá majá palná	My soul is filled
razlúkaju s tabój!	with your absence!
Dushá majá palná	My soul is filled
razlúkaju s tabój	with your absence
i gór'kikh sazhalénij.	and with bitter regrets.

TEXT. **Alekséy Tolstóy**, 1862. First set by Tchaikovsky; later by Rimsky-Korsakov (Op. 39/3, 1887).

METER. Binary. Iambic hexameter:

On yellow fields of grain the evening silence falls,
And in the air from distant villages darkening there,
A trembling gong resounds. Your absence fills my soul...

MUSIC. 1884. Op. 57, no. 2. F Minor. 4/4, Andante. For Baritone: d natural–g¹ flat. Dedicated to **Bogomír Kórsov**, to whom Tchaikovsky had earlier dedicated Song 37 (*q.v.*). Korsov sang Mazeppa at the opera's premiere in Moscow in February 1884.

RECORDINGS. Dolukhanova, Eizen, Fischer-Dieskau, Guliayev, Hvorostovsky, Aleksey Ivanov, Koshetz, Leiferkus, Lemeshev, Levko, Nesterenko, **Nortsov**, Ognivtsev, Pirogov, Reizen, Serkebayev, Slobodskaya, Vedernikov, Vishnevskaya.

Rimsky-Korsakov: Baikov, Borisenko.

70 *Не спрашивай*
Ask no question

Op. 57, No. 3

Another powerful song, this is Tchaikovsky's third song that uses a lyric from Goethe's novel *Wilhelm Meister*. He came upon it by chance. Spending the month of September 1884 at Mrs. von Meck's estate in Pleshcheyevo, he found the novel in her library. He wrote his brother Modest that he was reading it for the first time, and added "It's a revelation; I always thought it would be a terrible bore, but good God, how charming it is, and how glad I am that I happened to come across it" (*DG*, 324).

The two lyrics he had found earlier for Songs 9 and 21 (published separately from the novel in translations by Mey and Tyutchev) were known as "Mignon's songs," because the character Mignon sings them during the course of the novel. But now he encountered this mysterious character herself—think of her as a kind of early version of Gelsomina in Fellini's "La Strada"—when she first appears, and, sybil-like, delivers the words which are the lyric to this song. He recognized its power, and wrote a song that conveys that power with dramatic force.

The translation he used, by Aleksandr Strugovshchikov (1808-1878), is extraordinarily good. Strugovshchikov warned the reader that his translations of Goethe and Schiller were not strictly speaking translations, but Russian poems inspired by the originals (*Strugovshchikov*). Belinsky criticized him for it (*Etkind*, II, 397), but this practice was widely accepted in Russia and produced some outstanding poems. The repeated stresses on the broad Russian "a" and the tense "y" give the lyric a strong music of its own. Tchaikovsky changed the word *vershina* (height) to the plural (*vershiny*); the repetitions are his own. To the Adagio marking he added the words "con disperazione, ma quieto."

Не спрашивай, не вызывай признанья!
Молчания лежит на мне печать:
Всё высказать — одно моё желанье,
Но втайне я обречена страдать!

Там вечный лёд вершины покрывает,
Здесь на поля легла ночная тень:
С весною вновь источник заиграет,
С зарёю вновь проглянет Божий день,
С зарёю вновь проглянет Божий день.

И всем, и всем дано в час скорби утешенье,
Указан друг, чтоб сердце облегчить:
Мне с клятвой на устах дано одно терпенье,
И только Бог,
И только Бог их может разрешить!

Ne spráshyvaj, ne vyzyváj priznán'ja!	Ask no question, nor bid me bare my soul!
Malchánija lezhýt na mné pechát':	My vow of silence is unbreakable:
Fsjó výskazat'— adnó majó zhelán'je,	My one desire is to tell everything,
No ftájne ja abrechená stradát'!	But my fate is to suffer in secret!

Tam véchnyj ljót vershýny pakryvájet,	Eternal ice covers the heights above,
Zdes' na paljá leglá nachnája tén':	Here below, night's shadow lies on the fields:
S vesnóju vnof' istóchnik zaigrájet,	With spring the pure stream will flow again,
Z zarjóju vnof' pragljánet Bózhij dén',	With dawn God's daylight will shine forth,
Z zarjóju vnof' pragljánet Bózhij dén'.	With dawn God's daylight will shine forth.

I fsém, i fsém danó f chas skórbi uteshén'je,	All, all are given comfort in the hour of painful grief,
Ukázan drúk, shtop sérttse ablekchít':	A friend to ease the troubled heart:
Mné s kljátvaj na ustákh danó adnó terpén'je,	To me patience alone is ordained, with a vow on my lips,
I tól'ka Bókh,	And only God,
I tól'ka Bókh ikh mózhet razreshýt'!	And only God can unseal them!

TEXT. **Aleksándr Strugovshchikóv**, 1845. A translation of "Heiß mich nicht reden" from Book 3 of *Wilhelm Meisters Lehrjahre* (1795) by **Goethe**. First set by Gurilyov (1853). The German original has been set by several composers, including Schubert (twice), Schumann, and Wolf.

METER. Binary. Iambic pentameter:

> *The heights above are bound in solid ice,*
> *The fields below are hidden by the night...*

MUSIC. 1884. Op. 57, no. 3. D Minor. 3/4, Adagio molto sostenuto. For Middle Voice: a–g². Dedicated to the soprano **Emília Pavlóvskaya** (1853-1935), a favorite singer of Tchaikovsky's. She was a pupil of Camillo Everardi (see SINGERS & RECORDINGS, p. 297). She sang the first Tatyana at the Mariinsky, and was the first to sing Maria in *Mazeppa*. Tchaikovsky corresponded with Pavlovskaya, who wrote a short memoir about him (*Bortnikova* 172-5).

RECORDINGS. **Arkhipova**, Bogachova, Christoff, Dolukhanova, Kasrashvili, Kovalyova, Mkrtchyan, Obraztsova, Söderström, Vishnevskaya.

71 *Усни!*
Fall asleep!

Op. 57, No. 4

Tchaikovsky kept up, though not systematically, with the "fat" journals that were the principal forum of Russian literature—and Russian history, art, and philosophy, too—for a hundred years, from Pushkin's *Современник* (*Contemporary*) in the 1830s to Gorky's *Беседа* (*Colloquy*) in the 1920s. In recent issues of such journals he found poems by a new name, Dmitry Merezhkovsky (1865-1941), just beginning what turned out to be an influential career as a writer. He had never chosen texts by a young unknown poet before.

The lyric for this and the next song are both on the theme of death, or dying, but they treat the theme in original ways. The first line of this poem, with its images of grass and the cradle, makes one wonder if Merezhkovsky had been reading Walt Whitman. He certainly knew Lermontov, whose poem "I walk out alone onto the road" is one of the most famous in all of Russian poetry, a poem about dying, but not exactly losing consciousness; rather, falling asleep and hearing the rustling above him of a dark oak, forever green.

The song is tender and lyrical, a lullaby of sorts but treated freely. There are two outstanding recordings of it by Katulskaya and Kozlovsky. Kozlovsky holds the fermata notes on the last syllable of the word "усни" (fall asleep), marked "ad libitum," for a very long time, to beautiful effect.

> Уснуть бы мне навек в траве, как в колыбели,
> Как я ребёнком спал в те солнечные дни,
>   Когда в лучах полуденных звенели
>   Весёлых жаворонков трели
>   И пели мне они:
>   «Усни, усни, усни!»
>
> И крылья пёстрых мух с причудливой окраской
> На венчиках цветов дрожали, как огни,
>   И шум дерев казался чудной сказкой;
>   Мой сон лелея, с тихой лаской,
>   Баюкали они:
>   «Усни, усни, усни!»
>
> И убегая в даль, как волны золотые,
> Давали мне приют в задумчивой тени,
>   Под кущей верб, поля мои, поля родные,
>   Склонив колосья наливные,
>   Шептали мне они:
>   «Усни, усни, усни, усни!»

Usnúd' by mne navék f travé,
  kak f kalybéli,
Kak ja rebjónkam spál f te sólnechnyje dní,
Kagdá v luchákh palúdennykh zvenéli
Vesjólykh zhávarankaf tréli
I péli mne aní:
"Usní, usní, usní!"

I krýl'ja pjóstrykh múkh s prichúdlivaj
  akráskaj
Na vénchikakh tsvetóf drazháli, kak agní,
I shum deréf kazálsa chúdnaj
  skáskaj;
Moj son leléja, s tíkhaj láskaj,
Bajúkali aní:
"Usní, usní, usní!"

I ubegája v dál', kak vólny zalatýje,
Daváli mne prijút v zadúmchivaj tení,
Pat kúshchej vérp, paljá mají, poljá radnýje,
Sklaníf kalós'ja nalivnýje,
Sheptáli mne aní:
"Usní, usní, usní, usní!"

To fall asleep forever in the grass,
  as in the cradle,
When as a child I slept on sunlit days,
And in the bright rays of noon rang loud
The happy trills of the larks
And they sang to me:
"To sleep, to sleep, to sleep!"

And motley flies with irridescent
  wings
Trembled on the flower tops like lights,
And the rustling trees were like a magic
  fairy tale;
Rocking my sleep, with a soft caress,
They sang me a lullaby:
"To sleep, to sleep, to sleep!"

And stretching far like golden waves
That offer refuge in the pensive shade
Beneath a willow crest, my native fields,
Their ripe ears of grain bending down,
Kept whispering to me:
"To sleep, to sleep, to sleep, to sleep!"

TEXT. **Dmítry Merezhkóvsky**, 1884. Title: Усни (Fall asleep). First published in *Russkaia mysl'* (Russian Thought), 1884, no. 5, p. 351 (*Merezhkovskii*, 636). First set by Tchaikovsky; later by Nikolay Tcherepnin. Tchaikovsky inserted a few repetitions into the original text.

METER. Binary. Two hexameters followed by lines of 5, 4, 3, and 2 feet:

> *To fall asleep forever in the grass, the cradle,*
> *As when I was a child and slept on sunlit days,*
> *At noon the air was bright and filled with ringing,*
> *The happy trilling of the larks,*
> *Who sang a lullaby:*
> *"To sleep, to sleep!"*

MUSIC. 1884. Op. 57, no. 4. F Major. 3/4, Andante sostenuto. For Middle Voice: b–f². Dedicated to **Véra Butakóva** (1848-1923), née Davydova, a relative by marriage.

RECORDINGS. Katulskaya, Kozlovsky, Tugarinova.

72 Смерть
Death

Op. 57, No. 5

Even as a young man—Merezhkovsky was only 18 when he wrote this poem—he was already interested in "philosophical" questions which later characterized his poems, novels, and literary essays. This is one of those young man's "wise" poems that became fashionable in the early days of the Russian Symbolist movement in which Merezhkovsky was a principal leader.

Tchaikovsky saw the possibilities here for an original song on a subject usually associated with lamentation. Death is a gift of nature. The song he wrote is a slow waltz, with rising intonation. There are hints of drama in the second section but the basic mood is calm acceptance. It is an unusual and beautiful song that has been overlooked. The recordings of it are few but very fine.

Если розы тихо осыпаются,
Если звёзды меркнут в небесах,
Об утёсы волны разбиваются,
Гаснет луч зари на облаках,
Это смерть, смерть,

Это смерть — но без борьбы мучительной;
Это смерть, пленяя красотой,
Обещает отдых упоительный —
Лучший дар природы всеблагой.

У неё, наставницы божественной,
Научитесь, люди, умирать,
Чтоб с улыбкой кроткой и торжественной,
Чтоб с улыбкой кроткой и торжественной,
Свой конец безропотно встречать.

Jesli rózy tíkha asypájutsa,	If roses shed their petals quietly,
Jesli zvjózdy mérknut v nebesákh,	If stars grow dimmer in the sky,
Ab utjósy vólny razbivájutsa,	Waves against the cliffs are smashed to bits,
Gásnet lúch zarí na ablakákh,	Sunset's colors fade against the clouds,
Èta smért', smért',	That is death, death,

Èta smért' — no bez bar'bý   That is death — without the pain of
  muchítel'naj;   struggle,
Èta smért', plenjája krasatój,   That is death, with captivating beauty,
Abeshchájet óddykh upaítel'nyj —   Promising to ravish us with rest —
Lúchshij dár priródy fseblagój.   Best of gifts that blessed nature gives.

U nejó, nastávnitsy bazhéstvennaj,   Learn from her, divine mentor,
Nauchítes', ljúdi, umirát',   Learn, human folk, the way to die,
Shtop s ulýpkaj krótkaj   And with a smile of meekness
  i tarzhéstvennaj,   and of triumph,
Shtop s ulýpkaj krótkaj   And with a smile of meekness
  i tarzhéstvennaj,   and of triumph,
Svoj kanéts bezrópatna fstrechát'.   Face your end without complaint.

TEXT. **Dmítry Merezhkóvsky**, 1883. Untitled. First published in the journal *Otechestvennye zapiski* (Notes of the Fatherland), 1883, no. 11, p. 214 (*Merezhkovskii*, 633). First set by Tchaikovsky, who added the title and the repetitions; later set by Nikolay Tcherepnin (1909).

METER. Binary. Trochaic pentameter:

> *That is death, without the pain of struggle,*
> *That is death, with captivating beauty,*
> *Promising to ravish us with rest —*
> *Best of gifts that blessed nature gives.*

MUSIC. 1884. Op. 57, no. 5. F Major. 3/4, Moderato. For High Voice: d^1–g^2. Dedicated to **Dmítry Andréyevich Usátov** (1847-1913), Russian tenor. Son of a domestic serf of Count Sheremetev, he studied singing with Everardi at the St. Petersburg Conservatory. Sang at the Bolshoy 1880-89. He performed Song 15 in concerts at the Russian Music Society in 1877, 1880, 1882. He sang Lensky at the first Bolshoy production of *Eugene Onegin* in 1881, and Andrey in the premiere of *Mazeppa* in 1884. In April of that year, Tchaikovsky orchestrated Song 56 at his request. In later years, Usatov taught singing in Tiflis, where his most famous pupil was Chaliapin.

RECORDINGS. Leiferkus, Lisitsian, Lisovsky.

73   *Лишь ты один*
You alone

Op. 57, No. 6

Whatever prompted this choice of song, the feeling in it is very strong. The text by Aleksey Pleshcheyev is a translation of a German lyric that begins "Nur Du allein, Du schautest wie ich litt" (You alone saw how I suffered), by the Austrian poet Ada Christen (Christiane von Breden, 1844-1901). Her poem is vague; it hints darkly at the reason she has suffered, but there is no sure clue. She is an outcast without a home, unprotected, and struggling in her soul between light and darkness; she had no one to turn to, but the man to whom the poem is addressed stood by her—and never loved her.

Tchaikovsky sharpened the text, and made the conclusion more dramatic. It has been suggested that Pleshcheyev saw the poem as a variation on the theme of the "fallen woman" (*Engel-Braunschmidt*, 134). In his translation he brought out the theme of public condemnation, adding the phrase "My heart profusely bleeding, injured by the merciless crowd." Tchaikovsky saw Sarah Bernhardt in the Dumas play *La dame aux camélias*, and he knew Verdi's opera *La Traviata* based on the play, but he did not like the libretto and did not approve of a courtesan as heroine of an opera (*DG*, 409). For this reason, a connection in Tchaikovsky's mind between this song and the theme of the "fallen woman" is doubtful. He changed the second line of Pleshcheyev's text from "You alone knew how to read my troubled soul" to "You alone stood up for me when others falsely judged," which suggests that she is a woman wrongly accused. He also changed the second line of the last stanza, from "You never darkened my life" to "You never tried to poison my life... You alone spared me."

The dramatic final line comes almost as an accusation. Here, high friendship leads to what feels like a tragic realization. The song raises questions, but the force of feeling in it is completely convincing. Some very good singers have liked the song. Maria Kurenko brings out its power well in her splendid recording made in 1940 for the Tchaikovsky centennial.

> Лишь ты один в мои страданья верил,
> Один восстал на лживый суд людской
> И поддержал мой дух изнемогавший
> В те дни, как свет во мне боролся с тьмой.
>
> Лишь ты один простёр мне смело руку,
> Когда к тебе, отчаянья полна,
> Пришла я с сердцем кровью истекавшим,
> Безжалостной толпой оскорблена.

Лишь ты один мне в жизни ни мгновенья
Не отравлял... Один меня щадил,
Один берёг от бурь с участьем нежным...
И никогда меня ты не любил!
Нет, никогда, никогда меня ты не любил...

Lish ty adín v mají stradán'ja véril,	You and you alone believed in my suffering,
Adín vasstál na lzhývyj sút ljutskój	Stood up for me when others falsely judged
I padderzhál moj dúkh iznemagáfshyj	And gave support to my exhausted spirit
F te dní, kak svét va mné barólsa	On days when light and darkness fought
s t'mój.	within me.
Lish ty adín prastjór mne sméla rúku,	You alone held a hand out to me boldly,
Kagdá k tebé, atchájan'ja palná,	When, filled with despair, I came to you,
Prishlá ja s sérttsem króv'ju	My heart profusely
istekáfshym,	bleeding,
Bezzhálastnaj talpój askarblená.	Injured by the merciless crowd.
Lish ty adín mne v zhýzni ni	You alone never for a single
mgnavén'ja	moment
Ne atravljál... Adín menjá	Tried to poison my life... You alone
shchadíl,	spared me,
Adín berjók at búr' s uchást'jem	You alone protected me from storms
nézhnym...	with tender understanding...
I nikagdá menjá ty ne ljubíl!	And never did you love me!
Net, nikagdá, nikagdá menjá ty ne	No, never, never did you
ljubíl...	love me...

TEXT. **Alekséy Pleshchéyev**, 1884. Untitled. A translation of "Nur Du allein" by **Ada Christen**, 1872. Set first by Tchaikovsky; later by the Armenian composer G. O. Korganov (1858-1890).

METER. Binary. Iambic pentameter:
> *You gave support to my exhausted spirit*
> *At times when darkness struggled with the light.*

MUSIC. 1884. Op. 57, no. 6. G Major. 4/4, Andante non troppo. For Low Voice: a–f^2 sharp. Dedicated to the contralto **Aleksándra Krútikova** (see Song 19).

RECORDINGS. Bogachova, Borisenko, Isakova, Kruglikova, Kurenko, Maksakova, Moore (in French), Shpiller.

෴

12 Romances, Opus 60 (1886)

Six months after writing in his diary "it's time to live *in my own place* and *in my own way*," Tchaikovsky placed an ad in a Moscow newspaper: "Single person needs dacha-country house (for winter and summer residence), fully furnished, on riverbank, with good bathing and garden, no farther than three hours by railroad. Address letters with initials P. Tch. to Mr. Jurgenson's store at 10, Neglinny Lane" (*Davydov*, 10). A month later, in February 1885, he signed a lease for a house in Maidanovo, near Klin, at an annual rent of 1000 R.

Klin is an hour and a half by train from Moscow, on the railroad line that connects Moscow to Petersburg. The location was ideal—close enough to get to the city to do business, but far enough away to discourage unwanted visitors. He needed complete isolation to compose; he liked the woods and fields along the river, where he could take daily walks. He made this neighborhood his permanent base for the rest of his life, living finally in a secluded third house on the edge of Klin, with a large, cheerful upstairs room for his piano and books. That house is now the Tchaikovsky Home–Museum (Dom–muzei P. I. Chaikovskogo v Klinu) and the repository of the major portion of his archive.

Settled down near Moscow, he re-established working ties with the Conservatory, where Taneyev was now Director. He did not teach, but he sat on its board, attended final exams, and took part once again in the life of students and faculty at the Conservatory. He was elected Director of the Russian Musical Society and thus could play a leading role in deciding on concert programs and guest artists. At Maidanovo he began work by revising his earlier opera *Vakula the Smith*, giving it a new title *Cherevichki* (*The Slippers*), journeying to Petersburg in April to clear the changes with the poet Yakov Polonsky, who had written the original libretto (he would use three of Polonsky's poems for the Opus 60 romances). Next, he kept an old promise to Balakirev, writing his "Manfred" symphony, Op. 58, spending the summer under the gloomy spell of Byron's Romantic poem. The day he finished it, he started his eighth opera, *Charodeika* (*The Enchantress*). He wrote Mrs. von Meck that what attracted him to opera was its mass appeal to the public: "my 'Manfred' will be played once or twice, and then forgotten by all but a handful of specialists, whereas opera brings your music to the real public, not just to a small coterie, and, if everything turns out right, your music reaches all of the people" (*DG*, 353).

He found evidence of this the next year in Tiflis, where he spent April of 1886. Talented younger musicians were performing his music there: Mikhail Ippolitov-Ivanov (1859-1935), conductor of the Tiflis Opera, and his wife, the soprano Varvara Zarudnaya (1857-1939), who was a superb Maria in *Mazeppa* opposite an outstanding tenor named Pyotr Lodii (1855-1920) singing Andrey. They gave a concert of his works, including arias from *Eugene Onegin*, Songs 5 and 22 sung by Zarudnaya, and Songs 8 and 38 sung by Lodii; he was given an ovation (*DG*, 369). In Paris in May he finally met Pauline Viardot (1821-1910). One of the greatest singers of her time, she was retired from the stage but teaching at the Paris Conservatory. She made a strong impression on Tchaikovsky: "she's full of energy ... she's interested in everything, knows everything, and is exceedingly gracious. At her house I spent two hours leafing through the original score of Mozart's *Don Giovanni*. I can't express the emotion I felt examining this sacred treasure of music! It was as if Mozart and I had shaken hands and had a conversation" (*DG*, 374). When he returned to Moscow in July, he had another satisfying moment hearing his work performed in a setting accessible to "all of the people": he went to a service at Uspensky Cathedral in the Kremlin, where for the first time he heard one of his own hymns for choir being sung during the liturgy (*DG*, 378).

Earlier that spring, Grand Duke Konstantin, with whom he was in correspondence, told him the Empress had expressed the wish that Tchaikovsky might dedicate "one romance" to her. Maria Fyodorovna (1847-1928) was the daughter of King Christian IX of Denmark, born Princess Dagmar; her sister Alexandra was also Queen to a reigning monarch, Edward VII of England. Dedicating just one romance to the Empress was out of the question: he decided on a set of ten songs. He composed them at Maidanovo during the last ten days of August, writing a song a day, usually after his tea and daily walk. By the time he got to the last one, he felt he had run out of steam (*MN*, 457). But when these ten were done, he found two more poems by a different poet, Aleksey Khomyakov, writing them up to make it an even dozen. It would be hard to say which song was written when he was out of steam: all of them are good, and some of them are among his best songs. Grand Duke Konstantin wrote to express the gratitude of the Empress for his "charming" songs, adding that Song 75 had already been performed at court (*Romanov 1999*, 37-8).

There is a postscript to this dedication. The 1940 edition of Tchaikovsky's complete works (*PSS*) was undertaken as an authoritative, academic edition of the music, and, in most respects, it is a meticulous work of scholarship. But in Vol. 45, the space reserved for the dedication of the Opus 60 songs is blank. A close look, however, reveals faint erasure marks over each of the twelve songs. The date must explain this strange act of last-minute censorship. By 1940, Tchaikovsky had been elevated to the same status of cultural icon as Pushkin and Gorky. This edition of his work was "authorized by decree of 5 May 1940 of the Soviet of People's Commissars," as a special page at the beginning of each volume proclaims in large red letters. A revised, "Soviet" Tchaikovsky was ideologically incompatible with a composer who dedicated twelve songs to the woman who was the wife of Alexander III and the mother of Nicholas II. Her name had to be erased in all four thousand copies that were printed.

74 Вчерашняя ночь
Last night

Op. 60, No. 1

Night is a major theme in Opus 60. The image of *dark* night, often a dark autumn night, is common in folk songs, a well-known example being "Ноченька" (Night), sung without accompaniment in the drawn-out, melismatic style, with falling intonation, a lament, but sung by men rather than women (Chaliapin, Christoff, and Hvorostovsky have recorded it). Lyrics about the *bright* night sky full of stars are literary in origin, and constitute a different tradition. They go back to Lomonosov's "Evening Meditation on the Northern Lights" (1743), with its lines "an abyss is revealed, filled with stars; the stars are without number, the abyss is bottomless."

The present text by Aleksey Khomyakov (1804-1860) comes out of this literary tradition and is one of the earliest examples of such a lyric being made into a song. Khomyakov, an important Russian Orthodox thinker and philosopher of the Slavophile movement, certainly knew Lomonosov's ode, but for him the night sky was not only a theme that came out of his reading. Pyotr Bartenev (1829-1912), editor of the journal *Russkii arkhiv* (*Russian Archive*), who knew Khomyakov and provided a commentary to his poems, wrote of him: "For Khomyakov night was a time of introspection (самоуглубление), while his days were almost entirely taken up either by country activities (with hunting in first place), or, in town, by uninterrupted conversation with the diverse company of visitors who assembled at his house every day from morning on. He never went to sleep before 4 a.m. He saw a parallel between the dazzling brocade of the infinite night sky and the infinite treasure contained in the Gospels" (*Khomiakov 1900*, 417).

Tchaikovsky's song is in phrases that take upward flight, modelled exactly on the asymmetrical lines of Khomyakov's poem. Compared to these affirmative and confident lines, the last phrase, marked "ritenuto molto, quasi recitando" and intended to express the transition from earthly to heavenly thoughts, is a reflective rather than decisive conclusion—an unusual touch in a Tchaikovsky song. Its Orthodox spirituality made it a risky text in the Soviet period. As a result, it is little known and seldom sung. Nevertheless, the setting works well as a song and is more accessible than some of Tchaikovsky's other songs for singers who are approaching them for the first time.

Вчерашняя ночь была так светла,
Вчерашняя ночь все звёзды зажгла,
Так ясно,

Что, глядя на холмы и дремлющий лес,
На воды, блестящие блеском небес,
Я думал: о, жить в этом мире чудес
Прекрасно!

Прекрасны и волны, и даль степей,
Прекрасна в одежде зелёных ветвей
Дубрава;

Прекрасна любовь с вечно-свежим венком,
И дружбы звезда с неизменным лучом,
И песен восторг с озаренным челом,
И слава!

Взглянул я на небо, там твердь ясна:
Высоко, высоко восходит она
Над бездной;

Там звёзды живые катятся в огне...
И детское чувство проснулось во мне,
И думал я: лучше нам в той вышине
Надзвездной!

Vcheráshnjaja nóch bylá tak svetlá,
Vcheráshnjaja nóch fse zvjózdy zazhglá,
Tak jásna,

Shto, gljádja na khólmy i drémljushchij
    lés,
Na vódy, blestjáshchije bléskam
    nebés,
Ja dúmal: o, zhýt' v ètam míre
    chudés
Prekrásna!

Prekrásny i vólny, i dál'
    stepéj,
Prekrásna v adézhde zeljónykh vetvéj
Dubráva;

Last night was so bright,
Last night lit up all the stars,
So clearly,

That gazing at the hills and dreaming
    forest,
At the waters, shimmering under the
    bright sky,
I thought: oh, to live in this world of
    wonders
Is beautiful!

Fair are the waves, and the steppe
    stretching far,
Fair in its garment of green branches
Is the oak wood;

Prekrásna ljubóf' s véchna-svézhym
 venkóm,
I drúzhby zvezdá s neizménnym luchóm,
I pésen vastórk s azarjónnym chelóm,
I sláva!

Fair is love, its crown ever fresh,
And friendship's star with unchanging
 light,
And the bright face of songs of joy,
And glory!

Vzgljanúl ja na néba, tam tvért' jasná:
Vysóka, vysóka vaskhódit aná
Nad bézdnaj;

I looked up at heaven, the sky was clear:
High, so high it rises
Above the abyss;

Tam zvjózdy zhyvýje katjátsa v agné...
I détskaje chústva prasnúlas' va mné,
I dúmal ja: lúchshe nam
 f toj vyshyné
Nadzvézdnaj!

There living stars roll in fire...
And a childhood feeling awoke in me,
And I thought: it's better for us there
 in that height
Above the stars!

Text. **Alekséy Khomyakóv**, 1841. Part 1 of a poem in two parts entitled "Nachtstück" (Nocturne); first published in the journal *Moskvitianin* (Muscovite) in 1841. Set by Donaurov in 1873; after Tchaikovsky, by Arensky as a duet (Op. 29/2, 1893), and by Balakirev in "Ten Romances" of 1895-96 (discussed in *Ovchinnikov*, 182).

Nowadays, singers usually give the last word of the song its modern pronunciation "nadzvjozdnaj". In my transcription, I show the more old-fashioned pronunciation, because it is there for the rhyme: Khomyakov used it and Tchaikovsky retained it. In performance, however, this detail is of small importance since the rhyming words are so far apart.

Meter. Ternary. Amphibrachs of 4 feet, with short lines of 1 foot:

> *I looked up at heaven, the sky was so clear,*
> *Where rolling in fire there were millions of stars*
> *In glory!*

Music. 1886. Op. 60, no. 1. A-flat Major. 9/8, Allegro moderato. For High Voice: e¹ flat–a² flat. Dedicated to **Empress María Fyódorovna**.

Recordings. Isakova, Levinsky, Lisovsky, Martynov, Orfyonov, Rodgers, Söderström.

Balakirev: Christoff, Aleksey Ivanov.

☙

75 *Я тебе ничего не скажу*
I won't say anything to you

Op. 60, No. 2

This song became a favorite at court when the Empress received the Opus 60 songs dedicated to her. It shows again, as Tchaikovsky wrote in a letter to K. R., how Fet "avoids subject matter that can easily be expressed in words" (see Song 17). In this text, also a "night" poem, the subject is first awareness of being in love, when it is still an unspoken secret. The song celebrates the theme of undeclared love in the unusual metaphor of a flower that opens at night, used here as an image of a romantic feeling that cannot be put into words.

In the early 1890s, T. K. Tolstaya wrote a song to this same text. It became widely known and is still sung as the "popular" version of the song, though it lacks the delicacy and beautiful craftsmanship of Tchaikovsky's romance.

Я тебе ничего не скажу,
Я тебя не встревожу ничуть,
И о том, что я молча твержу,
Не решусь ни за что намекнуть.

Целый день спят ночные цветы,
Но, лишь солнце за рощу зайдёт,
Раскрываются тихо листы,
И я слышу как сердце цветёт.

И в больную, усталую грудь
Веет влагой ночной… я дрожу,
Я тебя не встревожу ничуть,
Я тебе ничего не скажу!
Я тебя не встревожу ничуть,
Я тебе ничего, ничего не скажу!

Ja tebé nichevó ne skazhú,
Ja tebjá ne fstrevózhu nichút',
I a tóm, shto ja mólcha tverzhú,
Ne reshús' ni za shtó nameknút'.

Tsélyj dén' spját nachnýje tsvetý,
No, lish sóntse za róshchu zajdjót,
Raskryvájutsa tíkha listý,
I ja slýshu kak sérttse tsvetjót.

I won't say anything to you,
I won't alarm you in any way,
And, what I silently repeat to myself,
I wouldn't mention even with a hint.

Nocturnal flowers sleep all day,
But when the sun has set behind the grove,
Their leaves open quietly,
And I can feel my heart flowering.

I v bal'núju, ustáluju grút'	And into my sick, weary breast
Véjet vlágaj nachnój...	Comes a moist breath of night air...
ja drazhú,	I tremble,
Ja tebjá ne fstrevózhu nichút',	I won't alarm you in any way,
Ja tebé nichevó ne skazhú!	I won't say anything to you!
Ja tebjá ne fstrevózhu nichút',	I won't alarm you in any way,
Ja tebé nichevó, nichevó ne skazhú!	I won't say anything, anything to you!

TEXT. **Afanásy Fet**, 1885. First published in *Vestnik Evropy* (The European Herald), 1886, no. 1. Title: Романс (Romance). First set by Tchaikovsky; later by several composers, including Rachmaninoff (1890). Tchaikovsky repeated the last two lines but otherwise made no changes in the text.

The metaphor of the heart blooming like a flower is highly unusual in Russian (for a discussion of this, see *Fet*, 54-7). Sergey Lemeshev thought it so unusual that in his recording he substitutes "поёт" (sing) for the word "цветёт" (blossom) in line 8, a substitution which destroys the metaphor. Other singers leave the text unchanged. The recording made by Georgy Vinogradov is especially fine.

The "popular" version of the song is by T. K. Tolstaya, about whom I have seen little information. She composed several popular romances, some of them to her own words. Her publisher, Nikolay Davingof in St. Petersburg, also published songs by Count M. L. Tolstoy (this is Lev Tolstoy's son Mikhail), with words by Countess A. V. Tolstaya.

METER. Ternary. Anapest, 3-foot, with masculine endings:
> *After sundown a breath of fresh air*
> *And my flowering heart is revived...*

MUSIC. 1886. Op. 60, no. 2. E Major. 6/8, Allegretto con moto. For High Voice: e^1–f^2 sharp. Dedicated to **Empress María Fyódorovna.**

RECORDINGS. Kozlovsky, Larin, Lemeshev, Levinsky, Maxwell, Migay, Tourel, Vinogradov.

Rachmaninoff: Söderström.

Tolstaya: Gmyria, Obukhova, Shcherbinina, Zykina.

76 *О, если б знали въг*
Oh, if you only knew

Op. 60, No. 3

Perhaps the first stanza of this poem by the French poet Sully Prudhomme in Aleksey Pleshcheyev's translation caught Tchaikovsky's eye as a statement of feelings he himself knew, as a single, and, at times, lonely man. He added a note to the score saying that the romance could be sung by a baritone if transposed down a tone or half tone (Tchaikovsky was himself a baritone). This is the only such note in all of his songs. In any case, he wanted it to appeal to as many singers as possible. It is a big, dramatic song, written for a mature, experienced singer.

О, если б знали вы, как много слёз незримых
Тот льёт, кто одинок, без друга и семьи, —
 Вы, может быть, порой, прошли бы мимо
 Жилища, где влачатся дни мои.

О, если б знали вы, что́ в сердце, полном тайной
Печали, чистый взор способен зародить, —
 В моё окно, порой, как бы случайно
 Вы, проходя, взглянули может быть.

О, если б знали вы, как сердцу счастья много
Дарит другого сердца близость, — отдохнуть
 У моего вы сели бы порога,
 Как добрая сестра, когда-нибудь.

О, если б знали вы, что я люблю вас, знали,
Как глубоко люблю, каким святым огнём
 Вы с давних пор мне душу согревали, —
 Вы может быть, может быть, ко мне вошли бы в дом!

O, jésli b ználi vý, kak mnóga sljós nezrímykh	Oh, if you only knew, how many unseen tears
Tot l'jót, kto adinók, bez drúga i sem'jí, —	Are shed by one alone, without a friend or family, —
Vy, mózhet být', parój, prashlí by míma	You, perhaps, some time, would pass
Zhylíshcha, gde vlachátsa dní mají.	The dwelling where my days are spent.

O, jésli b ználi vý, shtó f sérttse,
pólnam tájnaj
Pecháli, chístyj vzór spasóben zaradít', —
V majó aknó, parój, kak by
sluchájna
Vy, prakhadjá, vzgljanúli mózhet být'.

Oh, if you only knew, what in a heart
full of hidden
Sorrow, a pure gaze can bring to life, —
Into my window, some time, perhaps
by chance
You, passing by, would glance my way.

O, jésli b ználi vý, kak sérttsu
shchást'ja mnóga
Darít drugóva sérttsa blízast', —
addakhnút'
U majevó vy séli by paróga,
Kak dóbraja sestrá, kagdá-nibút'.

Oh, if you only knew, how much happiness
one heart
Finds in the gift of another heart's
proximity, —
You might sit down at my doorstep to rest,
Like a kind sister, some day.

O, jésli b ználi vý, shto ja ljubljú vas,
ználi,
Kak glubakó ljubljú, kakím svjatým
agnjóm
Vy z dávnikh pór mne dúshu sagreváli, —
Vy, mózhet být', mózhet být',
ka mne vashlí by v dóm!

Oh, if you only knew, that I love you,
knew,
How deeply I love, with what sacred
fire
You've long been warming my soul, —
You would perhaps, perhaps,
come into my house!

TEXT. **Alekséy Pleshchéyev**, 1883; published in *Ezhenedel'noe obozrenie* (Weekly Review), 1884, no. 1, p. 6. Translation of a poem entitled "Prière" (Ah! si vous saviez comme on pleure), in *Les Vaines Tendresses* (1875), by **René Sully Prudhomme** (1839-1907), French poet and critic, first laureate of the Nobel Prize in literature (1901). Not set by any other composers.

METER. Binary. Iambic, two hexameters followed by two pentameters:

Oh, if you only knew how many unseen tears
Are shed by one who lives alone without a friend,
Perhaps some time you'd think of walking past
The dwelling where my lonely days are spent.

MUSIC. 1886. Op. 60, no. 3. E-flat Major. 3/4, Allegro agitato. For High Voice: e^1 flat–a^2 flat. Dedicated to **Empress María Fyódorovna**.

RECORDINGS. Dolukhanova, Guliayev, Kozlovsky, Larin, Lemeshev, Levinsky, Maksakova, Martynov.

77 Соловей *Nightingale*

Op. 60, No. 4

Except for Song 2, written early in his career, this is Tchaikovsky's only song to a poem by the greatest of the Russian poets, Alexander Pushkin (1799-1837). It is a translation of a Serbian lyric song Pushkin found in Volume I of the three volumes of oral songs published in 1824 in Leipzig by the Serb philologist and collector of folk songs Vuk Stefanović Karadžić (1787-1864), a copy of which was in Pushkin's library, together with Vuk's Serbian dictionary (*Priima*, 107). In the song, the young hero, or "brave lad" as I have translated it, addresses the nightingale to draw a contrast between its "three songs" and his own "three sorrows." The title "Nightingale" was given to the poem by Pushkin; in Serbian, the song is known by a different title, "The Three Greatest Sorrows." The original Serbian text will be found below.

Pushkin's translation is nearly exact, but there are several differences, the most interesting of them being the way the first and third sorrows are described. The first sorrow, "my mother didn't marry me off young," is turned around by Pushkin to "I was married too early"; the third sorrow, "my sweetheart is angry at me," is changed and expanded into the two lines "evil folk separated my sweetheart from me." It is striking that these last two lines carry a suggestion of the troubles Pushkin himself had with regard to his wife at court—troubles that led to his duel and death.

The song Tchaikovsky wrote to Pushkin's text is one of his greatest stylizations of a folk song. It is another song of experience, a man's lament, and therefore similar, at least in genre, to the woman's lament of Song 51. The basic phrase is shaped by falling intonation, with the difference, however, that it is to be sung Allegro and "molto rubato e capriccioso": changes in the tempo are frequent, with the final phrase marked *ad libitum* for maximum freedom. The voice part calls for a rare expressiveness. It is sometimes performed as a weary complaint of a beaten man, but that is clearly not what either Pushkin or Tchaikovsky had in mind. Konstantin Lisovsky's strong tenor conveys very well the beauty of this song of a man in the full flower of his strength. It is a young man's song, and should be sung as such.

Соловей, мой соловейко!
Птица малая, лесная!
У тебя ль, у малой птицы,
Незаменные три песни,

У меня ли, у молодца,
Три великие заботы!
Как уж первая забота, —
Рано молодца женили;
А вторая-то забота, —
Ворон конь мой притомился;
Как уж третья-то забота, —
Красну девицу со мною
Разлучили злые люди.
Выкопайте мне могилу
Во поле, поле широком,
В головах мне посадите
Алы цветики-цветочки,
А в ногах мне проведите
Чисту воду ключевую.
Пройдут мимо красны девки,
Так сплетут себе веночки;
Пройдут мимо стары люди,
Так воды себе зачерпнут.

Salavéj, moj salavéjka!	Nightingale, my little nightingale!
Ptítsa málaja, lesnája!	Small bird, forest bird!
U tebjá l', u málaj ptítsy,	You have, little bird,
Nezaménnyje trí pésni,	Three unchanging songs,
U menjá li, u mólattsa,	I have, brave lad,
Trí velíkije zabóty!	Three great cares!
Kak ush pérvaja zabóta, —	The first care is this —
Rána mólattsa zheníli;	Too early was I married;
A ftarája-ta zabóta, —	The second care is this —
Vóran kón' moj pritamílsa;	My raven-black steed is weary;
Kak ush trét'ja-ta zabóta, —	And the third care is this —
Krásnu dévitsu sa mnóju	My fair lass and I
Razluchíli zlýje ljúdi.	Were separated by evil folk.
Výkapajte mne magílu	Dig me a grave
Vó pole, póle shyrókam,	In the field, the wide field,
V galavákh mne pasadíte	At my head plant
Ály tsvétiki-tsvetóchki,	Bright red flowers,
A v nagákh mne pravedíte	At my feet let flow
Chístu vódu kljuchevúju.	Pure spring water.
Prajdút míma krásny défki,	When fair girls pass by,
Tak spletút sebé venóchki;	Let them weave themselves garlands;
Prajdút míma stáry ljúdi,	When old folks pass by,
Tak vadý sebé zachérpnut.	Let them take a drink of water.

TEXT. **Aleksándr Púshkin**, between 1828 and 1834 (on dating, see *Priima*, 106). First published in 1835 in Book 15 of *Biblioteka dlia chteniia* (Library for Reading), then later that year in Pushkin's collected poems.

Translation of a Serbian folksong entitled "Три највеђе туге" (Tri najveće tuge, The three greatest sorrows), from Volume I, "Različne ženske pjesme" (Various women's songs) of "Narodne srpske pjesme" (Serbian Folk Songs), published by **Vuk Stefanović Karadžić** first in 1814 in Vienna, then, in the expanded edition which Pushkin owned, in Leipzig in 1824. In his introduction to the songs, Vuk (as he is known in Serbia) explains that by "women's songs" he means lyric songs, rather than epic songs; they can be sung by men, too, especially young men (*Wilson*, 395). There was confusion in Russia over Vuk's full name. When he made his visit to St. Petersburg in 1819, he used only his first name and patronymic Stefanović, rather than his surname: as a result, he came to be known in Russia as Vuk Stefanović rather than Vuk Karadžić (*Potepalov*, 9). Hence in Tchaikovsky's works (*PSS*) and the chronicle of Tchaikovsky's life (*DG*), the original author of this text is identified as "V. Stefanovich" (who is in any case not the author of the text, but the man who wrote it down when he heard it being sung). Vuk knew Goethe and Grimm, and had many Russian friends, but he and Pushkin never met.

Pushkin's "Nightingale" is the tenth poem in a cycle of 16 poems published under the title "Песни западных славян" (Songs of the Western Slavs—by which Pushkin meant both Serbs and Czechs). Pushkin's interest in Serbian folk songs goes back to the early 1820s when he was in Kishinyov, but was renewed by conversations he and Mickiewicz had in 1828 about Prosper Mérimée's "La Guzla" (1827), a collection of folk songs from Dalmatia, Bosnia, Croatia, and Herzegovina translated into French. The book turned out to be a hoax, with songs and commentary largely invented by Mérimée, but this did not deter Pushkin from carrying out his own intention to convey in Russian the style of Serb and Czech folk poetry. Some of his "Songs of the Western Slavs" he took from Mérimée, some were invented by him, but two of them, including "Nightingale," are genuine folk songs.

There is a discussion of these issues in *Priima*; a biography of Vuk in English by *Wilson*; and an article on the woman who first brought knowledge of Vuk's work to America in the 19th century by *Browne*. "The Three Greatest Sorrows" was translated into English in 1827 (*Bowring*, 165-6).

Pushkin's poem was first set by Nikolay Afanasiev (1821-1898), a minor composer, in 1870; after Tchaikovsky, by Cui (Op. 99/2, 1915).

METER. Binary. Trochaic tetrameter, not strictly adhered to in every line; the lines are unrhymed but invariably have a feminine ending:

> *Dig my grave in an open meadow,*
> *At my head plant bright red flowers,*
> *At my feet set water flowing…*

Music. 1886. Op. 60, no. 4. C Minor. 2/4, Allegro molto rubato e capriccioso. For High Voice: g^1–a^2 flat. Dedicated to **Empress María Fyódorovna**.

Recordings. Atlantov, Chaliapin, Ghiaurov, Hvorostovsky, Karolik, Lemeshev, **Lisovsky**, Martynov, Mkrtchyan, Mochalov, Nesterenko, Petrov, Reizen, Rodgers, Serkebayev, Söderström, Vedernikov.

Serbian Folk Song (used by Pushkin for his Russian translation)

ТРИ НАЈВЕЋЕ ТУГЕ

Славуј птица мала сваком покој дала,
а мени јунаку три туге задала:
прва ми је туга на срдашцу моме —
што ме није мајка оженила млада;
друга ми је туга на срдашцу моме —
што мој вранац коњиц пода мном не игра;
трећа ми је туга, ах, на срцу моме —
што се моја драга на ме расрдила!
Копајте ми раку у пољу широку,
два копља широку, четири дугачку;
више моје главе ружу усадите,
сниже моји ногу воду изведите:
које младо прође — нек се ружом кити,
које л' старо прође — нека жеђу гаси!
              —*Karadžić*, I, Song 542

THE THREE GREATEST SORROWS

The nightingale, little bird, gave peace to everyone,
but on me, brave lad, it inflicted three sorrows:
the first sorrow on my heart is this —
my mother didn't marry me off young;
the second sorrow on my heart is this —
my raven-black horse doesn't dance under me;
the third sorrow, alas, on my heart is this —
my sweetheart has grown angry at me!
Dig me a grave in the wide field,
two spear-lengths wide, four spear-lengths long;
at my head plant a rose,
at my feet set water flowing:
whatever young person passes by — may a rose adorn that person,
whatever old person passes by — may that one's thirst be slaked!

78 *Простые слова*
Simple words

Op. 60, No. 5

When Tchaikovsky wanted to write a song for which he had no text, he wrote his own words, as he did for Songs 15 and 38. This is the third and last such song. In all three of them, the words on the page are a means to an end— a musical end. In this case, Tchaikovsky wanted to write an allegro waltz that would express total devotion, forever, to a perfect and beloved *someone*. He wrote the text in two contrasting parts, using flowery language in the first half, then "simple words" that say the same thing better, with sincerity, and without hyperbole. True, these "plain" words include Slavonic diction from the church liturgy—"хлеб насущный" (daily bread), and its rhyme word "единосущный" (consubstantial), but to any Orthodox believer they are everyday words.

It has been suggested that the words were "devised as blatant tribute to his imperial dedicatee" (*Brown IV*, 88). If so, Tchaikovsky is guilty of the most abject flattery. Yet this is not in character: he was not a flatterer, but rather known for his sincerity. Tchaikovsky's dedications are a *gift* of music given to a friend or fellow musician or patron, but this does not mean the work is a message intended for that person. Could Tchaikovsky really think of the Empress as his "life," his "everything," his "double," his best friend, support, and joy?

If applied personally to the composer, this song could only be about one thing: his relationship with his "muse," which is to say, his relationship with music. On this subject, he wrote Mrs. von Meck in December 1877: "I really could have gone mad but for *music*. Here is heaven's greatest gift to humanity as it wanders in the dark. Only music illumines, reconciles, and soothes. Yet it is not a last straw to be grasped at, but a faithful friend, protector, and comforter, for whose sake alone life is worth living" (*von Meck 1993*, 81).

Ты звезда на полночном небе,
ты весенний цветок полей;
ты рубин, иль алмаз блестящий,
ты луч солнца во тьме светящий,
чаровница и царица красоты!

Так по струнам бряцая лирным,
тьмы певцов о тебе поют.
Славы нектар тобой изведан,
мне ж дар песен от Бога не дан,
я простые скажу слова.

Ты мой друг, ты моя опора,
ты мне жизнь, ты мне все и всё...
Ты мне воздух и хлеб насущный,
ты двойник мой единосущный,
ты отрада и услада дней моих!

Пусть, по струнам бряцая лирным,
тьмы певцов о тебе поют...
Славы нектар тобой изведан;
мне ж дар песен от Бога не дан,
как сумел, как сумел, так и сказал!

Ty zvezdá na palnóchnam nébe,
ty vesénnij tsvetók paléj;
ty rubín, il' almás blestjáshchij,
ty luch sóntsa va t'mé svetjáshchij,
charavnítsa i tsarítsa krasatý!

You're a star in the midnight sky,
you're a spring flower in the fields;
you're a ruby, or a sparkling diamond,
you're a sunbeam shining in the dark,
an enchantress and the queen of beauty!

Tak pa strúnam brjatsája lírnym,
t'mý peftsóf a tebé pajút.
Slávy néktar tabój izvédan,
mne sh dar pésen ad Bóga
  né dan,
Ja prastýje skazhú slavá.

So, plucking the strings of a lyre,
myriad poets sing your praises.
You have tasted the nectar of glory,
but God did not give me the gift of
  poetry,
I will say it in simple words.

Ty moj drúk, ty maja apóra,
ty mne zhýzn', ty mne fsé i fsjó...
Ty mne vózdukh i khlép nasúshchnyj,
ty dvajník moj jedinasúshchnyj,
ty atráda i usláda dnéj majíkh!

You're my friend, you're my support,
you're my life, you're my all and everything...
You are my air and daily bread,
you are my consubstantial twin,
you are the joy and delight of my days!

Pust', pa strúnam brjatsája lírnym,
t'mý peftsóf a tebé pajút...
Slávy néktar tabój izvédan;
mne sh dar pésen ad Bóga
  né dan,
kak sumél, kak sumél, ták i skazál!

So let myriad poets sing of you,
plucking the strings of a lyre...
You have tasted the nectar of glory;
but God did not give me the gift of
  poetry,
as well, as well as I knew how, I have said it!

TEXT. **N. N. [P. I. Tchaikovsky]**, 1886. Written by the composer for this song; not set by any other composers.

METER. Mixed ternary and binary; two anapests followed by an iamb, with the first strong downbeat on the third syllable:

> *you're a sunbeam in darkness shining,*
> *an enchantress and queen of beauty!*

MUSIC. 1886. Op. 60, no. 5. F Major. 3/4, Tempo di valse (allegro). For Middle Voice: d¹–f². Dedicated to **Empress María Fyódorovna**.

RECORDINGS. Arkhipova, Levinsky, Lisovsky, Söderström.

79 *Ночи безумные*
Frenzied nights

Op. 60, No. 6

This poem by Aleksey Apukhtin, dated 1876 by his editors (*Apukhtin*, 202), soon became widely known and was set to music many times. Chekhov has one of his characters sing it in his early novel *Драма на охоте* (*The Shooting Party*), written in 1884, two years before Tchaikovsky's song. Yakov Prigozhii (1840-1920), pianist and arranger at the gypsy night club "Yar" in Moscow, set a variant of Apukhtin's text to music (*Petrovskii 1997*, no. 185); A. A. Spiro (?-1917) wrote a duet to the text which is still sung today. Listings of other versions (*Ivanov*, I, 42) raise questions of dating, because some of those he cites are earlier than 1876, when Apukhtin supposedly wrote the poem. What is not in question is the enormous popularity of the poem as a song. A guest in the Tolstoy household reports being present one day when two of Lev Tolstoy's daughters sang a version of it. When the music ended, Tolstoy raised his head and twice exclaimed "How fine! (Как хорошо!)" (*Apukhtin*, 397).

"Frenzied Nights," also known as "Sleepless Nights," reads like a variation on another poem which earlier became famous as a song. In 1845, when the novelist Ivan Turgenev (1818-1883) was still writing poetry, he published a lyric entitled "В дороге" (On the road), which was sung as a "gypsy" romance. The song, called "Misty Morning," is a classic, still sung today:

> Утро туманное, утро седое,
> Нивы печальные, снегом покрытые...
> Нехотя вспомнишь и время былое,
> Вспомнишь и лица, давно позабытые.
>
> Вспомнишь обильные, страстные речи,
> Взгляды, так жадно, так робко ловимые,
> Первые встречи, последние встречи,
> Тихого голоса звуки любимые.
>
> Вспомнишь разлуку с улыбкою странной,
> Многое вспомнишь родное, далёкое,
> Слушая ропот колёс непрестанный,
> Глядя задумчиво в небо широкое.

> Misty morning, grey morning,
> Sad fields covered with snow...
> Involuntarily you remember the past,
> Remember faces forgotten long ago.

Remember the lavish, passionate speeches,
The glances, caught so eagerly, so shyly,
First meetings, final meetings,
The beloved sounds of a quiet voice.

Remember parting with a strange smile,
Remember so much that is dear and far away,
Hearing the unceasing murmur of the wheels,
Gazing pensively at the broad sky.

Apukhtin knew this poem by heart. Perhaps he found in it the impulse for his own original variation on the theme. Written to the very same music of four-foot dactyls, Apukhtin's verses turn Turgenev's day thoughts into night thoughts, and calm recollection into frenzied obsession. The mood is utterly different, but the two poems have in common the theme of the incessant way the past returns to haunt us: it will not let go, and we do not want it to let go. Whether these frenzied nights hold memories of passion, love, inspiration, or, as is likely, all of these together, they insist on searching for final answers and a willingness to hazard everything on that. The poem conjures up a "gypsy" mood that equates reality with extremes of passion.

Tchaikovsky's song translates this gypsy intensity into his own musical language. It has "profound passivity and melancholy" (*Al'shvang 1959*, 543), but it also expresses frenzy in the dramatic crescendo passage of the last stanza. The strong piano part frames it in a way that seems inevitable. The introduction leads to a place that sounds more like an ending than a beginning; when the song ends, we are back where we started, reinforcing the idea that from this particular state of mind, there can be no way out.

Ночи безумные, ночи бессонные,
Речи несвязные, взоры усталые...
Ночи, последним огнем озаренные,
Осени мертвой цветы запоздалые!

Пусть даже время рукой беспощадною
Мне указало, что было в вас ложного,
Всё же лечу я к вам памятью жадною,
В прошлом ответа ищу невозможного...

Вкрадчивым шепотом вы заглушаете
Звуки дневные, несносные, шумные...
В тихую ночь вы мой сон отгоняете,
Ночи бессонные, ночи безумные!
Ночи бессонные, ночи безумные!

Nóchi bezúmnyje, nóchi bessónnyje,
Réchi nesvjáznyje, vzóry ustályje...
Nóchi, paslédnim agnjóm azarjónnyje,
Óseni mjórtvaj tsvetý zapazdályje!

Frenzied nights, sleepless nights,
Incoherent speeches, tired gazes...
Nights lit by the last candle,
Dead autumn's late-blooming flowers!

Púst' dazhe vrémja rukój bespashchádnaju
Mné ukazála, shto býla v vas lózhnava,
Fsjó zhe lechú ja k vam pámjat'ju zhádnaju,
F próshlam atvéta ishchú
  nevazmózhnava...

Even if the unsparing hand of time
Has laid bare all that is false in you,
Still I fly to you in hungry memory,
Searching the past for an
  impossible answer...

Fkrátchivym shópatam vý zaglushájete
Zvúki dnevnýje, nesnósnyje, shúmnyje...
F tíkhuju nóch vy moj són atganjájete,
Nóchi bessónnyje, nóchi bezúmnyje!
Nóchi bessónnyje, nóchi bezúmnyje!

Your insinuating whispers muffle
The loud, unbearable noises of the day...
In the still night you drive away sleep,
Sleepless nights, frenzied nights!
Sleepless nights, frenzied nights!

TEXT. **Alekséy Apúkhtin**, 1876. Untitled; first published in 1886. Set before and after Tchaikovsky by many composers.

METER. Ternary. Dactyl, 4-foot:

> *Words incoherently spoken by candlelight,*
> *Searching the past for an answer impossible...*

MUSIC. 1886. Op. 60, no. 6. G Minor. 9/8, Andante non troppo, un poco rubato. For High Voice: d^1–a^2 flat. Dedicated to **Empress María Fyódorovna**.

RECORDINGS. Bogachova, Borodina, Kasrashvili, Kazarnovskaya, Leiferkus, Lemeshev, Lisitsian, Maksakova, Nelepp, Ognivtsev, Petrov, Preobrazhenskaya, Reizen, Rosing, Serkebayev, Vedernikov, Vishnevskaya, Vorvulev, Zbruyeva, Zlatogorova.

Spiro (duet): Obukhova and Kozlovsky, Maksakova and Katulskaya.

80 *Песнь цыганки*
Song of the gypsy girl

Op. 60, No. 7

The author of the words to this well-known song, Yakov Polonsky (1819-1898), was a man of Tchaikovsky's class but a generation older, born in a gentry family of modest means. He entered Moscow University to study law in 1838, the year after Pushkin's death, and began publishing lyrics in 1840, the year Tchaikovsky was born. There he knew Fet, who was his exact contemporary. Polonsky wrote his best lyrics in an eclectic, conversational style that included elements of folk song and gypsy romance (more than 75 of his poems were set to music, *PRP*, II, 19). Turgenev admired him for his "artless grace" (просто-душная грация) and the "freedom of his figurative language" (свободная образность языка).

This is one of those literary poems that is popularly known as a "folk song," because it is sung to music by an anonymous composer. Dates and names of composers of such songs are hard to find; if the sheet music shows a name at all, it is usually that of the arranger. The "folk" version of this song in all probability preceded Tchaikovsky's version, since Yakov Prigozhii published his arrangement of it in 1886 (*Ivanov*, I, 274). When Lemeshev sang all of Tchaikovsky's songs in a series of concerts broadcast over the radio in 1938-39, he received a letter from a listener in Novgorod province asking why he sang this song "to the wrong tune" (*Lemeshev 1968*, 176).

Tchaikovsky's excellent song is admired for its "sincerity" (задушевность) and "purity of feeling" (целомудрие чувства); like Pushkin's poem *The Gypsies* (see Song 2), it takes up a gypsy theme without resorting to gypsy "kitsch" (цыганщина) or other worn-out formulas (*Vasina-Grossman*, 292). It reminds us that *Carmen* was Tchaikovsky's favorite contemporary opera. In this song he does not imitate the style called "in modo romalesca" or "alla zingara" (discussed in *Shcherbakova*, 98-133), with its shouts and sudden changes of tempo, and a beat based not so much on pulse as on breathing. He does, however, vary the tempo from stanza to stanza, and in the marvelous Andante section he conveys the expressiveness of the "romalesca" style with its initial "parlando" intonation, followed by moody changes and a steep fall from the highest note in the song, on the word "friend" at the beginning of the second line, to the long low note held for two bars at the end of the section. The piano is used to establish a dancing rhythm at the outset and conclusion of the song, with triplets that suggest melismatic features of gypsy singing.

(Allegro moderato)
Мой костёр в тумане светит,
Искры гаснут на лету...
Ночью нас никто не встретит;
Мы простимся на мосту.

(poco meno mosso)
Ночь пройдёт—и спозаранок
В степь далёко, милый мой,
Я уйду с толпой цыганок
За кибиткой кочевой.

(tempo I)
На прощанье шаль с каймою
Ты на мне узлом стяни!
Как концы её, с тобою
Мы сходились в эти дни.

(poco meno mosso)
Кто-то мне судьбу предскажет?
Кто-то завтра, сокол мой,
На груди моей развяжет
Узел, стянутый тобой?

(Andante)
Вспоминай, коли другая
Друга милого любя,
Будет песни петь, играя
На коленях у тебя!

(Allegro moderato)
Мой костёр в тумане светит,
Искры гаснут на лету...
Ночью нас никто не встретит;
Мы простимся на мосту.

	(Allegro moderato)
Moj kastjór f tumáne svétit,	My campfire glows in the mist,
Ískry gásnut na letú...	The sparks fly up and burn out...
Nóchju nas niktó ne fstrétit;	No one will see us in the night;
My prastímsa na mastú.	We'll say farewell on the bridge.
	(poco meno mosso)
Nóch prajdjót — i spazarának	Night will end — and at first light
F stép' daljóka, mílyj mój,	Far into the steppe, my love,
Ja ujdú s talpój tsygának	I will leave with the crowd of gypsy girls,
Za kibítkaj kachevój.	Following the wandering caravan.

(tempo I)

Na prashchán'je shál' s kajmóju	At our farewell, wrap me with a gypsy shawl,
Ty na mné uzlóm stjaní!	Tie its ends in a tight knot!
Kak kantsý jejó, s tabóju	You and I have spent these days
My skhadílis' v èti dní.	Tied together tightly like that knot.

(poco meno mosso)

Któ-ta mne sud'bú pretskázhet?	Can anyone predict my fate?
Któ-ta záftra, sókal mój,	Tomorrow, my falcon, can anyone
Na grudí majéj razvjázhet	Untie the knot that's on my breast,
Úzel, stjánutyj tabój?	This knot, tied tight by you?

(Andante)

Fspaminái, kali drugája	Think of me, if another girl,
Drúga mílava ljubjá,	Taking you as her darling friend,
Búdet pésni pét', igrája	Sings her songs to you, playing
Na kalénjakh u tebjá!	As you hold her on your lap!

(Allegro moderato)

Moj kastjór f tumáne svétit,	My campfire glows in the mist,
Ískry gásnut na letú...	The sparks fly up and burn out...
Nóchju nas niktó ne fstrétit;	No one will see us in the night;
My prastímsa na mastú.	We'll say farewell on the bridge.

TEXT. **Yákov Polónsky.** Dated 1853, but that is the date he published it; Fet recalls first hearing it when he was a student in the early 1840s (*Polonsky*, I, 434). Title: Песня цыганки. An anonymous popular setting of the song existed in 1886 and probably preceded Tchaikovsky's song.

METER. Binary. Trochaic, 4-foot:

> *In the mist my campfire's glowing,*
> *Sparks rise up, burn out in flight,*
> *Not a soul will see us here,*
> *We're alone this one last night.*

MUSIC. 1886. Op. 60, no. 7. A Minor. 3/4, Allegro moderato, with changes in tempo indicated in the text. For High Voice: d^1-f^2. Dedicated to **Empress María Fyódorovna.** Transcribed for voice and orchestra by Taneyev (1891).

RECORDINGS. Arkhipova, Borodina, Fassbänder, Isakova, Kazarnovskaya, Kruglikova, Kurenko, Levko, Lodii, Maksakova, Mkrtchyan, **Obraztsova,** Obukhova, Rautio, Siniavskaya

Popular version: Kozin, Shcherbinina.

81 Прости
Forgive

Op. 60, No. 8

Between 1847 and 1860, Turgenev carried on a regular correspondence with Nikolay Nekrasov (1821-1878), a major "civic" poet and editor of leading journals like *Отечественные записки* (*Notes of the Fatherland*) and *Современник* (*The Contemporary*). They eventually fell out over a review of Turgenev's novel *On the Eve*, but while they were friends, Nekrasov respected Turgenev as a writer of first importance, and his letters to him are the warmest in all his correspondence. In a letter of 30 July 1856, Nekrasov sent this poem to Turgenev, saying it had just been written, and wondering if it was "tolerable, or just bad—in all conscience, I can't tell" (*Nekrasov*, Letters, 253-4). Turgenev's answer is not recorded, but if Nekrasov had any doubts, they did not last long: he published the poem later that year.

When Nekrasov died, Mrs. von Meck sent an edition of his poems to Tchaikovsky. He wrote back saying "I find it hard to forget that Nekrasov, defender of the weak and the oppressed, this democrat, this irate opponent of the aristocracy in all its manifestations, was in life a real aristocrat (барин)... There's something vaguely false in his poetry that bothers me" (*DG*, 176).

He evidently made an exception for this poem. He might have known some of the earlier settings, like the "allegro agitato" version of the song by Rimsky-Korsakov. Tchaikovsky takes an entirely different approach. It is one of his rarest songs, extremely somber but musically very beautiful. It is not easy to sing well. The voice has to express everything without sounding like impending doom; in the second half, there is an illumination.

> Прости! Не помни дней паденья,
> Тоски, унынья, озлобленья, —
> Не помни бурь, не помни слёз,
> Не помни ревности угроз!
> Не помни ревности, ревности угроз!
>
> Но дни, когда любви светило
> Над нами ласково всходило,
> И бодро мы свершали путь —
> Благослови и не забудь!
> Благослови и не забудь, и не забудь,
> не забудь!

Prastí! ne pómni dnéj padén'ja,	Forgive! Don't remember days of defeat,
Taskí, unýn'ja, azlablén'ja, —	Of longing, dejection, animosity, —
Ne pómni búr', ne pómni sljós,	Don't remember storms, don't remember tears,
Ne pómni révnasti ugrós!	Don't remember jealous fears!
Ne pómni révnasti, révnasti ugrós!	Don't remember jealous, jealous fears!
No dní, kagdá ljubví svetíla	But those days when love's star
Nad námi láskava fskhadíla,	Was rising tenderly above us,
I bódra my sversháli pút' —	And boldly we forged our way ahead —
Blagaslaví i ne zabút'!	Bless and do not forget them!
Blagaslaví i ne zabút', i ne zabút', ne zabút'!	Bless and do not forget them, do not forget, do not forget!

TEXT. **Nikoláy Nekrásov**, 1856; published in *Biblioteka dlia chteniia* (Library for Reading), 1856, no. 10. Untitled. The title of the song is sometimes mistranslated as "farewell" or "adieu". Set by dozens of composers, including Cui (Op. 5/3, 1859), Rimsky-Korsakov (Op. 27/4, 1883), and Nikolay Tcherepnin (Op. 22/5, 1904).

METER. Binary. Iambic, 4-foot:
Forget the storms, forget the tears,
Forget the hurtful jealous fears.

MUSIC. 1886. Op. 60, no. 8. F Major. 4/4, Moderato. For High Voice: c^1–a^2. Dedicated to **Empress María Fyódorovna**.

RECORDINGS. Descamps, Lemeshev, Milashkina, Pirogov, Reizen.
Cui: Christoff.
Rimsky-Korsakov: Gerasimova, Rozhdestvenskaya.

82 Ночь
Night

Op. 60, No. 9

Yakov Polonsky was thirty when he wrote this poem that proceeds from the strong impression made on him by the night sky as seen from the Crimean coast of the Black Sea, at the end of the summer of 1850. The image of "peace" at the beginning and end of the poem recalls one of Pushkin's most famous late lyrics "Пора, мой друг, пора! покоя сердце просит," ("It's time, my friend, it's time! the heart asks for peace," 1834), a poem about the desire to retire from active life and spend what remaining time is left on peaceful labors and contentment that is "pure." Polonsky stands dazzled by the beauty of night, drawn to its promise of "peace," but still very much immersed in life and not yet ready to retire from the world that he knows to be made up of tears, doubts, and the heart's quest. It is a deeply ambivalent poem, but, on balance, a young man's poem, tipped toward holding on to innocence rather than submitting to the inevitable too soon.

The song has always been a favorite of singers. It expresses the clean, honest melancholy of a person still young, contemplating seriously the implications of the idea that the journey of life on which he is embarked culminates in "peace." Tchaikovsky typically worked by sketching out quickly a key phrase in a poem, usually the first line. But here, in his copy of Polonsky's poems, it was the last line and a half he sketched out in the margin. This three-bar sketch is already in the song's key of G minor, "a key of earnest meditation" (*Slonimsky 1989*, 185). The music is a synthesis of spoken and sung intonations, with the rise and fall in melody at times as it would be in speech, the words articulated in the music as distinctly as if they were being spoken (*Al'shvang 1959*, 544-6). These speech intonations carry over into the piano part, which is in dialogue with the voice; the declamation in triple time gives the song echoes of melancholy meditation heard earlier in Songs 5 and 19 (*Vasina-Grossman*, 292).

Anton Chekhov is known to have liked the song: it is one of the songs his wife, the actress Olga Knipper, sang (*Balabanovich*, 142). Chekhov used it in one of his best stories, "My Life" (1896). He has his heroine, Masha, declare her intention to break free of life in a stifling provincial town by appearing at an amateur theatrical evening where she sings this song. The performance is admirable, seen through the eyes of her husband, who loves her; but the look of provocation on her face when it is over suggests that instead of bringing the audience into the song (which is what talent should do), she has used the song to make herself look good and to show her contempt for everyone else. This is a story where a young couple with talent and honesty are put to the hard test of making life in a provincial town real, starting with themselves; Masha deserts the town and leaves her husband. Chekhov uses the song to show that Masha's inherent artistic taste and talent really are worth something, but that her understanding of what the larger stakes are falls short.

Отчего я люблю тебя, светлая ночь?
Так люблю, что, страдая, любуюсь тобой!
И за что я люблю тебя, тихая ночь?
Ты не мне, ты другим посылаешь покой!

Что мне звёзды, луна, небосклон, облака,
Этот свет, что, скользя на холодный гранит,
Превращает в алмазы росинки цветка,
И как путь золотой через море бежит!

Ночь, за что мне любить твой серебряный свет?
Усладит ли он горечь скрываемых слёз?
Даст ли жадному сердцу желанный ответ?
Разрешит ли сомнений тяжёлый вопрос?

Сам не знаю, за что я люблю тебя, ночь,
Так люблю, что, страдая, любуюсь тобой!...
Сам не знаю, за что я люблю тебя, ночь...
Оттого, может быть, что далёк мой покой.

Atchevó ja ljubljú tebjá, svétlaja nóch?	Why do I love you, radiant night?
Tak ljubljú, shto, stradája, ljubújus' tabój!	Love you so, that I suffer as I drink you in!
I za shtó ja ljubljú tebjá, tíkhaja nóch?	And what is it I want from you, quiet night?
Ty ne mné, ty drugím pasylájesh pakój!	You send peace to others, not to me!
Shtó mne zvjózdy, luná, nebasklón, ablaká,	What to me are stars, moon, horizon, clouds,
Etat svét, shto, skal'zjá na khalódnyj granít,	This light, sliding over cold granite,
Prevrashchájet v almázy rasínki tsvetká,	Turning a flower's dewdrops to diamonds,
I kak pút' zalatój cherez móre bezhýt!	Running like a golden path across the sea!
Nóch, za shtó mne ljubít' tvoj serébrjanyj svét?	Night, why do I love your silver light?
Usladít li on górech skryvájemykh sljós?	Will it sweeten the bitterness of hidden tears?
Dást li zhádnamu sérttsu zhelánnyj atvét?	Give an avid heart the answer it desires?
Razreshýt li samnénij tjazhólyj vaprós?	Resolve the hard question posed by doubts?

Sam ne znáju, za shtó ja ljubljú tebjá, nóch,   I don't know why it is I love you, night,
Tak ljubljú, shto, stradája, ljubújus' tabój!   Love you so, that I suffer as I drink you in!
Sam ne znáju, za shtó ja ljubljú tebjá,   I don't know why it is I love you,
    nóch...   night...
Attavó, mózhet být', shto daljók moj pakój.   Maybe it's because my peace is far away.

TEXT. **Yákov Polónsky**, 1850; first published in the journal *Moskvitianin* (Muscovite) in 1851, part 1, no. 2. Title "Ночь" (Night). This is the only setting of the poem. Tchaikovsky cut eight lines of the original poem, and changed the word "doubt" to the plural.

METER. Ternary. Anapest, 4-foot:

> *What are stars and the moon, the horizon and clouds,*
> *And the light that turns dewdrops on flowers to diamonds?*

MUSIC. 1886. Op. 60, no. 9. G minor. 9/8, Moderato assai, molto espressivo. For High Voice: d^1–g^2. Dedicated to **Empress María Fyódorovna**.

RECORDINGS. Christoff, Gmyria, Kamionsky, Larin, Lemeshev, Lisovsky, Martynov, Mei-Figner, Obraztsova, Pirogov, Reizen, Shumskaya, Tourel, Vinogradov, Vishnevskaya.

ॐ

83 *За окном в тени мелькает*
Through the window in the shadows
Op. 60, No. 10

This spirited courting poem by Polonsky is a man's equivalent to the song of the gypsy girl. Though the poem lacks the depth that the theme of fate gives to Song 80, it is a finely realized sketch of a Don Juan, but a simpler, straight-forward, unsophisticated "Russian" Don, portrayed in the style of Russian realism. The music skillfully conveys the young man's seductive charm and ardent determination.

За окном в тени мелькает
Русая головка.
Ты не спишь, моё мученье!
Ты не спишь, плутовка!

Выходи ж ко мне навстречу!
С жаждой поцелуя,
К сердцу сердце молодое
Пламенно прижму я.

Ты не бойся, если звёзды
Слишком ярко светят:
Я плащом тебя одену
Так, что не заметят!

Если сторож наш окликнет —
Назовись солдатом;
Если спросят, с кем была ты, —
Отвечай, что с братом!

Под надзором богомолки
Ведь тюрьма наскучит;
А неволя поневоле
Хитрости научит!

Za aknóm f tení mel'kájet	Through the window in the shadows I glimpse
Rúsaja galófka.	That darling head of light brown hair.
Ty ne spísh, majó muchén'je!	You're not asleep, my torment!
Ty ne spísh, plutófka!	You're not asleep, my rascal!

Vykhadí sh ka mné nafstréchu!	Then come on out and see me!
Z zházhdaj patselúja,	Hungry for a kiss,
K sérttsu sérttse maladóje	I'll press my young heart to yours
Plámenna prizhmú ja.	In a burning embrace.
Tý ne bójsa, jésli zvjózdy	Don't fear if the stars
Slíshkam járka svétjat:	Are shining too brightly:
Ja plashchóm tebjá adénu	I'll wrap you in my cloak
Ták, shto ne zamétjat!	So no one will see us!
Jésli stórash nash aklíknet,	If the watchman calls "who goes there?",
Nazavís' saldátam;	Answer as a soldier;
Jésli sprósjat, s kém bylá ty,	If they ask you who was with you,
Atvecháj, shto z brátam!	Say it was your brother!
Pad nadzóram bagamólki	Under the eye of a chaperone
Vet' tjur'má naskúchit;	Prison life gets boring;
A nevólja panevóle	Sooner or later, willy-nilly,
Khítrasti naúchit!	It will teach you cunning!

TEXT. **Yákov Polónsky**, 1844; first published in *Otechestvennye zapiski* (Notes of the Fatherland) in 1845, no. 5. Title: Вызов (Invitation). Set by several composers before Tchaikovsky, including Dargomyzhsky (1858).

METER. Binary. Trochaic, alternating lines of 4 and 3 feet:

> *If they ask you who was with you,*
> *Say it was your brother!*

MUSIC. 1886. Op. 60, no. 10. F Major. 2/4, Allegro vivo (piano introduction), Allegro moderato, with variations (voice part). For High Voice: d^1–a^2. Dedicated to **Empress María Fyódorovna**.

RECORDINGS. Descamps, Guliayev, Karolik, Kozlovsky, Lemeshev, Levinsky, Lisovsky, Martynov, Rodgers, Shaposhnikov, Söderström, Tear.

Dargomyzhsky: Andrey Ivanov.

❧

84 *Подвиг*
Heroism

Op. 60, No. 11

The two songs to texts by Aleksey Khomyakov (Song 74 and this song) were the last written in the opus; Tchaikovsky thought them the best. The title of this song, which for convenience I have translated as "heroism," means a "heroic deed," "exploit," "feat." But these words are not used in English in the same way that "подвиг" (pronounced pódvik) is in Russian, where it denotes a concept essential to Russian thinking. (For comments on how this word is used, half ironically, in daily life in Russia today, see *Ries*, 53.)

The word implies the presence of that quality which in English is properly called "heroic virtue." Achievements worthy of the name are won with great difficulty over time, at a cost of significant sacrifice and suffering. In our own time, the achievement of an Alexander Solzhenitsyn or an Andrey Sakharov is what is meant by "подвиг." But theirs are public achievements; in this poem, Khomyakov defines heroic virtue in the private life of any man or woman. Tchaikovsky's very powerful song, where falling intonation is counterbalanced with rising crescendos, is subtitled "Monologue for Baritone."

> Подвиг есть и в сраженьи,
> Подвиг есть и в борьбе;
> Высший подвиг в терпеньи,
>   Любви и мольбе.
>
> Если сердце заныло
> Перед злобой людской,
> Иль насилье схватило
> Тебя цепью стальной;
> Если скорби земные
> Жалом в душу впились,
> С верой бодрой и смелой
> Ты за подвиг берись.
> Есть у *подвига* крылья,
> И взлетишь ты на них
> Без труда, без усилья
> Выше мраков земных,
> Выше крыши темницы,
> Выше злобы слепой,
> Выше воплей и криков
> Гордой черни людской.
>
> (repeat the first four lines)

Pódvik jést' i f srazhén'ji,	There is heroism in battle,
Pódvik jést' i v bar'bé;	Heroism in struggle too;
Výsshyj pódvik f terpén'ji,	The highest heroism is in endurance,
Ljubví i mal'bé.	In love and in prayer.

Jésli sérttse zanýla	If your heart aches
Pered zlóbaj ljutskój,	From the malice of man,
Il' nasíl'je skhvatíla	Or oppression seizes you
Tebjá tsép'ju stal'nój;	In a steel chain;
Jésli skórbi zemnýje	If the sorrows of this world
Zhálam v dúshu fpilís',	Have stung your soul to the quick,
S véraj bódraj i smélaj	With bold and active faith
Ty za pódvik berís'.	Commit yourself to heroism.
Jést' u pódviga krýl'ja,	Heroism has wings,
I vzletísh ty na níkh	And they will carry you up
Bez trudá, bez usíl'ja	Without toil, without effort,
Výshe mrákaf zemnýkh,	Higher than earthly darkness,
Výshe krýshy temnítsy,	Higher than the prison roof,
Výshe zlóby slepój,	Higher than blind malice,
Výshe vóplej i kríkaf	Higher than the cries and shouts
Górdaj chérni ljutskój.	Of the madding crowd.

Pódvik jést' i f srazhén'ji,	There is heroism in battle,
Pódvik jést' i v bar'bé;	Heroism in struggle too;
Výsshyj pódvik f terpén'ji,	The highest heroism is in endurance,
Ljubví i mal'bé.	In love and in prayer.

Text. **Alekséy Khomyakóv**, 1859. First published in the journal *Russkaia beseda* (Russian Colloquy) in 1859, no. 2. Untitled. Set only by Tchaikovsky.

Meter. Ternary. Anapest, lines of 2 feet, with frequent additional downbeats on the first syllable of the line:
Bravest deeds are in struggle,
Love, endurance, and prayer.

Music. 1886. Op. 60, no. 11. G Minor. 12/8, Andante. For Baritone: d¹–a². Dedicated to **Empress María Fyódorovna**.

Recordings. Burchuladze, Descamps, Fischer-Dieskau, Hvorostovsky, Karolik, Kastorsky, Maksakova, Mazurok, Mkrtchyan, Nesterenko, Petrov, Reizen, Tear.

85 *Нам звёзды кроткие сияли* / *Mild stars shone down on us*

Op. 60, No. 12

This attractive lyric to a song which has always been a favorite is a quintessential urban romance that looks back on youth to regret its passing. The first line of the second stanza, "we were young, we were in love," could be the theme-statement for dozens and dozens of late 19th and early 20th-century Russian songs.

It resembles the lyric of Song 19, "Reconciliation"; its final question may even be an allusion to Song 19. But it is not quite the same, because that lyric is a solitary, elegiac reflection on the past. This song is in the first person plural; the regret expressed here is for what *we* once had and now have lost. Musically, it is different, too, the markings in the score being "with tenderness," "cantabile," "dolce," all punctuated by throbbing little triplets that rise in crescendo.

The third stanza is sung to a different tempo, marked "agitato," culminating in the strange question "where's the bright swarm?", an original image which encapsulates the whole theme. In *War and Peace*, Tolstoy compared the swarming life of countless individuals to a hive of bees. Here, Pleshcheyev uses another bee-keeper's metaphor as an image of the "swarm" of innumerable hopes and dreams once shared by two young people when all of life lay before them. To the question at the end of the song, "when will you forget, oh heart, what spring once gave us?", there can be only one answer.

The song is a gentler sequel to the starker notes heard in Song 5, "Not a word, my friend," also by Pleshcheyev, but a translation. Here, in an original lyric, the poet acknowledges loss with the same tenderness and compassion, but he also elaborates on the poetry of the happiness that once was.

Нам звёзды кроткие сияли,
Чуть веял тихий ветерок,
Кругом цветы благоухали,
И волны ласково журчали
   У наших ног.

Мы были юны, мы любили,
И с верой вдаль смотрели мы;
В нас грёзы радужные жили,
И нам не страшны вьюги были
   Седой зимы.

Где ж эти ночи с их сияньем,

С благоухающей красой,
И волн таинственным журчаньем,
Надежд, восторженных мечтаний
   Где светлый рой?
   Где светлый рой?

Померкли звёзды, и уныло
Поникли блёклые цветы...
Когда ж, о сердце, всё, что было,
Что нам весна с тобой дарила,
   Забудешь ты,
   Забудешь ты?

Nam zvjózdy krótkije sijáli,	Mild stars shone down on us,
Chut' véjal tíkhij veterók,	A soft breeze barely stirred the air,
Krugóm tsvetý blagaukháli,	Flowers spread their fragrance all around,
I vólny láskava zhurcháli	And waves were gently lapping
U náshikh nók.	At our feet.
My býli júny, my ljubíli,	We were young, we were in love,
I s véraj vdal' smatréli mý;	With faith we looked to the future;
V nas grjózy ráduzhnyje zhýli,	Joyful dreams were alive in us,
I nam ne stráshny v'júgi býli	We weren't afraid of the blizzards
Sedój zimý.	Of grey-haired winter.
Gdé sh èti nóchi s ykh siján'jem,	Where, now, are those starlit nights,
Z blagaukhájushchej krasój,	Their beauty in all its fragrance,
I vóln taínstvennym zhurchán'jem,	The mysterious murmur of the waves,
Nadésht, vastórzhennykh mechtánij,	Of all those hopes, those joyous dreams,
Gde svétlyj rój?	Where's the bright swarm?
Gde svétlyj rój?	Where's the bright swarm?
Pamérkli zvjózdy, i unýla	The stars are dimmer now, and dejectedly
Poníkli bljóklyje tsvetý...	The faded flowers droop...
Kagdá sh o sérttse, fsjó, shto býla,	Can you forget, oh heart, all that used to be,
Shto nam vesná s tabój daríla,	The gifts spring gave the two of us,
Zabúdesh tý,	Can you forget,
Zabúdesh tý?	Can you forget?

TEXT. **Alekséy Pleshchéyev**, 1884. Title: Слова для музыки (Words for music). First published in the journal *Teatral'nyi mirok* (Theater World) in 1884, no. 34. First set by Tchaikovsky, later by Vasily Kalinnikov (1890). In the manuscript and published editions of the song before *PSS*, the author of the text is mistakenly identified as Polonsky.

METER. Binary. Iambic tetrameter, with a 2-foot line at the end:

> *Can you forget, when we were young,*
> *The gifts spring gave the two of us,*
> *Can you forget?*

MUSIC. 1886. Op. 60, no. 12. F Major. 4/4, Andante tenero; the third stanza is in 3/2 time, at a faster tempo. For Middle Voice: c^1–g^2 flat. Dedicated to **Empress María Fyódorovna**.

RECORDINGS. Borodina, Christoff, Gmyria, Isakova, Kasrashvili, Kazarnovskaya, Larin, Lemeshev, Maksakova, Milashkina, Nesterenko, Obraztsova, Obukhova, Petrov, Rautio, Schmitt-Walter (in German), Siniavskaya, Vinogradov, Vorvulev.

6 Romances, Opus 63 (1887)

The poet K. R. who wrote the lyrics to the six songs of Opus 63, and Grand Duke Konstantin Konstantinovich Romanov (1858-1915), to whom the songs are dedicated, were one and the same person. In 1880, this twenty-two-year-old grandson of Nicholas I and officer in the Emperor's suite asked to meet Tchaikovsky. He was a poet and a serious musician. Tchaikovsky had never met him, nor did he want to, but to his surprise, he found the young man very agreeable. After the meeting, the Grand Duke wrote in his diary: "19 March 1880. I spent a charming evening with Tchaikovsky, our best composer. Also present were his brother Anatoly [and the poet] Apukhtin... Pyotr Ilyich Tchaikovsky appears to be about 35, though his face and graying hair make him look older. He's short, rather thin, with a small beard and mild intelligent eyes. His movements, manner of speaking, and whole appearance show him to be a man extremely well brought up, educated, and kind. He went to school at the Law Academy, was very unhappy in his family life, and now devotes himself exclusively to music. Apukhtin is well known for his inordinate corpulence and his fine poems, which nothing can persuade him to publish: he knows them by heart and recites them aloud. He recited one of his less well-known poems 'Venice,' which is so good, your only thought is you fear it will end and you want it to go on and on. I was forced to play; I wanted to play a romance of Tchaikovsky's, but was afraid to. His brother sings; I accompanied him on 'A Tear Trembles' [Song 7], then played 'None but the Lonely Heart' [Song 9]... Tchaikovsky was asked to play something from his new opera *The Maid of Orleans*, not yet published; he sat down at the piano and played the prayer for chorus. We were all enraptured by the wonderful music: it's the moment when the people have realized Joan of Arc's prophetic gift, and she calls on the crowd to pray to God. Formally it resembles the prayer in the first act of *Lohengrin*: the voices gradually rise and grow stronger until chorus and orchestra reach *fortissimo* and the highest note... We went home at 2 a.m.—Tchaikovsky made the most pleasant impression on me" (*Romanov 1998*, 78-9). Two weeks later, Tchaikovsky was invited to the Marble Palace where the Grand Duke lived, and stayed late into the night talking. "We parted with frank mutual cordiality, as though we'd known each other a long time and were even friends. His near-sighted eyes sparkled with kindness, affection, and intelligence" (*ibid.*, 81).

What ensued was a friendship between two artists. They corresponded for the remainder of Tchaikovsky's life. Konstantin (as he signed his letters) presented him with a little book of songs published anonymously in Hamburg in 1880 called "Six Romances" (*Romanov 1999*, 33): two were to poems of Aleksey Tolstoy that Tchaikovsky himself had set to music (Songs 4 and 46). A few years later he published his first book of poems called "Стихотворения К. Р."

(Poems of K. R., St. Petersburg, 1886). This private edition, printed in 1000 copies, was not sold in shops but distributed personally by the poet as a gift to his friends and correspondents. K. R. was serious about his poetry: "I do not want to be a dilettante in literature," he wrote the critic Strakhov, who was one of the men he turned to for criticism of his poetry (*Romanov 1999*, 23). Tchaikovsky received his signed copy of K. R.'s first book in September 1886. Now in his archive at Klin, it shows sketches in the margins for some of the songs in this opus. At Maidanovo at the end of November 1887, when he finished orchestrating *The Sorceress*, he wrote the six romances of Opus 63, dedicating them to Konstantin. Jurgenson engraved them handsomely and they were published in 1888, with texts in Russian and German.

The Grand Duke also corresponded with Apollon Maikov, Yakov Polonsky, and Afanasy Fet. He rejoiced to hear that Tchaikovsky and "dear old Fet" had met at last at Fet's country estate in August 1891. Fet presented Tchaikovsky with a poem (*Fet*, 326), and Fet's wife, knowing Tchaikovsky liked flowers, gave him a bouquet (*Romanov 1999*, 79). The impression K. R.'s poetry first made on Fet was its "cordial sincerity" (задушевная искренность), a quality Tchaikovsky conveys well in the songs of Opus 63. The very fact of poetry coming from such a source was extraordinary. Here was a man whose daily routine began at nine when he went to his regiment, where he spent the greater part of the day, then caught a nap before the evening ball or other social duties. He embarked on a three-year cruise around the world on a navy frigate soon after meeting Tchaikovsky (whom he invited to go with him on the cruise!), but this was interrupted in Naples when Alexander II was assassinated in 1881. In middle life he was President of the Academy of Sciences and father of eight living children. When Polonsky asked him in a letter of 1894 how he spent his days, Konstantin replied: "I'm here in the Marble Palace, and do the same thing I do every day—the business of the Academy of Sciences and the Preobrazhensky Regiment; twice a day I go to memorial services, held during the day at the regiment or St. Isaac's, and in the evening at the Winter Palace" (*ibid.*, 26). Only his regular work habits (a trait he and Tchaikovsky had in common) enabled him to find time to write. He translated *Hamlet* and *Henry IV*, wrote a play about Christ called *The King of Judah* (a subject suggested to him by Tchaikovsky), and a long poem about the martyrdom of St. Sebastian. He also kept a diary from 1874 until his death (64 volumes) and carried on a voluminous correspondence: these private papers are only now being published, since during the Soviet period K. R. was a name rarely mentioned and almost unknown. In Vol. 45 of *PSS*, the name "K. R[omanov]" is given as the author of the lyrics to Opus 63, but, as was the case with the Empress in Opus 60, the dedication—"To His Imperial Highness Grand Duke Konstantin Konstantinovich"—has been erased.

86 *Я сначала тебя не любила*
I didn't love you at first

Op. 63, No. 1

In Athens in 1883 K. R. wrote nine lyrics which he grouped together in a cycle called "For a Groom and Bride." They are not linked to each other in any way except that they are poems about stages of love. Sometimes the speaker is a woman, sometimes a man; in some of them the lover is happy, in others not. They do not seem to be addressed to a particular couple: the title of the cycle indicates only that these are feelings any betrothed lovers might experience. In writing them, K. R. no doubt drew on his own experience, but he is not the speaker in these poems. In the text of this song, the speaker is a woman.

Я сначала тебя не любила,
Ты тревожил меня и пугал,
Меня новая участь страшила,
И неведомый жребий смущал.

Твоего я боялась признанья…
Но настал неминуемый час,
И, не помня себя, без сознанья,
Я навеки тебе отдалась.

И рассеялись вдруг опасенья,
Прежней робости нет и следа:
Под лучами зари во мгновенье
Так туманная тает гряда.

Словно солнце, любовь просияла,
И немеркнущий день заблистал:
Жизнью новою сердце взыграло,
И священный огонь запылал.

Ja snachála tebjá ne ljubíla,	I didn't love you at first,
Ty trevózhyl menjá i pugál,	You alarmed and frightened me,
Menja nóvaja úchast' strashýla,	I was afraid of how it might turn out,
I nevédamyj zhrébij smushchál.	Uncertain of the unknown future.

Tvajevó ja bajálas' priznán'ja...
No nastál neminújemyj chás,
I, ne pómnja sebjá, bes saznán'ja,
Ja navéki tebé addalás'.

I rasséjalis' vnóf' apasén'ja,
Prézhnej róbasti nét i sledá:
Pad luchámi zarí va mgnavén'je
Tak tumánnaja tájet grjadá.

Slóvna sóntse, ljubóf' prasijála,
I ne mérknushchij dén' zablistál:
Zhýzn'ju nóvaju sérttse vzygrála,
I svjashchénnyj agón' zapylál.

I feared your declaration of love...
But the inevitable hour arrived,
And, without reflection, instinctively,
I gave myself to you forever.

And at once my misgivings vanished,
My former shyness is completely gone:
So a cloud of fog in an instant
Dissolves in the first rays of dawn.

Love shone forth like the sun,
And unfading day gleamed bright:
My heart leaped up in new life,
And the sacred fire was kindled.

TEXT. **K. R.**, 15 February 1883, Athens. Untitled. Published in *Romanov 1886*. Poem 6 in the cycle "Жениху и невесте" (For a Groom and Bride). After Tchaikovsky, set by Rebikov (Op. 20/2, 1901).

METER. Ternary. Anapest, 3-foot:
> *I was frightened at first that you loved me,*
> *Of a future unknown, unforeseen...*

MUSIC. 1887. Op. 63, no. 1. B Flat Major. 6/8, Moderato mosso. For High Voice: f¹–f². Dedicated to **Grand Duke Konstantín Konstantínovich**.

RECORDINGS. Isakova, Preobrazhenskaya.

87 *Растворил я окно*
I opened the window wide

Op. 63, No. 2

The theme of the homesickness (тоска) of a Russian man in a "foreign land," on "another shore," far from home, is very common in Russian songs. Examples are everywhere, but this one in folk style (*PRP I*, 480) is by Ivan Lazhechnikov, on whose novel *Oprichnik* Tchaikovsky based his early opera:

… запел душа-соловушко	… the dear nightingale burst into song,
В чужой-дальней стороне;	In a distant foreign land;
Он всё горький сиротинушка,	He is still a bitter orphan there,
Он всё тот же, что и был;	He's the same as he always was;
Не забыл он песнь заветную,	He has not forgotten his one true song,
Всё про край родной поёт,	He still sings of his native land,
Всё поёт в тоске про милую,	He sings of his sweetheart, homesick still,
С этой песней и умрёт.	He will sing this song till he dies.

K. R.'s poem is, of course, completely different, stated in modern terms, from the point of view of a man who is abroad (he was in Germany when he wrote it). But the presence of these same images of the nightingale's song and over-whelming homesickness for Russia shows how well K. R. feels the tradition.

Tchaikovsky made a small change in the verb form in line 5 (from так пел to запел), and a significant change in the first line of the poem. In K. R.'s poem, the reason for opening the window is that it is "unbearably sad" in the room (стало грустно невмочь); the composer changed this to the more down-to-earth desire simply to get a breath of fresh air (стало душно невмочь).

Tchaikovsky considered this romance one of the two best in the opus. It has never dated or lost its poignancy, which is controlled, lyrical, and completely convincing.

Растворил я окно, стало душно невмочь,
Опустился пред ним на колени,
И в лицо мне пахнула весенняя ночь
Благовонным дыханьем сирени.

А вдали где-то чудно запел соловей;
Я внимал ему с грустью глубокой
И с тоскою о родине вспомнил своей,
Об отчизне я вспомнил далёкой,

Где родной соловей песнь родную поёт
И, не зная земных огорчений,
Заливается целую ночь напролёт
Над душистою веткой сирени.

Rastvaríl ja aknó, stála dúshna
nevmóch,
   Apustílsa pred ním na kaléni,
I v litsó mne pakhnúla vesénnjaja nóch
   Blagavónnym dykhán'jem siréni.

A vdalí gde-ta chúdna zapél
salavéj;
   Ja vnimál jemu z grúst'ju glubókaj
I s taskóju a ródine fspómnil svajéj,
   Ab atchízne ja fspómnil daljókaj,

Gde radnój salavéj pésn'
radnúju pajót
   I, ne znája zemnýkh agarchénij,
Zalivájetsa tséluju nóch napraljót
   Nad dushýstaju vétkaj siréni.

I opened the window wide for a
breath of air,
   I fell to my knees before it,
And I felt the spring night in my face
   With its fragrant scent of lilac.

Somewhere far off a nightingale began
a marvelous song;
   I listened with profound sadness,
And with longing I thought of home,
   Thought of my distant homeland,

Where a Russian nightingale sings a
Russian song,
   And, knowing no earthly sorrows,
Floods the night with music till dawn
   On a sweet-scented branch of lilac.

TEXT. **K. R.**, 13 May 1885, Meiningen. Untitled. Published in *Romanov 1886*. After Tchaikovsky, set by nine composers, including a "melodeclamation" by Arseny Koreshchenko, a student of Taneyev and Arensky.

METER. Ternary. Anapest, alternating lines of 4 and 3 feet:
   When I opened the window I fell to my knees,
   On the breeze came the scent of the lilacs…

MUSIC. 1887. Op. 63, no. 2. F Major. 9/8, Allegro. For Middle Voice: d^1–f^2. Dedicated to **Grand Duke Konstantín Konstantínovich.**

RECORDINGS. Gmyria, Hvorostovsky, Kasrashvili, Larin, Lemeshev, Martynov, Leokadiya Maslennikova, Mazurok, Mkrtchyan, Nesterenko, Obukhova, Ognivtsev, **Ots**, Petrov.

88 *Я вам не нравлюсъ*
You don't like me

Op. 63, No. 3

In theme, this song is a more sedate variation on a famous woman's song by Dargomyzhsky called Я всё ещё его, безумная, люблю (Crazy I am, but I love him still, 1851), which became very popular and widely known after Viardot sang it in 1853 (in *Viardot*). Another well-known song on this theme is the popular urban romance called Но я вас всё-таки люблю (But I love you all the same), written by N. A. Lensky, who worked with Yakov Prigozhii in the 1880s and 1890s—a song still sung today by singers like Nani Bregvadze (the text is in *Petrovskii 1997*, no. 37). This same phrase is the last line of the first stanza of K. R.'s poem. Of course his poem is quite different in feeling from the boulevard sentiments of the Lensky song, but it shows the impact of the urban romance tradition on Russian poetry at all levels, including the Romanov court.

The lyric is another poem from K. R.'s "Groom and Bride" cycle. It gives the impression it was written for the sake of the last line, with its participle six syllables long describing dead-end dreams, suffered through until nothing is left. The song, however, is heartfelt from the first note to the last, expressing vulnerability, a plea for understanding, and hope for reciprocity of feeling.

> Я вам не нравлюсь… Вы любили
> Лишь дружбу, не любовь мою;
> Мои надежды вы сгубили,
> И всё-таки я вас люблю!
>
> Когда же после, как-нибудь,
> Поймёте вы мои мученья,
> И не заметно в вашу грудь
> Проникнет капля сожаленья, —
>
> То будет поздно… Расцветают
> Лишь раз весенние цветы:
> Уж сердца вновь не приласкают
> Перестрадавшие мечты.

Ja vam ne nrávljus'… Vy ljubíli
Lish drúzhbu, ne ljubóf' majú;
Maji nadézhdy vy zgubíli,
I fsjó-taki ja vás ljubljú!

You don't like me… You liked
My friendship, not my love;
You dashed my hopes,
And still I love you!

Kagdá zhe pósle, kak-nibút',	But when, somehow, some day,
Pajmjóte vy maji muchén'ja,	You understand my torments,
I ne zamétna v váshu grút'	And a drop of pity
Praníknet káplja sazhalén'ja, —	Steals into your breast, —

To búdet pózna... Rastsvetájut	It will be too late... Only once
Lish rás vesénnije tsvetý:	Do spring flowers bloom:
Ush sérttsa vnóf' ne prilaskájut	A heart cannot be stirred again
Perestradáfshyje mechtý.	By dreams burned out in suffering.

TEXT. **K. R.**, 4 January 1883, Athens. Untitled. Published in *Romanov 1886*. Poem 1 in the cycle "Жениху и невесте" (For a Groom and Bride). After Tchaikovsky, set by several minor composers.

METER. Binary. Iambic tetrameter:

> *You liked my friendship, not my love,*
> *You dashed my hopes, but still I love you!*

MUSIC. 1887. Op. 63, no. 3. C Major. 4/4, Moderato; poco piu animato in stanza 2. For Middle Voice: d^1–f^2. Dedicated to **Grand Duke Konstantín Konstantínovich**.

RECORDINGS. Arkhipova, Borisenko, Isakova, Maksakova, Ognivtsev, Pirogov, Preobrazhenskaya, Reizen, Siniavskaya.

ॐ

89 *Первое свидание*
First meeting

Op. 63, No. 4

This is the last of three texts from the "Groom and Bride" cycle. The title refers to the first time lovers are reunited after a separation. Tchaikovsky wrote K. R. that he thought this romance turned out mediocre (очень неважен, *DG*, 448). It is not as bad as that, but the composer was not satisfied with it. It is a lively "allegro vivo" with rising intonation to express joy. Perhaps the composer was trying for something in the spirit of Mozart and felt the song had fallen short. However, there are several good recordings of it, showing that singers find it attractive.

Вот миновала разлука унылая,
Пробил свидания час, —
Светлое, полное счастие, милая,
Вновь наступило для нас.

Долго томилося, полно страдания,
Сердце твоё, но поверь:
Дни одиночества, дни испытания
Мы наверстаем теперь.

Нежные речи, любви выражения
Вновь потекут без конца,
И во единое снова биение
Наши сольются сердца.

Пусть сочетает созвучье единое
Наши две души, и вновь,
Словно весенняя песнь соловьиная,
Наша воспрянет любовь!

Vót minaвála razlúka unýlaja,
Próbil svidánija chás, —
Svétlaje, pólnaje shchástije, mílaja,
Vnóf' nastupíla dlja nás.

Our joyless separation is over now,
At last we're together again, —
Happiness, bright and complete, darling,
Has begun for us anew.

Dólga tamílasa, pólna stradánija,
Sérttse tvajó, no pavér':
Dní adinóchestva, dní ispytánija
Mý naverstájem tepér'.

Long did your heart pine, much did it suffer,
But this you must believe:
Days of loneliness, days of trial —
We're going to make up for them now.

Nézhnyje réchi, ljubví vyrazhénija	Tender speeches, expressions of our love,
Vnóf' patekút bes kantsá,	Will flow again without end,
I va jedínaje snóva bijénije	And, beating with one beat,
Náshy sal'jútsa serttsá.	Our hearts will be joined together.
Púst' sachetájet sazvúch'je jedínaje	Let that single harmony wed
Náshy dve dúshy, i vnóf',	Our two souls, and again,
Slóvna vesénnjaja pésn' salav'ínaja,	Like the spring song of the nightingale,
Násha vasprjánet ljubóf'!	Let our love take flight!

TEXT. **K. R.**, 7 March 1883. Title: Первое свидание (First meeting). Published in *Romanov 1886*. Poem 8 in the cycle "Жениху и невесте" (For a Groom and Bride). After Tchaikovsky, set by one minor composer as a duet.

The last word in the third stanza, "сердца" (hearts), is sometimes sung as "уста" (lips). Zara Dolukhanova sings it this way in her recording, for example. When Jurgenson first published Opus 63 in 1888, he printed "уста." The variant goes back to Tchaikovsky's manuscript, which has "уста" instead of "сердца." This is obviously an accidental slip, probably made by Tchaikovsky when he was copying out the words.

METER. Ternary. Dactyl, alternating lines of 4 and 3 feet:

> *Long were we parted, but that time is over now,*
> *And we're together again…*

MUSIC. 1887. Op. 63, no. 4. E Flat Major. 6/8, Allegro vivo. For High Voice: e[1] flat–g[2]. Dedicated to **Grand Duke Konstantín Konstantínovich**.

RECORDINGS. Borisenko, Borodina, Burchuladze, Dolukhanova, Krasnaya, Lemeshev, Milashkina, Söderström.

90 *Уж гасли в комнатах огни*
The lights were going out in the rooms

Op. 63, No. 5

With its theme "we were young and in love," this is a classic urban romance text, but K. R. chastely avoids sentimentality by using Fet's technique of writing about "what cannot be expressed in words." Not surprisingly, Fet told K. R. he thought this was one of the best poems in his book (*Romanov 1999*, 246). The result is a beautifully executed romance text with characteristic Russian imagery of the birch tree and the nightingale's song in the spring.

It elicited from Tchaikovsky one of his most perfect transformations of urban-romance material into musical language. Like Songs 40 and 85, it looks back on the past, but the mood is different, more serene. In its use of melodic lines followed by repeated notes, it seems to recapture something beautiful in the past and then hold on to it, sustain it on those repeated notes. Tchaikovsky considered the song one of the two best in the opus (*DG*, 448).

Уж гасли в комнатах огни...
　　Благоухали розы...
Мы сели на скамью в тени
　　Развесистой берёзы.

Мы были молоды с тобой!
　　Так счастливы мы были
Нас окружавшею весной,
　　Так горячо любили!

Двурогий месяц наводил
　　На нас своё сиянье;
Я ничего не говорил,
　　Боясь прервать молчанье;

Безмолвно синих глаз твоих
　　Ты опускала взоры:
Красноречивей слов иных
　　Немые разговоры.

Чего не смел поверить я,
　　Что в сердце ты таила,
Всё это песня соловья
　　За нас договорила.

Uzh gásli f kómnatakh agní...
　　Blagaukháli rózy...
My séli na skam'jú f tení
　　Razvésistaj berjózy.

My býli mólody s tabój!
　　Tak shchástlivy my býli
Nas akruzháfsheju vesnój,
　　Ták garjachó ljubíli!

The lights were going out in the rooms...
　　The roses smelled so fragrant...
We sat down on a bench in the shade
　　Of a wide-branching birch.

You and I were young!
　　We were so happy
In the spring that surrounded us,
　　How ardently we loved!

Dvurógij mésjats navadíl	The crescent moon sent down
Na nas svajó siján'je;	Its light on us;
Ja nichevó ne gavaríl,	I didn't say anything,
Bajás' prervát' malchán'je;	Afraid to interrupt the silence;
Bezmólvna sínikh glás tvajíkh	Saying nothing you lowered
Ty apuskála vzóry:	Your deep blue eyes:
Krasnarechívej slóf inýkh	More eloquent than any words
Nemýje razgavóry.	Are wordless conversations.
Chevó ne smél pavérit' ja,	What I did not dare believe,
Shto f sérttse ty tajíla,	What you kept hidden in your heart,
Fsjo èta pésnja salav'já	All this the song of the nightingale
Za nás dagavaríla.	Finished saying for us.

Text. **K. R.**, 30 July 1883, Pavlovsk. Untitled. Published in *Romanov 1886*. The first line is sometimes translated as the "fires" were going out, but I interpret these "fires" as lamps or candles, not logs burning in a fireplace. There is a minor textual variant in the last stanza, involving the way the first word of the first line is sung. In K. R. and Tchaikovsky, the word used is "Чего," a genitive form that naturally goes with the phrase "what I did not dare." Most singers, however, use the dative form "Чему" required by the verb "believe." Either form will work, without any change in meaning.

After Tchaikovsky, set by Yuly Bleikhman (a student of Rimsky-Korsakov); also by Alexander Blumental-Tamarin, author of popular romances, who published it in a songbook called "Gypsies in Kiev." This latter version, entitled "Былое" (Days gone by), omits the first stanza of K. R.'s poem. It was made famous by the gypsy contralto Varvara Panina (1872-1911), who recorded it.

Meter. Binary. Iambic, alternating lines of 4 and 3 feet:
More eloquent than any words
Are wordless conversations.

Music. 1887. Op. 63, no. 5. E Major. 4/4, Andantino. For High Voice: e[1]–f[2] sharp. Dedicated to **Grand Duke Konstantín Konstantínovich**.

Recordings. Arkhipova, Borodina, Dolukhanova, Lisitsian, Milashkina, Obraztsova, Obukhova, Ots, Preobrazhenskaya, Reizen, Vedernikov, **Vinogradov**.

↩

91 *Серенада*
Serenade

Op. 63, No. 6

This "allegretto" serenade moves along at such a lively tempo that it skips lightly over the rather wordy text, which has too much philosophy in it for a song meant to lull a girl to sleep. One of the stanzas in the original poem speaks of "the hour when inevitable fate will strike, and the world of sin gains power over you—you will know the curse of evil doubts and a time of trial will come." Tchaikovsky did not use this, and he made a few other small changes in wording.

As a song, it has always worked well. Tchaikovsky wrote "for tenor" on the score, and told K. R. he thought the public might like it if performed by a good singer like Nikolay Figner (*DG*, 449). Figner did not record it, but another very good tenor at the turn of the century, Ivan Yershov, did: it is the only recording by Yershov of a Tchaikovsky song.

О дитя! Под окошком твоим
Я тебе пропою серенаду.
Убаюкана пеньем моим,
Ты найдёшь в сновиденьях отраду.
　　Пусть твой сон и покой
　　В час безмолвный, ночной
Нежных звуков лелеют лобзанья.

Много горестей, много невзгод
Тебя в жизни, дитя, ожидает,
Спи же сладко, пока нет забот,
Пока сердце тревоги не знает.
　　Спи во мраке ночном
　　Безмятежным ты сном,
Спи, не зная земного страданья.

Пусть твой ангел хранитель святой,
Милый друг, над тобою летает,
И, лелея сон девственный твой,
Тебе райскую песнь напевает;
　　Пусть той песни святой
　　Отголосок живой
Тебе в душу вселит упованье.

Спи же, милая, спи, почивай
Под аккорды моей серенады!
Пусть приснится тебе светлый рай,
Преисполненный вечной отрады:
　　Пусть твой сон и покой
　　В час безмолвный ночной
Нежных звуков лелеют лобзанья.

O ditjá! Pad akóshkam tvajím
Ja tebé prapajú serenádu.
Ubajúkana pén'jem majím,
Ty najdjósh f snavidén'jakh atrádu.
　　Pust' tvoj són i pakój
　　F chás bezmólvnyj, nachnój
Nézhnykh zvúkaf lelèjut labzán'ja.

Oh child! Beneath your window
I will sing you a serenade.
Lulled by my singing,
Your dreams will be happy.
　　May your sleep and peace
　　In the silence of night
Be caressed by kisses of tender sounds.

Mnóga górestej, mnóga nevzgót	Many sorrows, many woes
Tebja v zhýzni, ditjá, azhydájet,	Await you, child, in life,
Spí zhe slátka, paká net zabót,	Sleep sweetly, now, while cares are absent,
Paka sérttse trevógi ne znájet.	And your heart knows no worry.
Spí va mráke nachnóm	Sleep in night's darkness
Bezmjatézhnym ty snóm,	Untroubled, undisturbed,
Spí, ne znája zemnóva stradán'ja.	Sleep in innocence of earthly suffering.
Púst' tvoj ángel khranítel' svjatój,	May your guardian angel,
Mílyj drúk, nad tabóju letájet,	Dear friend, fly over you,
I, leléja son défstvennyj tvój,	Caressing your innocent sleep,
Tebe rájskuju pésn' napevájet;	Singing you a heavenly song;
Púst' toj pésni svjatój	May this living echo
Adgalósak zhyvój	Of his divine song
Tebe v dúshu fselít upaván'je.	Fill your soul with hope.
Spí zhe, mílaja, spí, pachiváj	Then sleep, darling girl, sleep and slumber
Pad akkórdy majéj serenády!	To the chords of my serenade!
Púst' prisnítsa tebé svétlyj ráj,	May you dream of bright heaven,
Preispólnennyj véchnaj atrády:	Full of joy without end:
Pust' tvoj són i pakój	May your sleep and peace
F chás bezmólvnyj, nachnój	In the silence of night
Nézhnykh zvúkaf leléjut labzán'ja.	Be caressed by kisses of tender sounds.

TEXT. **K. R.**, 5 March 1882, Palermo. Title: "Серенада" (Serenade). Published in *Romanov 1886*. After Tchaikovsky, set by many composers, including a choral setting by Cui (Op. 46/2, 1893).

METER. Ternary. Anapest, lines of 3 feet, with short lines of 2 feet:
> *May your guardian angel protect you,*
> *While your heart knows no sadness or cares;*
> *With the sound of a kiss*
> *May his song give you bliss...*

MUSIC. 1887. Op. 63, no. 6. G Major. 6/8, Allegretto. For High Voice: d^1–a^2. Orchestrated by Taneyev for voice and symphony orchestra (published 1957: *MN*, 462). Dedicated to **Grand Duke Konstantín Konstantínovich**.

RECORDINGS. Arkhipova, Bogachova, Borisenko, Davydova, Dolukhanova, Gmyria, Kastorsky, Lemeshev, Levko, Lisovsky, Martynov, Milashkina, Nesterenko, Obukhova, Rodgers, Shumskaya, Söderström, Sterling, Vishnevskaya, Yershov, Zelenina.

6 Mélodies, Opus 65 (1888)

Of his failed earlier operas, the one closest to Tchaikovsky's heart was the comic opera *Vakula the Smith*, which he revised into *Cherevichki* (*The Slippers*). When it was given its premiere at the Bolshoy Theater on 31 January 1887, Tchaikovsky himself conducted it. It was his debut as a conductor. He was very nervous, but the performance went well. Conducting regularly, as he now began to do, brought a new dimension to his professional life. On 1 November 1887 he conducted the premiere of his newest opera, *Charodeika* (*The Enchantress*), in St. Petersburg. He liked the plot, which, though the action takes place in the 15th century, has a heroine with the spirit and charm of a Carmen, and for this soprano part especially he wrote some inspired music. But the problems with the opera became clear while he was composing it: it was too long, and the tragic outcome stretched belief. When the reviews came in, they were not favorable, though in this case Cui did put in a good word for him as a conductor: "the best performance was by the composer himself, a superlative, first-class conductor" (*DG*, 426).

At this time Tchaikovsky made the first of two grand tours of Europe as a conductor (1888, 1889), embarking for Leipzig, Hamburg, Berlin, Prague, Paris, and London. In Leipzig he met Brahms, whose music he respected but did not like ("the main thing—*beauty*—is missing!", *Romanov 1999*, 64). That same day he met Grieg, whom he liked and for whom he felt an immediate affinity as a composer who might be less of a master than Brahms, but who had a kindred "northern" soul that attracted him. Among others he met on this tour were Ferruccio Busoni, Richard Strauss, and Anton Dvořák. The whole tour was a great success, with Prague being a special triumph (*Brown IV*, 135-8). He returned to Prague in December to conduct the Czech premiere of *Eugene Onegin*, which was sung extremely well and brought one ovation after another (*DG*, 458).

Early on this first tour, in Berlin, he saw Désirée Artôt (1835-1907), the mezzo-soprano whom he had dreamed of marrying in 1868. They had not seen each other for twenty years. She asked him to write her a song. She was past fifty now, and teaching, but, having herself been a star pupil of Pauline Viardot, she was not about to quit singing yet. He promised to do this the next summer, but only after he finished the major works he was writing (his Fifth Symphony and the "Hamlet" overture, which he dedicated to Grieg). These were finished by early October. A few days later he had written not one, but six songs for her (the finished manuscript is dated "10/22 Octobre 1888"). The songs were all in French and written for the range of her voice.

Before they could be printed, they had to be translated into Russian. For this task Jurgenson engaged a singer, Aleksandra Santagano-Gorchakova (1842-

1913), who was best known for having translated *Carmen* into Russian, as well as innumerable other operas and romances to and from Russian. Tchaikovsky admired her for producing Glinka's *A Life for the Tsar* in Milan at her own expense (*MKS*, 324-9). When her translations were done, however, Tchaikovsky was not satisfied with them, but aside from revising a few phrases he let them stand. The songs were for Désirée, after all, who would sing them in French, not Russian. When she received them, she wrote "I only wanted one *Lied*, but you have written six for me. There is a saying 'generous as a king'— to which should be added 'or as an *artist*.'" She found the last three "splendid," and the first "charmingly fresh"; the third song was not mentioned, but she liked the second song too (*MN*, 462-5).

The six songs of Opus 65 come as a revelation. They are French in spirit, but shaped throughout by Tchaikovsky's genius for transforming feeling and subtle changes in feeling into his own musical language. The problem with the Russian translations is not that they need to be improved, but that the Russian language is not quite at home in these songs. They call for the *esprit*, the quickness, the shades of light and dark, the very sounds of the French language. With the exception of a few fine performances, Russian singers have not yet made these songs their own. Singers who can sing in French may rightly lay claim to them. Listening to Julia Varady's recording of the whole cycle straight through, one realizes what an engaging set of songs it is, now gay, now melancholy, never for a moment uninteresting or directionless. At least three of them are great songs.

The texts do not require extensive comment. They are by three minor 19th-century French poets: Augustine Malvine Blanchecotte (1830-1878), Édouard Turquety (1807-1867), and Paul Collin (1843-1915). Their verses were useful to Tchaikovsky not because they are memorable as poems, but because they provide good material to give musical expression to a range of different feelings evoked by the words, but stronger than just the words by themselves. The particular mood, sometimes quite intense, suggested by the poem is what both singer and listener need to keep in mind.

92 Sérénade
Serenade

Op. 65, No. 1

A serenade originally meant a song sung in the evening under a girl's window, but this frothy "souffle d'aurore" is a morning poem. The text is by Édouard Turquety, whose books published in the 1830s and 1840s have titles like *Amour et foi, Poésie catholique, Hymnes sacrées*, and *Fleurs à Marie*. Written as an allegretto waltz, this song bears a resemblance to the last song in Opus 63, also called a serenade, only here the basic piano figure is played staccato. It is a light and captivating confection. It was the first song Jessye Norman sang in Russia, at the Tchaikovsky gala in Leningrad in 1990, where she was accompanied by the excellent Yevgeny Shenderovich.

Où vas-tu, souffle d'aurore,	Where are you going, breath of dawn,
Vent de miel qui viens d'éclore,	Honeyed breeze that comes at daybreak,
Fraîche haleine d'un beau jour?	Fresh breath of a lovely day?
d'un beau jour?	of a lovely day?
Où vas-tu, brise inconstante,	Where are you going, fickle breeze,
Quand la feuille palpitante	When the trembling leaf
Semble frissonner d'amour?	Seems to quiver with love?
Est-ce au fond de la vallée,	Is it to the depths of the valley
Dans la cime échevelée	In the wild summit
D'un saule où le ramier dort,	Of a willow where the dove sleeps,
le ramier dort?	the dove sleeps?
Poursuis-tu la fleur vermeille,	Do you follow the vermilion flower,
Ou le papillon qu'éveille	Or a butterfly awakened
Un matin de flamme et d'or?	By a morning of flame and gold?
Va plutôt, souffle d'aurore,	Go instead, breath of dawn,
Bercer l'âme que j'adore:	To lull to sleep the soul I adore:
Porte à son lit embaumé	Carry to her perfumed bed
L'odeur des bois	The fragrance of the woods
et des mousses,	and the mosses,
Et quelques paroles douces	And some words as sweet
Comme les roses de mai,	As the roses of May,
L'odeur des bois	The fragrance of the woods
et des mousses,	and the mosses,
Et quelques paroles douces	And some words as sweet
Comme les roses de mai.	As the roses of May.

Ты куда летишь, как птица,
юный сын младой денницы,
свежий, чистый ветерок? ветерок?
В даль спешишь, того не зная,
что от страсти замирая,
каждый здесь дрожит листок!

Иль в долину хочешь мчаться,
в тёмных ивах покачаться,
где спит сладко соловей?
спит меж ветвей?
Хочешь к розе ты спуститься,
с мотыльком ли порезвиться,
в майский день, под блеском лучей?

Нет, лети зарёю ясной
к той, кого люблю я страстно,
к ложу её понеси:
запах роз и трав душистых,
поцелуй мой нежный, чистый,
как дуновенье весны;

запах роз и трав душистых,
поцелуй мой нежный, чистый,
как дуновенье весны.

Ty kudá letísh, kak ptítsa,	Where are you flying, like a bird,
júnyj sýn mladój dennítsy,	youthful son of young day,
svézhyj, chístyj veterók? veterók?	fresh, pure breeze? breeze?
V dál' speshýsh, tavó ne znája,	Do you hasten far, not yet aware,
shto at strásti zamirája,	that fainting from passion,
kázhdyj zdés' drazhýt listók!	here each leaf is trembling!
Il' v dalínu khóchesh mchátsa,	Or are you dashing to the valley,
f tjómnykh ívakh pakachátsa,	to swing in dark willows,
gde spit slátka salavéj?	where the nightingale sweetly sleeps?
spit mezh vetvéj?	sleeps in the boughs?
Khóchesh k róze ty spustítsa,	Do you want to come down to the rose,
s matyl'kóm li parezvítsa,	to gambol with the butterfly,
v májskij dén', pad bléskam luchéj?	on a May day, in sparkling sunlight?

Nét, letí zarjóju jásnaj
k tój, kavó ljubljú ja strásna,
k lózhu jejó panesí:
zápakh rós i tráv dushýstykh,
patselúj moj nézhnyj, chístyj,
kak dunavén'je vesný;

No, fly at clear light of dawn
to her whom I passionately love,
bring to her bed:
scent of roses and fragrant grasses,
my kiss, tender and pure
as a breath of spring;

zápakh rós i tráv dushýstykh,
patselúj moj nézhnyj, chístyj,
kak dunavén'je vesný.

scent of roses and fragrant grasses,
my kiss, tender and pure
as a breath of spring.

TEXT. **Édouard Turquety** (sometimes spelled Turquetiz). Title: "Aurore";
Tchaikovsky changed the title to "Sérénade." Published in *Borel*, page 176.
Tchaikovsky's copy of *Borel* is in his archive at Klin.

Russian translation by **Aleksándra Santagano-Gorchakóva**. Title:
Серенада (Serenade). In addition to being a prolific translator, Gorchakova, a
soprano, studied singing in Milan, sang at the Kiev Opera from 1867-71, then
organized her own opera company which performed Russian operas in Italy in
the 1870s. After that she became a highly regarded vocal teacher (Leonid
Sobinov studied with her). There is information about her in standard sources
(*Agin, ME, MES*), and also in *Altaev*, 125-32; obituaries appeared in *Istoricheskii
vestnik*, St. Petersburg, May 1913, pp. 749-50, and *Teatr i iskusstvo*, St. Petersburg, 1913, no. 13, p. 292. In 1901, Fred Gaisberg made some recordings of
her in Moscow. One of these, Aliabiev's "Nightingale", a favorite showpiece
for coloratura soprano, is on "The Yale Collection of Historical Sound Recordings," CD YHS 0001/2.

MUSIC. 1888. Op. 65, no. 1. D Major. 3/4, Allegretto quasi andantino. For
Middle Voice: b–f² sharp. Dedicated to **Madame Désirée Artôt de Padilla**.

RECORDINGS. Arkhipova (in Russian), Borodina, Lisovsky (in Russian),
Norman, Nortsov (in Russian), Obukhova, Shpiller (in Russian), Söderström,
Varady, Vishnevskaya.

93 *Déception*
Disappointment

Op. 65, No. 2

There is a touch of the sorrow of Orpheus losing Eurydice in Paul Collin's poem. The French text is well used by Tchaikovsky in laconic phrases that seem almost like recitative passages from Monteverdi. Melancholy is distilled here, concentrated in the last six lines of the song where the voice cries out and the piano provides simple sustained chords with arpeggios held back. The Russian version of the song works, but not as well as the French. When Fyodor Chaliapin recorded it in Russian in 1902, he substituted the word "longing" (тоскою) for the word "spring" in the third line.

Le soleil rayonnait encore.	The sun was still shining.
J'ai voulu revoir les grands bois	I wished to see again the great woods
Où nous promenions autrefois	Where we used to promenade
Notre amour à sa belle aurore.	Our love at its lovely beginning.
Je me disais: "Sur le chemin,	I said to myself: "On the road
Je la retrouverai, sans doute;	I will doubtless find her;
Ma main se tendra vers sa main,	My hand will reach for her hand,
Et nous nous remettrons	And on the way we will find
en route."	reconciliation."
Je regarde partout. En vain!	I look everywhere. In vain!
J'appelle! Et l'écho seul m'écoute!	I call! And only the echo hears me!
O, le pauvre soleil pâli!	Oh, poor pale sun!
O, les pauvres bois sans ramage!	Oh poor woods without birdsong!
O, mon pauvre amour,	Oh my poor love,
quel dommage!	what a pity!
Si vite perdu dans l'oubli!	So quickly lost to oblivion!

Ярко солнце ещё блистало,
увидать хотел я леса,
где с весною вместе любви
и блаженства пора настала.

Подумал я: "в лесной тиши
её найду опять, как прежде,
и руки подав мне свои,
пойдёт за мной полна надежды."
Я напрасно ищу... Увы!
Взываю! Лишь эхо мне отвечает!

О, как скуден стал солнца свет.
Как печален лес и безгласен!
О, любовь моя, как ужасно
так скоро утратить тебя!

Járka sóntse jeshchó blistála,	The sun still shone brightly,
uvidát' khatél ja lesá,	I went to see the woods,
gde s vesnóju vméste ljubví	where with spring the time
i blazhénstva pará nastála.	of love and bliss began.
Padúmal ja: "v lesnój tishý	I thought: "in the hush of the woods
jejó najdú apját', kak prézhde,	I will find her again, as before,
i rúki padáf mne svají,	and giving me her hands,
pajdjót za mnój palná nadézhdy."	she will follow me full of hope."
Ja naprásna ishchú... Uvý!	I look in vain... Alas!
Vzyváju! Lish èkho mne	I call her! Only the echo
atvechájet!	answers!
O, kak skúden stal sóntsa svét.	Oh, how faint now is the sun's light.
Kak pechálen lés i bezglásen!	How sad and still are the woods!
O, ljubóf' majá, kak uzhásna	Oh, my love, how awful
tak skóra utrátit' tebjá!	to lose you so soon!

Text. **Paul Collin**. Title: Déception. Published in Collin's book of poems *Du grave au doux*, Paris, 1878, on page 188. Collin wrote the libretto for César Franck's oratorio *Rebecca* (1881). He may have met Tchaikovsky; he gave Tchaikovsky two of his books, now at Klin. He also translated some of Tchaikovsky's romances into French (his French versions of Songs 22, 30, and 56 may be found in *Schindler*, and Song 76 is in *Huneker*).

Russian translation by **Aleksándra Santagano-Gorchakóva**. Title: Разочарование (Disappointment).

Music. 1888. Op. 65, no. 2. E Minor. 2/4, Moderato. For Middle Voice: a–e². Dedicated to **Madame Désirée Artôt de Padilla**.

Recordings. Arkhipova (in Russian), Chaliapin (in Russian), Christoff (in Russian), Descamps, Kozlovsky (in Russian), Larin, Mazurok (in Russian), Norman (on video only), Ots, Reizen (in Russian), Söderström, Tear (in Russian), Varady.

94   *Sérénade*
Serenade

Op. 65, No. 3

If Désirée's silence about this song implies a criticism, the fault lies not so much in Tchaikovsky's music as in Paul Collin's poem, made up of one extravagant comparison after another. Like Song 91, this serenade works well as a song despite the wordy text. There is beautiful material here for the singer, as many of the recordings show, such as those by Nadezhda Obukhova in French, and, in Russian, Vera Davydova and Sergey Shaposhnikov.

J'aime dans le rayon de la limpide aurore	I love in the bright rays of the clear dawn
Le reflet de tes jolis yeux,	The reflection of your pretty eyes,
Dans le chant matinal de l'oiseau j'aime encore	In the morning song of the bird I love again
L'écho de ton rire joyeux.	The echo of your joyous laughter.
Dans le calme des lys j'aime ta paix sereine,	In the calm of lilies I love your serene peace,
Dans leur pureté, ta blancheur;	In their purity, your whiteness;
J'aime dans le parfum des roses ton haleine	In the perfume of roses I love your breath
Et dans leur fraîcheur, ta fraîcheur.	And in their freshness, your freshness.
Dans la mer que le flux ou le reflux agite	In the sea stirred by the ebb and flow of tides
J'aime tes caprices d'enfant,	I love your childish whims,
Et j'aime les soupirs de ton sein qui palpite	And I love the sighs of your palpitating bosom
Dans les longues plaintes du vent.	In the long laments of the wind.
J'aime la fière ardeur dont ton coeur sent la flamme	I love the proud ardor whose flame your heart feels
Dans l'éclat du soleil qui luit;	In the burst of the gleaming sun;
Et j'aime les pudeurs charmantes de ton âme	And I love the charming modesty of your soul
Dans l'ombre chaste de la nuit.	In the chaste darkness of the night.
J'aime dans le printemps qui verdit, la folie	In the spring that turns everything green I love the foolishness
De ta jeunesse et ses espoirs;	Of your youth and its hopes;
Et j'aime la douceur de ta mélancolie	And I love the gentleness of your melancholy
Dans le vague déclin des soirs,	In the hazy approach of evenings,
Dans le vague déclin des soirs!	In the hazy approach of evenings!

В ярком свете зари, блистающем и ясном,
отблеск вижу дивных очей!
Мнится, будто звучит в пеньи птиц сладкогласных
лишь эхо твоих детских речей!

В лилии нахожу твой покой безмятежный,
твою чистоту в ней люблю!
Запах роз, как твоё дыханье, сладко нежен,
в розах я люблю свежесть твою.

И люблю я в волне в час бурный её прилива
горячность и вспышки твои,
люблю я твои вопли и горя порывы
в свисте ветра, в шуме грозы.

Страсти пылкой твоей я люблю проявленье,
жжёт она, точно солнца луч;
луна в своей красе стыдливой — твоё воплощенье,
когда блестит нам из-за туч.

В юной, светлой весне я люблю возрожденье
грёз чистых и надежд твоих;
люблю я твою печаль и страсть уединенья
в тихом мраке теней ночных,
в тихом мраке теней ночных!

V járkam svéte zarí, blistájushchem i jásnam,	In the bright light of dawn, clear and brilliant,
óddblesk vízhu dívnykh achéj!	I see the reflection of your wonderful eyes!
Mnítsa, bútta zvuchít f pen'i ptíts slatkaglásnykh	I think the sweet sound of birds singing
lish èkho tvajíkh détskikh rechéj!	is a mere echo of your childlike voice!
V lílii nakhazhú tvoj pakój bezmjatézhnyj,	In the lily I find your calm peace,
tvajú chistatú v nej ljubljú!	in it I love your purity!
Západh rós, kak tvajó dykhán'je, slátka nézhen,	The smell of roses, like your breathing, is sweetly tender,
v rózakh ja ljubljú svézhest' tvajú.	In roses I love your freshness.
I ljubljú ja v valné f chas búrnyj jejó prilíva	And I love in the stormy hour of a cresting wave
garjáchnast' i fspýshki tvají,	your heat and your vivacity,
ljubljú ja tvají vópli i górja parývy	I love your cries and bursts of grief
f svíste vétra, f shúme grazý.	in the whistling wind, in the loud thunderstorm.

Strásti pýlkaj tvajéj ja ljubljú   I love your fiery passion
prajavlén'je,   when it breaks out,
zhzhót aná, tóchna sóntsa lúch;   it burns, like a ray of the sun;
luná f svajéj krasé stydlívaj — tvajó   the moon in its chaste beauty is your
vaplashchén'je,   incarnation,
kagdá blestít nam iz-za túch.   when it shines on us from behind clouds.

V júnaj, svétlaj vesné ja ljubljú   In youthful, bright spring I love
vazrazhdén'je   the rebirth
grjós chístykh i nadésht tvajíkh;   of your pure dreams and hopes;
ljubljú ja tvajú pechál' i strást'   I love your sadness and passion
ujedinén'ja   for seclusion
f tíkham mráke tenéj nachnýkh,   in the quiet darkness of night shadows,
f tíkham mráke tenéj nachnýkh!   in the quiet darkness of night shadows!

TEXT. **Paul Collin.** Title: Sérénade. Published in *Collin*, page 174.

Russian translation by **Aleksándra Santagano-Gorchakóva.** Title: Серенада (Serenade).

MUSIC. 1888. Op. 65, no. 3. B Flat Major. 6/8, Andante non troppo, con noblezza. For Middle Voice: d^1–f^2. Dedicated to **Madame Désirée Artôt de Padilla.**

RECORDINGS. Arkhipova (in Russian), Davydova (in Russian), Isakova (in Russian), Kudriavtseva (in Russian), Nortsov (in Russian), Obukhova, Shaposhnikov (in Russian), Varady.

∾

95 *Qu'importe que l'hiver*
 What does it matter that winter

Op. 65, No. 4

This text by Paul Collin comes from a cycle called "Poèmes d'octobre". The comparisons are again extravagant, but here at least they have a three-part structure and move in a certain direction. For the two short phrases at the end of each stanza, the "allegro vivo" slows to "andante" marked *dolce*.

Musically, as a song, it is one of Tchaikovsky's most brilliant creations. There is a fine recording of it in Russian by Lyudmila Legostayeva.

Qu'importe que l'hiver éteigne
les clartés
Du soleil assombri
dans les cieux attristés?
  Je sais bien où trouver encore
  Les brillants rayons d'une aurore
  Plus belle que celle des cieux.
    Toi que j'adore,
    C'est dans tes yeux!

What does it matter that winter
smothers the brilliance
Of the sun darkened
in the saddened sky?
  I know well where to find again
  The bright rays of a dawn
  Lovelier than that of the heavens.
    You, whom I adore,
    It is in your eyes!

Qu'importe que l'hiver ait
des printemps défunts
Dispersé sans pitié les enivrants
parfums?
  Je sais où trouver, non flétrie,
  Malgré les bises en furie,
  Une rose encore tout en fleur.
    O ma chérie,
    C'est dans ton cœur!

What does it matter that winter
has dispersed without pity
The intoxicating perfumes
of the dead spring?
  I know where to find, unfaded,
  Despite the cold wind's fury,
  A rose still fully in bloom.
    Oh my dear,
    It is in your heart!

Ce rayon que, bravant les ombres
de la nuit,
Toujours splendide et pur au fond
de tes yeux luit;
  Cette fleur toujours parfumée
  Qui dans ton cœur est enfermée
  Et qui sait survivre
  à l'été,
    Ma bien aimée,
    C'est ta beauté!

This ray, which braves the shadows
of night,
Always shines splendid and pure,
deep in your eyes.
  This flower, always perfumed,
  Locked up in your heart,
  And which knows how to last
  until summer,
    My adored one,
    It is your beauty!

Пускай зима погасит солнца светлый луч
и покроет эфир цепью сумрачных туч...
Знаю я, где искать блеск света,
солнца и лучей и рассвета
прекрасней зари в небесах.
О, дорогая,
в твоих лишь глазах!

Пускай зима покроет снегом все цветы
и суровой рукой рассеет лепестки...
Знаю я, где искать цвет прекрасный,
несмотря на холод дней ненастных,
розу, в свежей, пышной красе.
О, дорогая,
в твоей лишь душе!

Этот луч, что в глазах твоих всегда блестит,
которого ничто не может погасить;
тот цветок, что душа сохраняет,
что никогда не увядает,
пережив весенние дни.
О, дорогая,
то блеск красы!

Puskáj zimá pagásit sóntsa svétlyj lúch
i pakrójet efír tsép'ju súmrachnykh
túch...
Znáju ja, gde iskád' blesk svéta,
sóntsa i luchéj i rassvéta
prekrásnej zarí v nebesákh.
     O, daragája,
     f tvajíkh lizh glazákh!

Puskáj zimá pakrójet snégam fse tsvetý
i suróvaj rukój rasséjet lepestkí...
Znáju ja, gde iskát' tsvét prekrásnyj,
nesmatrjá na khólad dnéj nenásnykh,
rózu, f svézhej, pýshnaj krasé.
     O, daragája,
     f tvajéj lizh dushé!

Let winter extinguish the sun's bright ray
and cover the ether with a row of sullen
clouds...
I know where to seek a bright glow of light,
fairer than the dawn's rays
at daybreak in the heavens.
     O, darling,
     only in your eyes!

Let winter cover all the flowers with snow
and scatter the petals with a stern hand...
I know where to seek a fair flower,
despite the cold of stormy days,
a rose in its fresh, splendid beauty.
     O, darling,
     only in your soul!

Ètat lúch, shto v glazákh tvajíkh	This ray, that always shines in your
fsegdá blestít,	eyes,
katórava nishtó ne mózhet pagasít';	which nothing can extinguish;
tot tsvetók, shto dushá sakhranjájet,	that flower, kept in your soul,
shto nikagdá ne uvjadájet,	that never fades,
perezhýf vesénnije dní.	outlasting spring days.
O, daragája,	Oh, darling,
to blésk krasý!	it is your bright beauty!

Text. **Paul Collin.** Untitled. Fourth poem in a cycle entitled "Poèmes d'octobre". Published in *Collin*, page 159.

Russian translation by **Aleksándra Santagano-Gorchakóva.** Title: Пускай зима... (Let winter...).

Music. 1888. Op. 65, no. 4. D Minor. 2/4, Allegro vivo e molto rubato. For Middle Voice: c^1–f^2. Dedicated to **Madame Désirée Artôt de Padilla.**

Recordings. Arkhipova (in Russian), **Legostayeva** (in Russian), Lisitsian (in Russian), Mazurok (in Russian), Söderström, Varady.

∾

96 *Les larmes*
Tears

Op. 65, No. 5

Again, out of another suggestive but far from perfect text, Tchaikovsky made an extraordinary song that moves us immediately and haunts us afterwards. It is his only song recorded by the splendid Maggie Teyte. In Russian, there is an outstanding recording by Sergey Shaposhnikov which uses an improved translation not heard elsewhere, by an unknown hand, that brings the text closer to a Russian elegy along the lines of "Reconciliation" (Song 19).

Si vous donnez le calme après tant de
    secouses,
Si vous couvrez d'oubli
    tant de maux dérobés,
Si vous lavez ma plaie et si
    vous êtes douces,
      O mes larmes, tombez! tombez!

If you give calm after so many
    alarms,
If you cover with forgetfulness
    so many concealed wrongs,
If you wash my wound and if you
    are gentle,
      Oh my tears, fall, fall!

Mais, si comme autrefois
    vous êtes meurtrières,
Si vous rongez un coeur qui déjà
    brûle en soi,
N'ajoutez pas au mal, respectez
    mes paupières:
      O larmes, laissez mois, laissez moi!

But if, as at other times,
    you are murderers,
If you gnaw a heart which already
    burns inside,
Don't make it worse, spare
    my eyes:
      Oh tears, leave me, leave me!

Oui, laissez moi! je sens ma peine
    plus cuisante,
Vous avez évoqué tous mes rêves perdus:
Pitié! pitié! pitié! laissez mourir
    mon âme agonisante!
    Larmes, ne tombez pas! ne
    tombez pas! non! non! ne tombez pas!

Yes, leave me! I feel my pain
    becoming more intense.
You have evoked all my lost dreams:
Have pity, pity, pity! Leave my
    tormented soul to die!
    Tears, do not fall! do not fall!
    no! no! do not fall!

Если покой дадите за все треволненья
и смоете теперь дней минувших тоску,
если ранам всем моим несёте облегченье,
    лейтесь, слёзы, я вас молю!

Но, если и теперь вы смерть с собой несёте,
если вы разжигать пламя сердца должны,
не мучьте же меня, зачем всю грудь мне рвёте:
    о, слёзы, скройтесь вы, скройтесь вы!

Да, скройтесь вы! моя тоска ещё ужасней;
пробудили вы вновь горе прошлых годов!
О, сжальтесь, о, сжальтесь ещё и дайте смерть
моей душе несчастной!
Слёзы, застыньте вновь, застыньте вновь!
да, да, застыньте вновь!

Jésli pakój dadíte za fse trevalnén'ja
i smójete tepér' dnej minúfshykh taskú,
jésli ránam fsem majím nesjóte
ablekchén'je,
    léjtes', sljózy, ja vás maljú!

If you bring peace to all disquieting times
and wash away now the anguish of days past,
if you bring relief to all my
wounds,
    flow, tears, I beg you!

No, jésli i tepér' vy smért' s sabój nesjóte,
jésli vy razzhygát' plámja sérttse dalzhný,
ne múchte zhe menjá, zachém fsju grút'
mne rvjóte:
    O, sljózy, skrójtes' vy, skrójtes' vy!

But if you bring death now,
if you must fan the flame of the heart,
do not torment me, why tear my
breast:
    Oh, tears, vanish, vanish!

Da, skrójtes' vy! majá taská jeshchó
uzhásnej;
prabudíli vy vnof' góre próshlykh
gadóf!
O, zzhál'tes', o, zzhál'tes' jeshchó i
dájte smért' majéj dushé neshchásnaj!
    Sljózy, zastýn'te vnof', zastýn'te
vnof'! da, da, zastýn'te vnof'!

Yes, vanish! my anguish is even more
    terrible;
you have awakened again the grief of
years past!
Oh, have pity, have pity again and
give death to my unhappy soul!
    Tears, dry up again, dry up again!
    yes, yes, dry up again!

TEXT. **Augustine Malvine Blanchecotte**. Title: Les Larmes. Published in *Borel*, page 370. Tchaikovsky omitted the second stanza of the original poem; all the repetitions in the fourth line of each stanza are his.

Russian translation by **Aleksándra Santagano-Gorchakóva**. Title: Слёзы (Tears).

MUSIC. 1888. Op. 65, no. 5. G Major. 4/4, Andante doloroso. For Middle Voice: d^1–e^2. Dedicated to **Madame Désirée Artôt de Padilla**.

RECORDINGS. Arkhipova (in Russian), Golodiayevskaya (in Russian), Ots, Shaposhnikov (in Russian), Söderström, Teyte, Varady.

97 *Rondel*
Rondel

Op. 65, No. 6

Gorchakova's Russian translation skillfully preserves the rondel form of Paul Collin's poem. As used here, this involves repeating the first two lines in each stanza and using only two rhymes throughout.

Il se cache dans ta grâce
Un doux ensorcellement.
Pour leur joie et leur tourment
Sur les cœurs tu fais main basse.

In your grace is hidden
A gentle enchantment.
To their joy and torment
All hearts are taken prisoner
by your force.

Tous sont pris. Nul ne se lasse
De ce servage charmant.
Il se cache dans ta grâce
Un doux ensorcellement.

All are caught. None can resist
This charming bondage.
In your grace is hidden
A gentle enchantment.

C'est l'affaire d'un moment,
Ton regard qui sur nous passe
Est le filet qui ramasse
Nos âmes; Dieu sait comment!
Il se cache dans ta grâce
Un doux ensorcellement.

It only takes a moment;
Your gaze glancing over us
Is the net which gathers
Our souls; God knows how!
In your grace is hidden
A gentle enchantment.

Ты собою воплощаешь
силу чар и волшебства:
радость, счастье и тоска
от тебя придут, ты знаешь,

но всем тем, кого пленяешь,
рабства цепь не тяжела.
Ты собою воплощаешь
силу чар и волшебства!

Да, победа не трудна:
взглядом, что ты нам бросаешь,
ты, как сетью, обнимаешь
и ловишь у всех сердца...
Ты собою воплощаешь
силу чар и волшебства.

Ty sabóju vaplashchájesh
sílu chár i valshepstvá:
rádast', shchást'je i taská
at tebjá pridút, ty znájesh,

You are the embodiment
of charms and enchantment:
joy, happiness, and longing
are what you bring, you know,

no fsem tém, kavó plenjájesh,
rápstva tsép' ne tjazhelá.
Ty sabóju vaplashchájesh
sílu chár i valshepstvá!

but to everyone you captivate,
the chain of bondage is not heavy.
You are the embodiment
of charms and enchantment!

Da, pabéda ne trudná:
vzgljádam, shto ty nam brasájesh,
ty, kak sét'ju, abnimájesh
i lóvish u fsékh serttsá...
Ty sabóju vaplashchájesh
sílu chár i valshepstvá.

Yes, you conquer easily:
with the glance you cast over us,
you embrace us with a net
and catch the hearts of all...
You are the embodiment
of charms and enchantment.

TEXT. **Paul Collin.** Title: Rondel. Published in *Collin*, page 176.

Russian translation by **Aleksándra Santagano-Gorchakóva.** Title: Чаровница (Enchantress).

MUSIC. 1888. Op. 65, no. 6. G Major. 2/4, Allegretto grazioso, with markings "giocoso" in the introduction, "misterioso" at the beginning of the third stanza, and "parlando" on the words "Dieu sait comment!". For Middle Voice: d^1–e^2. Dedicated to **Madame Désirée Artôt de Padilla.**

RECORDINGS. Arkhipova (in Russian), Borisenko (in Russian), Descamps, Larin, Mazurok (in Russian), Norman, Söderström, Varady.

6 Romances, Opus 73 (1893)

Mrs. von Meck sent Tchaikovsky 6000 R. in July 1890, telling him she was paying him his full year's stipend all at once. Such an advance payment for a whole year had never happened before. Then in September she wrote him saying that financial difficulties would no longer permit her to send him any stipend in future years, but asked him not to forget her friendship. Whether in her letter she declared an end to their correspondence is doubtful, though exactly what it said is not known, because it so upset Tchaikovsky that he tore the letter up (*von Meck 1993*, xxxv). On her part, her failing health, her fear of bankruptcy (which was real, though it did not come to pass), and pressure from members of her household all persuaded her that she could no longer sustain her role as Tchaikovsky's patron. In his reply to her it is clear that he did not think of this as the end of their friendship, but in fact that is what it was. He received no reply to his letter, and intermediaries in her household effectively kept her from receiving messages from him or sending him any communication on her own (*Poznansky 1991*, 511-529). Of all the thoughts that passed through his mind after this shock—distress at the loss of income he thought of as essential, the wish that he could help her if she truly was in need, dismay at what seemed her fickle change of heart, and his deeply hurt pride at the implication that she had viewed his attachment to her all along as based on the fact that she was a source of money to him (which was not true)—the hardest thing of all was the void where there had been a "best friend," a friendship with a woman who had embodied in his life an "ideal." It would have been easier if she had simply died.

Despite this loss, Tchaikovsky was a contented man in his private and professional life at the beginning of the nineties. He was one of the most famous composers in the world; he had not written himself out as the critics had predicted. He wrote the *Sleeping Beauty* in 1889, and a short opera *Iolanthe* as part of a double bill with *The Nutcracker* in 1892. Between them, he undertook his second opera to a libretto based on Pushkin, *The Queen of Spades*, one of his best works for the stage, written in Florence in 1890 in only seven weeks of inspiration and hard work. In the spring of 1891 he sailed to New York, where he was the biggest celebrity invited by Andrew Carnegie for the opening of Carnegie Hall. He was hopelessly homesick, but was kept busy conducting concerts of his music in New York, Baltimore, and Philadelphia, with visits to Washington and Niagara Falls; much that he saw pleased him, and his American hosts and audiences liked him enormously (*Yoffe*). Cambridge University was hoping he would come to accept an honorary degree in the spring of 1893.

In August 1892, he received a letter from an unknown poet whose name was Daniil Ratgauz, a law student at the St. Vladimir University in Kiev. He was twenty-four years old. This letter, now lost, contained a poem called "We sat together," and presumably another one called "Night," plus several other poems, none of which had been published. He asked Tchaikovsky to consider them as possible lyrics for songs. Tchaikovsky answered promptly that he received many such requests, almost never with anything he could use, but for once he could say a sincere thank you. He was busy and could not say when he would write music for them, but he did promise to use some of them, saying that one of them, "We sat together," "especially begs to be set to music" (*MN*, 466). Ratgauz thanked the composer and sent him five more poems, of which Tchaikovsky eventually chose four. The young man was certainly not shy about promoting his own poetry.

Tchaikovsky did not get around to writing the new romances until he finished the major project he was working on the next spring, which was his Sixth Symphony, Opus 74, the "Pathétique"; he also had to write some new pieces for piano he had promised, Opus 72. When these were done, he wrote the songs of Opus 73 to six of the poems Ratgauz had sent a year earlier. He worked on them between 22 April and 5 May 1893, taking the night of 27 April off to go to the Bolshoy Theater for the premiere of *Aleko*, a short opera by the young Sergei Rachmaninoff, who had just graduated from the Conservatory. Before departing for honorary degree ceremonies at Cambridge, he sent the finished songs to Jurgenson, who had them printed in July 1893, with texts in Russian and translations into German as was the custom.

These songs are sometimes referred to outside Russia as "German songs," but there is nothing German about them except the name of the poet (Rathaus). Daniil Maksimovich Ratgauz (1868-1937) was born in a German family in Kharkov (his father was a banker), but he was thoroughly Russianized and wrote only in Russian (*Nechaev*). He published his first book of poems, perhaps at his own expense, exactly at the time Jurgenson published the songs. This volume was passed by the censor in Kiev on 9 July 1893 (*Ratgauz 1893*). Among the 74 poems in the book are the six poems of Opus 73, each one asterisked with a note that reads "Set to music by P. I. Tchaikovsky." He paid careful attention to typography, layout, and punctuation; there is an errata slip at the back with two misprints duly corrected. He dedicated the book to his parents. On the first page is an epigraph from Edgar Allan Poe: "Melancholy is the most legitimate of all the poetical tones."

Tchaikovsky and Ratgauz never met, but they did exchange photographs and a few letters. Tchaikovsky asked him why his poetry was so melancholy: "You're talented, you're very handsome; judging by the elegant suits you wear, you have means, and people surely like you—in a word, you have everything needed to be happy. But your poems are in the minor key, your lyre is tuned to mournful music. Is there a reason for this?" (*LPP*, 135). When Ratgauz told him he was completely sincere—he was melancholy by temperament and could write best by being true to that—Tchaikovsky assured him he did not question his sincerity and begged forgiveness for prying. He said "in my music I'm also inclined to sad songs, even though like you, at least in the last few years, I am well enough off and consider myself a happy person" (*ibid.*, 154).

After Tchaikovsky set his poems to music, Ratgauz quickly became one of the most popular Russian poets among composers high and low, from the conservatories to the gypsy clubs. In number of poems set to music before 1917 (*Ivanov*), Ratgauz is in the top ten, with more than Aleksey Tolstoy, Pleshcheyev, and Apukhtin, and fewer only than Pushkin, Fet, Lermontov, and Konstantin Balmont. His sadness and romantic pessimism struck a chord in a very wide audience, making his lyrics ideal for the urban romance, which enjoyed a boom at the turn of the century. It is indicative of their "Russianness" that they have something in common with the lyrics of Ivan Surikov (Song 51), a poet who was purely Russian and born of peasant stock:

Я один, и не с кем	I'm alone, and have no one
Слова мне сказать…	To say a word to…
За окном скрипит берёза,	Outside the window a birch creaks,
В комнате темно…	In my room it's dark…
Где ты в это время,	Where are you right now,
Друг далёкий мой?	My friend so far away?

Lines like these by Surikov from 1868 are not very far from the images out of which Ratgauz wrote the lyric which became Song 103. Ratgauz made his melancholy more modern and more urban, but it had the accents of the same Russian melancholy in Surikov and many others, including streaks of it which run through the writings of Anton Chekhov. Tchaikovsky recognized inspiration here as soon as he saw it.

When the new songs were finished, Tchaikovsky dedicated them to Nikolay Figner, who sang Gherman in the premiere of *Queen of Spades* in 1890. As a song cycle, Opus 73 is a perfectly realized work of art and one of Tchaikovsky's most important vocal compositions. It is a cycle about love and solitude, expressed in the free and laconic musical language of a master. Each song finds its own powerful moment of breakthrough or resolution. The mood changes from song to song, but its point of constant anchor is the recurring image of an absent "friend" (друг). It was the last work he undertook and carried through to completion before his death in St. Petersburg on 25 October 1893 Old Style.

98 *Мы сидели с тобой*
We sat together

Op. 73, No. 1

During the Symbolist revival of poetry in the 1890s, along with the interest in aestheticism and mysticism and verbal "music"—this is the period of Chekhov's *Seagull*—Valery Bryusov, the Moscow maître of poetic practice, laid down a formula for writing a poem. This consisted of choosing as your subject a *moment*, and squeezing every last drop of life out of it: "берём мы миги, их губя" (we seize moments, using them up). These moments had to be *original*: he favored the offbeat or the morbid, and avoided sentiment at all costs. In his reviews of the new poets, he was merciless in his judgments. When Ratgauz published his "Collected Poems" in 1906, Bryusov wrote that it ought to be called the "Collected Banalities of D. Ratgauz" (*Briusov*, VI, 352-5). As an example of the poet's lack of originality, he cites the line "И тебе ничего, ничего не сказал" (nothing, nothing did I say to you), which happens to be line 8 of the present text. He gives a line from Fet as the model for this: "Ничего, ничего не ответила ты" (nothing, nothing did you answer). Bryusov's own poems were so original that when Osip Mandelstam was compiling an anthology, he complained that he could not find a single poem by Bryusov good enough to include (*Mandelstam*, 237).

But Bryusov was right, Ratgauz had read Fet, and he certainly knew the text of Song 75, which he used as a jumping-off point for the present poem, turning it in a different direction. He also knew Bryusov's formula for constructing a poem around a "moment"—the moment when "I didn't say what I could have said and should have said then." The first stanza sets the stage where the moment occurred, the second conveys the emotional thunderstorm of the moment, and the third stanza is the recall, with agonizing regret.

Tchaikovsky saw this moment as fateful. His musical language is direct but lyrically varied, impelled by the wave-like pulse of the initial four piano chords, and swelling to the dramatic outcry in the last line which expresses the finality of fate itself. Others have remarked the presence of "fate" as a theme in the music here (*Vasina-Grossman*, 295, *Brown IV*, 463); the former also sees a certain similarity with Schubert's great late song to a text by Heine, "Der Doppelgänger," from *Schwanengesang*.

> Мы сидели с тобой у заснувшей реки.
> С тихой песней проплыли домой рыбаки.
> Солнца луч золотой за рекой догорал.
> И тебе я тогда ничего не сказал.

Загремело вдали, надвигалась гроза,
По ресницам твоим покатилась слеза.
И с безумным рыданьем к тебе я припал,
И тебе ничего, ничего не сказал.

И теперь, в эти дни, я, как прежде, один,
Уж не жду ничего от грядущих годин.
В сердце жизненный звук уж давно отзвучал...
Ах, зачем, ах, зачем, я тебе ничего, ничего не сказал!

My sidéli s tabój u zasnúfshej rekí.   We sat together by the still river.
S tíkhaj pésnej praplýli damój rybakí.   With a quiet song the fishermen rowed home.
Sóntsa lúch zalatój za rekój   Across the river the gold ray of the sun
   dagarál.   was dying out.
I tebé ja tagdá nichevó ne skazál.   And all that time I said nothing to you.

Zagreméla vdalí, nadvigálas' grazá,   There was distant thunder as a storm moved in,
Pa resnítsam tvajím pakatílas' slezá.   A tear rolled down your eyelashes.
I z bezúmnym rydán'jem k tebé ja pripál,   And sobbing madly I fell at your feet,
I tebé nichevó, nichevó ne skazál.   And said nothing to you, nothing at all.

I tepér', v èti dní, ja, kak prézhde, adín,   And now once again, as before, I'm alone,
Ush ne zhdú nichevó   No longer expecting anything
   ad grjadúshchikh gadín.   from the coming years.
F sérttse zhýznennyj zvúk uzh davnó   In my heart all cries of life long ago
   adzvúchal...   died out...
Akh, zachém, akh zachém   Oh why, oh why,
   ja tebé nichevó,   did I say nothing to you,
   nichevó ne skazál!   nothing at all!

TEXT. **Daniíl Ratgáuz**, 1892. Published in *Ratgauz 1893*, page 15.
METER. Ternary. Anapest, 4-foot:
      On the bank of the river together we sat,
      As the fishermen rowed their way home with a song...
MUSIC. 1893. Op. 73, no. 1. E Major–C-sharp Minor. 12/8, Andante non
troppo (dotted quarter note = 66). For High Voice: e^1–g^2 sharp. Dedicated to
Nikoláy Fígner.
RECORDINGS. Arkhipova, Gmyria, Guliayev, Hvorostovsky, Larin,
Lemeshev, Levko, **Lisitsian**, Lisovsky, Maksakova, Martynov, Mishura, Nelepp,
Nesterenko, Nortsov, Obukhova, Rosing, Serkebayev, Söderström, Varady,
Zhadan.

99 *Ночь*
Night

Op. 73, No. 2

This song introduces the theme of night into the cycle. It is another poem built around a "moment" (миг), with the word itself occurring in line 7. The text is brief and concentrated. The image in the third line of "longing" (тоска) uses a common Russian word which is difficult to render in English with the full force of its meaning. It implies the absence of someone or something central to one's sense of well-being. It is longing for the absent friend in the last line, but it is also an overall mood. This feeling is not a melancholy pose, but strikes a chord in many a Russian soul (Lenin is said to have liked listening to this song when he lived in exile in Geneva—see the notes to the Mark Reizen recording below on "Lenin's Favorite Songs"). Chekhov expresses this condition succinctly in "My Life," when the hero has been deserted by his wife: "какая это была тоска ночью, в часы одиночества" ("what agony it was [without her] in the lonely hours of the night"). The song is somber, laconic, and powerful; it is sometimes performed with "cello obbligato."

Меркнет слабый свет свечи,
Бродит мрак унылый,
И тоска сжимает грудь
С непонятной силой.

На печальные глаза
Тихо сон нисходит,
И с прошедшим в этот миг
Речь душа заводит.

Истомилася она
Горестью глубокой…
Появись же, хоть во сне,
О мой друг далекий!

Mérknet slábyj svét svechí,	Dim grows the weak light of the candle,
Bródit mrák unýlyj,	Beyond roams wretched darkness,
I taská zzhymájet grút'	And my heart's gripped by longing
S nepanjátnaj sílaj.	Strong past understanding.

Na pechál'nyje glazá	Eyes filled with sorrow
Tíkha són niskhódit,	Yield to sleep's quiet descent,
I s prashétshym v ètat mík	And at this moment, with the past,
Réch dushá zavódit.	My soul starts a conversation.

Istamílasa aná	It is weary and worn out
Górest'ju glubókaj,	With sadness profound;
Pajavís' zhe, khot' va sné,	Appear now, if only in a dream,
O moj drúk daljókaj!	Oh my friend far away!

Text. **Daniíl Ratgáuz**, 1892. Published in *Ratgauz 1893*, page 34.
Meter. Binary. Trochee, alternating lines of 4 and 3 feet:
> *Dimmer grows the candle's light,*
> *Wretched darkness wanders...*

Music. 1893. Op. 73, no. 2. F Minor. 3/2, Adagio (half note = 54). For High Voice: c^1–g^2 flat. Dedicated to **Nikoláy Fígner**.

Recordings. Arkhipova, Atlantov, Baikov, Borodina, Bozhkova, Burchuladze, Christoff (with cello), Descamps, Andrey Ivanov, Kasrashvili, Lemeshev, **Levko** (with cello), Martynov, Mazurok, Mishura, Mkrtchyan, Nelepp, Obraztsova, Obukhova, Preobrazhenskaya, Reizen, Varady, Vishnevskaya, Zimmermann.

100 *В эту лунную ночь*
On this moonlit night

Op. 73, No. 3

This is a different moment, a moment of being together, rather than apart. It is an ecstatic moment, but it will not last. Night is ending as dawn approaches, and the day promises more "longing and sorrow."

В эту лунную ночь, в эту дивную ночь,
В этот миг благодатный свиданья,
О мой друг! я не в силах любви превозмочь,
Удержать я не в силах признанья.

В серебре чуть колышется озера гладь,
Наклонясь, зашепталися ивы ...
Но бессильны слова! — как тебе передать
Истомлённого сердца порывы?

Ночь не ждёт, ночь летит. Закатилась луна,
Заалело в таинственной дали ...
Дорогая! прости, — снова жизни волна
Нам несёт день тоски и печали.

V ètu lúnnuju nóch, v ètu dívnuju nóch,
V ètat mik blagadátnyj svidán'ja,
O moj drúk! ja ne f sílakh ljubví prevazmóch,
Uderzhát' ja ne f sílakh priznán'ja.

On this moonlit night, on this wondrous night,
In this blessed moment of being together,
O my friend! I cannot contain my love,
I cannot hold back this declaration.

F serebré chut' kalýshetsa ózera glát',
Naklanjás', zasheptálisa ívy...
No bessíl'ny slavá! — kak tebé peredát'
Istamljónnava sértsa parývy?

The smooth silver lake is slightly stirring,
Bending down, the willows start to whisper...
But words are powerless! — how can I convey
The thrills my exhausted heart feels?

Nóch ne zhdjót, nóch letít. Zakatílas' luná,
Zaaléla f tajínstvennaj dáli...

Night won't wait, it flies. The moon is down,
The sky glows red in the mysterious distance...

Daragája! prastí, — snóva zhýzni	Darling! forgive me, — again life's
valná	wave
Nam nesjót den' taskí i pecháli.	Is bringing us a day of longing and sorrow.

TEXT. **Daniíl Ratgáuz**, 1892. Published in *Ratgauz 1893*, page 72. After Tchaikovsky, set by Yuly Bleikhman (Op. 32/2, 1900).

METER. Ternary. Anapest, alternating lines of 4 and 3 feet:

> *On this night in the moonlight, this wonderful night,*
> *In this moment of being together...*

MUSIC. 1893. Op. 73, no. 3. A-flat Major. 9/8, Andante con moto (dotted quarter note = 76). For High Voice: d^1 natural–a^2 flat. Dedicated to **Nikoláy Fígner**.

RECORDINGS. Arkhipova, Borisenko, Gedda, Jadlowker (in German), Kasrashvili, Kozlovsky, Larin, Lemeshev, Martynov, Mishura, Nelepp, Nortsov, Petina, Pirogov, Schock, Varady, Vinogradov, Vishnevskaya.

101 *Закатилось солнце*
The sun has set

Op. 73, No. 4

This song is the brightest in the cycle, with a bolero beat prominent in the piano part (*Vasina-Grossman*, 266). Night is beginning, a night together, bringing attainment of happiness, expressed unmistakably with rising intonation.

Закатилось солнце, заиграли краски
Лёгкой позолотой в синеве небес.
В обаяньи ночи сладострастной ласки
Тихо что-то шепчет задремавший лес.

И в душе тревожной умолкают муки,
И дышать всей грудью в эту ночь легко.
Ночи дивной тени, ночи дивной звуки,
Нас с тобой уносят, друг мой, далеко . . .

Вся объята негой этой ночи страстной,
Ты ко мне склонилась на плечо главой . . .
Я безумно счастлив, о мой друг прекрасный,
Бесконечно счастлив в эту ночь с тобой!

Zakatílas' sóntse, zaigráli kráski	The sun has set, a play of colors has begun,
Ljókhkaj pazalótaj f sinevé nebés.	Light streaks of gold in a dark blue sky.
V abaján'ji nóchi sladostrásnaj láski	In the magic of night's voluptuous caress
Tíkha shtó-ta shépchet zadremáfshyj lés.	The sleeping forest whispers something softly.
I v dushé trevózhnaj umalkájut múki,	And torments in an anxious soul subside,
I dyshát' fsej grúd'ju v ètu nóch lehkó.	And tonight one's whole being breathes easier.
Nóchi dívnaj téni, nóchi dívnaj zvúki,	Shadows of this wondrous night, sounds of this wondrous night,
Nás s tabój unósjat, drúk moj, dalekó...	Carry the two of us, my friend, far away...
Fsja objáta négaj ètaj nóchi strásnaj,	Wrapped in night's passionate languor,
Ty ka mné sklanílas' na plechó glavój...	You lean your head on my shoulder...
Ja bezúmna shchástlif, o moj drúk prekrásnyj,	I'm insanely happy, oh my friend so lovely,
Beskanéchna shchástlif v ètu nóch s tabój!	Boundlessly happy on this night with you!

TEXT. **Daniíl Ratgáuz**, 1892. Published in *Ratgauz 1893*, page 36. Set only by Tchaikovsky. He changed "приутихший лес" (the stilled forest) to "задремавший лес" (the sleeping forest) in the last line of the first stanza.
METER. Binary. Trochaic, 6-foot:

> *Shadows of the evening, dreaming forest murmurs,*
> *Carry us, my darling, far away tonight...*

MUSIC. 1893. Op. 73, no. 4. E Major. 9/8, Andante (quarter note = 66). For High Voice: e¹–a². Dedicated to **Nikoláy Fígner**.

RECORDINGS. Arkhipova, Atlantov, Borisenko, Borodina, Burchuladze, Guliayev, Kazarnovskaya, Kruglikova, Larin, Lemeshev, Levko, Lisovsky, Martynov, Leokadiya Maslennikova, Mishura, Nelepp, Obraztsova, Siniavskaya, Söderström, Varady, Vishnevskaya.

102 *Средь мрачныхъ дней*
On gloomy days

Op. 73, No. 5

As in Song 99, the theme is absence, but here there is a breakthrough from darkness to light, from confusion to clarity. It is a summarizing poem, which steps back to find strong affirmation and belief.

Средь мрачных дней, под гнётом бед,
Из мглы туманной прошлых лет,
Как отблеск радостных лучей,
Мне светит взор твоих очей.

Под обаяньем светлых снов
Мне мнится, я с тобою вновь.
При свете дня, в ночной тиши
Делюсь восторгами души.

Я вновь с тобой! — моя печаль
Умчалась в пасмурную даль ...
И страстно вновь хочу я жить —
Тобой дышать, тебя любить!

Sred' mráchnykh dnéj,
  pad gnjótam bét,
Iz mglý tumánnaj próshlykh lét,
Kak ódblesk rádasnykh luchéj,
Mne svétit vzór tvajíkh achéj.

Pad abaján'jem svétlykh snóf,
Mne mnítsa, já s tabóju vnóf'.
Pri svéte dnjá, v nachnój tishý,
Deljús' vastórgami dushý.

Ja vnóf' s tabój! — majá pechál'
Umchálas' f pásmurnuju dál'...
I strásna vnóf' khachú ja zhýt' —
Tabój dyshát', tebjá
  ljubít'!

On gloomy days,
  when cares oppress,
Out of the vague dimness of the past,
Like rays of light bringing gladness,
The gaze of your eyes shines on me.

Under this spell of bright dreams,
I imagine being with you once more.
In the light of day, in the still of night,
Again I know these raptures of the soul.

I am with you once more! — my sadness
Has vanished in a gray distance...
And again I passionately want to live —
With you each breath I take, with you
  to love!

TEXT. **Daniíl Ratgáuz**, 1892. Published in *Ratgauz 1893*, page 40.
METER. Binary. Iambic tetrameter:
> *And once again I want to live,*
> *With you to love, each breath I take.*

MUSIC. 1893. Op. 73, no. 5. A-flat Major. 4/4, Allegro moderato (quarter note = 112). For High Voice: e^1 flat–a^2 double flat. Dedicated to **Nikoláy Fígner**.

RECORDINGS. Arkhipova, Larin, Lemeshev, Lisitsian, Martynov, Leokadiya Maslennikova, Mishura, Nelepp, Ognivtsev, Varady.

∾

103 *Снова, как прежде, один*
Again, as before, alone

Op. 73, No. 6

Here the theme of night, complete with stars and moonlight, comes together with a final moment of solitude to close the cycle.

The very first line is a restatement of a phrase heard earlier, in the last stanza of the first song in the cycle: "once again, as before, I'm alone." The motif of "longing" (тоска) encountered in Songs 99 and 100 is stated in the second line.

Then the absent friend is evoked by the tree seen outside the window, its leaves "whispering something." The poplar is an image from Ukrainian folklore, used by Shevchenko in his poems, where it represents a young woman, isolated, standing alone, bending with the wind, who has met with a misfortune in which love is lost.

The sky blazing with stars is shorthand in Russian poetry for eternity, an image that inevitably calls to mind Lermontov's "I walk out alone onto the road." The prayer at the end is a new theme in the cycle. It affirms the past, despite the loneliness and difficulty of the moment, in a spiritual bond which, if it does not defeat solitude, holds it at bay.

Снова, как прежде, один,
Снова объят я тоской.
Смотрится тополь в окно,
Весь озарённый луной.

Смотрится тополь в окно,
Шепчут о чём-то листы.
В звёздах горят небеса...
Где теперь, милая, ты?

Всё, что творится со мной,
Я передать не берусь...
Друг! помолись за меня,
Я за тебя уж молюсь.

Snóva, kak prézhde, adín,	Again, as before, I'm alone,
Snóva obját ja taskój.	Again I'm filled with longing.
Smótritsa tópal' v aknó,	A poplar stands by the window,
Vés' azarjónnaj lunój.	Flooded with moonlight.

Smótritsa tópal' v aknó,	A poplar stands by the window,
Shépchut a chóm-ta listý.	The leaves are whispering about something.
V zvjózdakh garját nebesá…	The sky is aflame with stars…
Gdé, teper', mílaja, tý?	Where, now, darling, are you?
Fsjó, shto tvarítsa sa mnój,	I couldn't begin to tell you
Já peredát' ne berús'…	All that's happening to me…
Drúk! pamalís' za menjá,	Friend! say a prayer for me,
Já za tebjá ush maljús'.	I am praying for you.

TEXT. **Daniíl Ratgáuz**, 1892. Published in *Ratgauz 1893*, page 28.

The text was sometimes, though not always, censored in the Stalin period. The recording by Solomon Khromchenko shows religious language in the last two lines edited out:

Друг мой, повспомни меня,	My friend, think of me from time to time,
Сердцем к тебе я стремлюсь.	In my heart I yearn to be with you.

METER. Ternary. Dactyls, 3-foot:

> *Stars in the sky are aflame,*
> *Darling, where are you tonight?*

MUSIC. 1893. Op. 73, no. 6. A Minor. 3/4, Andante mosso (quarter note = 69). For High Voice: a^1–g^2 sharp. Dedicated to **Nikoláy Fígner**.

Transcribed for orchestra by Leopold Stokowski.

RECORDINGS. Arkhipova, Atlantov, Bolshakov, Borodina, Christoff, Davrath, Descamps, Hvorostovsky, Karolik, Kasrashvili, Khromchenko, Kozlovsky, Larin, Lemeshev, Lisovsky, Martynov, Mishura, Mkrtchyan, **Nelepp**, Nesterenko, Obraztsova, Ognivtsev, Petrov, Pirogov, Ropskaya, Stokowski (orchestral transcription), Tear, Varady, Verrett, Vishnevskaya.

Afterword

I.

My interest in Tchaikovsky's songs began in Moscow in the winter of 1991-92. The Soviet period had just ended and a new era was beginning. All winter long the lines at the milk store formed well before dawn. Never in visits to the country going back to 1968 was the contrast so striking between the hardship of daily life and the compensating strength to be drawn from cultural and spiritual resources. Many of my days were spent in reading rooms of libraries, museums, and archives, and quite a few of my evenings at concerts in the Great Hall and Small Hall of the Moscow Conservatory.

That winter I listened to the radio. The programming was entirely new. I heard songs and singers I had never heard before. They played "old romances"—popular songs by Gurilyov, Varlamov, and Bulakhov, sometimes with Glinka and Dargomyzhsky alongside them. Many were "Russian songs," not real folk songs, but "urban" folk songs, ditties about village life written for a town audience. All these went back to the first half of the 19th century, but they did not seem outdated. They played gypsy songs, "cruel" romances, and other sentimental songs, tangos, and foxtrots. These had been very popular until the 1930s, and now in 1992 they were back just as if there had never been an interruption. I heard singers like Varya Panina and Tamara Tsereteli, Vialtseva and Plevitskaya, Vertinsky and Kozin, and, singing songs in nearly all categories, Nadezhda Obukhova, who became my favorite singer.

Among this stream of neglected but much-loved songs were frequent romances by Tchaikovsky—not Rimsky or Musorgsky, but Tchaikovsky. It was striking to hear them in that context of popular songs rather than in a program of art songs. No matter who was visiting me while these songs were coming over the radio, friends who were literary and musical, or friends who were not literary or musical—a biologist, a physicist, a doctor, neighbors who took in laundry or drove a cab—it seemed all these people knew these songs, including those by Tchaikovsky. They knew the music and they knew the words. I now realize how fitting it was that his songs were remembered in that context, especially after the Soviet period, when not only were his texts censored but his music was appropriated for official purposes of state, like the ballet music played during the recent "putsch" which had led to the downfall of Soviet power. That winter of scarcity and long lines, with hours of good Russian songs coming over the radio every day, gave way to better times and worse fare over the radio, but while it lasted, it was an interval when Tchaikovsky's songs were being heard by "all the people," who knew them and understood them and liked them—the very audience he hoped his vocal music would reach.

Those who knew Tchaikovsky in life were the last to see him as he truly was. By that I mean see him as a contemporary, his personality sometimes puzzling but most often charming and attractive, his public life in the conservatory or backstage or on the podium concentrated on making music of high standards, and—not least important—his right to keep his private life private still respected. His sudden death during a cholera epidemic at the height of his powers changed all that forever. It gave rise to speculation that cholera was a convenient story invented to cover up something else. Rumors of a suicide, fabricated out of other rumors based on the composer's sexual orientation, can be traced back to the time of his death; later, when all the witnesses themselves were dead, these rumors were revived for embellishment and recirculation, sometimes by respectable scholars. Seldom has closeted sexual orientation caused so much biographical mischief. When his correspondence with Mrs. von Meck was published in the 1930s, Nina Berberova wrote a book about the composer subtitled "the history of a solitary life." It is a shrewd portrait of the man from "inside," which first sought the key to his personality by implying his homosexuality but not dwelling on it in detail (*Berberova 1936*). This has been followed by Alexander Poznansky's biography subtitled "The Quest for the Inner Man" (*Poznansky 1991*), a book which leaves no stone unturned. A second well-documented contribution to the composer's biography is Poznansky's book *Tchaikovsky's Last Days* (*Poznansky 1996*), which is a judicious examination of all the evidence pertaining to the suicide myth and a convincing refutation of it. Nevertheless, all this has placed in the foreground the composer's private life, deflecting attention from his creative life in music, how he saw his culture, and how his own genius interacted with it. In my commentary to his songs, I have tried to turn the discussion back to the culture out of which his music arose, in the belief that the "inner man" we wish to understand is the man who wrote the music. What matters about Tchaikovsky's sexual orientation is not its presumed erotic content, but its affective content: love was something he needed to feel, and did feel throughout his life, for many people (of both sexes) and in many ways. It was this, not eros, that drove the "warmth" he sought when he composed. In his songs (and operas), in the music he brought to a text, he conveys publicly, to his audience, what he wanted to say about love.

Of all the works Tchaikovsky never lived to write, one I wish for is the opera he and Chekhov talked about doing together, to "Bèla," a Lermontov story from *Hero of Our Time*. Bèla was going to be a soprano, Pechorin a baritone, Kazbich a bass, and Maxim Maximych a tenor (*Balabanovich*, 99). When Tchaikovsky first happened on a Chekhov story in 1887, it so excited him he set out to find the author to thank him personally. They met in 1888, liking each other greatly and each admiring the other's work. In 1889 Chekhov dedicated his book of stories *Gloomy People* to him. Tchaikovsky knew right away after reading a story like "Gusev" when it came out in a newspaper how good it was. Chekhov was one who truly did see Tchaikovsky for who he was, as a contemporary, as an *artist*. They were different as artists but had much in common. They had a conscience and they believed in work. They idolized Tolstoy's art but they hated his preaching. They did not let the critics get them down. Nothing they wrote was ever phony or forced or boring or based on clever tricks. They were 19th-century men, but what they created found a lasting audience in the 20th century and beyond.

Chekhov joked in a letter to the composer's brother on 16 March 1890 that in the ranks of Russian artists, the first place had long been taken by Lev Tolstoy, while he himself occupied a spot down around ninety-eight. But he was not joking when he ranked Tchaikovsky number two, adding "I am prepared to stand as honor guard day and night at the door of the house where Pyotr Ilyich lives."

Six Duets, Opus 46 (1880)

1 *Вечер*
Evening

Op. 46, No. 1

The six duets of Opus 46 were written in the summer of 1880, which Tchaikovsky spent at his sister's at Kamenka and at Mrs. von Meck's estate at Brailov and in her cottage three miles away in Simaki. That Easter he, his sister Sasha, her daughter Tanya, and his brother Anatoly sang together at mass the Lord's Prayer from his own liturgy of St. John Chrysostom, along with some of the traditional Orthodox liturgical songs he had arranged. When writing these duets, he could have had in mind his sister and niece in those for soprano and mezzo-soprano, with Anatoly or himself as baritone in no. 2, the Scottish ballad (*Brown III*, 107-9). He dedicated them all to his niece Tanya. On 30 August Anatoly took them to Jurgenson, who published them in 1881 (*MN*, 478). The texts given here are those published in Vol. 43 of *PSS*, 1941.

Солнце утомилось,
Ходя день денской;
Тихо догорая,
Гаснет за рекой.

Край далёкий неба
Весь зарёй облит,
Заревом пожара
Блещет и горит.

В воздухе смолкает
Шум дневных тревог;
Тишь ночную с неба
Шлёт на землю Бог.

Ходят огневые
Полосы в реке;
Грустно где-то песня
Льётся вдалеке.

Тихо... Отчего же
В сердце у меня
Не стихает горе
Прожитого дня?

Отчего ж так больно
Скорбь сжимает грудь?
Боже мой! Боже мой!
Дай мне отдохнуть!

The sun is tired now,
On the move all day;
Quietly burning down,
It sets across the river.

The far edge of the sky
Is awash in sunset,
Like a reflection of a fire
It glows and burns.

The noise dies down
Of loud busy day;
God sends down to earth
Night stillness from the sky.

Fiery stripes
Dance on the river;
Someone sings a sad song
Somewhere far away.

It's quiet... Then why
Can't my heart
Let the grief of today
Quiet down and be stilled?

Why this painful weight
Of sorrow in my breast?
Dear God! Dear God!
Let me rest!

TEXT. **Iván Súrikov**. Tchaikovsky pieced together the text using two poems by Surikov: "Солнце утомилось" (1865) and "В воздухе смолкает" (1866), making some changes in the wording and adding repetitions.

MUSIC. 1880. Op. 46, no. 1. A Flat Major. 3/2, Andante non troppo. For High and Middle Voices. Dedicated to **Tatyána Lvóvna Davýdova** (1862-1886), Tchaikovsky's niece, daughter of his sister Aleksandra and Lev Davydov.

RECORDINGS. Arkhipova & Kasrashvili, Lear & Stewart.

2 *Шотландская баллада*
Scottish ballad

Op. 46, No. 2

The source for this translation by Aleksey Tolstoy is "Edward," the Scottish ballad that begins "Why dois your brand sae drap wi bluid, Edward, Edward." A critic wrote Tchaikovsky that the words to the ballad were "impossible: 'I killed my father'—brrr!" (*Iakovlev*, 462), but he did not agree. He wrote Mrs. von Meck that it was one of his favorite creations, adding he was sure no one would perform it as he imagined it: "it should not be sung, but declaimed, with the greatest intensity" (*MN*, 478).

«Чьей кровию меч свой ты так обагрил,
    Эдва́рд, Эдва́рд?
Чьей кровию меч свой ты так обагрил?
Зачем ты глядишь так сурово?»
 «То сокола я, рассердяся, убил,
То сокола я, рассердяся, убил,
И негде добыть мне другого!»

"Whose blood has turned your sword so red,
    Edward, Edward?
Whose blood has turned your sword so red?
Why is your look so grave?"
"In anger I killed my hawk,
In anger I killed my hawk,
And another one like him I'll never find!"

«У сокола кровь так красна не бежит,
    Эдва́рд, Эдва́рд!
У сокола кровь так красна не бежит,
Твой меч окровавлен краснее!»
«Мой конь краснобурый был мною убит,
Мой конь краснобурый был мною убит,
Тоскую по добром коне я!»

"The blood of a hawk runs not so red,
    Edward, Edward!
The blood of a hawk runs not so red,
Your sword is bloodied redder!"
"I've killed my roan-red steed, I have,
I've killed my roan-red steed,
I'm longing now for that good steed!"

«Конь стар у тебя, эта кровь не его,
    Эдва́рд, Эдва́рд!
Конь стар у тебя, эта кровь не его,
Не то в твоём сумрачном взоре!»
«Отца я сейчас заколол моего,
Отца я сейчас заколол моего,
И лютое жжёт меня горе!»

"Your steed was old, this blood is not his,
    Edward, Edward!
Your steed was old, this blood is not his,
Some other dole is in your look!"
"My father have I killed just now,
My father have I killed just now,
And cruel is the woe that pains me!"

«А грех чем тяжёлый искупишь ты свой,
    Эдва́рд, Эдва́рд?
А грех чем тяжёлый искупишь ты свой?

"And how will you repent your dreadful sin,
    Edward, Edward?
And how will you repent your dreadful sin?

Чем сымешь ты с совести ношу?»	How take the load from your conscience?"
«Я сяду в ладью непогодой морской,	"I'll ride a boat out in an ocean gale,
Я сяду в ладью непогодой морской,	I'll ride a boat out in an ocean gale,
И ветру все парусы брошу!»	And raise all sails to the wind!"

«Что ж будет с твоими детьми	"What will become of your bairns
и с женой,	and your wife,
Эдва́рд, Эдва́рд!	Edward, Edward?
Что ж будет с твоими детьми	What will become of your bairns
и с женой	and your wife,
В их горькой, беспомощной доле?»	In their bitter, helpless dole?"
«Пусть по миру ходят за хлебом с	"Let them go beg in the world for their
сумой,	bread,
Пусть по миру ходят за хлебом с	Let them go beg in the world for their
сумой,	bread,
Я с ними не свижуся боле!»	No more will I ever see them!"

«А матери что ты оставишь своей,	"And what will you leave to your mother,
Эдва́рд, Эдва́рд?	Edward, Edward?
А матери что ты оставишь своей	And what will you leave to your mother,
Тебя что у груди качала?»	Who rocked you at her breast?"
«Проклятье тебе до скончания дней,	"A curse on you to the end of your days,
Проклятье тебе до скончания дней,	A curse on you to the end of your days,
Тебе, что мне грех нашептала!»	Who whispered that sin to me!"
— «Эдва́рд! Эдва́рд!»	— "Edward! Edward!"

TEXT. **Alekséy Tolstóy**, 1871. A translation of "Edward," from Thomas Percy's *Reliques*, first published in 1765 (*Child*). Tolstoy did not use the Scottish original but a German translation by Theodor Fontane (1819-1898). Tchaikovsky omitted the fifth stanza, and also the phrase "Мать моя, мать" (Mother of mine, mother) from each stanza.

MUSIC. 1880. Op. 46, no. 2. A Minor. 6/8, Allegro agitato, ma non troppo. For Soprano and Baritone. Dedicated to **Tatyána Lvóvna Davýdova**.

RECORDINGS. Arkhipova & Pashinsky, Fischer-Dieskau & de los Angeles.

3 *Слёзы*
Tears

Op. 46, No. 3

This impromptu lyric by Fyodor Tyutchev has been very popular with Russian composers. The poem came to Tyutchev on a rainy autumn night riding home in a cab.

Слёзы людские, о слёзы людские,
Льётесь вы ранней и поздней порой...
Льётесь безвестные, льётесь незримые,
Неистощимые, неисчислимые, —
Льётесь, как льются струи дождевые
В осень глухую порою ночной.

Human tears, oh human tears,
You flow at all hours, early and late...
Flow unknown and flow unseen,
Inexhaustible, innumerable, —
Flow like flowing streams of rain
In barren autumn at a late night hour.

TEXT. **Fyódor Tyútchev**, 1849. Set by many composers, including Glière, Goldenweiser, Grechaninov, Cui, Rebikov, Nikolay Tcherepnin, and Medtner. MUSIC. 1880. Op. 46, no. 3. G Minor. 9/8, Andante molto sostenuto. For High and Middle Voices. Dedicated to **Tatyána Lvóvna Davýdova**. RECORDINGS. Arkhipova & Kasrashvili, Söderström & Meyer (in French).

В огороде, возле броду
In the garden, by the ford

4

Op. 46, No. 4

В огороде, возле броду,	In the garden, by the ford,
Маков цвет не всходит,	Poppies aren't growing,
И до броду за водою	Nor does the maiden go
Девица не ходит.	To the ford to fetch water.
В огороде хмель зелёный	In the garden green hop-vines
Сохнет на тычине;	Are drying on the fence;
Черноброва, белолица	Black of brow and white of face
Девица в кручине.	The maiden sorrows.
В огороде, возле броду,	In the garden, by the ford,
Верба наклонилась, —	Willows bend low, —
Загрустилась черноброва,	Sad she is, the black-browed maid,
Тяжко загрустилась.	Heavy is her sadness.
Она плачет, плачет и рыдает,	She weeps, weeps and sobs,
Словно рыбка бьётся,	Like a fish that's caught,
А над нею, молодою,	And, looking at the young maid,
Молодец смеётся.	A lad is laughing at her.

TEXT. **Iván Súrikov.** Translated in 1868 or 1869 from a Ukrainian poem by **Taras Shevchenko,** "Но вгороді коло броду" written in 1848.

MUSIC. 1880. Op. 46, no. 4. A Major. 3/4, Allegro moderato. For High and Middle Voices. Dedicated to **Tatyána Lvóvna Davýdova.** Orchestrated by Taneyev in 1898 at the request of Modest Tchaikovsky for a memorial concert for the composer (*MN*, 480).

RECORDINGS. Arkhipova & Kasrashvili, Dolukhanova & Sakharova, Söderström & Meyer (in French).

5 *Минула страсть*
Passion has cooled

Op. 46, No. 5

This lyric is another of the love poems by Aleksey Tolstoy which turned out to be such inspired choices as texts for Tchaikovsky's romances. Tolstoy wrote it the same year as "A Tear Trembles" (Song 7). The present text, which has three stanzas, ends in a long simile which takes up the whole of the last stanza. Tchaikovsky used only the first two stanzas for the duet.

Минула страсть, и пыл её тревожный	Passion has cooled, and its disturbing fire
Уже не мучит сердца моего,	No longer torments my heart,
Но разлюбить тебя мне невожможно!	But to stop loving you would be impossible!
Всё, что не ты, — так суетно и ложно,	Everything that isn't you is vain and false,
Всё, что не ты, — бесцветно и мертво.	Everything that isn't you is drab and dead.
Без повода и права негодуя,	No longer does my blood rebel
Уж не кипит бунтующая кровь, —	For no good right or reason, —
Но с пошлой жизнью слиться не могу я,	But life's dull banality is not for me,
Моя любовь, о друг, и не ревнуя,	So even if I don't feel jealousy, darling,
Осталась та же прежняя любовь.	My love remains just as it was before.

TEXT. **Alekséy Tolstóy**, 1858. First used for a song setting by Baron Vietinghoff-Schell in 1878; after Tchaikovsky, set by some minor composers.

MUSIC. 1880. Op. 46, no. 5. F Minor. 4/4, Allegro agitato. For Soprano and Tenor. Dedicated to **Tatyána Lvóvna Davýdova**.

RECORDINGS. Arkhipova & Kasrashvili, Lemeshev & Kudriavtseva.

Stanza 3, omitted from the song

Так от высот нахмуренной природы,	So, from frowning nature's heights,
С нависших скал сорвавшийся поток	Off overhanging cliffs, a flood released
Из царства туч, грозы и непогоды	From realm of storm clouds and thunder
В простор степей выносит те же воды	Pours its waters onto the broad steppe
И вдаль течёт, спокоен и глубок.	And flows into the distance, serene and deep.

6 *Рассвет*
Dawn

Op. 46, No. 6

Занялася заря —	Dawn is breaking —
Скоро солнце взойдёт.	The sun will be up soon.
Слышишь... чу! соловей	Hear that? hark! a nightingale
Громко песни поёт.	Sings his songs loud.
Всё ярчей и ярчей	Brighter and brighter
Переливы зари;	Are the colors of dawn;
Словно пар над рекой	See, it looks like the river
Поднялся, посмотри.	Is sending up steam.
От цветов, на полях,	From the flowers in the fields
Льётся запах кругом,	Come sweet smells all around,
И сияет роса	And the dew shines
На траве серебром.	Like silver on the grass.
И к воде наклонясь,	Reeds bend toward the water,
Что-то шепчет камыш;	Whispering something;
А кругом, на полях,	All around, in the fields,
Непробудная тишь... Ах!	There's a deep, deep stillness... Ah!
Как отрадно, легко,	How gladly, how lightly,
Широко дышит грудь!	How deeply you can breathe!
Ну, молись же скорей!	Well, say your prayers quickly!
Ну молись да и в путь!	Say your prayers and let's hit the road!

TEXT. **Iván Súrikov**, 1865. Untitled. Tchaikovsky made some changes in wording and added the title.

MUSIC. 1880. Op. 46, no. 6. E Major. 3/4, Allegro moderato. For High and Middle Voices. Dedicated to **Tatyána Lvóvna Davýdova**. Tchaikovsky orchestrated the duet, by request, for a court concert at Gatchina Palace in 1889 (*MN*, 479).

RECORDINGS. Arkhipova & Kasrashvili, Söderström & Meyer (in French).

Singers & Recordings

Recordings of Tchaikovsky's songs go back more than a hundred years to the dawn of the recording age. One of the first is a recording of Song 11 made by Lavrovskaya in 1892 (there is a copy in Pushkinsky Dom in St. Petersburg). In the list below, the earliest ones, made between 1900 and World War I, are by famous singers like Schumann-Heink, Nezhdanova, Chaliapin, Sobinov, and Caruso. At the end of the century, excellent new recordings have been made by Sergei Leiferkus, Dmitri Hvorostovsky, Nina Rautio, Ilya Levinsky, Galina Gorchakova, Olga Borodina, Joan Rodgers, Ewa Podleś, and many other singers working today. In between are all the recordings made by the marvelous singers who flourished between the 1920s and the 1980s. Hence, the list below covers the whole of the 20th century.

It is, of course, not complete (no such list can ever be complete), but most of the recordings of Tchaikovsky's songs made between 1900 and 2000 will be found here. The list consists primarily of recordings in LP or CD format released from 1950-1999. Records issued in 78 rpm format which have not been transferred to LP or CD are indicated when they are important historically. The list does not include recordings made for radio broadcasts unless they have been issued as records (unreleased recordings by major singers remain in the vaults of Gosteleradio in Moscow). Sources consulted—*Bennett, The Record Collector (TRC)*, the Russian State Archive of Sound Recordings in Moscow (*RGAFD*), and others—are cited in the bibliography, but I have used them primarily as guides. My final authority has been the actual record or CD itself. For information about singers, I have used standard sources listed in the bibliography (*Agin, Baker's, BT, Hamilton, ME, MES*), as well as the more detailed references cited as *Pruzhansky, TRC, The Record of Singing*, and *Levik*.

The continuity of the singing tradition in Russia is very striking. Many singers in their prime in the first third of the 20th century were taught by contemporaries of Tchaikovsky—Lavrovskaya, Usatov, Galvani, Viardot—or by singers who were taught by them. The "Russian school" of singing as it was formed and passed on in the conservatories at the turn of the century reaches back in its main line to Manuel Garcia (1805-1906), Viardot's brother and the most famous vocal teacher of the 19th century. His pupil Henrietta Nissen-Saloman (1819-1879), who studied also with Viardot and whose piano teacher was Chopin, taught singing at the St. Petersburg Conservatory when Tchaikovsky was a student there; her pupils included Lavrovskaya and Natalia Iretskaya (1845-1922) who taught with Nissen-Saloman and then took her place at the conservatory. Garcia's methods were brought to Russia also by his pupil Camillo Everardi (1825-1899), an Italian bel canto baritone, who taught in St. Petersburg (1870-88), Kiev (1890-97), and Moscow (1898-9). His pupils included well-known singers like Dmitry Usatov and Fyodor Stravinsky, and also Stanislav Gabel, who taught Everardi's methods at the St. Petersburg Conservatory from 1879-1923. In Moscow, a related academic tradition of the Italian school was instituted when Nikolay Rubinstein brought Giacomo Galvani to teach at the conservatory from 1869-1887. He was the teacher of Mikhail Medvedev, who sang the first Lensky as a raw youth, and who in turn became Sergey Levik's teacher. This Italian line found brilliant continuation in Umberto Masetti, who, like Galvani, was trained in Bologne and taught at the Moscow Conservatory from 1899-1919. Masetti was renowned for teaching techniques of breath control and evenness and naturalness of tone. He never forced the voice, but found ways of developing it gradually. He was also known for inculcating the highest standards of vocal culture while bringing out the individuality of each singer. His pupils included Nezhdanova, Obukhova, Kurenko, and the Italian baritone Riccardo Stracciari, who was Boris Christoff's teacher. Solidly established prior to the October Revolution, these pedagogical traditions in the Russian school of singing did not entirely die out in the twentieth century. Genealogical ties within these traditions are evident in the biographies of many of the singers named below.

It has been harder to find information on the pianists. The very term used in Russian for accompanist—*kontsertmeister*—shows the respect given to these artists who are full partners in any good performance of a song. The high level of musical training in Russia (which so struck Yehudi Menuhin when he first visited the country in 1945) is evident in their work. For every singer it is a matter of first importance to find a skilled and steady *kontsertmeister*. The singers never forgot them, but the historians of music often have. In the case of only some of them—Sakharov, Kozel, Makarov, Goldenweiser, Boshniakovich, Oborin, Ashkenazy and a few others—have I been able to include biographical information below. In most cases I have omitted mention of the honors singers and accompanists alike have received: Honored Artist of Russia, People's Artist of Russia (or other republic), People's Artist of the USSR (the highest award), State Prize Laureate, and so on. Nearly every Soviet artist named here has been so honored. These awards, wholly deserved but sometimes late in coming, are listed in *Agin*, *MES*, and other standard references.

In the compilation below, there are two recordings that occur so frequently they are cited in shorthand form. These are the two "complete" collections of Tchaikovsky's songs released by Melodiya.

The first of these is designated by the short title **Complete Romances** (1969). It contains all of the songs except the sixteen songs for children, Opus 54. The full citation for this set of six records is **LP Melodiya D 026111-22**.

The second is called **Complete Songs and Duets** (1980). This set of eight records contains all 103 songs, including Opus 54, as well as songs for two, three, and four voices, including the duets, Opus 46. Its full citation is **LP Melodiya S10 13475-13490**. Individual singers and performances on these two sets may coincide but often do not, so a singer's contribution to each set is listed separately.

Finally, a note on how the name "Melodiya" is used in this discography. The Melodiya label was not in use until 1964 (*Bennett*, x). Before that, records bore various names on the label, such as "Akkord," or "Aprelevskii zavod," which designated the factory that manufactured the record; earlier, in the 78 era, records were labeled "MuzTrest," "SovSong," "SSSR," or by factory or other designation. But in the list below, all records issued during the period of Soviet monopoly of the recording industry are identified simply as Melodiya, whatever the actual label on the record may read. When the Soviet Union was dissolved in 1991, independent labels like "Russian Disc" (a company organized by former Melodiya staff) began to issue records and compact discs, sometimes making new recordings, but often drawing on pre-existing Melodiya stock. The proliferation of new labels continues, though Melodiya still exists.

Anders, Peter. German tenor, 1908-1954. In *Record of Singing*, vol. 4.
• LP Telefunken 069 485-6 (HT 36). Also Telefunken 6.48064 DP. Hubert Giesen, piano, 1951. Songs 7, 8, 9, 14, 15, 24, 41 (all in German).

Anderson, Marian. African American contralto, 1897-1993. She won fame in Europe in the 1930s, visiting Russia in 1935, where she sang Song 45 in the first of her sold-out concerts in Leningrad; when she went to Moscow, Nezhdanova attended all her recitals there (*Keiler*, 144-7). Though no commercial recordings of her performances of Tchaikovsky's songs were issued, her concert repertoire included Songs 8, 9, 36, 45, 50, 73, 92, 93. Her one studio recording (Song 9, in English, 1955) was not issued, but a 1946 recording of it for the Bell Telephone Hour is extant (*Keiler*, 379). In addition, one of her favorite concert pieces was the aria "Adieu, forêts" from *Maid of Orleans*. In *Record of Singing*, vol. 3.

Arkhipova, Irina Konstantinovna. Russian mezzo-soprano, born 1925 in Moscow. She took music lessons at the Gnesin Institute as a girl, but trained as an architect while singing in amateur groups. In 1946 she studied with Nadezhda Malysheva, a gifted teacher who had worked in Stanislavsky's opera studio; in 1948 she enrolled as an external student at the Moscow Conservatory, where her teacher was Leonid Savransky. She graduated in 1953 in the same class as Gennady Rozhdestvensky and Gennady Pishchayev. After a season at the Sverdlovsk Opera she came to the Bolshoy where she made her debut as Carmen in 1956. Her voice of firm, pure, polished tone, and her capacity for hard work made her one of the finest Russian singers of her generation. She debuted at the Met at age 71 (*Opera News*, 19 April 1997). Published memoirs in 1992 (*Arkhipova*).
• LP Melodiya S 01179-80. Semyon Stuchevsky, piano. Songs 9, 17, 19, 35, 40, 44, 45, 70, 78, 80, 88, 90, 91, 92 (in Russian), 94 (in Russian).
• Complete Romances. Songs 17, 19, 44, 70, 78, 92 (in Russian).
• LP Melodiya SM 03167-8. Natalia Rassudova, piano. With Makvala Kasrashvili, soprano, and Vladislav Pashinsky, baritone. Six Duets, Op. 46.
• LP Melodiya S10 10779-80. "Arkhipova at Klin," 1977-78. Igor Guselnikov, on Tchaikovsky's piano. Songs 92-97 (in Russian), 98-103.
• Complete Songs and Duets. Songs 17, 93 and 96 (in Russian), 102. Six Duets, Op. 46.
• CD Melodiya SUCD 10-00010. "Musical Festival in Polotsk," concert recording (1988). Natalia Bogilava, piano. Song 9.

Ashkenázy, Vladímir Davídovich. Pianist, born 1937 in Moscow, son of the well-known pianist and arranger of popular romances David Ashkenazi (see the singer Valentina Shcherbinina below). Pupil of Lev Oborin (*q.v.*) and others. First Prize (tied with John Ogdon), Tchaikovsky Competition, 1962. Soloist and conductor, he is also an excellent accompanist. The recordings of Tchaikovsky and Rachmaninoff songs he made with Elisabeth Söderström are indispensable—intelligent and ever fresh after repeated hearings.

Atlántov, Vladímir Andréyevich. Russian tenor, born 1939 in Leningrad. His father was a singer at the Kirov (bass). Studied at the Leningrad Conservatory (1963, class of N. D. Bolotina) and La Scala (1963-65). First Prize, Tchaikovsky Competition, 1966. Kirov Opera 1963-67, after 1967 at the Bolshoy; also Vienna, Berlin, La Scala, Covent Garden, and with the Bolshoy at the Met. Concert tours of Canada, Europe, Japan.
• LP Melodiya SM 03203-4. Farida Khalilova, piano. Songs 9, 39, 50, 77, 99, 101, 103.
• Complete Songs and Duets. Song 103.

Baikóv, Sergéy Vladímirovich. Russian bass, born 1955 in a town on the Volga. Trained at the Russian Academy of Music (Gnesin), pupil of Konstantin Lisovsky. Soloist, Moscow Philharmonic, Minin Chamber Choir.
• CD A&E (MCA) AED-10320. Ilya Sheps, piano. Songs 7, 38, 39, 41, 49, 99.
• CD Le Chant du Monde LDC 288 038/40. Ilya Sheps, piano. Song 69 (Rimsky-Korsakov).

Bákhchiev, Aleksándr Geórgievich. Russian pianist, born 1930 in Moscow. Pupil of Lev Oborin. Classmate of Gennady Pishchayev, with whom he has made recordings. Noted for educational "concert-talks" and original concert programs with other pianists of rarely performed works. Honored Artist of Russia.

Bársova, Valériya Vladímirovna. Russian lyric-coloratura soprano, 1892-1967. Moscow Conservatory 1919, where she graduated both in voice (class of Umberto Masetti) and piano (Alexander Goldenweiser); took further lessons from her older sister Maria Vladimirova, also a soprano and pupil of Masetti. Moscow Zimin Opera 1917; sang Rosina in *Barber of Seville* with Chaliapin as Don Basilio in Moscow in 1919 and 1920, and again in Riga in 1930. Bolshoy 1920-48; People's Artist 1937. One of the greatest singers of her generation, with a velvety, soft, elastic voice, technically very strong. Toured in Europe.
• LP Melodiya D 08937-8. Pianist not indicated. Songs 55, 60.

Belmás, Ksénia Aleksándrovna. Russian soprano, 1890-1981. Born in Chernigov, father of French origin, mother Ukrainian. Studied in Kiev with Martin Petz (in *Levik*), sang in Kharkov (1910), Odessa (1913-14). When her husband was killed in the Civil War, she fled Kiev and resumed her career in Europe. Sang at the Paris Opera, gave recitals there and in Berlin, where she made most of her recordings (1927-30). In 1934 she settled in South Africa, where she taught singing (*TRC*, vol. 38, no. 4). In *Record of Singing*, vol. 3.
• LP Club "99" CL 99-13. Alexander Kitschine, piano (1929). Songs 45, 51. Also on • CD Memoir Classics CD MOIR 422.

Bogachóva, Irína Petróvna. Russian mezzo-soprano, born 1939. Leningrad Conservatory 1965, class of I. P. Timonova-Levando; graduate training at La Scala. Kirov Opera since 1964; Professor, Leningrad Conservatory. Sang in Kirov seasons at the Met in 1998, 1999.
• CD Russian Compact Disc RCD 26001. Songs 44, 73 (1980, Sofia Vakman, piano). Song 91 (1981, Andreev Folk Orchestra). Songs 70, 79 (1991, Yelena Gaudasinskaya, piano).

Bolshakóv, Alekséy Alekséyevich. Russian baritone, 1914-1979. Born in Samara. Sang in the Red Army Chorus during the war. Sverdlovsk Opera 1947-53; Bolshoy 1953-75.
• CD Russian Compact Disc RCD 16038. Grigory Zinger, piano, 1963. Song 103.

Borg, Kim. Finnish bass, 1919-2000. Born in Helsinki. Operatic career included three seasons at the Met (1959-62). Sang Boris Godunov at the Bolshoy, Gremin in *Eugene Onegin* at Glyndebourne (1968). In *Record of Singing*, vol. 4.
• LP Supraphon 50499. Alfred Holeček, piano, 1979. Songs 9, 39, 41, 49. Also on • LP Artia ALP-704.

Borisénko, Véra (Veroníka) Ivánovna. Russian mezzo-soprano, born 1918. Sverdlovsk Conservatory, class of Yegor Yegorov (taught by Varvara Zarudnaya, who was trained by Nissen-Saloman and Everardi). Kiev Opera (1944-46), Bolshoy (1946-63, 1967-77).
• **78 Melodiya 14005**. Georgy Orentlikher, piano. Song 73.
• **78 Melodiya 15854.** Abram Makarov, piano. Song 89.
• **78 Melodiya 026138-9.** Nikolay Korolkov, piano. Songs 26, 28.
• **LP Melodiya D 4100-01**. Pianist not indicated. Songs 26, 28, 97, 100, 101. Songs 40, 42, 69 (Rimsky-Korsakov).
• **LP Melodiya SM 02089-90**. Nikolay Korolkov, piano. Songs 10, 11, 73, 88, 91.
• **Complete Romances**. Nikolay Korolkov, piano. Song 73.
• **LP Melodiya SM 03661-2**. Nikolay Korolkov, piano. Song 2 (Verstovsky). Song 29 (Varlamov).

Borodiná, Olga Vladímirovna. Russian mezzo-soprano, born 1963. Leningrad Conservatory, pupil of Irina Bogachova (*q.v.*). Kirov Opera 1987-present. Major roles at Covent Garden (since 1992), San Francisco (since 1995), and the Met (since 1997).
• **CD Philips 442 013-2**. "Tchaikovsky Romances," 1993. Larissa Gergieva, piano. Songs 1, 4, 5, 8, 9, 11, 17, 19, 38, 40, 79, 80, 85, 89, 90, 92, 99, 101, 103.

Boshniakóvich, Olég Dragomírovich. Russian pianist, born 1920. Pupil of Konstantin Igumnov (*q.v.*): poetic, every detail worked out. Accompanied Obukhova after Sakharov died, and Hvorostovsky on his first album of Tchaikovsky and Rachmaninoff romances.

Bozhkova, Nelly. Bulgarian mezzo-soprano, born 1949. Sofia Conservatory, 1971, pupil of Christo Brymbarov; soloist, Sofia National Opera.
• **LP Melodiya S10 10775-6** (Tchaikovsky Competition, 1978). Yelena Manova, piano. Song 99.

Burchuládze, Paata. Georgian bass, born 1951. Studied at La Scala 1978-80. First Prize, Tchaikovsky Competition, 1982. Principal singer at the Tbilisi Opera. Strong, dynamic voice with wide range. People's Artist of Georgia. Has sung at Covent Garden and the Met.
• **CD London 421 417-2**. "Russian Songs," 1987. Ludmilla Ivanova, piano. Songs 7, 9, 41, 43, 84, 89, 99, 101.

Caruso, Enrico. Italian tenor, 1873-1921. In *Record of Singing*, vol 1.
• **CD RCA 60495-2**. "The Complete Caruso." Song 8 (in French), orch. conducted by Josef Pasternack, 3 Nov. 1916. Song 39 (in French), orch. conducted by Gaetano Scognamiglio, 21 Jan. 1914. Song 44 (in Italian), Gaetano Scognamiglio, piano, 17 Jan. 1913.
• **CD Memoir Classics CD MOIR 422**. Song 44, as above.

Celine, Annette. Brazilian soprano of Polish heritage. Began musical studies with her mother, a well-known pianist and accompanist on this recording, who emigrated to Brazil in 1942.
• **CD Olympia OCD 629**. "Chopin: 19 Polish Songs, Op. 74." Felicja Blumental, piano. Song 32 (Chopin).

Chaliápin, Fyódor Ivánovich (pronounced Shaljápin). Russian bass, born in Kazan in 1873, died in Paris in 1938. Sang in provincial opera companies in Volga towns in 1890; in 1892-3 he studied in Tiflis with Dmitry Usatov (see Song 72, dedicated to him). Debut at Mariinsky (St. Petersburg) in 1895, Mamontov Opera (Moscow) in 1896, Bolshoy 1899 (he regularly sang in both capitals until leaving Russia in 1922); then La Scala, Monte Carlo, Rome, Berlin, Paris, the Met (1907). Incomparable singer and dramatic actor of the operatic stage (Boris Godunov, King Philip, Mephistopheles), he sang his first Prince Gremin in *Eugene Onegin* on 22 October 1893 in Tiflis, three days before Tchaikovsky's death, singing the part not as a set piece but with a naturalness and sincerity that made the character come alive, showing why Tatyana is loyal to him. Though he recorded only Songs 49, 77, and 93, he also performed Songs 5, 25, 82, and 87 in concerts. In addition to the sessions below, there is an earlier January 1902 take of Songs 77 and 93, and Song 49 was recorded again in Camden in 1927. Discography in *Borovsky*. People's Artist of the Republic (1918).

Close friend of Gorky and Rachmaninoff. The vast literature in Russian begins with his own writings (*Shaliapin*), the chronicle of his life and work (*Kotliarov*), and memoirs and correspondence (*Grosheva*). In *Levik*; in *Record of Singing*, vols. 1, 2, 3.

• **LP EMI EX 7 61065 1**. "Chaliapin," 4-record set transferred from 78s by Keith Hardwick. Song 93 (in Russian), with unknown pianist, recorded in Moscow in January 1902. Song 77, Max Rabinowitsch, piano, recorded in Hayes 9 Oct. 1921.

• **CD Nimbus NI 7823/4**. "Chaliapin (Prima Voce Series)." Song 49, orch. conducted by Rosario Bourdon, violin solo by Schmidt, recorded in Camden 3 Jan. 1924.

• **CD Memoir Classics CD MOIR 422**. Max Rabinowitsch, piano (1921). Song 77.

• **CD Pearl GEMM CD 9921**. "Feodor Chaliapin sings Russian Music," vol. 2. Song 49 (1924, as above). D. I. Pokhitonov, piano: Song 77 (1913).

Choi, Hans. American baritone, born 1958 in Seoul. First Prize, Tchaikovsky Competition, 1990. His teachers included Carlo Bergonzi and Igor Chichagov.

• **CD Melodiya SUCD 10-00116** (Tchaikovsky Competition, 1990). Igor Chichagov, piano. Song 9.

Christoff, Boris. Bulgarian bass, born 1914 in Plovdiv. A matchless singer, he has recorded well over 150 songs by the major Russian composers, and all his recordings are important. Trained as a lawyer, he was noticed in a choir by the King of Bulgaria, who gave him a scholarship and sent him to Italy, where he studied with Riccardo Stracciari (in *Record of Singing*, vols. 2 and 3), a pupil of Masetti. He made his debut at La Scala in 1947, then in the U.S. in 1956 at San Francisco, where he sang Boris, a part he also sang at the Bolshoy. He learned more than forty roles in six languages. An heir to Chaliapin, he is a versatile singer whose expressive voice has great color and dramatic power, but he also has a lighter touch, as he shows in Song 67. He died in Rome in 1993. In *Record of Singing*, vol. 4.

• **LP Capitol G 7236**. Alexandre Labinsky, piano; Gaston Marchesini, cello. (Paris, 1959 and 1960). Songs 9, 11, 22, 24, 27, 39, 56, 67, 70, 82, 85, 93, 99 (with cello), 103.

• **CD EMI CZS 7 67496 2**. "Mélodies Russes," 5 CDs. As above.

• **same**. Alexandre Tcherepnine, piano (Paris, 1967). Songs 24, 74 (Balakirev).

• **same**. Serge Zapolsky, piano (Paris, 1967). Song 81 (Cui).

• **CD EMI CHS 7 63025 2**. "Moussorgsky: Complete Songs," 3 CDs. Alexandre Labinsky, piano (Paris 1955-57). Songs 25, 46 (Musorgsky).

Daunoras, Vatslovas. Lithuanian bass, born 1937. Trained at the Vilnius Conservatory, where he now teaches, and at La Scala; soloist, Vilnius Opera. Fourth Prize, Tchaikovsky Competition, 1966. People's Artist USSR (1986).

• **LP Melodiya D 018247-8** (Tchaikovsky Competition, 1966). Song 49. Also on • **CD Russian Disc RDCD 00379**.

Davrath, Netania. Israeli soprano, 1931-1987, born in Ukraine. Among her voice teachers was Jennie Tourel (*q.v.*) at Juilliard. Operatic roles in Tel Aviv, Boston, and Chicago. Her recitals included appearances with Leopold Stokowski (*q.v.*) and Leonard Bernstein.

• **CD Vanguard Classics 08 9081 72**. Erik Werba, piano. Songs 10, 50, 51, 103.

Davýdova, Véra Aleksándrovna. Russian mezzo-soprano, 1906-1993. Leningrad Conservatory 1930, class of Yelena De Vosse-Soboleva (a pupil of Everardi). Mariinsky Opera 1929-32, Bolshoy 1932-56. Tall, stately, beautiful (Stalin was said to be in love with her), she had a splendid, even voice throughout her whole range. Her roles included Lyubov (*Mazeppa*), and Marfa (*Khovanshchina*), for which she was coached by Ivan Yershov (*q.v.*). Her early retirement to teach at the Tbilisi Conservatory was seen as a major loss for the Bolshoy.

• **RGAFD Catalogue**. Abram Makarov, piano. Song 91.

• **Complete Romances**. Aleksandr Yerokhin, piano. Song 94 (in Russian).

DeGaetani, Jan. American mezzo-soprano, 1933-1989. A virtuoso singer admired for her performances of difficult (especially modernist) works.

• **CD Arabesque Z6674**. "Russian Songs," 1984. Gilbert Kalish, piano. Songs 5, 9, 17, 18, 22, 27, 31, 40, 48, 51. Also on • **LP Nonesuch Digital 9 79103-1 F**.

De Reszke, Edouard. Polish bass, 1853-1917. Sang Songs 9 and 39 in Paris in 1888 at concerts of Tchaikovsky's music which the composer attended, and Song 39 in Petersburg in 1891 (*DG* 441, 443, 514). His brother **Jean de Reszke**, famous tenor (1850-1925), also sang in the 1888 Paris concerts (Songs 8 and 50), *pace* Michael Scott, "... Jean de Reszke rarely appeared in concert, and then only in excerpts from opera; throughout his entire career he never sang a song" (*Scott I*, 141). Both in *Record of Singing*, vol. 1.
- **LP Odyssey Y-35067** (from the Columbia 1903 Grand Opera series). Song 39 (in French).

Descamps, Paul. Belgian bass-baritone.
- **CD ADDA 590041**. Xavier Rivera, piano, 1989. Songs 1, 4, 9, 19, 20, 23, 24, 29, 32, 37, 39, 41, 49, 81, 83, 84, 93, 97, 99, 103.

Dolukhánova, Zára Aleksándrovna. Russian-Armenian mezzo-soprano (later, soprano). Born 1918 in Moscow in a musical family: her parents and her sister Dagmar, who married Pavel Lisitsian, were accomplished musicians. She studied violin as a girl, at 16 began voice training with Vera Beliayeva-Tarasevich. Debuted at Yerevan Opera in 1939 but soon decided on a concert career in order to have the freedom to explore music of all periods. Soloist at All-Union Radio from 1944-1957 and the Moscow Philharmonic from 1959-1982. Her fame rose rapidly after she won a gold medal in Budapest in 1949; she was awarded a State Prize (then called Stalin Prize) in 1951, an unusual honor for a concert singer. Vast repertoire from Bach to Shostakovich; sang concert performances of operas rarely performed in Russia, including coloratura mezzo roles; toured extensively, including recitals in the U.S. in 1959, 1962, 1970. In the early 1960s she made a transition to soprano with Yevgeny Kanger, a pianist, whom she names today as her most important teacher. A brilliant concert singer in the tradition of Zoya Lodii (*q.v.*) and Pauline Viardot, to whom she has been compared. Her concerts were eagerly anticipated musical events because she kept to her rule of never singing the same song twice in a city no matter how many times she appeared there. Her farewell concert was at the Great Hall of the Moscow Conservatory in the spring of 1983. Currently on the faculty at the Russian Academy of Music (Gnesin), where she has taught since 1972. In *Record of Singing*, vol. 4. Biography by *Iakovenko*.
- **Complete Romances**. Berta Kozel, piano. Songs 6, 28.
- **Complete Songs and Duets**. Song 6.
- **LP Melodiya M10 48659 003**. Berta Kozel, piano, Galina Sakharova, soprano. Duet 4.
- **CD Melodiya SUCD 10-00202**. Songs 5, 17, 28, 29, 40, 47, 48, 50, 68, 70.
- **CD Russian Disc RD CD 11 342**. Alexander Dolukhanian, piano (1948): Songs 2, 3. Berta Kozel, piano (1950-58): Songs 5, 6, 17, 28, 40, 41, 50, 68, 89, 90, 91.
- **LP Melodiya S10 10519-20**. Vladimir Khvostin, piano (1977). Songs 11, 69, 76.

Eddy, Nelson. American baritone, 1901-1967. Sang in the Philadelphia Opera, then on the radio and in successful Hollywood films. *WERM* also lists Songs 39, 56 (in English).
- **CD Memoir Classics CDMOIR 436**. Orch. cond. Nathaniel Finston, 1939. Songs 9, 49 (in English).

Èizen, Artúr Artúrovich. Russian bass, born 1927. Student of Vladimir Politkovsky (*q.v.*). Soloist with the Red Army Chorus 1949-57, at the Bolshoy from 1957. After 1975 on the faculty of solo singing at the Russian Academy of Music (Gnesin Institute).
- **LP Melodiya SM 02573-4**. State Symphony, cond. A. Stasevich. Songs 7, 9, 38, 39, 41, 49, 69.

Estes, Simon. African American bass-baritone, born 1938. Third Prize, Tchaikovsky Competition, Moscow, 1966. Has sung with major opera companies including the Met, La Scala, Bayreuth, Covent Garden, Berlin, Zurich, Geneva, Hamburg.
- **LP Melodiya D 018247-8** (Tchaikovsky Competition, 1966). Song 5.

Fassbänder, Brigitte. German mezzo-soprano, born 1939.
- **LP Electrola C063-29085**. Song 80 (in German).

Fígner, Nikoláy Nikoláyevich. Russian tenor, 1857-1918. Born in Kazan province, brother of Vera Figner, remembered in Russian history as a member of "People's Will," a terrorist group which assassinated Alexander II in 1881. Served as a naval officer, then went to

Italy, where he studied singing and made his debut in Naples in 1882. While in Italy he met the Italian soprano Medea Mei (*q.v.*), whom he brought to St. Petersburg in 1887 and married in 1889. Figner and Mei were stars of the Mariinsky Opera from 1887 until 1904 (Figner) and 1912 (Mei). Despite his nasal tone, he was a favorite of the public for his stage presence and intelligence as a singer (*Nezhdanova*, 39). Both he and his wife were admired by Tchaikovsky; they created the roles of Gherman and Liza in the first *Queen of Spades* (1890). Tchaikovsky dedicated the songs of Opus 73 to him. He made about forty recordings, including some with his wife. Described at length in *Levik*, who considered his Gherman inferior to his "unrivalled" performances as Verdi's Otello, and as Andrey in *Oprichnik*. In *Record of Singing*, vol. 1.

• **LP Melodiya M10 45313 004.** Songs 8 (1909) and 38 (1901).

Fischer-Dieskau, Dietrich. German baritone, born 1925. Celebrated singer of lieder, unequalled in the scope of his recordings of the German song repertoire. His choice of Tchaikovsky romances includes several rare songs, and he brings his artistry to his performances of all of them, but the recordings would have been better had he tried harder to learn how Russian words are supposed to sound. A cautionary example. In *Record of Singing*, vol. 4.

• **LP Philips 6514 116.** "Tchaikovsky Lieder." Aribert Reimann, piano. Songs 1, 7, 13, 16, 20, 23, 24, 29, 32, 37, 39, 41, 42, 43, 49, 69, 84.

• **LP Angel 35963.** Gerald Moore, piano, Victoria de los Angeles, soprano. Duet 2.

Fominá, Nína Víktorovna. Russian soprano, born 1937. Moscow Conservatory 1971, pupil of A. S. Sveshnikova, went directly to the Bolshoy.

• **Complete Songs and Duets.** Alexander Pokrovsky, piano. Songs 12, 31, 36.

Frijsh, Povla. Danish soprano, 1881-1960, admired concert singer. In *Record of Singing*, vol. 3.

• **CD Pearl GEMM CDS 9095.** Song 41 (in French), Elof Nielsen, piano, 1933.

Gedda, Nicolai. Swedish tenor, born 1925 in Stockholm. A truly international opera star who has sung in all the major European opera houses and in all the major European languages; in the U.S., he sang at the Met for 23 seasons from 1957-80. His father, Mikhail Ustinov, was a Russian who emigrated after the Civil War and, as a singer with the Don Cossack choir, became choir master in a Russian church in Leipzig; Gedda first sang there as a child. Studied in Stockholm, including lessons with Swedish tenor Karl Öhmann. His fluency in Russian allowed him to sing the role of Lensky in *Eugene Onegin* in Moscow and Leningrad in 1980 and to acquire a large repertoire of Russian songs (he made a special study of Russian songs with Paola Novikova in New York). In 1980-81 he gave concerts in Russia and made studio recordings for Melodiya. In *Record of Singing*, vol. 4.

• **LP HMV SLS-5250.** Gerald Moore, piano (1969). Songs 39, 41.

• **LP Electrola C 063-28023.** Jan Eyron, piano. Songs 39, 56, 100.

• **CD Gala GL 332.** "Nicolai Gedda Sings French & Russian Songs." Geoffrey Parsons, piano (1971). Songs 39, 41, 56, 100.

• **LP Melodiya S10 13977-8.** Liya Mogilevskaya, piano (1980). Songs 8, 41.

• **LP Melodiya S10 14631-2.** "Recital in the Leningrad Philharmonic Grand Hall." Erik Werba, piano (1981). Song 40 (Rimsky-Korsakov).

Gerásimova, Natália Borísovna. Russian soprano, born 1950 in Moscow, where she graduated from the Gnesin Institute in 1977, class of A. D. Kilchevskaya. Soloist, Moscow Chamber Choir (1971-93), and independent concert artist who has worked with many ensembles and appeared in Europe and the U.S. She has recorded unusual 20th-c. songs (Lurie, Mosolov, Shcherbachov), and revived songs by rarely heard composers of the late 18th and early 19th cc. (Zhilin, Kashin, Dubiansky, Vielgorsky). People's Artist of Russia.

• **CD Rossijsky Instrument RI 002.** "I See Your Image." Chamber Ensemble "Barokko" (1993). Song 2 (Vielgorsky).

• **CD Russian Compact Disc (Russian Romance) RCD 16017.** "Romances by Mikhail Glinka," 1996. Igor Zhukov, piano. Song 32 (Glinka).

• **CD Le Chant du Monde LDC 288 038/40.** "Rimsky-Korsakov, Complete Songs," 1991-

92. Vladimir Skanavi, piano. Songs 46, 81 (Rimsky-Korsakov).

Ghiaúrov, Nicolai. Bulgarian bass, born 1929. Studied in Sofia with Christo Brymbarov and went on to the Moscow Conservatory. Brilliant career as a singer of Italian, French, and Russian opera. Debuts at Sofia (1956), Bolshoy (1957), La Scala (1959), Covent Garden (1962), Chicago (1963), Met (1965). Married to Mirella Freni (I heard him sing Gremin to her Tatyana in *Eugene Onegin* at the Met 22 Dec. 1992). His fine "basso cantante" and clean, expressive delivery of the lyrics make him an excellent singer of Russian songs.
   • **LP Melodiya M10 44687-004**. Zlatinka Mishakova, piano (Moscow, May 15, 1961). Songs 7, 39.
   • **CD London 443 024-2**. "Russian Songs," 1971. Zlatina Ghiaurov, piano. Songs 5, 9, 39, 40, 41, 49.
   • **CD RCA Victor 09026-62501-2**. "Russian Romances," 1993. Pavlina Dokovska, piano. Songs 9, 39, 41, 49, 77.

Ghiuselev, Nicola. Bulgarian bass, born 1936. Pupil of Christo Brymbarov; soloist at the Sofia Opera since 1960.
   • **CD Balkanton 040099**. "Songs by Russian Composers." Theodor Mousev, piano. Song 49.

Gmýria, Borís Románovich. Russian-Ukrainian bass, 1903-1969. A stevedore and merchant sailor in the Black Sea, he took an engineering degree before deciding to study voice. Graduated from the Kharkov Conservatory in 1939 (class of P. V. Golubev) and went to the Kiev Opera, where he was a principal singer until retirement. One of the finest recitalists of his time, with a repertoire of more than 500 Russian, Ukrainian, and Western European songs. In *Record of Singing*, vol. 4.
   • **78 Melodiya 20380-81**. [Lev Ostrin, piano]. Songs 89, 98.
   • **LP Melodiya 33 ND 1595**. [Lev Ostrin, piano]. Songs 41, 82, 87.
   • **LP Melodiya D 011997-8**. Lev Ostrin, piano. Songs 8, 9, 19, 25, 38 (with cello), 39, 49, 65, 85, 87, 91, 98.
   • **LP Melodiya D 033119**. Lev Ostrin, piano. Songs 41, 91.
   • **Complete Romances**. Lev Ostrin, piano. Song 8.
   • **LP Russian Disc R10 00163-4**. Lev Ostrin, piano. Songs 9, 25, 87.
   • **LP Melodiya M10 36765-6**. Lev Ostrin, piano, 1969. Song 75 (Tolstaya).

Goldenweiser, Aleksándr Borísovich (in Russian, Gol'denvéizer). Pianist and teacher, 1875-1961. Pupil of Pabst and Siloti (piano), Ippolitov-Ivanov, Arensky, and Taneyev (composition). Taught at the Moscow Conservatory from 1906 until his death, as an eminent exponent of the Russian piano school, "seeking the inner meaning of the music while achieving technical brilliance" (*Baker's*). Close to Rachmaninoff, Medtner, and also Lev Tolstoy, about whom he wrote memoirs.

Golodiáyevskaya, Irma. Russian mezzo-soprano.
   • **Complete Romances**. L. Dundukova, piano. Song 96 (in Russian).

Golovín, Dmítry Danílovich. Russian baritone, 1894-1966. Sang in church choirs as a boy; joined operetta theatre in Sevastopol in 1915; in 1919 at Sevastopol Opera sang the title role of Anton Rubinstein's *Demon*, later one of his best roles. Moscow Conservatory 1921-24, pupil of N. G. Raisky. Zimin Opera 1923, Bolshoy 1924-43. Sang in Monte Carlo, Milan, Paris 1928-29. Unusually full and powerful voice.
   • **LP Melodiya D 032713-4**. Song 34 (with altered text purged of religious references).

Gorchakóva, Galína Vladímirovna. Russian soprano, born 1963 in Novokuznetsk. Studied at the Novosibirsk Conservatory; Sverdlovsk Opera 1988-91; Kirov Opera since 1991. Brilliant performances with Kirov at Covent Garden and the Met in Russian operas of Borodin, Rimsky-Korsakov, Prokofiev, and Tchaikovsky, some of which she has recorded. Her Tchaikovsky heroines include Iolanta (*Iolanthe*), Maria (*Mazeppa*), Tatyana (*Eugene Onegin*) and Liza (*Queen of Spades*).
   • **CD Philips 446 720-2**. "Memories of Love," 1996. Larissa Gergieva, piano. Songs 10, 11, 36, 40.

Guliáyev, Yúry Aleksándrovich. Russian baritone, 1930-1986. Urals Conservatory 1949-53. Sang at Sverdlovsk 1955-6, Donetsk 1956-60, Kiev 1960-75, the Bolshoy 1975-86. He was a popular concert singer, whose recordings of Tchaikovsky's songs are often heard on the radio; he also wrote songs.
- **LP Melodiya S10 10839-40**. Rosalia Trokhman, piano. Songs 25, 41, 69, 76, 83, 98, 101.
- **Complete Songs and Duets**. Rosalia Trokhman, piano. Song 41.

Homer, Louise. American contralto, 1871-1947. Distinguished career in opera 1900-1929, primarily at the Met; famous as Orfeo in Gluck's opera (with Toscanini, 1909), and as Dalila opposite Caruso. In *Record of Singing*, vol. 1.
- **CD Pearl GEMM CD 9950**. "Louise Homer." Song 9 (1929, in German).

Hvorostóvsky, Dmítri Aleksándrovich. Russian baritone, born 1962. Krasnoyarsk Institute of Arts 1987, pupil of Yekaterina Iofel; Krasnoyarsk Opera 1984-90. Glinka Prize 1987, "Singer of the World" Prize at Cardiff 1989, after which he was invited to sing in major opera houses in Russia and the West, including the Met. Recitals in Europe, the U.S., and Russia, where he is highly regarded. His idiomatic, expressive performances of Russian songs show his voice to fine advantage; his recordings of Tchaikovsky's songs are outstanding.
- **CD Philips 432 119-2**. "Russian Romances," 1990. Oleg Boshniakovich, piano. Songs 7, 9, 19, 38, 39, 77, 84, 87, 103.
- **CD Philips 442 536-2**. "My Restless Soul," 1993. Mikhail Arkadiev, piano. Songs 1, 5, 25, 40, 41, 42, 43, 49, 50, 69, 98.

Igúmnov, Konstantín Nikoláyevich. Russian pianist and pedagogue (1873-1948). Student of Pavel Pabst (1854-97, to whom Tchaikovsky dedicated his "Concert Polonaise", Op. 72, no. 7). Noted for his interpretations of Tchaikovsky's piano work.
- **CD Dante HPC 068**. "L'Art de Konstantin Igumnov," vol. 1. Song 11 (Tchaikovsky piano transcription, 1935).

Isákova, Nína Sergéyevna. Russian mezzo-soprano, born 1928 near Pskov. Moscow Conservatory 1958, where she studied with contralto Faina Petrova, a pupil of Zarudnaya and Goldenweiser who sang at the Met from 1930-33 and at the Bolshoy from 1933-49. Stanislavsky Opera Theatre 1958-85; concert singer, teacher at the Moscow Conservatory after 1978; now residing in the U.S.
- **LP Melodiya D 6995-6**. Yevgeniya Bruk, piano. Songs 1, 29, 74, 96, 102.
- **Complete Romances**. Yevgeniya Bruk, piano. Songs 1, 26, 27, 30, 80, 85, 88.
- **Complete Songs and Duets**. Aleksandr Bakhchiev, piano: Songs 1, 73. Yevgeniya Bruk, piano: Songs 26, 27, 28, 29, 30, 48, 80, 86, 88, 94 (in Russian).

Ivanóv, Alekséy Petróvich. Russian baritone, 1904-82. Leningrad Conservatory 1932, class of Walter Bosse (in *Levik*); also studied with Ivan Yershov (*q.v.*). Sang in Leningrad (Maly) until 1936, two years in Saratov and Gorky, then at the Bolshoy 1938-67. A versatile artist, he sang lyric, dramatic, and comic parts, including the Devil in Tchaikovsky's opera *The Slippers*.
- **LP Melodiya M10 36033-38**. "The Art of Aleksey Ivanov." Aleksey Zybtsev, piano. Songs 13, 69. Song 74 (Balakirev).
- **Complete Romances**. Song 13.

Ivanóv, Andréy Alekséyevich. Russian baritone, 1900-1970. Born near Lublin (now Poland, then part of the Russian empire). Sang in a children's choir led by his father, a school teacher. The family evacuated to Kiev when the First World War began. A voice teacher in Kiev realized his talent and gave him free lessons; joined the Kiev Opera as an extra. Though not enrolled in the conservatory, he was invited to sing Onegin in a student production, performing so well he was awarded a diploma. After the Civil War he joined a "traveling opera collective" that performed in towns up and down the Volga and in the Caucasus, learning 22 roles on the road: Prince Igor, the Demon, Rigoletto, Escamillo (*Carmen*), Germont (*La Traviata*), Valentin (*Faust*), Amonasro (*Aida*). (It is something to marvel at, this caravan of singers putting on grand opera in the Soviet provinces during the period of NEP and *The Twelve Chairs*.) In 1926 he went on to sing in Baku, Odessa, and Sverdlovsk, finally returning to Kiev where he sang from 1934-49. By the time he went to the Bolshoy in 1950, he was already a People's Artist of Ukraine (1941) and the Soviet Union (1944). He sang at the Bolshoy for six years; later gave recitals and toured, including a concert tour to England. One of the best Russian baritones of his day, his singing is distinguished by perfect diction and a clear, ringing tone. In *Record of Singing*, vol. 4.

• **LP Melodiya M10 36235-40.** "The Art of Andrei Ivanov." Georgy Orentlikher, piano. Songs 7, 35.

• **LP Melodiya M10 41247-50.** Georgy Orentlikher, piano: Songs 7, 35, 49. Naum Walter, piano: Songs 38, 41, 99.

• **Complete Romances.** Song 7.

• **LP Melodiya D 029539-40.** "Romances to Lyrics by Y. Polonsky." Pianist not indicated. Song 83 (Dargomyzhsky).

Jadlowker, Hermann. Latvian-Jewish tenor, born in Riga, 1877-1953. Unusual "coloratura-heldentenor" voice. In *Record of Singing*, vol. 2.

• **CD Marston 52017-2.** Pianist not indicated, 1924. Songs 8, 37, 39, 100 (in German).

Kamiónsky, Oskar Isáyevich. Russian baritone, 1869-1917. St. Petersburg Conservatory (1891), pupil of Camillo Everardi and Stanislav Gabel. Encouraged by Tchaikovsky and Anton Rubinstein to study in Italy, he went to Europe in 1891, made his debut in Naples, sang in Siena, Florence, Athens. Back home he sang for twenty years, mostly in the provincial opera houses of the empire, in Kharkov, Kiev, Kazan, Rostov-on-the-Don, Tiflis, Saratov, Nizhny-Novgorod, Yekaterinoslav (Dnepropetrovsk), Odessa, Baku. Gave a concert tour of Siberia and Japan in 1909. Famous bel canto singer known as "the Russian Battistini." Described in *Levik*.

• **78 Gramophone Concert Record (Moscow). GC 3-22921.** Songs 5, 49.

• **CD Symposium 1151.** "Singers of Russia 1900-1917: Sergei Levik & His Contemporaries." Song 82.

Karolik, Maxim. Jewish tenor from Bessarabia, c. 1900-1963. A passionate amateur and friend of Nicolas Slonimsky in Boston. His surname was probably invented, taken from King Karol of Romania. Aristocratic bearing, friendly with Boston society, guest at wedding of Jacqueline and John Kennedy (*Slonimsky 1988*, 109-10).

• **LP Unicorn UNS-2 (1055-57).** "Thirty Russian Art Songs." Robert Pettitt, piano. Articles, Comments and Translations by Maxim Karolik and Nicolas Slonimsky. Illustrated booklet with portraits of the singer and the composers. Songs 12, 34, 77, 83, 84, 103.

Kasrashvíli, Makvalá Filimónovna. Russian-Georgian soprano, born 1942. Pupil of Vera Davydova (*q.v.*); graduated Tbilisi Conservatory in 1966 and went directly to the Bolshoy.

• **CD Melodiya SUCD 10-00264.** Liya Mogilevskaya, piano. Songs 5, 10, 15, 35, 38, 40, 41, 45, 50, 51, 68, 70, 79, 85, 87, 99, 100, 103.

Kastórsky, Vladímir Ivánovich. Russian bass, 1870-1948. Son of a village priest, sang in church choirs, educated in parochial school in Kostroma. In 1893 studied with Gabel, who dismissed him (Gabel later admitted his mistake); advised and coached by Antonio Cotogni (whose pupils included Jean de Reszke, Battistini, Gigli). Sang at the Mariinsky 1898-1930; seasons in Paris and London (with Diaghilev, 1907-9), Moscow (1918-23); tours of Europe and the provinces, including Harbin (1922-4). He had a voice of rare beauty, with velvety, soft timbre. Most admired in Russian roles (Ruslan, Pimen, Dosifey, Gremin, which he sang 500 times), but also in Wagner (Wotan, Hagen, King Mark). He made about 150 recordings (1901-39, some under the name Torsky). In *Record of Singing*, vols. 1, 2; in *Levik*.

• **RGAFD Catalogue:** Songs 41 (1915), 49 (1915), 84 (1911, with orchestra), 91 (1912).

• **LP Rubini GV2.** Songs 41, 49.

Katúlskaya, Yeléna Kliméntievna. Russian soprano, 1888-1966. Born in Odessa, finished the St. Petersburg Conservatory 1909, pupil of Natalia Iretskaya. Sang many times opposite Sobinov, Yershov, Tartakov, and Chaliapin (in *Boris Godunov* and *Barber of Seville*) early in her career; was a soloist at the Bolshoy from 1913-46. A classic representative of the Russian school, her repertoire included 46 parts in Russian, Italian, and French opera; she was also a connoisseur of songs (of which she knew more than 600), including 19th-c. urban romances. Her voice was esteemed for its noble, expressive, silvery timbre. Sang in concerts at the front during the war; after the war, taught at the Moscow Conservatory.

- **RGAFD Catalogue:** Songs 22 (1932), 51 (1915).
- **78 Melodiya 10302-3.** Matvey Sakharov, piano. Song 45.
- **78 Melodiya 20404.** Pianist not indicated. Song 61.
- **LP Melodiya M10 38693-4.** Boris Yurtaikin, piano. Songs 12, 71.

Kazarnóvskaya, Ljubóv Yúrevna. Russian soprano, born 1956. Moscow Conservatory 1981, pupil of Yelena Shumilova. Stanislavsky Opera 1981-86, Kirov 1986-89.
- **CD Legato Classics LCD 220-1.** Ljuba Orfenova, piano. Songs 2, 41, 51, 101.
- **CD Naxos 8.554357.** "Tchaikovsky: Complete Songs," vol. 1, 1997. Ljuba Orfenova, piano. Songs 2, 3, 10, 11, 12, 17, 20, 29, 36, 45, 46, 47, 50, 51, 79, 80, 85.

Khrómchenko, Solomón Márkovich. Russian-Ukrainian tenor, born 1907 near Kiev. Studied in Odessa, then at the Lysenko Institute in Kiev, and the Moscow Conservatory, where he was a pupil of Ksenia Dorliak. Soloist at the Bolshoy 1934-57. Soft, expressive lyric tenor, fine diction and phrasing. He gave a radio concert on his 70th birthday.
- **LP Melodiya M10 40121-24.** "The Art of Solomon Khromchenko." Aleksey Zybtsev, piano. Songs 25, 103 (with bowdlerized text). Song 32 (Rimsky-Korsakov).

Korjus, Miliza. Coloratura soprano of Swedish and Russian-Polish parentage, born 1908 in Warsaw. Debuted in Tallinn in 1929. Sang in Poland, Kiev, and Budapest, but primarily in Germany until 1936 where she made her early recordings (mostly in German, though *Bennett* shows one recording in Estonian). She made a film in Hollywood ("The Great Waltz," 1938) and thereafter sang in San Francisco, Carnegie Hall, and the Hollywood Bowl. In the 1940s she recorded Strauss waltzes in English; her late recordings made between 1964-68 include the Tchaikovsky song below. She died in Los Angeles in 1980.
- **LP Voce 52.** "Miliza Korjus: Unpublished Recordings." Song 10.

Kóshetz, Nína Pávlovna (in Russian spelled Koshits). Russian soprano, 1894-1965. One of the most influential singers of the Russian modernist movement during the period of revolution and civil war. Graduated Moscow Conservatory 1913 in piano and voice, pupil of Umberto Masetti (later, in Paris, Félia Litvinne). Her operatic career reached its height at the Zimin Opera in Moscow 1913-17, though she continued to sing in productions later, including the premiere of Prokofiev's *Love for Three Oranges* (Chicago, 1921). She achieved her greatest success as a concert artist. She performed with Rachmaninoff, who dedicated his last songs to her (Opus 38, 1916). The impact of her concerts on her contemporaries in Russia at the time was very great. Boris Yanovsky, a composer, wrote of the "simplicity" (a very positive word in Russian contexts) of her singing, its intimacy, delicacy, elegance of line, its soft, tender colors, and the good taste in which it was all delivered (*Rampa i zhizn'*, 1918, no. 8, 26 (13) Feb., p. 9). A year later in Kiev, Lev Nikulin heard her sing Prokofiev's song cycle to poems by Anna Akhmatova, Opus 27, and noticed something similar in her performance: "Prokofiev is considered almost a Futurist in music, but in Akhmatova's poems he found a keen, limpid tenderness and sadness, and N. P. Koshits sang the charming, wayward, utterly simple words exactly as they would come across if they were being spoken" (*Katz & Timenchik*, 51). Prokofiev later dedicated his Opus 35 to her. Medtner and Grechaninov wrote songs for her, and accompanied her in recitals in Europe and America. After she emigrated to the U.S. in 1920, she gave concerts and was a champion of Russian vocal music, but the kind of impact she had in Russia did not last and could not have continued outside Russia. In 1935 she moved to Hollywood, gave singing lessons to Marlene Dietrich, acted in some films, and gradually lost her voice and figure (*TRC*, vol. 39, no. 1, Jan.-Mar. 1994). Her earliest known recording session in 1914 included Tchaikovsky's lullaby, Song 11 (in *Record of Singing*, vol. 2); then in what was probably her last session, at Schirmer's in New York in 1941, she attempted Song 69, a difficult song. She had not recorded it before. But it did not work; it was no good and was never published. Even its identity was lost to those who lovingly restored her recordings.
- **LP EMI RLS 743.** "Record of Singing," vol. 2. Song 11 (recorded in Kiev, 1914).

• **CD OPAL (Pearl) CDS 9855.** "The Nina Koshetz Edition, Recordings 1916-1941." Brunswick sessions, 1922: Nicolai Stember, piano, with cello obbligato. Songs 9, 41. Schirmer sessions, 1941: Nina Koshetz, piano. Songs 9, 41, 69 (listed in the CD booklet and Koshetz discography as "Russian song, title unknown").
• **CD Nimbus NI 7839.** "Prima Voce Party." Song 9 (Brunswick, 1922). Also on • **CD Memoir Classics CD MOIR 422.**

Kovalyóva, Galína Aleksándrovna (spelled Kovalëva). Russian coloratura soprano, 1932-1995. Came from the Saratov Conservatory to the Kirov in 1960, where she quickly became a star. First Prize, Toulouse, 1962. Admired for her technique and purity of intonation in cantilena and coloratura passages. Taught at the Leningrad Conservatory after 1971.
• **LP Melodiya D 14971-2.** Yevgeny Shenderovich, piano. Songs 11, 68.
• **LP Melodiya S10 19189-90.** "Goethe and Heine in Works of Russian Composers" (1982). Semyon Skigin, piano. Songs 8, 9, 18, 25, 70.

Kozél, Bérta Márkovna. Pianist, pupil of Heinrich Neuhaus. A respected accompanist of the "active" school (plays a role in shaping the performance rather than passively following the singer). Worked with Dolukhanova for about eight years until forced to retire due to illness. They met at All-Union Radio in 1944 when they both got a job on the same day. Each was looking for a partner; they found a practice room, and after two hours of intense music-making they were a team (interview with Zara Dolukhanova 17 Jan. 2000). She also made recordings with Lemeshev.

Kózin, Vadím Alekséyevich. Russian gypsy singer (tenor), 1903-1994. Grandson of the gypsy contralto Varvara Panina. Enormously popular in the thirties and forties, he knew 3000 songs including 200 he wrote himself. At the Teheran summit in 1943, Churchill asked Stalin if Kozin could join the two other singers—Marlene Dietrich and Maurice Chevalier— being brought in to sing for Churchill on his birthday; Stalin had him flown to Teheran for one day (*Savchenko*, 74-5). In 1944 he was arrested and sent to the Gulag. His records were banned until perestroika, when he was rediscovered, still alive, in Magadan.
• **LP Melodiya M60 46669 007.** Accompanied by Boris Krupyshev's Hawaiian Ensemble (1938; Krupyshev is in *Starr*). Song 80 (folk version).

Kozlóvsky, Iván Semyónovich. Russian-Ukrainian lyric tenor, 1900-1993. Studied in Kiev at the Institute of Music and Drama 1917-19, a pupil of Yelena Muravyova (trained by Aleksandra Kochetova and Emilia Pavlovskaya, to whom Tchaikovsky dedicated Songs 6 and 70). Sang in Poltava, Kharkov, and Sverdlovsk before joining the Bolshoy, where he sang from 1926-54. A sweet, pungent voice, technically very fine. He had no peers in the role of the Yurodivy (Simpleton) in *Boris Godunov*; he made many fine recordings. Kozlovsky was one of the two most popular tenors at the Bolshoy during the mid-century: female fans in those years were jokingly divided into "Kozlovitianki" and "Lemeshistki," after rival Sergey Lemeshev. Author of a book of memoirs and articles (*Kozlovsky*). Biography and discography in *TLC*, vol. 44, no. 3, Sept. 1999; in *Record of Singing*, vol. 4.
• **LP Melodiya D 2008-9.** Songs 41, 44 (in Russian), 100.
• **LP Melodiya D 16899-900.** Naum Walter, piano. Songs 7, 41, 44 (in Russian), 71, 75, 76, 83, 93 (in Russian), 100, 103. Song 41 is also on • **LP Colosseum CRLP 10400.** Songs 75, 76, 93 are also on • **LP Colosseum CRLP 10401.**
• **LP Melodiya D 029539-40.** "Romances to Lyrics by Y. Polonsky." Song 83.
• **Complete Romances.** Naum Walter, piano. Songs 46, 75, 76.
• **LP Melodiya D 020557-8**, reissued as **M 60 20557 009.** Song 79 (Spiro version, duet with Obukhova).

Krásnaya, Nadézhda Sergéyevna. Russian lyric soprano, born in Kyzyl, Tuva, 1947. Moscow Conservatory 1971. Fourth Prize, Tchaikovsky Competition, 1970. Young artist at Bolshoy 1972-76; soloist with the Moscow Philharmonic from 1976. Sang all Tchaikovsky's romances in a series of concerts at Klin.
• **LP Melodiya M10 39657-8.** Natalia Rassudova, piano. Songs 40, 50, 89.
• **CD Russian Disc RD CD 11 078**, "Tchaikovsky: Complete Romances," vol. 1, 1990. Vadim Fedorovtsev, piano. Songs 1-25.

Krúglikova, Yeléna Dmítrievna. Russian soprano, 1907-1982. Moscow Conservatory 1933, pupil of Ksenia Dorliak. All-Union Radio 1931-33; Bolshoy 1932-56, where, with Shumskaya and Shpiller, she was one of the three leading sopranos at mid-century. State Prize Laureate 1943. Sang Wagner (Sieglinde, Elsa), Rimsky-Korsakov (Fevronia), and a much-admired Tatyana in *Eugene Onegin*. She did not record Song 34, but is known to have sung it in concert (*BT*, 362)—a rare instance of that song being sung by a woman. After 1958, she taught at the Gnesin Institute and the Moscow Conservatory.
- **78 Melodiya 3517-8**. G. I. Kats, piano. Songs 12, 80.
- **78 Melodiya 6255-6**. Semyon Stuchevsky, piano. Songs 10, 101.
- **78 Melodiya 9771-2**. E. Smirnova, piano. Songs 35, 73.
- **78 Melodiya 9883-4**. Alexander Goldenweiser, piano. Songs 4, 12.
- **LP Melodiya D 27427-8**. E. Smirnova, piano. Songs 5, 8, 15.

Kudriávtseva, Véra Nikoláyevna. Russian soprano, born 1911. Studied at the Leningrad Conservatory with Sofia Akimova and Ivan Yershov (*q.v.*). Sang at the Maly (Leningrad) 1944-55, then in Moscow at the Stanislavsky Opera 1955-68. Wife of Sergey Lemeshev.
- **LP Melodiya M10 41033-36**. Berta Kozel, piano. Songs 4, 36, 94 (in Russian). Duet 5 (with Lemeshev).

Kudryávchenko, Yekaterína. Russian-Ukrainian soprano, born 1958. Studied at the Moscow Conservatory with Vera Kudriavtseva-Lemesheva.
- **CD M-Classic MTMCD 95 042**, "Golden Duet: Romances." Yekaterina Sarantseva, piano. Songs 44, 46, 50, 51.

Kurénko, María Mikháilovna. Russian soprano, 1890-1980. Graduate of Law School, Moscow University, and the Moscow Conservatory, 1913, class of Umberto Masetti. Kharkov Opera 1914; Bolshoy 1918-22; Kiev Opera 1922-23; Riga Opera 1924-25. She came to the U.S. in 1925 and settled permanently. New York debut at Carnegie Hall in January 1926. Primarily a concert singer, for twenty years she gave recitals and sang on radio. Sang Parasha in the American premiere of Stravinsky's *Mavra* in Philadelphia in 1934, and in 1950 she recorded Stravinsky's "Cats' Lullabies" and other songs with the composer's son Soulima as accompanist. Her recordings span the long period 1914-1955 and include important recordings of Grechaninov (accompanied by the composer) and Rachmaninoff. She conveys each song as a whole, with crystalline delivery of the lyrics. Like some other singers of the older generation (Chaliapin, Sobinov, Slobodskaya, Kozlovsky), she sings certain songs in a freer, more expressive style, making use of *fermate*, whether or not they are in the score, to linger on a telling note, but she always does it with taste and finesse. Taught at Juilliard. Essay and discography in *TRC*, vol. 42, no. 3, Sept. 1997 (showing that she recorded Songs 9 and 11 in 1927); in *Record of Singing*, vol. 3.
- **78 Victor Album M 678**. Sergei Tarnowsky, piano (1940). Songs 5, 9, 10, 38, 41, 51 (second verse omitted), 67, 73, 80.
- **CD Pearl GEMM CD 9228**. Sergei Tarnowsky, piano. As above, except Song 10.
- **CD Sanctus SCSH 004**. As above, including Song 10.
- **LP Lyrichord LL 23** (reissued as **Concert Artist LPA 1040**). Robert Hufstader, piano (1952). Song 32 (Chopin).

Kuuzik, Tiit (Dietrich) Janovich. Estonian baritone, 1911-1990. Graduate of the Tallinn Conservatory 1938, Vienna Opera 1938-40, Tallinn Opera 1940-41 and from 1944.
- **LP Melodiya S10 06215-6**. Valdur Roots, piano. Songs 5, 9, 49.

Lanskóy, Mikhaíl. Russian baritone, born 1954. Graduate of the Gnesin Institute and Moscow Conservatory. Soloist, Moscow Philharmonic.
- **CD Le Chant du Monde LDC 288 038/40**. Ilya Scheps, piano. Song 48 (Rimsky-Korsakov).

Lanza, Mario. American-Italian tenor, 1921-1959.
- **CD M-Classic Records MK CD 99069**. Orch. cond. by Ray Sinatra. Song 9 (in English).

Lárin, Sergéj. Russian tenor, born 1956. Western debut in Vienna, 1990; has sung in Europe and America including Covent Garden, San Francisco, and the Met.

• **CD Chandos Chan 9428**. "Tchaikovsky Songs," 1995. Bekova Sisters Trio (piano, violin, cello). Songs 3, 5, 7, 8, 9, 10, 25, 35, 39, 40, 41, 50, 68, 75, 76, 82, 85, 87, 93, 97, 98, 100, 101, 102, 103.

Lavróva, Tatyána Nikoláyevna. Russian soprano, born 1911. Leningrad Conservatory, class of S. V. Akimova. At Leningrad Maly 1944-62; after 1958 on the faculty of the Leningrad Conservatory.
• **LP Colosseum CRLP 10400**. E. D. Lebedev, piano. Song 36.

Lear, Evelyn. American soprano, born in Brooklyn in 1926. Studied with Sergius Kagen at Juilliard and Maria Ivogün in Berlin. Sang in Europe, then at the Met from 1967 for 13 seasons. Married to baritone Thomas Stewart, her partner on the duet below.
• **LP Deutsche Grammophon 139 303**. Erik Werba, piano, Thomas Stewart, baritone. Duet 1.

Legostáyeva, Lyudmíla Ivánovna. Russian mezzo-soprano. Born 1902 in Kharkov region of Ukraine. After musical training in Moscow she was much admired as a soloist for All-Union Radio from 1930 to 1960. She sang cantatas, romances, and concert performances of operas; was outstanding in many roles, including Boyarina Morozova in *Oprichnik*, Lyubov in *Mazeppa*, the Princess in *The Enchantress*, and the Warrior in Tchaikovsky's "Moscow Cantata." The latter, sung in a wartime concert in 1942, inspired the famous sculptor Vera Mukhina to use Legostayeva as model for a sculpture of "Mother Russia."
• **LP Melodiya M10 41619-20**. Georgy Orentlikher, piano. Song 29.
• **Complete Romances**. Georgy Orentlikher, piano. Song 95 (in Russian).

Léiferkus, Sergéi Petróvich. Russian baritone of Baltic German heritage, born 1946 in Leningrad. Graduate of the Leningrad Conservatory 1972, class of Yu. A. Barsov. Soloist, Leningrad Musical Comedy Theater (1970-72), Maly Opera (1972-78), Kirov Opera (since 1978). He has sung in Russian and Western operas at Covent Garden, the Met, and other major opera houses; has recorded over 100 romances from Glinka to Rachmaninoff. His diction, acting skill, and polished singing make him a superb interpreter of Russian songs.
• **CD Conifer 75605 51266 2**, "Tchaikovsky: The Complete Songs," vol. I (1995). Semyon Skigin, piano. Songs 1, 4, 5, 7, 8, 9, 19, 25, 37, 39, 40, 41, 43, 47, 48, 49, 69, 72, 79.

Lémeshev, Sergéy Yákovlevich. Russian tenor, 1902-1977. Born a peasant in a village near Tver, he had no musical education until 1919 when a Moscow couple who summered nearby heard him singing folk songs and took him under their wing. He entered the Moscow Conservatory in 1921; finished 1925 in the class of N. G. Raisky. Studied, like many singers headed for the operatic stage, with Stanislavsky after the famous director and teacher of acting method had returned from his American tour in 1924. Sang in Sverdlovsk in 1926, then for two seasons in Harbin 1927-29, where he made his first recordings for American Victor in Peking (for a sketch of cultural life in Harbin in those years, see *Karlinsky*). Learned most at the Tbilisi Opera 1929-31, an outstanding house since Tchaikovsky's day, where young singers (Chaliapin was one) became mature artists, and where top singers from Moscow and Petersburg came regularly as guest artists. Went to the Bolshoy in 1931 where he was a major star. Sang there until 1956, returning on his 70th birthday to sing Lensky, his most famous role, in *Eugene Onegin*. He heard or sang with most of the major Russian singers of the first half of the 20th century, and his memoirs are interesting because they contain observations about the artistic practice of his time and his fellow artists (*Lemeshev*); for articles by and about him, and discography, see *Lemeshev 1987*. He was the first singer to sing all of Tchaikovsky's songs in a series of five concerts in 1938-39, with Semyon Stuchevsky as accompanist. He recorded 52 of them, sometimes more than once. His fine 1966 recital of Tchaikovsky songs is shown periodically on Russian television. In *Record of Singing*, vol. 3.
• **78 Melodiya 6476**. Semyon Stuchevsky, piano (1937). Song 69.
• **78 Melodiya 7776**. (Stuchevsky, 1938). Song 6. Also on • **LP Colosseum CRLP 10400**.
• **78 Melodiya 7778**. (Stuchevsky, 1938). Song 15.
• **78 Melodiya 9443**. (Stuchevsky, 1939). Song 61. Also on • **LP Colosseum CRLP 10401**.
• **78 Melodiya 9446**. (Stuchevsky, 1939). Song 63. Also on • **LP Colosseum CRLP 10401**.

- **78 Melodiya 9865, 9870.** (Stuchevsky, 1939). Songs 59, 67.
- **78 Melodiya 14161-2.** Abram Makarov, piano (1946). Songs 39, 98. Song 39 is also on
- **LP Colosseum CRLP 10400.**
- **78 Melodiya 14286-7.** (Makarov, 1946). Songs 100, 103. Also on • **LP Colosseum CRLP 10401.**
- **78 Melodiya 14392.** (Makarov, 1947). Song 52. Also on • **LP Colosseum CRLP 10401.**
- **78 Melodiya 14396.** (Makarov, 1947). Song 54. Also on • **LP Colosseum CRLP 10401.**
- **78 Melodiya 15083-4.** (Stuchevsky, 1947). Songs 20, 81.
- **78 Melodiya 17301.** Naum Walter, piano (1949). Song 89.
- **78 Melodiya 19453.** (Makarov, 1951). Song 37. Also on • **LP Colosseum CRLP 10400.**
- **78 Melodiya 019987.** (Walter, 1951). Song 91. Also on • **LP Colosseum CRLP 10401.**
- **78 Melodiya 019988.** (Makarov, 1951). Song 12. Also on • **LP Colosseum CRLP 10400.**
- **78 Melodiya 20384-5.** (Makarov, 1951). Songs 10, 102.
- **78 (LP) Melodiya D 00691-2.** (Makarov, Walter). Songs 68, 77, 101, 102.
- **78 (LP) Melodiya D 00693-4.** (Makarov, Walter). Songs 37, 40, 50, 91.
- **78 (LP) Melodiya D 00747-8.** (Makarov, Walter, Stuchevsky). Songs 9, 30, 33, 87.
- **LP Melodiya D 2850-1.** Berta Kozel, piano. Songs 52, 54, 55, 57, 59, 60, 61, 63, 64, 65, 67.
- **LP Melodiya D 6083-4.** (Kozel). Songs 9, 10, 12, 30, 34, 35, 41, 82.
- **LP Melodiya D 010307-8.** (Walter). Songs 8, 11, 19, 39, 40, 41, 44, 75, 76, 79, 83, 85, 87, 99, 102.
Song 44 is on • **LP Colosseum CRLP 10400.** Song 85 is on • **LP Colosseum CRLP 10401.**
- **LP Melodiya D 012223-4.** (Kozel). Songs 10, 25, 35, 37, 38, 40, 61, 68, 77, 98, 100, 101,
103. Duet 5 (with Kudriavtseva).
- **LP Melodiya D 013331-2.** Pianist not indicated. Song 40 (Rimsky-Korsakov).
- **LP Melodiya D 029713-4.** (Kozel, Walter). Songs 25, 35, 38, 39, 40, 41, 68, 102.
- **Complete Romances.** (Walter, Makarov, Stuchevsky). Songs 12, 33, 50, 91, 98, 102.
- **Complete Songs and Duets.** (Kozel, Walter). Songs 8, 44, 75, 76, 79, 100.
- **CD Arlecchino ARL 98.** (Kozel, Walter). Songs 8, 11, 12, 34, 44, 75, 79, 85, 87.

Levínsky, Ilyá. Russian tenor, born 1963 in Baku, where he studied piano and voice at the conservatory and began his career at the Baku Opera in 1987. Won a Glinka Prize in Riga in 1989. He has sung in Israel and at the Berlin Comic Opera. This is only the second time Opus 54 has been recorded in its entirety (the first was by Gennady Pishchayev).
- **CD Conifer 75605 51268 2.** "Tchaikovsky: The Complete Songs," vol. III, 1995. Semyon Skigin, piano. Songs 35, 52-67 (Opus 54), 74, 75, 76, 78, 83.

Levkó, Valentína Nikoláyevna. Russian contralto, born 1926. Graduate of the Gnesin Institute 1953 and the Moscow Conservatory 1962; graduate training with Maksakova (*q.v.*). Sang at the Stanislavsky Opera 1957-60, Bolshoy 1960-83. Since 1977 at the Russian Academy of Music (Gnesin) where she chairs the department of solo singing.
- **LP Melodiya D 00011113-4.** V. Podolskaya, piano. Song 80.
- **LP Melodiya SM 02143-4** (c. 1970). Grigory Zinger, piano (and Viktor Stolin, cello, on Song 99). Songs 5, 19, 36, 41, 50, 51, 69, 80, 91, 98, 99, 101.
- **LP Melodiya S20 08065-68** "Lenin's Favorite Songs." Song 41.

Lisitsián, Pável Gerásimovich. Russian baritone of Armenian heritage, born 1911 in Vladikavkaz. Sang in amateur choirs while working as a driller in the Caucasus. Admitted to the Leningrad Conservatory in 1930 but his voice "broke" after three months. Stayed in Leningrad, worked as a welder, joined the Bolshoy Drama Theater as an extra; there the famous actor Nikolay Monakhov recognized his talent, coached him, let him sing on stage (Lisitsian later said he learned mastery of diction and phrasing from Monakhov, who was a fine baritone himself). Resumed studies in 1933 at a Musical Technical School; sang at the Maly Theater as a young artist under Samuil Samosud 1935-37. By the time he went to Yerevan to sing at the Armenian Opera from 1937-40, Lisitsian had a good musical education acquired largely through his own efforts, in the rich milieu of the theaters, museums, and concert halls of Leningrad. His appearance at an Armenian Arts Festival in Moscow in 1939 attracted immediate attention. In April 1940 he made his debut at the Bolshoy as Onegin, and was a principal singer there until 1966. First Soviet artist to sing at the Met, where he sang Amonasro (one performance only) in 1960. Married to the sister of Dolukhanova; three of their children are singers, including the two "Lisitsian Sisters,"

Karina and Ruzana, famed as singers of duets. Biography, repertoire, partial discography in *Iakovenko 1989*. Lisitsian recorded with various accompanists from 1939-1961: a complete list with year of recording is on the CD below. One of the greatest baritones of the century, he is much admired both in Russia and the West. In *Record of Singing*, vol. 4.
- **LP Melodiya D 06943-4**. Naum Walter, piano. Songs 9, 38, 98.
- **LP Melodiya D 0007421-2**. Naum Walter, piano. Songs 38, 98.
- **LP Melodiya M10 35910**. Songs 9, 38, 39, 72, 79, 95.
- **Complete Romances**. Naum Walter, piano. Songs 9, 39.
- **CD Russian Disc RD CD 15 021**. Naum Walter, piano: Songs 9, 20, 38, 98. Alexander Dolukhanian, piano: Song 19. Matvey Sakharov, piano: Song 39. Alexander Yerokhin, piano: Songs 79, 90, 102. Boris Abramovich, piano: Song 72. Nikolay Korolkov, piano: Song 95.

Lisóvsky, Konstantín Pávlovich. Russian tenor, born 1932 in Leningrad. Graduate of the Gnesin Institute 1967, pupil of Anna Shtein; later studied with Gennady Aden. Third Prize, Tchaikovsky Competition, Moscow, 1966. A fine concert singer, he was invited to join the Bolshoy but preferred working with the Red Army Chorus (1954-65) and as soloist with the Moscow Philharmonic (1965-92), where his frequent concert appearances included two major concerts a year of new material. Tours in Russia and abroad including the U.S. Has taught at the Russian Academy of Music (Gnesin) since 1979; was visiting professor at the Izmir Conservatory (Turkey) from 1992-97. As a student, he first sang Tchaikovsky romances at the suggestion of pianist Abram Makarov (*q.v.*); though his early favorites were Songs 40 and 77, Makarov persuaded him to work also on Song 34, a rare song, which was among the first he recorded (interview with the singer in Moscow, 18 Jan. 2000).
- **LP Melodiya D 018247-8** (Tchaikovsky Competition, 1966). Song 77.
- **LP Melodiya D 20145-6**. Vladimir Schreibman, piano. Songs 34, 77, 82, 83, 101.
- **LP Melodiya D 26629-30**. Orchestra of Russian Folk Instruments of Central TV and Radio, cond. Vladimir Fedoseyev. Song 44 (in Italian).
- **LP Melodiya D 030863-4**. Vladimir Schreibman, piano. Songs 5, 34, 47, 72, 77, 98, 103.
- **Complete Romances**. Vladimir Schreibman, piano. Songs 5, 34, 47, 72, 77, 82, 83, 98, 101.
- **Complete Songs and Duets**. Vladimir Schreibman, piano: Songs 5, 34, 47, 72, 77, 82, 83, 98, 101. Svetlana Zvonaryova, piano: Songs 15, 18, 33, 38, 46, 74, 78, 91, 92 (in Russian).

Lódii, Zóya Petróvna. Russian lyric soprano, 1886-1957. A highly regarded concert singer who flourished from 1912 to the end of the 1920s, then became a teacher at the Moscow Conservatory (1929-35) and the Leningrad Conservatory (1932-57). She studied first with her father the tenor P. A. Lodii, a pupil of Everardi, then with Natalia Iretskaya. She saw the heir to her art in Zara Dolukhanova, who was inspired by her and corresponded with her.
- **RGAFD Catalogue**: Song 80 (1928).

Magomáyev, Muslím Magométovich. Russian-Azeri baritone, born 1942 in Baku. Grandson of composer Abdul Magomaev. Studied at La Scala 1964-65, graduated Baku Conservatory 1968, pupil of Shevket Mamedova. Soloist at the Baku Opera since 1963. Popular concert singer who has toured widely at home and abroad.
- **LP Melodiya SM 03205-6**. Boris Abramovich, piano. Songs 25, 39, 40, 41, 44, 49, 50.
- **Complete Songs and Duets**. Boris Abramovich, piano. Song 50.

Makárov, Abrám Davídovich. Russian pianist of Ukrainian-Jewish heritage, 1897-1984. Accompanist, Moscow Philharmonic, 1925-67; Honored Artist of Russia, 1961. Born in Lugansk (Ukraine) where he met Mark Reizen in high school; the two became lifelong friends. Accompanied Nezhdanova and Sobinov on tour; made recordings with Barsova, Borisenko, Davydova, Kastorsky, Kruglikova, Lemeshev, Irina Maslennikova, Preobrazhenskaya, Reizen, Vishnevskaya, and with violinists Yehudi Menuhin, David Oistrakh, Leonid Kogan, Igor Bezrodny. A legendary accompanist, he could play and transpose at sight and from memory. When Menuhin arrived late for his first concert in Moscow (Nov. 1945), Makarov accompanied him with no advance knowledge of the program and without any rehearsal. As a first-year student at the St. Petersburg Conservatory (c. 1915), his dream was to become a violinist. Eavesdropping on a class being taught by the famous violinist Leopold Auer (who knew Tchaikovsky), Auer asked him if he could play at sight and sat him down at the piano. After the lesson Auer told him "forget the violin, young man—you are a good pianist!" (interview with A. A. Makarov, 18 Jan. 2000). He performed often in ensembles on tour at home and abroad. Taught ensemble at the Moscow Conservatory 1968-84. Filmed at Tchaikovsky's piano in Klin accompanying Mark Reizen in a recital of Tchaikovsky romances (1974). When he died, Reizen sang Song 5 at his memorial service. He is remembered in memoirs (*Reizen, Lemeshev, Kozlovsky*).

Maksákova, María Petróvna. Russian mezzo-soprano, 1902-1974. Born in Astrakhan, joined a church choir at ten, sang Olga in *Eugene Onegin* in local opera in 1919. Given voice training by Maximilian Maksakov (described in *Levik*), whom she married. Sang at the Bolshoy 1923-1956. "Small, refined, had taste; crystal-clear intonation; everyone fell in love with her Carmen; created a new Marfa (*Khovanshchina*) who was aristocratic, with inner power—she brought out the words so you never forgot them" (*Lemeshev*).
- **78 Melodiya 10037-8.** S. S. Pogrebov, piano. Songs 80, 93.
- **78 Melodiya 12898.** N. Kruchinin, guitar. Song 79 (Spiro version, duet with Katulskaya).
- **78 Melodiya 15806.** Boris Yurtaikin, piano. Song 1. Also on • **LP Colosseum CRLP 10400.**
- **LP Melodiya D 032243-48.** "The Art of M. P. Maksakova." Yurtaikin and Pogrebov, piano. Songs 45, 48, 73, 84, 85.
- **LP Melodiya M10 44137-40.** "The Art of M. P. Maksakova." Yurtaikin and Pogrebov, piano. Songs 10, 36, 76, 79, 80. Song 80 is also on • **LP Melodiya D 029539-40.**
- **LP Melodiya M10 45608.** Boris Yurtaikin, piano. Songs 73, 79, 88, 98.
- **Complete Romances.** Boris Yurtaikin, piano. Song 48.

Marsh, Jane. American soprano, born 1944 in San Francisco. Studied with Ellen Repp at Oberlin College, and with Lili Wexburg and Otto Guth in New York. First Prize, Tchaikovsky Competition, Moscow, 1966. Has sung in major opera theaters including Dusseldorf, Salzburg, San Francisco, Naples, Hamburg, and Prague.
- **LP Melodiya D 018247-8** (Tchaikovsky Competition, 1966). Song 11.

Martýnov, Alekséy. Russian tenor, born 1948 in Moscow. Studied violin at the Gnesin Institute, then singing at the Moscow Conservatory. Soloist with the Moscow Philharmonic and at the Stanislavsky Opera Theater.
- **CD Mezhdunarodnaya Kniga MK 417054.** Aristotel Konstantinidi, piano. Songs 5, 8, 10, 12, 15, 25, 33, 35, 39, 40, 41, 46, 47, 61, 74, 76, 77, 82, 83, 87, 91, 98, 99, 100, 101, 102, 103.
- **CD Le Chant du Monde LDC 288 038/40.** Aristotel Konstantinidi, piano. Songs 4, 32, 40 (Rimsky-Korsakov).

Máslennikova, Irína Ivánovna. Russian soprano, born 1918 in Kiev, where she studied at the Conservatory (1938-41) with Maria Donets-Tesseir. At Kiev Opera 1941-43, Bolshoy 1943-60.
- **LP Melodiya D 2008-9.** Abram Makarov, piano. Songs 36, 68.
- **Complete Romances.** Songs 36, 68.

Máslennikova, Leokádiya Ignátievna. Russian lyric-dramatic soprano, born 1918. Studied at the Minsk Conservatory 1938-41, graduated Kiev Conservatory 1946, class of D. G. Yevtushenko. Kiev Opera 1944-46, Bolshoy 1946-69.
- **78 Supraphon C 23336/46276-7.** Tamara Fidlerova, piano. Songs 50, 68.
- **78 Supraphon C 23337/46278-9.** Tamara Fidlerova, piano. Songs 101, 102.
- **LP Melodiya S10 06103-4.** Nikolay Korolkov, piano. Songs 10, 87.

Maxwell, Linn. American mezzo-soprano, born 1945.
- **CD Albany Records Troy 072.** "Romances of the Russian Masters," 1991. Robert McCoy, piano. Songs 8, 9, 12, 49, 51, 75.

Mazurók, Yúry Antónovich. Russian baritone of Polish heritage, born in the Lublin district of Poland in 1931. Graduated Moscow Conservatory 1960, pupil of Sergey Migay (*q.v.*) and A. S. Sveshnikova. Joined the Bolshoy in 1963; has sung at the Met, Covent Garden, Vienna.
- **LP Melodiya D 026393-4.** N. Afanasyeva, piano. Songs 16, 23, 24, 25, 37, 41, 43, 49, 84, 87, 93 (in Russian), 95 (in Russian), 97 (in Russian), 99.
- **Complete Romances.** Songs 16, 23, 24, 25, 37, 41, 43, 49, 84, 87, 93, 97.

• **Complete Songs and Duets**. Songs 7, 13, 16, 23, 24, 25, 32, 37, 43, 49, 84, 87, 95, 97.

McCormack, John. Famous Irish tenor, 1884-1945. In *Record of Singing*, vols. 2, 3.
  • **LP EMI EX 2900563**. Gerald Moore, piano. Song 56 (in English).

Mei-Figner, Medea. Italian soprano, 1859-1952. Born in Florence, but made her career in Russia when she married Nikolay Figner (*q.u.*). She had an even, full voice, with a wide range, "free top notes and velvety low ones"; when she made her debut at 16 as Azucena, a mezzo role, the audience released a flock of doves on stage to show its approval (*Levik*, 108). She found a warm reception in Russia as an artist with "temperament" who tried hard to become a genuine Russian singer. First sang Liza in *Queen of Spades*, and Iolanta a year later, under Tchaikovsky's direction. She sang at the Mariinsky until 1912. She taught singing in St. Petersburg after the Revolution, then moved to Paris in 1930 or possibly earlier. In *Record of Singing*, vol. 1.
  • **LP Rubini RS-301**. Hélène Polivanoff, piano. Song 41 (Moscow, 1930?). A recording of this song in *RGAFD*, pianist not indicated, • **78 MuzTrest 3455**, is dated "c. 1928."
  • **LP Melodiya M10 45191-2**. Song 82 (Moscow, 1930?).

Migáy, Sergéy Ivánovich. Russian baritone, 1888-1959. Son of a priest, sang in church choir as a child. Studied in Petersburg (with Gabel) and Odessa; had lessons with Battistini 1911-13 when he was in Russia. Nezhdanova set him up at the Bolshoy where he sang from 1912-24. Sang with Chaliapin and Katulskaya in *Boris Godunov* (1914, 1915), and in *Faust* as Valentin with Chaliapin as Mephistopheles (1918). Later sang in Leningrad and Tbilisi. Retired from the stage in 1941, then directed the vocal group on All-Union Radio and taught at the Moscow Conservatory. He was an exceptionally appealing singer: Lemeshev reports once in Tbilisi the Georgian audience (known for their "Italian" temperament) made him repeat Onegin's last-act aria "Alas, no doubt" five times.
  • **78 Melodiya 10104-5**. Semyon Stuchevsky, piano (1939). Songs 23, 33.
  • **LP Melodiya D 034025-6**. Pianist not indicated. Songs 23, 33, 37, 41, 75.

Miláshkina, Tamára Andréyevna. Russian soprano, born 1934 in Astrakhan. Moscow Conservatory 1959, class of Yelena Katulskaya; at the Bolshoy 1958-89.
  • **LP Melodiya D 026395-6**. Vladimir Viktorov, piano. Songs 2, 3, 4, 10, 11, 29, 51, 68, 81, 85, 89, 90, 91.
  • **Complete Romances**. Songs 2, 3, 4, 10, 29, 51, 81, 89.
  • **Complete Songs and Duets**. Songs 2, 3, 4, 10, 11, 81, 89.

Mishúra, Irína. Russian-Jewish mezzo-soprano, born in Krasnodar. Graduate of the Gnesin Institute, Moscow. Sang in the Moldavian Opera and in Europe before emigrating to the U.S. in 1992, where she has sung in Detroit, San Francisco, Dallas and other cities.
  • **CD VAI Audio VAIA 2003**. "In the Silence of the Night." Valery Ryvkin, piano (1996). Songs 9, 19, 35, 41, 50, 98-103.

Mkrtchyan, Lina. Armenian contralto, born in Odessa.
  • **CD Opus 111 OPS 30-219**. Yevgeny Talisman, piano (1998). Songs 4, 5, 7, 8, 9, 10, 11, 19, 25, 40, 41, 45, 49, 50, 51, 70, 77, 80, 84, 87, 99, 103.

Mochálov, Aleksey. Russian bass, born 1956.
  • **CD a-ram ltd OCD 027**. Maria Barankina, piano. Song 77.

Moore, Grace. American soprano, 1898-1947. Sang at the Met (1927-32, 1935-46), Paris, Covent Garden, Chicago, and was in several films.
  • **CD Pearl 9116**. Song 73 (in French).

Morózov, Alekséy Dmítrievich. Russian baritone, born 1946. Leningrad Conservatory 1975, class of Galina Kovalyova (*q.u.*).
  • **LP Melodiya S10 10775-6** (Tchaikovsky Competition, 1978). Yevgeny Shenderovich, piano. Song 25.

Nèlepp, Geórgy Mikháilovich. Russian dramatic tenor, 1904-57, born in Ukraine. Graduate of the Leningrad Conservatory 1930, class of Iosif Tomars (a pupil of Gabel); soloist at the

Kirov until 1944, then at the Bolshoy to 1957. Outstanding representative of well-schooled, "academic" Russian singing: the voice fine-timbred, even throughout its wide range, with good diction and control; gives intelligent expression to a wide range of feelings from the plaintive to the heroic. In *Record of Singing*, vol. 4.
  • **LP Melodiya D 12279-80.** Pianist not indicated. Songs 9, 20, 34, 35, 38, 79, 98, 99, 100, 101, 102, 103. Song 20 is also on • **LP Colosseum CRLP 10400.**
  • **Complete Romances.** N. Reznikov, piano: Song 20. Matvey Sakharov, piano: Songs 35, 38, 79, 99, 100, 103.

Nesterénko, Yevgény Yevgénievich. Russian bass, born 1938 in Moscow. Graduate of the Leningrad Conservatory. First Prize, Tchaikovsky Competition, 1970. Sang in Leningrad (Maly 1963-67, Kirov 1967-71), then in Moscow at the Bolshoy, where he sang and recorded many major bass roles. Author of a book about his singing career (*Nesterenko*).
  • **CD Melodiya SUCD 10-00298.** Yevgeny Shenderovich, piano. Songs 8, 9, 13, 25, 38, 39, 41, 49, 50, 69, 77, 84, 85, 87, 91, 98, 103.

Nezhdánova, Antonína Vasílievna. Lyric-coloratura soprano of mixed Russian-Ukrainian-Polish heritage, 1873-1950. Born near Odessa in 1873, daughter of a school teacher; sang in church and village choirs from age 7. Educated in Odessa, where she first heard the Italian coloratura sopranos Luisa Tetrazzini and Olimpia Boronat, and, in Russian operas, Nikolay Figner and his wife Medea Mei. A natural singer, she was twice turned down in St. Petersburg for study at the Conservatory because her voice was small. Auditioned by Masetti at the Moscow Conservatory in 1899 (he asked her to sing Song 61, and to play a few bars of the piano part to Song 91), he understood her vocal potential and extraordinary charm, and over the next three years his careful training brought out her full range, strength, and confidence. She sang at the Bolshoy 1902-34; had a brilliant stage career in Russian, Italian, and French opera, also singing showpiece roles from Mozart (Queen of the Night) and Wagner (the Woodbird). In addition to her mastery of coloratura technique, she had a warm, sweet, true tone, and a winning simplicity and directness. Also brilliant and original as a recitalist,she gave a series of concerts of early songs before Bach, with Wanda Landowska accompanying her on the harpsichord—the first time the harpsichord had been played in concert in Moscow (1912-13). Her repertoire of songs was large. She sang 34 of Tchaikovsky's romances; her interpretations were carefully worked out (Migay and Bogdanov-Berezovsky in *Nezhdanova* discuss some of them in detail). Her accompanist on her earliest recordings was Masetti, but, after 1919, Nikolay Golovanov, who was her husband. That she recorded only two of Tchaikovsky's songs is a major loss. Author of memoirs (*Nezhdanova*). Discography in *TRC*, vol. 24, nos. 1-2. In *Record of Singing*, vol. 1; in *Levik*.
  • **78 Melodiya 012075/0313.** Song 10. (RGAFD Catalogue: recorded 1914).
  • **LP Melodiya D 028361-62.** Pianist not indicated. Song 10.
  • **LP Club "99" CL 99-71.** Pianist not indicated. Songs 10, 11.

Norman, Jessye. African American soprano, born 1945. Brilliant career in opera (Berlin, Rome, Florence, La Scala, Met and others) and as a recitalist. The concert below (in complete form on video) was her first appearance in Russia: she sang three songs of Opus 65 and "Adieu, forêts" from *Maid of Orleans* (all in French).
  • **CD RCA Victor 60739.** Tchaikovsky Gala in Leningrad (1990). Yevgeny Shenderovich, piano. Songs 92, 97.

Nortsóv, Pantéleimon Márkovich. Russian baritone, 1900-1993. Graduate of the Kiev Conservatory 1925, class of Vasily Tsvetkov (a pupil of Lavrovskaya); studied at Stanislavsky's opera studio. Sang in Kiev and Kharkov 1926-27; at the Bolshoy 1927-54. His most famous role was Onegin, which he sang more than 600 times.
  • **78 Melodiya 9899-9900.** Boris Abramovich, piano. Songs 69, 98.
  • **LP Melodiya M10 36829-30.** Naum Walter, piano (1968-73). Songs 94 (in Russian), 100.
  • **LP Melodiya M10 40415-18.** Naum Walter, piano (1948-49). Songs 69, 92 (in Russian).
  • **LP Melodiya M10 46507 002.** Naum Walter, piano. Songs 39, 94 (in Russian).
  • **Complete Romances.** Song 69.

Obórin, Lev Nikoláyevich, 1907-1974. Greatly admired Russian pianist, he performed both as a soloist and in ensemble (as accompanist to Natalia Shpiller, and with violinist David Oistrakh, for example). Pupil of Igumnov (*q.v.*); taught at the Moscow Conservatory from 1928. Close friend of Shostakovich.

Obraztsóva, Yeléna Vasílievna. Russian mezzo-soprano, born in Leningrad in 1939. Graduated from the Leningrad Conservatory 1964, pupil of A. A. Grigorieva; went to the Bolshoy the same year. First Prize (tied with Siniavskaya), Tchaikovsky Competition, 1970 (the jury included Maria Callas). International operatic career at the Met, San Francisco, La Scala, Barcelona, Vienna. Her brilliant, dramatic, rich-timbred voice is impressive in recital. She works with the outstanding accompanist Vazha Chachava. Interviews (in Russian), a discography, and photos in *Sheiko*.

• **LP Melodiya D 016143-4.** Violin Ensemble and Cello Quartet of the Bolshoy Theater, cond. Yuli Reentovich, 1965. Songs 6, 26, 50.

• **LP Melodiya S10 12265-6**, 1979. Vazha Chachava, piano. Songs 9, 19, 40, 41, 45, 51, 70, 80, 82, 90, 101, 103.

• **CD Russian Compact Disc RCD 16007.** Acad. Orch. of Russian Folk Instruments of All-Union Radio, cond. Nikolay Nekrasov. Live Concert, 1980. Song 2 (Verstovsky).

• **LP Melodiya A10 00521 006.** Live Recital, Chachava, 1986. Songs 9, 40, 51, 85, 99, 101.

• **Complete Songs and Duets**, Chachava. Songs 9, 19, 40, 45, 51, 70, 85, 90, 99.

Obúkhova, Nadézhda Andréyevna. Russian mezzo-soprano, 1886-1961. Born in Moscow, she graduated from the Moscow Conservatory in 1912 in the class of Umberto Masetti, with whom she continued to study in 1914-15. Under Masetti she perfected a technique which enabled her to produce deep, even, beautiful tone to the end of her life. Her repertoire included Fricka, Amneris, Carmen, Dalila as well as fifteen Russian roles; German, French, and Neapolitan songs, and hundreds of Russian romances and folk songs. She made her debut in 1916 as Polina in *Queen of Spades* at the Bolshoy, where she sang until 1943. Alongside her career in the theater she was incomparably great as a concert artist. She sang Polina's romance on the first concert broadcast over Soviet radio on 17 September 1922; her singing was heard over the radio throughout her life, including the war years, when she did programs for the home front and for the allies in England and France. Her song recitals began in 1931 with a program of Tchaikovsky's romances, and continued until a few weeks before her death in Feodosia in the summer of 1961. With her accompanist Matvey Sakharov (*q.v.*), she continually enlarged her song repertoire, performing a great many Russian and Western classical songs, and reviving forgotten urban romances of the 19th and early 20th centuries. Sakharov accompanied her on all the recordings below, made between 1940-1962, except Song 79. Memoirs, tributes, and repertoire in *Obukhova*; in *Record of Singing*, vol. 4.

• **LP Melodiya D 2008-09.** Songs 8, 85.

• **LP Melodiya D 10203-4.** Songs 19, 44, 87, 92, 94.

• **LP Melodiya D 011835-6.** Songs 5, 9, 19, 38, 40, 44, 51, 85, 87, 90, 91, 92, 94, 99.

• **LP Colosseum CRLP 10400.** Songs 8, 9, 38, 40, 51.

• **LP Colosseum CRLP 10401.** Songs 80, 90, 98.

• **LP Westminster XWN 18510.** Songs 8, 80, 85, 90, 91, 92, 94.

• **LP Melodiya D 022647-8.** "Obukhova in Concert." Song 2 (Verstovsky). Song 75 (Tolstaya). Song 2 is also on • **LP Melodiya M10 35697-35700**, and on • **CD Arlecchino ARL 124**.

• **LP Melodiya D 020557-8**, reissued as • **LP Melodiya M 60 20557 009.** P. Veshchitsky, N. Alekseyev, guitars. Song 79 (Spiro version, duet with Kozlovsky).

• **CD EMI CHS 7 69741 2.** "The Record of Singing," vol. 4. Song 8.

• **CD Pearl GEMM CD 9200.** Songs 5, 19, 91. Also on • **CD Eclectra ECCD-2029**.

Ógnivtsev, Aleksándr Pávlovich. Russian bass, 1920-1981. Graduate of the Kishinyov Conservatory, 1949. Soloist at the Bolshoy 1949-81. Sang Boris Godunov, Gremin, Don Basilio; appeared in films "Rimsky-Korsakov" (1953) and "Aleko" (1954).

• **LP Melodiya SM 04309-10.** Nikolay Korolkov, piano. Songs 8, 9, 10, 11, 38, 47, 68, 69, 79, 87, 88, 102, 103.

Oleinichénko, Galína Vasílievna. Russian soprano, born 1928 in Odessa where she finished the conservatory in 1953. Odessa Opera 1952-55, Kiev 1955-57, Bolshoy 1957-81.
• **LP Melodiya D 016143-4.** Violin Ensemble and Cello Quartet of the Bolshoy Theater, cond. Yuli Reentovich. Songs 11, 22.

Olszewska, Maria. German mezzo-soprano, 1892-1959. In *Hamilton* (as Olczewska); biography and discography in *TRC*, vol. 40, no. 3: 178-203.
• **78 The Gramophone Co. (Berlin).** Item 65 in *TRC* (not seen): Song 9 (in German).

Orfyónov, Anatóly Ivánovich (spelled Orfënov). Russian lyric tenor, 1908-87. Graduate of the Stanislavsky Music Institute 1934, soloist at the Stanislavsky Opera 1934-42, Bolshoy 1942-55. Artistic Director of the vocal group at All-Union Radio 1954-59.
• **Complete Romances.** D. Galkin, piano. Songs 18, 74.

Ots, Geórg Kárlovich. Estonian lyric baritone, 1920-75. Born in Petrograd, studied at the Tallinn Conservatory with Tiit Kuuzik (*q.v.*). Sang from 1945 in the Estonian Opera. An elegant singer, he had a wide repertoire in opera and operetta, classic and popular songs; he also appeared in several films.
• **LP Melodiya D 028449-50.** Eugen Kelder, piano. Songs 7, 9, 41, 43, 44, 87, 90, 93, 96.

Page-Green, Jacqueline. African American soprano, born 1951.
• **LP Melodiya S10 10775-6** (Tchaikovsky Competition, 1978). Ludmila Ivanova, piano. Song 8.

Pears, Peter. English tenor, 1910-1986. Creator of leading roles in many of Benjamin Britten's operas. In *Record of Singing*, vol. 4.
• **CD BBCB 8002-2.** "Britten the Performer, Volume 2: Tchaikovsky" (1962). Song 56 (version for tenor and orchestra made by Tchaikovsky for Dmitry Usatov). English Chamber Orchestra, cond. Benjamin Britten. Sung in English.

Pechkóvsky, Nikoláy Konstantínovich. Russian tenor, 1896-1966. Studied in Moscow under L. D. Donskoy (whose teachers were Everardi and Musorgsky). Studied acting with Stanislavsky. Sang in Leningrad at the Mariinsky (later, Kirov) from 1924-41. Known as the best Gherman of his day; also admired as a recitalist, especially of Tchaikovsky's songs. Trapped by chance behind enemy lines outside Leningrad in 1941, he was arrested after the war and sent to the Gulag. Survived and returned; wrote memoirs (*Pechkovsky*).
• **CD Laserfilm LF 93 018.** S. Davydova, piano. Songs 25, 38.

Pedrotti, Mark. Canadian baritone, born in New Zealand.
• **CD CBC Records MVCD 1051.** Stephen Ralls, piano. Songs 7, 9, 39, 49.

Petína, Irra (Irína Stefánovna). Russian mezzo-soprano, born 1907 in St. Petersburg. Her father was an aide to the Tsar; in 1917 the family fled to Harbin, where her voice teacher was Aleksandra Matsulevich-Solovyova, a pupil of Galvani (*Taskina*, 195). Petina sang in the Harbin Opera and was known for her Carmen (*Karlinsky*, 286). Came to the U.S. in 1930, studied at the Curtis Institute; sang Carmen, Suzuki, and other roles at the Met from 1933-50; also sang at the New York City Opera. She sang in the 1956 premiere of Leonard Bernstein's *Candide* as the Old Lady; was also in some Hollywood films. The performances below sound like what a Hollywood arranger might do with a Tchaikovsky song, but they are sung by a good Russian singer in Russian. They are unlike any others.
• **Columbia Masterworks MM 712 (78 rpm set).** With orchestra cond. by Walter Hendl, arranged by Hershey Kay. Songs 4, 9, 25, 40, 41, 50, 51, 100.

Petróv, Iván Ivánovich. Russian bass, born 1920 in Irkutsk. (Real surname Krauze). Graduate, Glazunov Academy, Moscow, 1943; during student years he sang in Ivan Kozlovsky's opera workshop productions. He sang at the Bolshoy from 1943-70: one of the best Russian basses in his prime.
• **78 Melodiya 026822-3.** Semyon Stuchevsky, piano. Songs 47, 49.
• **LP Melodiya 08555-6.** Semyon Stuchevsky, piano. Song 49.
• **LP Melodiya D 015301-2.** Semyon Stuchevsky, piano. Songs 7, 10, 13, 20, 25, 38, 39, 41, 42, 43, 49, 79, 84, 87, 103. Also on • **LP Melodiya S 01177-8**, except Song 103.

• **LP Melodiya M10 39215** "The Art of Ivan Petrov." Semyon Stuchevsky, piano. Songs 47, 49. Georgy Orentlikher, piano. Song 42 (Rimsky-Korsakov).
• **LP Melodiya D 016143-4.** Violin Ensemble and Cello Quartet of Bolshoy Theatre, cond. B. Reentovich. Songs 77, 85.
• **Complete Songs and Duets.** Semyon Stuchevsky, piano. Songs 20, 42.

Piatigórsky, Gregor (Grigóry Pávlovich). Russian-American cellist, 1903-1976. Born in Yekaterinoslav, died in Los Angeles. Studied at the Moscow Conservatory from age 11, played in the Bolshoy orchestra from age 16; original cello, Lenin String Quartet. Berlin Philharmonic 1924-28; came to the U.S. in 1929. During his concert career he performed with Toscanini, Rachmaninoff, Horowitz, Heifitz, Artur Rubinstein and others; many composers wrote music for him, including Stravinsky, Prokofiev, Copland, Barber. His transcription of Tchaikovsky's song gives the voice part to the cello, adding a short phrase near the beginning and another at the end, but otherwise leaving the song entirely intact.
• **CD Music & Arts CD-674.** Karol Szreter, piano. Song 9, transcribed for cello.

Pirogóv, Aleksándr Stepánovich. Russian bass, 1899-1964. Born in Ryazan, youngest of four brothers, all basses, all opera singers; the others were Grigory, Aleksey, and Mikhail (the brothers considered Mikhail the best, though Grigory was the most famous). Studied and sang in various theaters in Moscow from 1917. Accepted into the Bolshoy in 1924, he sang there until 1954. On stage he acted with "temperament," sometimes overacting, but always showing character in a striking way. His gravelly bass is also striking; he was a master of crescendo who could make a note grow to powerful effect.
• **LP Melodiya D 2699-2700.** Boris Yurtaikin, piano. Songs 13, 47. Aleksey Zybtsev, piano. Song 88.
• **LP Melodiya D 3686-7.** Boris Yurtaikin, piano. Songs 42, 81, 82, 100.
• **LP Melodiya D 029539-40.** "Romances to Lyrics by Y. Polonsky." Song 82.
• **LP Melodiya D 035048.** Orchestra of the Bolshoy Theater, cond. Alexander Orlov. Song 49 (Taneyev orchestration).
• **Complete Romances.** Song 42.
• **CD Multisonic 31 0273-2** (Czech Republic). Russian Treasures Series (Recordings from Moscow Radio). Vladimir Reztsov, Aleksey Zybtsev, piano. Songs 69, 88, 103.

Pishcháyev, Gennády Mikháilovich. Russian tenor, born 1927. Graduated Moscow Conservatory 1953, class of S. P. Yudin (a pupil of Alexander Dodonov, who studied with Manuel Garcia: see Song 34). Admired soloist, Moscow Philharmonic. Like Lemeshev, he performed all Tchaikovsky's romances in a series of concerts in 1963-64, and again in 1965, 1971, 1975. His recordings include the first complete recording of Opus 54, an exemplary performance in which he is accompanied by his classmate Aleksandr Bakhchiev (*q.v.*).
• **Complete Songs and Duets.** Aleksandr Bakhchiev, piano. Songs 35, 52-67.

Podleś, Ewa. Polish contralto, born 1952 in Warsaw. Third Prize, Tchaikovsky Competition, 1978. Has sung in leading opera houses of Europe since 1983, especially France, but also in the U.S. and Canada; acclaimed in the Rossini repertoire and as a recitalist.
• **LP Melodiya S10 11239-40** (Tchaikovsky Competition, 1978). G. Khristenko, piano. Songs 45, 68.
• **CD Forlane UCD 16683.** Graham Johnson, piano, 1993. Songs 2, 45, 50, 51.

Politkóvsky, Vladímir Mikháilovich. Russian bass-baritone, 1892-1984. Moscow Conservatory 1918, pupil of Masetti. Among his roles at the Bolshoy from 1920-48 were Onegin, Godunov, Scarpia, Iago, Iokanaan. He taught at the Moscow Conservatory, where his students included Artur Eizen (*q.v.*).
• **LP Melodiya M10 38739-40.** Georgy Orentlikher, piano. Songs 7, 39.

Polyánsky, Valéry Kuzmích. Russian conductor, born 1949 in Moscow. Graduate of the Moscow Conservatory in 1973, pupil of Gennady Rozhdestvensky. Organized the State Chamber Choir in 1971 which he led for 20 years, then in 1992 he and Rozhdestvensky co-founded the State Symphonic Choir of Russia. A leader in many important productions and music festivals; Honored Artist of Russia.

• **CD Melodiya SUCD 10-00015**. "P. Tchaikovsky: Choral Works." Ministry of Culture Chamber Choir, led by Valery Polyansky. Song 56 (choral version).
• **CD Russian Disc RCD 22106**. Song 27 (choral version), State Chamber Choir; Song 56 (choral version), State Chamber Choir; Song 56 (Arensky variations), Belorussian Chamber Orchestra.

Ponselle, Rosa. American soprano, 1897-1981. In a distinction drawn by Will Crutchfield between the "pioneers" of singing (in the 20th century this means Caruso, Chaliapin, and Callas) and the "paragons" of singing, Ponselle is a supreme example of the latter (*Hamilton*, 341). After she retired from the Met in 1937, she sang the German text of Song 9 in concert and later recorded it. In *Record of Singing*, vols. 2, 3.
• **LP OASI-635**. With unidentified orchestra. Song 9.
• **CD Eklipse EKR CD 51**. "Rosa Ponselle in Concert, 1936-52." Song 9.
• **CD Romophone 81022-2**. "Rosa Ponselle: The 1939 Victor and 1954 'Villa Pace' Recordings." Igor Chichagov, piano (1954). Song 9.

Postávnicheva, Nína Konstantínovna. Russian mezzo-soprano, born 1919. Graduate of the Moscow Conservatory, pupil of Yelizaveta Petrenko (who studied with Iretskaya and Carolina Ferni-Giraldoni, Caruso's teacher). Concert artist with the Moscow Philharmonic and All-Union Radio; taught at the Moscow Conservatory until 1980.
• **Complete Romances**. Olga Tomina, piano. Song 31.

Preobrazhénskaya, Sófia Petróvna. Russian mezzo-soprano, 1904-66. Born in St. Petersburg, graduate of the conservatory in 1928, pupil of Ivan Yershov. At the Mariinsky (Kirov) Opera 1928-59, where she was greatly admired for over 30 years, a matchless Amneris, Azucena, Lyubov (*Mazeppa*), Marfa (*Khovanshchina*), Countess (*Queen of Spades*), and Nurse (*Eugene Onegin*). Her recordings of Tchaikovsky's songs are very fine, despite the claim (*Gamalei*, 34) that her voice lost some of its color on records.
• **78 Melodiya (Tashkentskii Zavod) 477**. Abram Makarov, piano. Song 2 (Verstovsky).
• **78 Melodiya 5720**. Abram Makarov, piano. Song 99.
• **78 Melodiya 17167-8**. Adolph Merovich, piano. Songs 31, 90.
• **78 Melodiya 17182-3**. Adolph Merovich, piano. Songs 10, 79.
• **LP Colosseum CRLP 10401**. Adolph Merovich, piano. Song 88.
• **LP Melodiya D 1165-6**. Adolph Merovich, piano. Songs 30, 86.
• **Complete Romances**. Song 86.

Price, Margaret. Welsh soprano, born 1941. Brilliant career in opera, especially Mozart.
• **LP Classics for Pleasure (EMI) CFP 40078**. James Lockhart, piano. Songs 4, 9, 41.
• **CD EMI 7243 5 68578 2 7**. Same.

Rachmáninoff, Sergéi Vasílievich. Russian composer and pianist, 1873-1943.
• **CD RCA Victor 7766-2-RG**. "Rachmaninoff plays Rachmaninoff: Solo Works and Transcriptions." Song 11, transcribed by Rachmaninoff for piano, recorded 26 Feb. 1942.

Ráutio, Nina. Russian soprano, born 1957. Graduate, Leningrad Conservatory. Fourth Prize, Tchaikovsky Competition, 1986. Has sung at the Kirov, Bolshoy, La Scala, Pittsburgh, Paris, Florence, Berlin.
• **CD Conifer 75605 51267 2**. "Tchaikovsky: The Complete Songs," vol. 2, 1995-96. Semyon Skigin, piano. Songs 2, 6, 10, 11, 12, 17, 22, 27, 29, 30, 36, 38, 45, 50, 51, 68, 80, 85.

Rebróff, Iván. Russian bass.
• **LP Saphir (Intercord) 120.871**. "Russische Lieder von Liebe und Tod." Herbert Seidemann, piano. Songs 7, 39, 41.

Réizen, Mark Ósipovich. Russian bass of Ukrainian-Jewish heritage, 1895-1992. Studied at the Kharkov Conservatory with Federico Bugamelli, a pupil of Masetti. From Kharkov he went to the Leningrad Opera 1925-30, then the Bolshoy 1930-54. Returned on his 90th birthday to sing Gremin in *Eugene Onegin*. A superb singer and powerful actor with a highly expressive, rich voice of astonishing color and range. His forte was legendary, but he also had a pianissimo so expressive it could stop a rehearsal to allow Natalia Shpiller singing opposite him to regain her composure, while the rest of the cast were drying their eyes (*Reizen*, 225). Recorded many operas including a 1952 *Eugene Onegin* with Kruglikova, Maksakova, Andrey Ivanov and Kozlovsky; made films of *Khovanshchina* and *Aleko*. Memoirs, photographs, and partial discography in *Reizen*. A fuller discography is in *TRC*, vol. 28, nos. 1-2, May-June 1983; but other recordings exist as well, including a tape of Song 81 in the Bakhrushin Museum in Moscow. Except as indicated, the Tchaikovsky songs were recorded with Abram Makarov (*q.v.*). In *Record of Singing*, vols. 3, 4.

- **CD EMI Classics CHS 7 69741 2**. "Record of Singing," vol. 4. Albert Coates, piano, 1929. Song 49 (minus piano intro and coda).
- **78 Melodiya 02584**. Song 49 (1933).
- **78 Melodiya 07518-9**. Songs 49, 82 (1938).
- **78 Melodiya 9601-2**. Songs 77, 79 (1938).
- **78 Melodiya 18583-4**. Songs 9, 88 (1950).
- **LP Melodiya D 00616-17**. Songs 7, 65.
- **LP Melodiya D 00618-19**. Naum Walter, piano. Songs 47, 69, 88.
- **LP Melodiya D 1346-7**. Song 19.
- **LP Melodiya D 2008-9**. Songs 39, 69.
- **LP Melodiya D 016337-8**. Songs 9, 19, 38, 41, 47, 65, 77, 88, 90, 99.
- **LP Melodiya D 023227-8**. Song 84.
- **LP Melodiya D 035105-12**. "The Art of M. O. Reizen." Songs 19, 38.
- **LP Melodiya S10 05797-8**. Vladimir Khvostin, piano (1974). Songs 5, 40, 41, 47, 49, 77, 79, 82, 84, 90, 99.
- **LP Melodiya S20 08065-68**. "Lenin's Favourite Songs." Song 99 (Khvostin).

Resnik, Regina. American soprano, later mezzo-soprano, born 1922. Sang at the Met from 1944 for 30 seasons.
- **CD Sony SMK 60784**. Richard Woitach, piano. Songs 41, 50, 51.

Rethberg, Elisabeth. German soprano, 1894-1976. In *Record of Singing*, vols. 2, 3.
- **CD Romophone 81012-2**. "Elisabeth Rethberg: the Complete Brunswick Recordings (1924-29)." Willem Willeke, cello, with orchestra (1925). Song 9 (in German).

Rodgers, Joan. English soprano. A fine recitalist with excellent Russian, which she studied at Liverpool University.
- **CD Hyperion CDA66617**. "Tchaikovsky Songs," 1992. Roger Vignoles, piano. Songs 4, 5, 8, 9, 10, 11, 22, 35, 38, 40, 41, 45, 50, 51, 59, 60, 61, 74, 77, 83, 91.

Rópskaya, Aleksándra Dmítrievna (1897-1957). Russian mezzo-soprano, trained in Saratov. After the Civil War she was in a traveling opera collective, then sang in Odessa and Kharkov, and from 1928 at the Kiev Opera. People's Artist of Ukraine (1941).
- **LP Melodiya M10 48921**. Pianist not indicated. Song 103.

Rósing, Vladímir Sergéyevich. Russian tenor, 1890-1963. Born in St. Petersburg, studied with Tartakov and Jean de Reszke. Sang Lensky and Gherman on the stage but was primarily a concert singer. After 1913 in Britain and the U.S. In 1923, at the Eastman School in Rochester, he brought Nicolas Slonimsky to America: "Rosing was a remarkable person. He had an expressive but not very strong tenor voice, and he sang Russian songs in a mesmerizing manner, with his eyes closed and his entire body tense with emotion" (*Slonimsky 1988*, 81). He was admired by George Bernard Shaw, who rated him second only to Chaliapin. Biography and discography in *TRC*, vol. 36, no. 3 (this shows that Fred Gaisberg recorded him singing Song 98 in St. Petersburg in 1912; others were recorded in London after 1915, but only Songs 39 and 79 were released). In *Record of Singing*, vol. 3.
- **LP Melodiya M10 46475**. Hans Gellhorn, piano, 1937. Songs 5, 8, 41, 103.
- **CD Pearl GEMM CD 9021**. Hans Gellhorn, piano, 1937. Songs 5, 8.

Rozhdéstvenskaya, Natália Petróvna. Russian soprano, 1900-1997. Born in Nizhny-Novgorod, graduate of Moscow GITIS (1929). Soloist at All-Union Radio 1929-60, where she was a favorite both in operas and in programs of Russian romances with partner Sergey Migay (*q.v.*). She recorded songs by Russian and European composers (Schumann, Ravel,

Grieg); her son, the conductor Gennady Rozhdestvensky, sometimes accompanied her. She also translated librettos into Russian, including Stravinsky's *Rake's Progress*.
- **LP Melodiya M10 41883-4**. Anton Bernar, piano. Songs 4, 60.
- **CD Arlecchino ARL 53**. Gennady Rozhdestvensky, piano. Song 81 (Rimsky-Korsakov).

Savénko, Vasily. Russian bass-baritone, born in Ukraine. Graduate of the Moscow Conservatory, pupil of Aleksey Bolshakov (*q.v.*).
- **CD Hyperion CDA 67105**. Alexander Blok, piano. Songs 39, 41, 49.

Sákharov, Matvéy Ivánovich. Pianist, accompanist of Obukhova, 1894-1958. His mother was an amateur singer trained by Tchaikovsky's friend Aleksandra Kochetova (see Song 6, dedicated to her); as a boy, he accompanied his mother at musical evenings. Studied at the Moscow Conservatory with Igumnov. Accompanist at the Bolshoy 1924-41, where he met Obukhova. They gave their first concert in 1933, and thereafter for 25 years performed, recorded, and worked out new repertoire together. Indispensable partner in one of the most important Russian song legacies on record. He also worked with Katulskaya, Kozlovsky, Lisitsian, Nelepp, Zhadan, Zlatogorova. Biographical articles by Obukhova and T. I. Sakharova in *Obukhova*.

Schmitt-Walter, Karl. German baritone, 1900-1985. In *Record of Singing*, vol. 4.
- **LP Acanta BB 23.072**. Song 85 (in German).

Schock, Rudolf. German tenor, born 1915. In *Record of Singing*, vol. 4.
- **LP Acanta 40.23550**. Erhard Michel, piano. Songs 41, 50, 100 (in German), 44 (in Italian).

Schumann-Heink, Ernestine. Austrian-American contralto, 1861-1936. In *Record of Singing*, vol. 1.
- **CD Romophone 81029-2**. "The Complete Recordings," vol. I, 1900-09. Song 9 (in German). Orchestra with cello, 21 Oct. 1906 (earliest recording of the song known to me).

Schwarzkopf, Elisabeth. German soprano, born 1915. In *Record of Singing*, vol. 4.
- **CD EMI Classics 7243 5 65860 2 4**. "The Elisabeth Schwarzkopf Songbook." Gerald Moore, piano, 1956. Song 9 (in German).
- **CD EMI CDM 7 63654 2**. "Encores." Geoffrey Parsons, piano, 1967. Song 44.

Serkebáyev, Yermék Bekmukhamédovich. Kazak baritone, born 1926. Graduated Alma-Ata Conservatory 1951, pupil of A. M. Kurganov. Sang from 1947 at the Alma-Ata Opera, has toured widely and appeared in films.
- **LP Melodiya SM 04191-2**. Vladimir Viktorov, piano. Songs 5, 25, 39, 41, 49, 69, 77, 79, 98.
- **Complete Songs and Duets**. Songs 39, 69.

Sháposhnikov, Sergéy Nikoláyevich. Russian baritone, 1911-1973. Leningrad Conservatory 1935, class of A. N. Ulyanov (a pupil of L. D. Donskoy, whose teachers were Everardi and Musorgsky). A leading singer at the Leningrad Maly after 1935, his warm-timbred, even voice, and his perfect diction made him one of the finest Russian baritones at mid-century.
- **78 Melodiya 18569**. E. D. Lebedev, piano. Songs 32, 83. Song 32 is also on • **LP Colosseum CRLP 10400**. Song 83 is also on • **LP Colosseum CRLP 10401**.
- **78 (LP) Melodiya D 00693-4**. E. D. Lebedev, piano. Songs 32, 94 (in Russian).
- **LP Colosseum CRLP 10401**. E. D. Lebedev, piano. Song 96 (in Russian).
- **Complete Romances**. E. D. Lebedev, piano. Song 32.

Sharónova, Valentína Alekséyevna. Russian soprano, born 1951. Graduate of the Gnesin Institute 1983, pupil of Zara Dolukhanova; soloist, Moscow Philharmonic.
- **CD Russian Disc RD CD 11 021**. Vladimir Yurigin-Klevke, piano. Song 32 (Cui).

Sharúbina, Nina. Russian soprano. Graduate, Belarus Music Academy, Minsk, 1994.
- **CD Erasmus Muziek WVH 161**. Larissa Keda, piano. Songs 45, 50. Song 2 (Verstovsky).

Shcherbínina, Valentína Mikháilovna. Russian mezzo-soprano, born 1947. Moscow Conservatory (1973), La Scala (1975-6); Stanislavsky Opera since 1979. Charming performances of popular romances arranged by David Ashkenazi in the "old-fashioned"

style.
- **LP Melodiya S10 26473 005**. "My Bonfire: Old Russian Romance," 1986. David Ashkenazi, piano, with Alexander Chernov, violin, and Sergei Lebedev, guitar. Song 75 (Tolstaya). Song 80 (folk version).

Shpíller, Natália Dmítrievna. Russian lyric soprano, born 1909 in Kiev. Graduate of Kiev Conservatory 1931, class of A. N. Shperling (a pupil of Lavrovskaya). Samara Opera 1931-34. Debut as Micaela in *Carmen* at the Bolshoy in 1934; sang there until 1958. Wrote reviews and popular articles about music; taught at the Gnesin Institute. A highly regarded singer of the Russian school admired for her musicality and warm, polished expressiveness.
- **78 Melodiya 9901-2**. Semyon Stuchevsky, piano. Songs 55, 60.
- **LP Melodiya D 5978-9**. Songs 68, 73.
- **LP Melodiya D 033953-56**. "The Art of N. D. Shpiller." Lev Oborin, piano. Songs 11, 14.
- **LP Melodiya M10 46733 003**. Lev Oborin, piano. Songs 14, 92 (in Russian).
- **Complete Romances**. Lev Oborin, piano. Songs 11, 15.

Shúmskaya, Yelizavéta Vladímirovna. Russian lyric-coloratura soprano, 1905-88. Studied singing in Moscow with D. B. Beliavskaya. From a start in provincial opera she came to the Bolshoy in 1944 and sang there until 1958, where she was a great favorite with the public. Taught singing at the Moscow Conservatory.
- **LP Melodiya D 11617-8**. Nikolay Korolkov, piano. Songs 50, 68, 82, 91.
- **Complete Songs and Duets**. Nikolay Korolkov, piano. Song 68.
- **CD Russian Compact Disc RCD 16005**. Georgy Orentlikher, piano, 1952. Song 6.

Sinatra, Frank. American singer of popular songs (lyric baritone), 1915-1998. No formal training, though he acknowledged Mabel Mercer as the singer from whom he learned the most. He made at least four recordings of "None But the Lonely Heart" for V-Disc and Columbia in the 1940s (details in *O'Brien*); all these were sung to an orchestral arrangement by Axel Stordahl that uses a theme from Tchaikovsky's Sixth Symphony as prelude to the vocal. Much later in 1959 Sinatra recorded the song again with Gordon Jenkins, who wrote a new arrangement based solely on the original piano part; it was made to stand as the last song on "No One Cares," an album of songs about romantic breakup. This last version with Jenkins's dark strings is his best recording of the song. Its qualities are not unlike those that characterize the Russian school of singing Tchaikovsky's songs: clean and heartfelt articulation of the words, respect for the music as written, and total sincerity.
- **CD Columbia Legacy C2K 66135**. "Frank Sinatra: The V-Discs," vol. 2. Arranged for orchestra and conducted by Axel Stordahl. CBS broadcast of "The Frank Sinatra Show," 31 Jan. 1945. Song 9 (in English, Westbrook translation).
- **CD Columbia Legacy CXK 48673**. "Frank Sinatra: The Columbia Years 1943-1952. The Complete Recordings." Vol. 5, 31 Oct. 1946. Vol. 7, 26 Oct. 1947.
- **CD Capitol CDP 7 94519 2**. "No One Cares." Arranged for orchestra and conducted by Gordon Jenkins, 24 Mar. 1959.

Siniávskaya, Tamára Ilínichna. Russian mezzo-soprano, born 1943. Graduate of the Russian Academy of Theater Arts in Moscow (GITIS), class of D. B. Beliavskaya. First Prize (tied with Obraztsova), Tchaikovsky Competition, 1970 (the jury included Maria Callas). Soloist at the Bolshoy since 1964; sang at La Scala 1973-74; People's Artist USSR 1982.
- **LP Melodiya SM 03725-6**. Violinists of the Bolshoy Theater, cond. Yuli Reentovich. Songs 9, 10, 11, 80, 85, 101.
- **CD Russian Disc RDCD 00532**. State Academic Symphony Orchestra, cond. Yevgeny Svetlanov. Songs 8, 9, 10, 50, 51, 88.

Slobódskaya, Oda Abrámovna. Russian soprano, born in Vilno in 1888 (*Baker's*) or 1895 (*Russia Abroad, Agin*), died in London in 1970. Studied five years at the St. Petersburg Conservatory, a pupil of Natalia Iretskaya; made her debut at the Mariinsky as Liza in *Queen of Spades*. From 1918-21 a soloist at the Mariinsky; sang with Chaliapin there and at the Narodny Dom. In emigration since 1922, when she sang Parasha in the premiere of Stravinsky's *Mavra* in Paris. Settled in London in 1931; there she established herself as "an authoritative interpreter of Russian songs in recital" and voice teacher (*Baker's*). Interview

and discography in *Recorded Sound*, 1969, 495-507. In *Record of Singing*, vol. 3.
- **LP Saga XID 5050**. Ivor Newton, piano, 1951. Songs 5, 9, 41, 61.
- **LP London OS 25312**. Ivor Newton, piano; with English introduction. Song 67.
- **CD Pearl GEMM CD 9021**. Ivor Newton, piano, 1938. Songs 5, 10, 45, 51 (second verse omitted), 69.

Sóbinov, Leoníd Vitálievich. Russian tenor, 1872-1934. With Chaliapin and Nezhdanova, one of the three greatest Russian singers of the early 20th century. Studied singing in Moscow from 1892 (while completing a law degree in 1894): his teachers included Alexander Dodonov (see Song 34) and Alexandra Gorchakova (see Opus 65). Sang in *Pagliacci* with a visiting Italian opera troupe, was accepted into the Bolshoy in 1897. Celebrated career followed with triumphs in St. Petersburg, Milan, Berlin, London, Paris, Madrid, Monte Carlo. A famous Lensky and Lohengrin; an elegant, expressive singer with a voice of rare beauty. In February 1917 when the Romanov regime collapsed he was elected Director of the Bolshoy. His handsome appearance and committed concert singing made him a huge favorite with the public. In addition to the two recordings below, his concert repertoire included Songs 5, 6, 7, 8, 10, 12, 25, 68, 75, 79, 87, 90, 91, 100, 102, 103. In *Record of Singing*, vol. 1; in *Levik*.
- **LP Melodiya M10 45309**. Song 83 (1901).
- **LP Melodiya M10 49003 000.** "Collected Recordings III." Song 41 (1911).
- **CD Memoir Classics CD MOIR 422**. Song 41, as above.

Söderström, Elisabeth. Swedish soprano, born 1927. Renowned opera singer at the Swedish Royal Opera, Covent Garden, Glyndebourne, Salzburg, the Met, in operas by Mozart, Strauss, Tchaikovsky, Janáček, and others. A versatile and committed singer of the greatest delicacy, warmth, and honesty. Her music teacher and mentor was Adelaide Andreeva von Skilondz (in *Levik*, 190), who gave a brilliant finish to Söderström's affinity for Russian material. Her repertoire includes 35 songs of Tchaikovsky and all 83 songs of Rachmaninoff.
- **CD Decca 436 204-2**. Vladimir Ashkenazy, piano. Songs 1, 2, 3, 4, 8, 9, 10, 11, 14, 17, 20, 30, 35, 38, 40, 41, 45, 50, 59, 60, 74, 77, 78, 92, 93, 95, 96, 101. Transferred to CD from **LP Decca SXL 6972** and **LP Decca SXL 7606**. The latter has, in addition, Songs 51, 55, 70, 83, 89, 91, 97, 98.
- **CD BIS CD-17**. With Kerstin Meyer, mezzo-soprano, and Jan Eyron, piano, 1974. Duets 3, 4, 6 (in French).
- **CD London 436 920-2**. Rachmaninoff Songs (Complete). Vladimir Ashkenazy, piano. Songs 4, 75 (Rachmaninoff).

Soloviánenko, Anatóly Borísovich. Ukrainian tenor, 1932-1999. Trained at La Scala 1963-65, graduated from the Kiev Conservatory 1978; since 1965, soloist at the Kiev Opera.
- **CD Melodiya SUCD 10-00201**. Rita Bobrovich, piano, with Siberian Violinists Ensemble, cond. by Mikhail Parkhomovsky, 1990. Songs 8, 40, 41, 50.

Souzay, Gérard. French baritone, born 1918. He sang in opera, but is primarily known as a fine performer of songs. In *Record of Singing*, vol. 4.
- **CD Dutton CDLX 7036**. Irene Aïtoff, piano (1948). Songs 9, 41 (in French).
- **LP RCA Stereo LSC 3082**. Dalton Baldwin, piano. Songs 39, 41 (in Russian).

Stepánova, Yeléna Andréyevna. Russian lyric-coloratura soprano, 1891-1978. Born in Moscow, daughter of a singing teacher, sang in church choirs. Studied at the Moscow Conservatory with Ya. Losev, then two years with M. Polli. At the Bolshoy 1908-1944. With Nezhdanova, Katulskaya, and Barsova, one of the finest sopranos of the older generation at the Bolshoy.
- **LP Melodiya M10 38793-4**. Pianist unknown. Song 11.

Stérling (Korolkóva), Tatiána Sergéyevna. Russian mezzo-soprano, born 1942. Graduate, Gnesin Institute Moscow, 1972; since then, soloist, Moscow Philharmonic.
- **CD A&E AED-10157**. Anatoly Spivak, piano. Songs 8, 11, 22, 40, 41, 44, 68, 91.

Stokowski, Leopold. "Celebrated, spectacularly endowed, and magically communicative English-American conductor" (*Baker's*), 1882-1977.
• **CD Biddulph WHL 015.** "Stokowski Conducts Tchaikovsky." Philadelphia Orchestra, 19 Apr. 1937. Song 103 (transcription for orchestra by Stokowski).

Svéshnikov, Aleksándr Vasílievich. Russian choir director, 1890-1980. Founder, Sveshnikov Chorus. Rector and teacher of choral singing at the Moscow Conservatory 1948-74. (Not to be confused with A. S. Sveshnikova, his wife, who taught solo singing at the conservatory.)
• **LP Melodiya-Angel SR 40039.** Song 27 (1863 choral version).

Tartakóv, Ioákim Víktorovich. Russian baritone, 1860-1923. Pupil of Everardi. Sang at the Mariinsky from 1882. Discography and good analysis of his vocal interpretation of Songs 5, 41, 49, 93, 103 in *Tartakov*, 54-7. In *Record of Singing*, vols. 1, 2; in *Levik*.
• **LP OASI 630.** "Russian Basses and Baritones of the Acoustic Era." Songs 39, 49.
• **CD Yale University Library YHS 0001/2.** "The Yale Collection of Historical Sound Recordings." Song 41 (recorded by Fred Gaisberg in Moscow in June 1901).

Tauber, Richard. Austrian tenor, 1891-1948. Operatic and concert singer, most renowned in operetta, very popular in Europe, in England, where he settled in 1938, and in the U.S., where he gave his last concert in Carnegie Hall in 1947. In *Record of Singing*, vols. 2, 3. Discography in *TRC*, vol. 18, nos. 8-10. Only the two songs discussed in *Jackson* are listed here.
• **78 Parlophone-Odeon RO 20518.** Song 9, in English, with orchestra.
• **78 Parlophone-Odeon RO 20549.** Song 44, in English ("Fifinella"), with orchestra.

Tear, Robert. Welsh tenor, born 1939. A singer at Covent Garden who has made many fine recordings, including operas by Benjamin Britten and romances of Rachmaninoff.
• **LP Argo ZRG 707.** Philip Ledger, piano. Songs 1, 4, 9, 10, 11, 12, 15, 19, 20, 24, 29, 32, 37, 39, 41, 83, 84, 93 (in Russian), 103.

Teyte, Maggie. English soprano and famous recitalist, 1888-1976. Pupil of Jean de Reszke; performed with Debussy. In *Record of Singing*, vols. 3, 4. The recording below was made in 1948 (*TRC*, vol. 9 no. 6).
• **78 Gramophone Shop (NY) GSC.24, 2EA 12454.** Gerald Moore, piano. Song 96.

Tibbett, Lawrence. American baritone, 1896-1960. At Met 1923-1950, where he was a great favorite for his fine singing, diction, and acting; also sang on popular radio shows. In addition to the song below, *WERM* lists a recording of Song 9 (in English). In *Record of Singing*, vol. 3.
• **CD Memoir Classics CD MOIR 422.** Orch. cond. by Nathaniel Shilkret. Song 49.

Tourel, Jennie. American mezzo-soprano of Russian-Jewish heritage, 1900?-1973. Born Zhenya Davidovich (?) in St. Petersburg (*Baker's*) or Vitebsk (*Hamilton*); other sources claim she was Canadian, born in Montreal. Studied in Paris with Reynaldo Hahn and Anna El-Tour; by reversing the syllables of her teacher's surname, she renamed herself Tourel. Sang in Chicago (1930), at Opéra Russe and Opéra-Comique in Paris (1931-40); Met debut in 1937. Sang at the Met and the New York City Opera in the 1940s; sang the first Baba the Turk in Venice in the premier of Stravinsky's *Rake's Progress* in 1951. Noted recitalist; taught at Juilliard. In *Record of Singing*, vol. 4.
• **LP Decca DL 9981.** "None But the Lonely Heart: Jennie Tourel sings Russian Love Songs." Brooks Smith, piano, George Ricci, cello obbligato. Songs 9, 10, 40 41.
• **LP Odyssey 32 160070.** "Jennie Tourel Sings Russian Songs." Allen Rogers, piano, Gary Karr, double bass. Songs 9, 11, 12, 75.
• **LP Columbia M 32231.** "Jennie Tourel, Leonard Bernstein at Carnegie Hall." Leonard Bernstein, piano. Songs 12, 82.
• **CD Vox CDX 5126.** "Jennie Tourel Live at Alice Tully Hall," 19 April 1970. James Levine, piano. Song 9.

Tugárinova, Tatyána Fyódorovna. Russian soprano, 1925-83. Graduated Moscow Conservatory 1957, pupil of Nina Dorliak. Bolshoy 1956-80.

• **LP Melodiya D 030863**. Nikolay Korolkov, piano. Songs 14, 21, 22, 45, 71.
• **Complete** Romances. (Korolkov). Songs 14, 21, 22, 45, 71.
• **Complete Songs and Duets**. (Korolkov). Songs 14, 21, 22, 71.

Tyler, Veronica. African American soprano. Studied at Peabody, Juilliard. Second Prize, Tchaikovsky Competition, 1966. Has sung at New York City Opera.
• **LP Melodiya D 018247-8** (Tchaikovsky Competition, 1966). Song 4.

Varady, Julia. Romanian soprano, born 1941. Married to Fischer-Dieskau.
• **CD Orfeo C 053 851 A**. "Tschaikowsky Lieder," 1981. Aribert Reimann, piano. Songs 4, 8, 25, 35, 45, 46, 92-97, 98-103.

Vaughan, Sarah. American jazz singer, 1924-1990. On her "classical" album below, in addition to "None But the Lonely Heart," she sings popular songs based on themes by Rachmaninoff ("Full Moon and Empty Arms") and Anton Rubinstein ("If You Are But a Dream").
• **CD Roulette CDP 7 95977 2**. "Sarah Slightly Classical." Arranged for orchestra and conducted by Marty Manning, 1963. Song 9 (in English).

Vayne, Kyra. Russian soprano,1916-2001. Born in Petrograd, she lived in London after 1924; received vocal training there from Maria Kuznetsova and Oda Slobodskaya. Her opera career was interrupted by the war, but resumed after it. Biography and discography in *TRC*,vol. 37, no. 4; note by Vayne herself in vol. 40, no. 4.
• **CD Preiser 89996**. Colin Tilney, piano, c. 1964. Songs 6, 10, 56.

Vedérnikov, Aleksándr Filíppovich. Russian bass, born 1927. Graduated Moscow Conservatory 1955, class of R. Al'per-Khasina. Kirov Opera 1955-58, graduate training at La Scala 1961, soloist at the Bolshoy 1958-90. He was awarded a State Prize in 1969 for his concert programs, which included appearances in Europe and Canada.
• **LP Melodiya D 6165-6**. I. Naumova, piano. Songs 7, 49, 69, 77, 79, 90.
• **LP Melodiya D 021568**. Orchestra of the Bolshoy Theater, cond. Mark Ermler. Song 49 (Taneyev orchestration).
• **LP Melodiya S10 21307 001**. Naum Shtarkman, piano. Songs 5, 7, 38, 40, 41, 49, 69, 77, 79, 90.

Verhaeghe, Claudie. French soprano.
• **CD Discover International DICD 920272**. "Frédéric Chopin: 19 Polish Songs, Op. 74." Jean Micault, piano, 1992. Song 32 (Chopin).

Verrett, Shirley. American mezzo-soprano, born 1931 in New Orleans. Studied with Lotte Lehmann, went on to Juilliard to study with Anna Fitziu and Marion Székely-Frescki. Toured Russia in 1963, where she sang Carmen at the Bolshoy; made her Met debut as Carmen in 1968. A splendid, versatile singer who has sung both soprano and mezzo roles.
LP RCA LM/LSC 2835. "Shirley Verrett, Carnegie Hall Recital, January 30, 1965". Charles Wadsworth, piano. Songs 51, 103.

Vinográdov, Geórgy Pávlovich. Russian lyric tenor, 1908-1980. Born in Kazan, where he sang in a Russian church choir and studied violin and viola. At the Army Communications Academy in Moscow, amateur singing led to study with N. G. Raisky (Lemeshev's teacher). Professional recognition came when he finished in the top ten at the first All-Union Vocal Competition held in December 1938 in an unheated hall; Migay encouraged him, saying "Never mind, the frost makes your voice sound even better!" (*Iakovleva*). The jury was chaired by Barsova, who later recorded Tchaikovsky's "Romeo and Juliet" duet with him. He worked his entire career as a concert singer with All-Union Radio, the Defense Band, the State Jazz Group, the Red Banner Ensemble of Song and Dance, and the State Concert Guild. Unusually versatile, he could sing Tchaikovsky and Rachmaninoff, Schubert and Schumann, popular tangos and foxtrots, as well as operas performed in concert. His recordings number in the hundreds. He never appeared on stage and thus never rivalled Lemeshev and Kozlovsky, but his pure intonation, perfect diction, taste, genuine musicality, and lyrical voice which he never forced made him one of the most popular singers of his

day. Honored Artist of Russia (1949). He was forced into retirement in 1951 for "disciplinary infractions on a concert tour." He spent his retirement years as a teacher at the All-Union Creative Studio of the Variety Arts. In *Record of Singing*, vol. 4.
  • **78 Melodiya 13241**. Alexander Goldenweiser, piano. Song 35. (Seen and heard at *RGAFD*, Apr. 2000; erroneously listed in Western discographies as Song 8).
  • **78 ESTA D 2012 (Supraphon B 23041)**. K. Vinogradov, piano. Songs 41, 44 (in Russian). (Not seen but cited in *Jackson, WERM*, and *Gramophone Shop*.)
  • **78 ESTA 2104 (Supraphon B 23042)**. K. Vinogradov, piano. Song 100. (Not seen, cited in *WERM* and *Gramophone Shop*.)
  • **78 Melodiya 16278-9**. Songs 62, 65. (Not seen, cited in *WERM*).
  • **LP Melodiya D 2590-91**. Georgy Orentlikher, piano. Songs 10, 54, 55, 60, 61, 64, 75, 82, 85.
  • **LP Melodiya M10 40761-64**. Georgy Orentlikher, piano. Songs 10, 17, 75, 82, 90.
  • **Complete Romances**. Georgy Orentlikher, piano. Song 90.
  • **CD Preiser 89118**. Georgy Orentlikher, piano. Songs 10, 17, 75, 82, 90.

Vishnévskaya, Galína Pávlovna. Russian soprano, born 1926 in Leningrad. She began with hopes of becoming a popular singer like the famous Klavdiya Shulzhenko, and got her first singing job in the Leningrad Operetta in 1944. She found a rare music teacher in Vera Garina, who understood her talent and trained her voice. Accepted into the Bolshoy in 1952, where she was a star until she and her husband Mstislav Rostropovich left the Soviet Union in 1974. Has sung at the Met, Covent Garden, La Scala and elsewhere. Shostakovich and Britten wrote music for her. She has recorded over 100 Russian romances, sometimes more than once. Author of lively and outspoken memoirs (*Vishnevskaya*).
  • **LP Melodiya D 4499**. Boris Abramovich, piano. Songs 8, 11, 19, 40.
  • **Complete Romances**. Boris Abramovich, piano. Song 40.
  • **LP RCA Victor LM 2497**. Alexander Dedyukhin, piano. Songs 8, 11, 51.
  • **LP London OS 26141**. Mstislav Rostropovich, piano. Songs 8, 35, 41, 69, 91, 99.
  • **CD Melodiya SUCD 10-00259**. Mstislav Rostropovich, piano. Songs 4, 5, 9.
  • **CD EMI 5 65716 2**. "The Rostropovich Edition." Songs 4, 8, 11, 38, 40, 41, 45, 48, 51, 100, 103. Also on • **LP EMI SLS 5055**.
  • **LP DG 2530 725**. Song 32 (Glinka).
  • **CD Erato 2292-45643-2**. Mstislav Rostropovich, piano. Songs 5, 9, 10, 19, 36, 41, 50, 61, 68, 70, 79, 82, 92, 101. Song 46 (Musorgsky).

Vladímirov, Yevgény Nikoláevich. Russian bass. Sang in the Red Banner Ensemble and for All-Union Radio. Sang in the premiere of Shostakovich's 14th Symphony.
  • **LP Melodiya S10 05517-8**. Valentina Strzhizhovskaya, piano. Song 25.

Voigt, Deborah. American dramatic soprano, born 1960 in Chicago. First Prize, Tchaikovsky Competition, 1990. Met debut 1991. Has sung in Florence, Vienna, Cologne, Covent Garden, Buenos Aires, San Francisco, Boston, and elsewhere, in opera and recitals.
  • **CD Melodiya SUCD 10-00116** (Tchaikovsky Competition, 1990). Igor Chichagov, piano. Song 50.

Vórvulev, Nikoláy Dmítrievich. Russian baritone, 1917-1967. Sang in the Belorus Army Ensemble during the war, then trained at the Minsk Conservatory, where he graduated in 1954 in the class of Yevgeny Viting. At the Minsk Opera 1946-57, then the Kiev Opera 1957-67. People's Artist of USSR (1956).
  • **LP Melodiya M10 39269**. Pianist not indicated. Songs 79, 85.

Walter, Naúm Gennádievich (in Russian spelled Vál'ter). Pianist, born 1902. Student of Felix Blumenfeld and Heinrich Neuhaus. Honored Artist of Russia. Accompanist and soloist at All-Union Radio 1928-61. Worked with Andrey Ivanov, Kozlovsky, Lemeshev, Lisitsian, Nortsov, Reizen, Shpiller, Shumskaya, Vinogradov.

Yershóv, Iván Vasílevich. Russian dramatic tenor, 1867-1943. Student of Stanislav Gabel (1893), with a further year of study in Milan with Ernesto Rossi. Sang at the Mariinsky 1895-1929. In *Record of Singing*, vol. 1, where his voice is described as "limpid, brilliant,

integrated, [with a] seemingly inexhaustible range and variety of nuances." Professor at the Petrograd (later, Leningrad) Conservatory 1916-1941. Extensively described in *Levik*, "the most brilliant jewel in the Mariinsky's Wagnerian crown."
• LP Melodiya M10 45189. Song 91 (recorded 1903).

Zakhárov, Sergéy. Russian baritone of Ukrainian background, born 1950. A popular singer who emulated Georg Ots and achieved fame in the 1970s in the music halls of Leningrad. Frequent appearances on TV and concerts at home and abroad.
• CD Russian Disc RCD 26004. "Oh, You My Ancient Romance." Solovyov-Sedoy Variety Orchestra conducted by Sergey Gorkovenko (1987). Songs 39, 41.

Zbrúyeva, Yevgénia Ivánovna. Russian contralto, 1868-1936. Born in Moscow, discovered by Nikolay Rubinstein, taught piano by Kashkin, voice by Lavrovskaya. Sang at the Bolshoy from 1894 and the Mariinsky from 1905-1917; frequently sang with Chaliapin including Diaghilev's Paris concerts. Her recordings of songs have a special interest because (despite her patronymic) she was the daughter of Pyotr Petrovich Bulakhov, a well-known composer of urban romances. In *Record of Singing*, vols. 1, 2. Her recording of Song 9 changes the gender of the singer to feminine, a unique instance in recordings of the song.
• LP Club "99" CL 99-78. "Eugenia Zbrujewa." Songs 9, 79.

Zelénina, Maria. Russian soprano (Odessa).
• CD Sonora SO 22587 CD. "In the Kingdom of Roses and Wine." Oleg Petrov, piano. Songs 21, 91.

Zhadán, Iván Danílovich. Ukrainian-Russian tenor, born in Lugansk in 1902. Sang in church choir from age 10. Went to Moscow in 1923, studied at the conservatory with Professor Yegorov and with Stanislavsky. Sang at the Bolshoy 1928-41. Developed his song repertoire with Matvey Sakharov. Fled Russia in 1941, came to the U.S. in 1948. In *Record of Singing*, vol. 4.
• 78 Melodiya (Noginsky Zavod) 4603. Matvey Sakharov, piano. Songs 25, 98.
• CD Private Label DIDX-025756. "Ivan Jadan: Great Russian Tenor of the Century." Songs 25, 98 as above (erroneously described as recorded in Germany). Adele Gonzmart, piano: Songs 9, 10, recorded in Florida in 1953-54.

Zimmermann, Margarita. Russian-Argentinian mezzo-soprano.
• CD Sony SK 57482. Dalton Baldwin, piano (1991). Songs 4, 9, 11, 25, 51, 99.

Zlatogórova, Bronisláva Yákovlevna (real name Goldberg). Russian contralto, born 1905 near Kiev. Trained in Odessa and at the Kiev Conservatory, where, like Kozlovsky, she took singing lessons from Yelena Muravyova. Sang in Kharkov, then at the Bolshoy 1929-1953. People's Artist of Russia (1951).
• LP Melodiya 40882. G. I. Kats, piano. Song 82.

Zýkina, Lyudmíla Geórgievna. Russian singer of folk and popular songs, born 1929. Soloist with the Piatnitsky Choir and with All-Union Radio. Her ringing mezzo is known everywhere in Russia. She is a good example of the folk as opposed to the academic style of Russian singing: chest tones at the low end, throat sounds at the top, with a "flying" voice that moves easily between the two extremes. People's Artist of the USSR (1973), Hero of Socialist Labor (1987).
• LP Melodiya S20 20643 001. Russian Folk Ensemble "Rossiya", cond. Viktor Gridin, 1983. Song 75 (Tolstaya).

Bibliography

Short Titles

BT. *Bol'shoi Teatr SSSR* [The Bolshoy Theater of the USSR], ed. I. F. Bèlza et al. Moscow: Gosudarstvennoe muzykal'noe izdatel'stvo, 1958.

Baker's. *Baker's Biographical Dictionary of Musicians.* Seventh Edition, revised by Nicolas Slonimsky. New York: Schirmer Books, 1984.

DG. *Dni i gody P. I. Chaikovskogo: Letopis' zhizni i tvorchestva* [Days and Years of P. I. Tchaikovsky: A chronicle of his life and work], ed. V. V. Iakovlev. Moscow-Leningrad: Muzgiz, 1940.

Dnevniki. *Dnevniki P. I. Chaikovskogo 1873-1891* [Diaries of P. I. Tchaikovsky 1873-1891], ed. I. I. Chaikovskii. Moscow-Petrograd, 1923.

LPP. P. I. Chaikovskii. *Literaturnye proizvedeniia i perepiska* [Literary works and correspondence], vol. XVII. Ed. K. Iu. Davydova and G. I. Labutina. Moscow: Muzyka, 1981.

ME. *Muzykal'naia èntsiklopediia* [Musical encyclopedia], ed. Iu. V. Keldysh. Six volumes. Moscow, 1973-1982.

MES. *Muzykal'nyi èntsiklopedicheskii slovar'* [Musical encyclopedic dictionary], ed. G. V. Keldysh. Moscow, 1990.

MKS. P. I. Chaikovskii. *Muzykal'no-kriticheskie stat'i* [Music Criticism], 4th edition. Leningrad: Muzyka, 1986.

MN. *Muzykal'noe nasledie Chaikovskogo: Iz istorii ego proizvedenii* [Musical legacy of Tchaikovsky: From the history of his compositions], ed. K. Iu. Davydova, V. V. Protopopov, and N. V. Tumanina. Moscow, 1958.

PRP. *Pesni russkikh poètov v dvukh tomakh* [Songs of Russian poets in two volumes], ed. V. E. Gusev. Third Edition. Biblioteka poèta, Bol'shaia seriia. Leningrad, 1988.

PSS. P. I. Chaikovskii. *Polnoe sobranie sochinenii* [Complete collected works]. *Romansy i pesni* [Romances and songs], ed. Ivan Shishov and N. Shemanin. Moscow-Leningrad, 1940. Vols. 44, 45. The Duets, Op. 46, are in Vol. 43, *Khory i ansambli* [Choruses and ensembles], 1941.

RGAFD. Rossiiskii Gosudarstvennyi Arkhiv Fono-Dokumentov [Russian State Archive of Sound Recordings], Moscow.

Record of Singing. Recordings of vocal artists from the earliest sound recordings to the end of the 78 rpm era. The last two volumes are on CD. Vol. 3: Testament SBT 0132; Vol. 4: EMI Classics CHS 7 69741 2. See *Scott* below for volumes 1 and 2.

RP. *Russkie pisateli 1800-1917: biograficheskii slovar'* [Russian writers 1800-1917: biographical dictionary], ed. P. A. Nikolaev et al. Four volumes to date. Moscow: Sovetskaia èntsiklopediia, 1989 (vol. 1); Bolshaia rossiiskaia èntsiklopediia, 1992-99 (vols. 2-4).

TRC. *The Record Collector.* A Magazine for Collectors of Recorded Vocal Art. Vols. 1-41 (May 1946-December 1996).

WERM. *The World's Encyclopædia of Recorded Music*, ed. Francis F. Clough and G. J. Cuming. London, 1952.

Select Bibliography

Abraham, Gerald. *Essays on Russian and East European Music.* Oxford. 1985.

⸻, ed. *The Music of Tchaikovsky.* New York, 1946.

⸻. "Russia." In *A History of Song*, ed. Denis Stevens. Westport, 1982.

⸻. *Slavonic and Romantic Music.* New York, 1968.

Agin, M. S. *Vokal'no-èntsiklopedicheskii slovar'. Biobibliografiia* [Vocal Encyclopedia. Biobibliography]. Five vols. Moscow: Gnesin Music Academy, 1991-1994.

Aikhenval'd, Iulii I. *Siluèty russkikh pisatelei.* Moscow: Respublika, 1994.

Al'shvang, Arnold A. *Opyt analiza tvorchestva P. I. Chaikovskogo (1864-1878).* Moscow and Leningrad, 1951.

_____ . *P. I. Chaikovskii*. Moscow: Gosudarstvennoe muzykal'noe izdatel'stvo, 1959.

_____ . "The Songs" in *The Music of Tchaikovsky*, ed. Gerald Abraham. New York, 1946.

Altaev, Al. (Altaeva-Iamshchikova, Margarita Vl.). *Pamiatnye vstrechi*. Moscow, 1955.

Apukhtin, A. N. *Polnoe sobranie stikhotvorenii*, ed. R. A. Shatseva. Biblioteka poèta, Bolshaiia seriia. Leningrad, 1991.

Arkhipova, Irina. *Muzy moi*. Moscow: Molodaia gvardiia, 1992.

Asaf'ev, Boris Vl. *Russkaia muzyka XIX i nachalo XX veka*. Leningrad: Muzyka, 1979.

Balabanovich, E. Z. *Chekhov i Chaikovskii*. Moscow: Moskovskii rabochii, 1973.

Balakirev, M. *Romansy i pesni dlia golosa s fortepiano* [Romances and songs for voice and piano]. Two vols. Moscow: Muzyka, 1978, 1979.

Batser, D. and B. Rabinovich, eds. *Russkaia narodnaia muzyka: notograficheskii ukazatel' (1776-1973)*. Two Parts. Moscow: Sovetskii kompozitor, 1981, 1984.

Bartlett, Rosamund. "Tchaikovsky, Chekhov, and the Russian Elegy." In *Tchaikovsky and His World*, ed. Leslie Kearney. Princeton: Princeton University Press, 1998.

Belonovich, Galina Ivanovna and S. Kotomina. *Chaikovskii 1840-1893. Al'bom*. Moscow: Muzyka, 1990.

Bennett, John R. *Melodiya: A Soviet Russian L. P. Discography*. Westport and London: Greenwood Press, 1981.

Berberova, Nina Nikolaevna. *Chaikovskii*. Berlin, 1936 (republished in St. Petersburg, 1993).

_____ . *Kursiv moi*. München: Wilhelm Fink Verlag, 1972.

Berg, Nikolai Vasil'evich. *Perevody iz Mitskevicha*. Warsaw, 1865.

Blagoi, D. D. "Tiutchev v muzyke." In *Literaturnoe nasledstvo*, "Fedor Ivanovich Tiutchev." Vol. 97, Book 2, Moscow: Nauka, 1989.

Bogdanov-Berezovskii, V. *Ivan Yershov*. Moscow-Leningrad: Gosudarstvennoe muzykal'noe izdatel'stvo, 1951.

Borel, Eugène, ed. *Album lirique de la France moderne par Eugène Borel*. Cinquième édition revue et augmentée par A. Peschier. Stuttgart, 1874.

Borovsky, Victor. *Chaliapin: A Critical Biography*. New York: Alfred A. Knopf, 1988.

Bortnikova, E. E., Davydova, K. Iu., Pribegina, G. A., eds. *Vospominaniia o P. I. Chaikovskom*. Second ed. Moscow: Muzyka, 1973.

Botstein, Leon. "Music as the Language of Psychological Realism: Tchaikovsky and Russian Art." In *Tchaikovsky and His World*, ed. Leslie Kearney. Princeton: Princeton University Press, 1998.

Bowring, John. *Servian Popular Poetry*. London: 1827.

Briusov, Valerii. *Sobranie sochinenii v semi tomakh*, ed. P. G. Antokol'skii et al. Seven vols. Moscow: Khudozhestvennaia literatura, 1973-5.

Brown, David (I). *Tchaikovsky: The Early Years 1840-1874*. New York: W. W. Norton, 1978.

_____ (II). *Tchaikovsky: The Crisis Years 1874-1878*. New York and London: W. W. Norton, 1983.

_____ (III). *Tchaikovsky: The Years of Wandering (1878-1885)*. London: Victor Gollancz Ltd, 1986.

_____ (IV). *Tchaikovsky: The Final Years (1885-1893)*. New York and London: W. W. Norton, 1991.

Brown, Malcolm Hamrick. "Native Song and National Consciousness in Nineteenth-Century Russian Music." In *Art and Culture in Nineteenth-Century Russia*, ed. Theofanis George Stavrou. Bloomington: Indiana University Press, 1983.

Browne, Wayles. "Talvyj, Kopitar and the American Public's First Introduction to the Slavic Literatures." In *Kopitarjev Zbornik*: Ljubljana, 1996, pp. 505-511.

Chaikovskii, Modest Il'ich. *Zhizn' Petra Il'icha Chaikovskogo* [The Life of Peter Ilyich Tchaikovsky]. Three vols. Moscow-Leipzig: P. Jurgenson, censor's dates 1900-02; (reprinted, Moscow: Algoritm, 1997).

Chekhov, Anton. *Sobranie sochinenii v dvenadtsati tomakh*, ed. V. V. Ermilov et al. Twelve vols. Moscow: Gosudarstvennoe izdatel'stvo khudozhestvennoi literatury, 1960-64.

_____ . *Letters of Anton Chekhov*, translated by Michael Henry Heim, selected and with commentary by Simon Karlinsky. New York: Harper & Row, 1973.

Child, Francis James. *English and Scottish Popular Ballads*, ed. Helen Child Sargent and

George Lyman Kittredge. Boston and New York: Houghton, Mifflin and Company, 1904.

Christian, David. *"Living Water": Vodka and Russian Society on the Eve of Emancipation.* Oxford: Clarendon Press, 1990.

Collin, Paul. *Du grave au doux.* Paris, 1878.

Dargomyzhskii, A. *Polnoe sobranie romansov i pesen* [Complete collection of romances and songs], ed. M. S. Pekelis. Two vols. Moscow-Leningrad: Gosudarstvennoe muzykal'noe izdatel'stvo, 1947.

Davydov, Iurii L'vovich. *Klinskie gody tvorchestva Chaikovskogo.* Moscow: Moskovskii rabochii, 1964.

Dombaev, G. S. *Tvorchestvo P. I. Chaikovskogo v materialakh i dokumentakh.* Moscow, 1958.

Douglas, Nigel. *More Legendary Voices.* New York: Limelight Editions, 1995.

Dowler, Wayne. *An Unnecessary Man: The Life of Apollon Grigor'ev.* Toronto: University of Toronto Press, 1995.

Edgerton, William. "One More Look at the Problem of Transliteration." *Slavic Review* 48, No. 1 (Spring 1989): 97-99.

Engel-Braunschmidt, Annelore. "Ada Christens 'Nur Du allein' und P. I. Tschaikowskys Vertonung." In *Sodalicium Slavizantium Hamburgense in honorem Dietrich Gerhardt,* 121-139. Amsterdam, 1971.

Etkind, E. G., ed. *Mastera russkogo stikhotvornogo perevoda.* Biblioteka poèta, Bol'shaia seriia. Two vols. Leningrad, 1968.

Evlampios, Georgii. *Amarantos ili rozy vozrozhdennoi Èllady.* Sankt-Peterburg, 1843. Reprinted as *O Amarantos* in Athens, 1973.

Fet, A. A. *Stikhotvoreniia i poèmy,* ed. B. Ia. Bukhshtab. Biblioteka poèta, Bol'shaia seriia. Leningrad, 1986.

Finck, Henry T., ed. *One Hundred Songs by Ten Masters in Two Volumes. For Low Voice.* Boston: Oliver Ditson Company, 1917; also New York, Chas. H. Ditson & Co., and Chicago, Lyon & Healy.

Frank, Joseph. *Dostoevsky: The Seeds of Revolt, 1821-1849.* Princeton: Princeton University Press, 1976.

———. *Dostoevsky: The Years of Ordeal, 1850-1859.* Princeton: Princeton University Press, 1983.

Gaisberg, Frederick William. *The Music Goes Round.* New York: Macmillan, 1942.

Gamalei, Iu. V. *"Mariinka" i moia zhizn'.* St. Petersburg: Papirus, 1999.

Gershuni, Evgenii Pavlovich. *Rasskazyvaiu ob èstrade.* Leningrad: Iskusstvo, 1968.

Gippius, Zinaida. *Zhivye litsa.* Tbilisi: Merani, 1991.

Girardin, Émile de. *Poésies Complètes de Madame Émile de Girardin (Delphine Gay).* Paris, 1846.

Glinka, Mikhail I. *Polnoe sobranie romansov i pesni dlia odnogo golosa s fortepiano* [Complete romances and songs for one voice with piano], ed. N. N. Zagornyi. Leningrad: Gosudarstvennoe muzykal'noe izdatel'stvo, 1955.

———. *Memoirs.* Translated by Richard B. Mudge. Westport: Greenwood Press, 1980.

Gramophone Shop Encyclopedia of Recorded Music, Third Edition, ed. Robert H. Reid. New York: Crown Publishers, 1948.

Grekov, Nikolai Porfir'evich. *Stikhotvoreniia N. P. Grekova.* Moscow, 1860.

Grosheva, E. A., ed. *Fedor Ivanovich Shaliapin: sbornik.* Two vols. Moscow: Iskusstvo, 1960.

Hamilton, David, ed. *The Metropolitan Opera Encyclopedia.* New York: Simon and Schuster, 1987.

Hartmann, Moritz. *Zeitlosen.* Braunschweig: Friedrich Bieweg und Sohn, 1858.

Heine, Heinrich. *Heine Werke 1,* ed. Stuart Atkins. München: C. H. Beck, 1973.

———. *Heine Werke 1I,* ed. Stuart Atkins. München: C. H. Beck, 1977.

———. *The Complete Poems of Heinrich Heine: A Modern English Version by Hal Draper.* Boston: Suhrkamp/Insel and Oxford University Press, 1982.

Hemans, Felicia. *Poetical Works,* Six vols. Edinburgh and London: William Blackwood and Sons, 1854.

Herzen, Alexander. *My Past and Thoughts: The Memoirs of Alexander Herzen.* Translated by Constance Garnett. Berkeley: University of California Press, 1982.

Huneker, James, ed. *Forty Songs by Peter Ilyitch Tchaikovsky. For Low Voice.* Boston: Oliver Ditson Company, 1912.

Iakovenko, Sergei Borisovich. *Volshebnaia Zara Dolukhanova.* Moscow: SOBA, 1996.

_____. *Pavel Gerasimovich Lisitsian: Uroki odnoi zhizni.* Moscow: Muyzka, 1989.

Iakovlev, Vasilii. *Chaikovskii na moskovskoi stsene.* Moscow-Leningrad: Iskusstvo, 1940.

Iakovleva, L. "Georgii Vinogradov." In *Pevtsy sovetskoi èstrady,* ed. Liudmila G. Bulgak. Moscow, 1977.

Ippolitov-Ivanov, Mikhail M. *50 let russkoi muzyki v moikh vospominaniiakh.* Moscow, 1934.

Ivanov, Georgii Konstantinovich. *Russkaia poeziia v otechestvennoi muzyke (do 1917 goda)* [Russian poetry in music of the fatherland (to 1917)]. Vypusk I. Moscow: Muzyka, 1966. Vypusk II. Moscow: Sovetskii kompozitor, 1969.

Jackson, David M. "Tchaikovsky: Ten songs" in *Song on Record 2,* ed. Alan Blyth. Cambridge: Cambridge University Press, 1988.

Jurgenson, P. I. *P. I. Chaikovskii. Perepiska s P. I. Iurgensonom,* ed. V. A. Zhdanov and N. T. Zhegin. Two vols. Moscow: Muzgiz, 1938.

Kandinskii, A. I. et al, eds. *P. I. Chaikovskii: k 100-letiiu so dnia smerti.* Materialy nauchnoi konferentsii. Nauchnye trudy Moskovskoi gosudarstvennoi konservatorii im. P. I. Chaikovskogo. Sbornik 12. Moscow, 1995.

Karadžić, Vuk Stefanović. *Srpske narodne pjesme.* Four vols. Beograd: Prosveta, 1953.

Karlinsky, Simon. "Memoirs of Harbin", in *Slavic Review,* vol. 48 no. 2 (Summer 1989): 284-290.

Katz, B. and Timenchik, R. *Anna Akhmatova i muzyka: Issledovatel'skie ocherki.* Leningrad: Sovetskii kompozitor, 1989.

Kearney, Leslie. "Truth vs. Beauty: Comparative Text Settings by Musorgsky and Tchaikovsky." In *Tchaikovsky and His Contemporaries,* ed. Alexandar Mihailovic. Westport and London: Greenwood Press, 1999.

Keiler, Allan. *Marian Anderson: A Singer's Journey.* New York: Scribner, 2000.

Khomiakov, A. S. *Stikhotvoreniia.* Moscow, 1861.

_____. *Polnoe sobranie sochinenii.* Vol. 4, "Stikhotvoreniia." Moscow, 1900.

_____. *Stikhotvoreniia i dramy,* ed. B. F. Egorov. Biblioteka poèta, Bol'shaia seriia. Leningrad, 1969.

Kimball, Robert. *Cole.* New York, Chicago, San Francisco, 1971.

_____, ed. *The Complete Lyrics of Ira Gershwin.* New York: Alfred A. Knopf, 1993.

Klimenko, I. A. *Moi vospominaniia o P. I. Chaikovskom.* Riazan', 1908.

Kol'tsov, A. V. *Polnoe sobranie sochinenii A. V. Kol'tsova,* ed. A. I. Leshchenko. St. Petersburg, 1911.

Kondratowicz, Ludwik. *Wybór poezyj,* ed. Stanisław Cywiński. Vol. I. Wilno, 1923.

Kopytova, Galina. "Neizvestnyi nabrosok Chaikovskogo," in *Skripichnyi kliuch,* No. 3, 1998: 48-51.

Kotliarov, Iu. and Garmash, V. *Letopis' zhizni i tvorchestva F. I. Shaliapina.* Two vols. Leningrad: Muzyka, 1989.

Kozlovskii, Ivan S. *Muzyka – radost' i bol' moia,* ed. I. Safronova and N. Slezina. Moscow: Kompozitor, 1992.

K. R. See Romanov, Konstantin.

Kreid, Vadim, ed. *Slovar' poètov Russkogo Zarubezh'ia.* Sankt-Peterburg: Izdatel'stvo Khristianskogo gumanitarnogo instituta, 1999.

Kuzin, Nikolai. *Pleshcheev.* Moscow: Molodaia gvardiia, 1988.

Larosh [Laroche], G. A. *Sobranie Muzykal'no-kriticheskikh statei.* Two vols. Moscow: Gosudarstvennoe muzykal'noe izdatel'stvo, 1922-1924.

Lemeshev, S. Ia. *Put' k iskusstvu.* Moscow, 1968.

_____. *S. Ia. Lemeshev. Iz biograficheskikh zapisok. Stat'i. Besedy. Pis'ma. Vospominaniia o S. Ia. Lemesheve,* ed. E. A. Grosheva. Moscow: Sovetskii kompozitor, 1987.

Lermontov, M. Iu. *Izbrannye proizvedeniia v dvukh tomakh,* ed. B. M. Eikhenbaum and E. E. Naidich. Biblioteka poèta, Bol'shaia seriia. Two vols. Moscow-Leningrad, 1964.

Levik, Sergei. *The Levik Memoirs: An Opera Singer's Notes*, translated by Edward Morgan. London: Symposium Records, 1995.

Linnell, Norman. "Mark Reizen–Russian Bass Extraordinary." *The Record Collector*, vol. 28, nos. 1 & 2 (1983): 5-31.

Lischke, André. *Piotr Ilyitch Tchaikovski*. Paris: Fayard, 1993.

Maikov, A. N. *Polnoe sobranie sochinenii A. N. Maikova*. Vols. 1-3. St. Petersburg, 1884.

————. *Izbrannye proizvedeniia*, ed. L. S. Geiro. Biblioteka poèta, Bol'shaia seriia. Leningrad, 1977.

Mandelstam, Nadezhda. *Hope Against Hope: A Memoir*. Translated from the Russian by Max Hayward. New York: Atheneum, 1983.

Manuilov, V. A., ed. *Lermontovskaia èntsiklopediia*. Moscow, 1981.

Mashinskii, S. I., ed. *Poèty kruzhka N. V. Stankevicha*. Biblioteka poèta, Bol'shaia seriia. Moscow-Leningrad, 1964.

Meck: see von Meck.

Mei, L. A. *Polnoe sobranie sochinenii*, ed. P. V. Bykov. Vol. I. St. Petersburg, 1911.

————. *Stikhotvoreniia i dramy*, ed. S. A. Reiser. Biblioteka poèta, Bol'shaia seriia. Leningrad, 1947.

Menuhin, Yehudi. *Unfinished Journey*. New York, 1977.

Merezhkovskii, Dmitrii. *D. S. Merezhkovskii. Sobranie stikhotvorenii*, ed. A. V. Uspenskaia and G. G. Martynov. Sankt-Peterburg: Folio-Press, 2000.

Metropolitan Opera Annals, compiled by William H. Seltsam. New York: The H. W. Wilson Company, 1947 (Second Printing with Corrections, 1949).

Mihailovic, Alexandar, ed. *Tchaikovsky and His Contemporaries: A Centennial Symposium*. Westport and London: Greenwood Press, 1999.

Miliukov, A. P. "A. A. Grigor'ev i L. A. Mei." *Istoricheskii vestnik* 11 (1883): 98-109.

Mirsky, D. S. *A History of Russian Literature*, ed. Francis J. Whitfield. New York: Vintage Books, 1958.

Moore, Gerald. *Am I Too Loud? Memoirs of an Accompanist*. London: Penguin Books, 1966.

Morozova, L. I. and B. M. Rozenfel'd. *Lermontov v muzyke*. Moscow: Sovetskii kompozitor, 1983.

Muratova, K. D. *Istoriia russkoi literatury XIX veka*. Moscow-Leningrad, 1962.

————. *Istoriia russkoi literatury kontsa XIX-nachala XX vv.* Moscow-Leningrad, 1963.

Musset, Alfred de. *Poésies complètes*. Paris, 1951.

Mussorgsky, Modest. *Complete Songs*. New York: G. Schirmer, 1995.

Nechaev, V. P. "Ratgauz," in *Literaturnaia èntsiklopediia russkogo zarubezh'ia (1918-1940)*. Tom I. *Pisateli russkogo zarubezh'ia*. Moscow: Rossiiskaia politicheskaia èntsiklopediia (ROSSPEN), 1997.

Neishtadt, Vladimir, ed. *Grecheskie narodnye pesni*. Moscow, 1957.

Nekrasov, N. A. *Pis'ma 1840-1877*, ed. V. E. Evgen'eva-Maksimova. Moscow-Leningrad, 1930.

Nesterenko, Evgeny. *Razmyshleniia o professii*. Moscow, 1985.

Nezhdanova, A. V. *Antonina Vasil'evna Nezhdanova. Materialy i issledovaniia*, ed. V. A. Vasina-Grossman et al. Moscow: Iskusstvo, 1967.

Obolensky, Dimitri, ed. *The Heritage of Russian Verse*. Bloomington, London: Indiana University Press, 1976. (Originally published in 1962 as *The Penguin Book of Russian Verse*).

O'Brien, Ed. *Sinatra: The Man and His Music*. Austin, 1992.

Obukhova, Nadezhda A. *N. A. Obukhova: Vospominaniia, stat'i, materialy*, ed. Igor Bèlza. Moscow: Vserossiiskoe teatral'noe obshchestvo, 1970.

Ogarev, N. P. *Stikhotvoreniia N. Ogareva*. Izd. K. Soldatenkova i N. Shchepkina. Moscow, 1856.

Orlova, Elena Mikhailovna. *Romansy Chaikovskogo*. Moscow-Leningrad: Gosudarstvennoe muzykal'noe izdatel'stvo, 1948.

Ovchinnikov, Mikhail A. *Tvortsy russkogo romansa*, second edition. Moscow: Muzyka, 1991.

Oxford Book of Carols, ed. Percy Dearmer, Ralph Vaughan Williams, and Martin Shaw. Oxford: Oxford University Press, 34th impression, 1987.

Palmer, Christopher. *The Composer in Hollywood*. London, New York: Marion Boyars, 1990.

Paxson, Margaret. *Configuring the Past in Rural Russia: An Essay on the Symbolic Topography of Social Memory*. Ph. D. Dissertation, University of Montreal, 1999.
Pechkovskii, N. K. *Vospominaniia opernogo artista*. Sankt-Peterburg: Izdatel'stvo na Fontanke, 1992.
Petrovskii, Miron. "'Ezda v ostrov liubvi', ili chto est' russkii romans." *Voprosy literatury*, no. 5 (1984): 55-90.
‗‗‗‗‗‗‗ and Valentina Morderer, eds. *Russkii romans na rubezhe vekov*. Kiev, 1997.
Pleshcheev, A. N. *Podsnezhnik: Stikhotvoreniia dlia detei i iunoshestva A. N. Pleshcheeva*. St. Petersburg, 1878.
‗‗‗‗‗‗‗ . *Stikhotvoreniia A. N. Pleshcheeva*. Fourth edition, ed. P. V. Bykov. St Petersburg, 1905.
‗‗‗‗‗‗‗ . *Polnoe sobranie stikhotvorenii*, ed. M. Ia. Poliakov. Biblioteka poèta, Bolshaiia seriia. Moscow-Leningrad, 1964.
Polonskii, Iakov P. *Sochineniia v dvukh tomakh*, ed. I. B. Mushina. Two vols. Moscow: Khudozhestvennaia literatura, 1986.
Potepalov, S. G. "Puteshestvie P. I. Keppena po slavianskim zemliam," in *Iz istorii russko-slavianskikh literaturnykh sviazei XIX v*. Moscow-Leningrad: Akademii nauk SSSR, 1963.
Poznansky, Alexander. *Tchaikovsky: The Quest for the Inner Man*. New York: Schirmer Books, 1991.
‗‗‗‗‗‗‗ . *Tchaikovsky's Last Days*. Oxford: Clarendon Press, 1996.
‗‗‗‗‗‗‗ , ed. *Tchaikovsky Through Others' Eyes*. Bloomington and Indianapolis: Indiana University Press, 1999.
Priima, F. Ia. "Iz istorii sozdaniia 'Pesen zapadnykh slavian' A. S. Pushkina," in *Iz istorii russko-slavianskikh literaturnykh sviazei XIX v*. Moscow-Leningrad: Akademiia nauk SSSR, 1963.
Proshloe russkoi muzyki. Materialy i issledovaniia (I). P. I. Chaikovskii. Peterburg: Knigoizdatel'stvo "Ogni," 1920.
Pruzhanskii, A. M. *Otechestvennye pevtsy 1750-1917*. Vol. 1 [A through P; vol. 2 exists only as author's notes at the Glinka Museum]. Moscow: Sovetskii kompozitor, 1991.
Pushkin, A. S. *Polnoe sobranie sochinenii v desiati tomakh*, ed. B. V. Tomashevskii. Ten vols. Moscow: Nauka, 1962-66.
Rakhmaninov, S. V. *Romansy: polnoe sobranie* [Romances: complete collection], ed. P. Lamm. Moscow: Gosudarstvennoe muzykal'noe izdatel'stvo, 1957.
Ratgauz, Daniil. *Stikhotvoreniia*. Kiev, 1893.
‗‗‗‗‗‗‗ . *Polnoe sobranie stikhotvorenii*. Three volumes. St. Petersburg and Moscow: M. O. Vol'f, no date [1906].
Reizen, Mark O. *Avtobiograficheskie zapiski. Stat'i. Vospominaniia*, ed. E. A. Grosheva. Second edition. Moscow: Sovetskii kompozitor, 1986.
Richter, Laurence R. "Russian Songs & Arias" (review). *Slavic and East European Journal* 38, no. 2, Summer (1994): 401-404.
‗‗‗‗‗‗‗ . *Tchaikovsky's Complete Song Texts*. Russian Texts of the Complete Songs of Peter Ilyich Tchaikovsky with phonetic transcriptions, literal and idiomatic English translations. Geneseo, New York: Leyerle Publications, 1999.
Riemens, Leo, and K. J. Kutsch. *Großes Sängerlexicon*. Bern and München, 1997.
Ries, Nancy. *Russian Talk*. Ithaca and London: Cornell University Press, 1997.
Rimskii-Korsakov, N. A. *Polnoe sobranie sochinenii, tom 45: Romansy* [Complete works, vol. 45: Romances], ed. M. O. Shteinberg and A. N. Rimskii-Korsakov. Moscow-Leningrad: Gosudarstvennoe muzykal'noe izdatel'stvo, 1946.
Rodgers, Richard. *Musical Stages*. New York, 1975.
Romanov, Konstantin Konstantinovich (K. R.). *Stikhotvoreniia K. R.*, Third edition. 1879-1885. St. Petersburg, 1996.
‗‗‗‗‗‗‗ . *K. R. Velikii kniaz' Konstantin Romanov. Dnevniki. Vospominaniia. Stikhi. Pis'ma*, ed. Ella E. Matonina. Moscow: Iskusstvo, 1998.
‗‗‗‗‗‗‗ . *K. R. Izbrannaia perepiska*, compiled by L. I. Kuz'mina. Rossiiskaia akademiia nauk, Institut russkoi literatury. Sankt-Peterburg: Izdatel'stvo "Dmitrii Bulanin," 1999.

Rosen, Charles. *The Romantic Generation.* Cambridge: Harvard University Press, 1995.

Rostopchina, Evdokiia. *Stikhotvoreniia. Proza. Pis'ma,* ed. Boris Romanov. Moscow, 1986.

"Russia Abroad." *Russkoe zarubezh'e. Zolotaia kniga emigratsii. Pervaja tret' XX veka.* Moscow: Rossiiskaia politicheskaia èntsiklopediia (ROSSPEN), 1997.

Russkie klassicheskie vodevili. Repertuarnaia biblioteka dlia khudozhestvennoi samodeiatel'nosti, Vypusk III. Moscow: Iskusstvo, 1945.

Savchenko, Boris A. *Vadim Kozin.* Moscow: Iskusstvo, 1993.

Schindler, Kurt, ed. *The Golden Treasury of Music: A Century of Russian Song from Glinka to Rachmaninoff.* New York: G. Schirmer, Inc., 1911.

Scott, Michael. *The Record of Singing. Vol I: to 1914; Vol 2: 1914-1925.* Boston: Northeastern University Press, 1993.

Shaliapin, F. I. *Maska i dusha: Moi sorok let na teatrakh.* Moscow, 1989 (first published in Paris, 1932).

Shcherbakova, Taisiya A. *Tsyganskoe muzykal'noe ispolnitel'stvo i tvorchestvo v Rossii.* Moscow: Muzyka, 1984.

Shcherbina, N. F. *Izbrannye proizvedeniia,* ed. G. Ia. Galagan. Biblioteka poèta, Bol'shaia seriia. Leningrad, 1970.

Sheiko, Rena. *Elena Obraztsova. Zapiski v puti. Dialogi.* Moscow, 1984.

Shevchenko, Taras. *The Poetical Works of Taras Shevchenko, The Kobzar,* ed. C. H. Andrusyshen & Watson Kirkconnell. Toronto: University of Toronto Press, 1964 (reprinted 1977).

Sices, David, ed. *Alfred de Musset: Comedies & Proverbs.* Baltimore and London: The Johns Hopkins University Press, 1994.

Slonimsky, Nicolas. *50 Russian Art Songs From Glinka to Shostakovich, for Voice and Piano* (Am-Rus Vocal Series). Three vols. New York: Leeds Music Corporation, 1949-1951.

_____ . *Perfect Pitch: A Life Story.* Oxford and New York: Oxford University Press, 1988.

_____ . *Lectionary of Music.* New York: McGraw-Hill, 1989.

Smit, Leo. "The Classic Cole Porter." *Saturday Review,* 1971, no. 25.

Smith, R. E. F. and David Christian. *Bread and Salt: A social and economic history of food and drink in Russia.* Cambridge, 1984.

Snyder, Lawrence D. *German Poetry in Song: An Index of Lieder.* Two vols. Berkeley: Fallen Leaf Press, 1995.

Sobolevskii, Aleksei Ivanovich, ed. *Velikorusskie narodnye pesni.* Seven vols. Sankt-Peterburg, 1895-1902.

Sokolov, V. S. Notes on "Khvostovy" and "A. A. Khvostova" in the Name Catalogue, Tchaikovsky Archive, Klin.

Solov'ëv, Vladimir S. *Stikhotvoreniia i shutochnye p'esy,* ed. Dmitrij Tschizewskij. Slavische Propyläen, Vol. 18. München: Wilhelm Fink Verlag, 1968.

Spitz, Sheryl A. "Social and Psychological Themes in East Slavic Folk Lullabies." *Slavic and East European Journal,* vol. 23, no. 1 (Spring 1979): 14-24.

Starr, S. Frederick. *Red and Hot: The Fate of Jazz in the Soviet Union, 1917-1980.* New York and Oxford: Oxford University Press, 1983.

Stoddard, Richard Henry. *Songs of Summer.* Boston: Ticknor and Fields, 1857.

Strugovshchikov, A. N. *Stikhotvoreniia Aleksandra Strugovshchikova, zaimstvovannye iz Gëte i Shillera.* Kniga pervaia. Sanktpeterburg, 1845.

Surikov, Ivan Z. *Stikhotvoreniia I. Z. Surikova.* Moscow: Tipografiia A. I. Mamontova, 1871.

_____ . *Sobranie stikhotvorenii,* ed. A. Dymshits. Biblioteka poèta, Bol'shaia seriia. Leningrad, 1951.

Taneev, S. I. *P. I. Chaikovskii, S. I. Taneev. Pis'ma,* ed. V. A. Zhdanov. Moscow: Goskul't-prosvetizdat, 1951.

Tartakov, G. *Kniga o I. V. Tartakove.* Leningrad: Muzyka, 1987.

Taruskin, Richard. *Defining Russia Musically.* Princeton: Princeton University Press, 1997.

_____ . *Musorgsky.* Princeton: Princeton University Press, 1993.

_____ . *Stravinsky and the Russian Traditions: A Biography of the Works through Mavra.* Two vols. Berkeley, Los Angeles: University of California Press, 1996.

Taskina, E. P., ed. *Russkii Kharbin.* Moscow: Izd. Moskovskogo Universiteta "CheRo," 1998.

Tchaikovsky, Modeste. *The Life & Letters of Peter Ilich Tchaikovsky*, ed. [and considerably abridged] by Rosa Newmarch. London and New York, 1905 (reprinted 1924; reprinted 1970 by Haskell House Publishers Ltd., New York).

Tiutchev, F. I. *Lirika*, ed. K. V. Pigarev. Two vols. Moscow: Nauka, 1965.

_____ . *Polnoe sobranie stikhotvorenii*, ed. A. A. Nikolaev. Biblioteka poèta, Bolshaiia seriia. Leningrad, 1987.

_____ . *Stikhotvoreniia. Pis'ma*, ed. K. V. Pigarev. Moscow, 1957.

Tolstoi, A. K. *Polnoe sobranie stikhotvorenii v dvukh tomakh*, ed. E. I. Prokhorov. Two vols. Biblioteka poèta, Bolshaiia seriia. Leningrad, 1984.

Tolstoy, Nikolai. *The Tolstoys: Twenty-Four Generations of Russian History, 1353-1983*. New York, 1983.

Turgenev, I. S. *Polnoe sobranie sochinenii i pisem v dvadtsati vos'mi tomakh*, ed. M. P. Alekseev et al. Twenty-eight vols. Moscow: Izdatel'stvo Akademii nauk SSSR, 1960-68.

Tumanina, Nadezhda V. *Chaikovskii: Put' k masterstvu, 1840-1877*. Moscow: AN SSSR, 1962.

_____ . *P. I. Chaikovskii: Velikii master, 1878-1893*. Moscow: Nauka, 1968.

Unbegaun, Boris O. *Russian Versification*. Oxford: Clarendon Press, 1956.

Vaidman, P. E. *Tvorcheskii arkhiv P. I. Chaikovskogo*. Moscow: Muzyka, 1988.

_____ , and B. Ia. Anshakov, eds. *P. I. Chaikovskii i russkaia literatura*. Izhevsk: Udmurtiia, 1980.

_____ , and Galina I. Belonovich, eds. *P. I. Chaikovskii: Zabytoe i novoe*. Al'manakh. Vypusk I. Trudy gosudarstvennogo doma-muzeia P. I. Chaikovskogo v Klinu. Moscow, 1995.

Vasina-Grossman, Vera A. *Russkii klassicheskii romans XIX veka*. Moscow: AN SSSR, 1956.

Viardot, Pauline. *Muzykal'nyi portret Poliny Viardo*, ed. G. Preobrazhenskaia. Moscow, 1994.

Vinokur, N. G. and R. A. Kagan. *Pushkin v muzyke*. Moscow: Sovetskii kompozitor, 1974.

Vishnevskaya, Galina. *Galina: A Russian Story*. Translated by Guy Daniels. San Diego, New York, London: Harcourt, Brace, Jovanovich, 1984.

Vol'man, Boris L. *Russkie notnye izdaniia XIX-nachala XX veka*. Leningrad: Muzyka, 1970.

von Meck, N. F. *P. Chaikovskii: perepiska s N. F. von Meck*, ed. V. A. Zhdanov and N. T. Zhegin. Three vols. Moscow-Leningrad, 1934-6.

_____ . *."To my best friend": Correspondence between Tchaikovsky and Nadezhda von Meck 1876-1878*, ed. Edward Garden and Nigel Gotteri. Oxford: Clarendon Press, 1993.

Weintraub, Wiktor. *The Poetry of Adam Mickiewicz*. 'S-Gravenhage: Mouton, 1954.

Wigmore, Richard, ed. *Schubert: The Complete Song Texts*. New York: Schirmer, 1988.

Wilder, Alec. *American Popular Song: The Great Innovators, 1900-1950*. New York and Oxford: Oxford University Press, 1990.

Wiley, Roland John. *Tchaikovsky's Ballets*. Oxford: Clarendon Press, 1985.

Wilson, Duncan. *The Life and Times of Vuk Stefanović Karadžić, 1787-1864*. Oxford: At the Clarendon Press, 1970.

Yoffe, Elkhonon. *Tchaikovsky in America: The Composer's Visit in 1891*. Translated by Lidya Yoffe. New York and Oxford: Oxford University Press, 1986.

Zgorzelski, Czesław, ed. *Ballada polska*. Biblioteka narodowa, Seria I, No. 177. Wrocław-Warszawa-Kraków, 1962.

Index of Song Titles in Russian

Али мать меня рожала — Song 31
Бабушка и внучек (Под окном чулок старушка) — Song 52
Благославляю вас, леса — Song 49
В огороде возле броду — Duet 4
В тёмном аде под землёю — Song 16
В эту лунную ночь — Song 100
Весенняя песня (В старый сад выхожу я) — Song 64
Весна (Травка зеленеет) — Song 54
Весна (Уж тает снег) — Song 60
Вечер (Вишнёвый садик возле хаты) — Song 30
Вечер (Солнце утомилось) — Duet 1
Вчерашняя ночь — Song 74
Глазки весны голубые — Song 18
Горними тихо летела душа — Song 46
День ли царит — Song 50
Детская песенка (Мой Лизочек) — Song 67
За окном в тени мелькает — Song 83
Забыть так скоро — Song 10
Закатилось солнце — Song 101
Зачем? (Зачем же ты приснилася) — Song 35
Зима (Дед, поднявшись спозаранку) — Song 63
Зимний вечер (Хорошо вам, детки) — Song 58
И больно, и сладко — Song 6
Кабы знала я — Song 45
Как над горячею золой — Song 20
Как наладили: «Дурак — Song 24
Канарейка (Говорит султанша канарейке) — Song 22
Колыбельная песнь в бурю (Ах! уймись ты, буря) — Song 61
Колыбельная (Спи, дитя моё) — Song 11
Корольки (Как пошёл я с казаками) — Song 34
Кукушка (Ты прилетел из города) — Song 59
Ласточка (Идёт девочка сиротка) — Song 66
Легенда (Был у Христа младенца сад) — Song 56
Лишь ты один — Song 73
Любовь мертвеца (Пускай холодною землёю) — Song 43
Минула страсть — Duet 5
Мой гений, мой ангел, мой друг — Song 1

Мой костёр в тумане светит — Song 80
Мой Лизочек — Song 67
Мой садик (Как мой садик свеж и зелен!) — Song 55
Моя баловница — Song 32
Мы сидели с тобой — Song 98
На берегу (Домик над рекою) — Song 57
На землю сумрак пал — Song 47
На нивы жёлтые — Song 69
На сон грядущий (Ночная тьма безмолвие приносит) — Song 27
Нам звёзды кроткие сияли — Song 85
Не верь, мой друг — Song 4
Не долго нам гулять — Song 26
Не отходи от меня — Song 29
Не спрашивай — Song 70
Нет, никогда не назову — Song 33
Нет, только тот, кто знал — Song 9
Ни отзыва, ни слова, ни привета — Song 37
Ни слова, о друг мой — Song 5
Новогреческая песня (на тему "Dies irae") — Song 16
Ночи безумные — Song 79
Ночь (Меркнет слабый свет свечи) — Song 99
Ночь (Отчего я люблю тебя, светлая ночь) — Song 82
О, если б знали вы — Song 76
О, если б ты могла — Song 42
О, спой же ту песню — Song 14
Он так меня любил — Song 36
Осень (Скучная картина!) — Song 65
Отчего? (Отчего побледнела весной) — Song 8
Первое свиданье (Вот миновала разлука) — Song 89
Песнь Земфиры (Старый муж, грозный муж) — Song 2
Песнь Миньоны (Ты знаешь край) — Song 21
Песнь цыганки (Мой костёр в тумане светит) — Song 80
Погоди! — Song 12
Подвиг — Song 84
Пойми хоть раз — Song 13
Полночь (Mezza notte) — Song 3
Примиренье (О, засни моё сердце глубока) — Song 19
Прости! — Song 81
Простые слова (Ты звезда на полночном небе) — Song 78
Птичка (Птичка Божия проснулася с зарёю) — Song 53
Пускай зима — Song 95

Разочарование (Ярко солнце ещё блистало) — Song 93

Рассвет (Занялася заря) — Duet 6

Растворил я окно — Song 87

Серенада (В ярком свете зари) — Song 94

Серенада Дон Жуана (Гаснут дальней Альпухары) — Song 39

Серенада (О, дитя) — Song 91

Серенада (Ты куда летишь) — Song 92

Скажи, о чём в тени ветвей — Song 68

Слеза дрожит — Song 7

Слёзы (Если покой дадите) — Song 96

Слёзы (Слёзы людские) — Duet 3

Смерть (Если розы тихо осыпаются) — Song 72

Смотри, вон облако — Song 28

Снова, как прежде, один — Song 103

Соловей, мой соловейко — Song 77

Средь мрачных дней — Song 102

Средь шумного бала — Song 41

Страшная минута (Ты внимаешь) — Song 38

Так что же? (Твой образ светлый) — Song 15

То было раннею весной — Song 40

Уж гасли в комнатах огни — Song 90

Уноси моё сердце — Song 17

Усни (Уснуть бы мне навек) — Song 71

Усни, печальный друг — Song 48

Флорентинская песня — Song 44

Хотел бы в единое слово — Song 25

Цветок (Весело цветики в поле пестреют) — Song 62

Чаровница (Ты собою воплощаешь) — Song 97

Шотландская баллада (Чьей кровию меч свой) — Duet 2

Я вам не нравлюсь — Song 88

Я ли в поле да не травушка была — Song 51

Я с нею никогда не говорил — Song 23

Я сначала тебя не любила — Song 86

Я тебе ничего не скажу — Song 75

Index of Song Titles in English

A soul flew quietly in the heavenly heights — Song 46
A tear trembles — Song 7
Again, as before — Song 103
Amid gloomy days — Song 102
Amid the din of the ball — Song 41
As over darkly glowing embers — Song 20
As they harped their tune: "You fool" — Song 24
Ask no question — Song 70
At first I didn't love you — Song 86
Autumn — Song 65
Bedtime prayer — Song 27
Beyond the window — Song 83
Birdie — Song 53
Blue eyes of spring — Song 18
By the river — Song 57
Canary — Song 22
Carry my heart away — Song 17
Child's song — Song 67
Christ-child had a garden — Song 56
Coral beads — Song 34
Cradle song — Song 11
Cuckoo — Song 59
Dawn — Duet 6
Day or night — Song 50
Day-dreaming in the shade — Song 68
Dead man's love — Song 43
Death — Song 72
Deception (Déception)— Song 93
Did mother give me life — Song 31
Dies irae — Song 16
Disappointment — Song 93
Do you know the land? — Song 21
Does the day reign — Song 50
Don Juan's serenade — Song 39
Don't ask — Song 70
Don't believe, my love — Song 4
Don't leave me — Song 29
Drunkard's song — Song 24
Dusk fell on the earth — Song 47

Enchantress — Song 97
Evening (A cherry orchard by a peasant house) — Song 30
Evening (The sun is tired) — Duet 1
Exploit — Song 84
Fall asleep — Song 71
Fearful minute — Song 38
First meeting — Song 89
Florentine song — Song 44
Flower — Song 62
Fool's song — Song 24
Forgive — Song 81
Frenzied nights — Song 79
Garden — Song 55
Go to sleep, sad friend — Song 48
Granny and grandson — Song 52
Gypsy girl's song (My campfire glows in the mist) — Song 80
He loved me so — Song 36
Heroism — Song 84
Human tears — Duet 3
I bless you, forests — Song 49
I didn't love you at first — Song 86
I don't attract you — Song 88
I never spoke to her — Song 23
I opened the window wide — Song 87
I was not a blade of grass — Song 51
I wish I could pour into a single word — Song 25
I won't say anything to you — Song 75
If I could pour into a single word — Song 25
If only I had known — Song 45
In the garden by the ford — Duet 4
It was in early spring — Song 40
It's painful, it's sweet — Song 6
Know you the land — Song 21
Last night — Song 74
Legend — Song 56
Les Larmes — Song 96
Let winter — Song 95
Lights were going out in the rooms — Song 90
Little bird — Song 53
Little blue eyes of spring — Song 18
Look: that cloud there — Song 28
Love of a dead man — Song 43
Lullaby in a storm — Song 61

Lullaby — Song 11
Midnight (Mezza notte) — Song 3
Mignon's song — Song 21 (see also Songs 9, 70)
Mild stars shone down on us — Song 85
Modern Greek song — Song 16
My campfire glows in the mist — Song 80
My darling girl — Song 32
My garden — Song 55
My genius, my angel, my friend — Song 1
My Lizzie-lad — Song 67
Night (Dim grows the weak light) — Song 99
Night (Why do I love you, bright night) — Song 82
Nightingale — Song 77
Nights of madness — Song 79
No response, no word, no greeting — Song 37
No, never will I name her — Song 33
No, only one who knows — Song 9
None but the lonely heart — Song 9
Not a word, my friend — Song 5
Nursery song — Song 67
Oh, if only you knew — Song 76
Oh, if you could for a moment — Song 42
Oh, sing that song — Song 14
Old husband, cruel husband — Song 2
On gloomy days — Song 102
On the riverbank — Song 57
On this moonlit night — Song 100
On yellow fields of grain — Song 69
One small word — Song 38
Orphan girl — Song 66
Painful and sweet — Song 6
Passion has cooled — Duet 5
Pilgrim's song — Song 49
Pimpinella — Song 44
Plain words — Song 78
Prayer at bedtime — Song 27
Qu'importe que l'hiver — Song 95
Reconciliation — Song 19
Rondel — Song 97
Say of what, in the shade of branches — Song 68
Scottish ballad — Duet 2
See, that cloud there — Song 28
Sérénade (J'aime) — Song 94

Serenade (Oh child) — Song 91
Sérénade (Où vas-tu, souffle d'aurore) — Song 92
Serenade of Don Juan — Song 39
Simple words — Song 78
Sleep — Song 71
Sleep, sad friend — Song 48
Sleepless nights — Song 79
So soon forgotten — Song 10
So what more can I say? — Song 15
Song of the gypsy girl — Song 80
Spring (Grass is greening) — Song 54
Spring (Snow's melting) — Song 60
Spring song (I walk out into the old garden) — Song 64
Stay a while! — Song 12
Sun went down — Song 101
Swallow — Song 66
Tear trembles — Song 7
Tears (Les Larmes) — Song 96
Tears — Duet 3
The lights were going out in the rooms — Song 90
This moonlit night — Song 100
Through the window in the shadows — Song 83
To forget so soon — Song 10
Understand just once — Song 13
Wait a while! — Song 12
Was I not a blade of grass — Song 51
We haven't long to stroll — Song 26
We sat together — Song 98
What does it matter that winter — Song 95
Whether day reigns — Song 50
Whose blood has turned your sword so red — Duet 2
Why? (Why has the rose grown pale) — Song 8
Why? (Why did I dream of you) — Song 35
Winter evening (It's nice for you, children) — Song 58
Winter (Granddad, up at crack of dawn) — Song 63
Yellow fields of grain — Song 69
You alone — Song 73
You don't like me — Song 88
Zemfira's Song — Song 2

INDEX OF NAMES

Singers are not included here unless mentioned in the text. A complete list of singers and their accompanists will be found in SINGERS & RECORDINGS.

Abraham, Gerald, xiv, 144, 146
Afanasiev, Nikolay, 216
Akhmatova, Anna, 59, 308
Aksakov, Konstantin, 187-9
Albrecht, Konstantin, 49, 127, 151
Aleksandrova-Kochetova, A. D., 17, 19, 107, 119, 309, 322
Alexander I, 69
Alexander II, 128, 154, 238, 303
Alexander III, 190, 206, 237
Aliabiev, Alexander, 6, 45, 59, 130, 255
Alshvang, Arnold, xiv, 29-30, 45, 47, 77, 96, 221, 228
Anderson, Marian, 26, 299
Antsev, Mikhail, 63
Apukhtin, Aleksey, 29-32, 102-5, 108, 128, 144-6, 220-2, 237, 270
Arensky, Anton, 37, 135, 165, 209, 242, 305
Ariosto, Lodovico, 69
Arlen, Harold, 130
Artôt, Désirée, 9, 251-2, 255-267
Asafiev, Boris, 47, 96
Ashkenazi, David, 300, 322-3
Ashkenazy, Vladimir, 3, 298, 300
Auer, Leopold, 313-14
Bakaleinikoff, Constantin, 26
Bakhchiev, Alexander, 300, 319
Balakirev, Mily, 10, 25, 33-4, 67, 73-4, 119, 205, 209
Balmont, Konstantin, 270
Baratynsky, Yevgeny, 59
Barrymore, Ethel, 25
Barsova, Valeriya, 300, 326
Bartenev, Pyotr, 207
Bartok, Bela, xviii
Beethoven, Ludwig von, 27, 33, 40-1, 50, 66, 116
Belinsky, Vissarion, 152, 197
Bellini, Vincenzo, 7, 33
Benardaki, Maria, 146-7
Berberova, Nina, 32, 109, 284
Berg, Alban, 66

Berg, Nikolay, 136-8
Bergman, Ingrid, 26
Berlin, Isaiah, 20
Berlioz, Hector, 47
Bernard, Matvey, 51, 99, 160
Bernard, Nikolay, 51, 54, 56, 58, 76, 78
Bernhardt, Sarah, 203
Bernstein, Leonard, 302, 318, 325
Bessel, Vasily, 34, 44, 45, 51, 57-8
Bizet, Georges, 223, 251-2
Blanchecotte, Augustine, 252, 264-5
Bleikhman, Yuly, 248, 276
Blok, Alexander, 40, 55, 59
Blumenfeld, Felix, 21, 327
Blumental-Tamarin, Alexander, 248
Boccacio, Giovanni, 69
Borodin, Alexander, 9, 10, 67
Borodina, Olga, 297
Bortniansky, Dmitry, 151
Boshniakovich, Oleg, 20, 60, 298, 301
Brahms, Johannes, 35, 251
Bregvadze, Nani, 243
Britten, Benjamin, 106, 165, 318, 327
Brodsky, Joseph, 59
Brown, David, xiv, 29, 47, 96, 114, 144, 147, 154, 218, 271, 289
Brüll, Ignaz, 76
Bryusov, Valery, 271
Bulakhov, Pyotr, 59, 283, 328
Bülow, Hans von, 58
Busoni, Ferruccio, 251
Butakova, Vera, 200
Byron, Lord, George Gordon, 3, 67, 69, 205
Callas, Maria, 317, 320, 323
Carnegie, Andrew, 7, 163, 268
Caruso, Enrico, 125, 297, 301, 320
Catoire, Georgi, 63
Chaliapin, Fyodor, 202, 207, 256, 297, 301-2, 320
Chekhov, Anton, 59, 77, 152, 220,

228-9, 270, 271, 273, 284-5
Chesnokov, Pavel, 135
Chevalier, Maurice, 309
Chichagov, Igor, 302, 320, 327
Chopin, Frederic, 51, 82, 91, 93, 297
Christen, Ada, 203-4
Christoff, Boris, 35, 73, 207, 298, 302
Churchill, Winston, 309
Collin, Paul, 252, 256-63, 266-7
Cui, César, 10, 13, 14, 16, 25, 30, 47,
    50-1, 66, 91-3, 104, 124, 135, 190,
    216, 227, 250, 251, 293
Dante Alighieri, 91, 122
Daragan, D. G., 193
Dargomyzhsky, Alexander, 18, 148,
    232, 243, 283
Davingof, Nikolay, 211
Davydov, Bob, 190
Davydov, Lev (Tchaikovsky's brother-
    in-law), 86, 190-1, 290
Davydov, Vasily (Decembrist), 191
Davydova, Alexandra Ilyinichna
    (Sasha, Tchaikovsky's sister), 86,
    108-9, 128, 190-2, 289-90
Davydova, Alexandra (widow of
    Decembrist), 190
Davydova, Tatyana, 289-96
Davydova, Vera, 258, 302, 307
De Reszke, Edouard, 25, 303
De Reszke, Jean, 303, 307, 321, 325
Derfeldt, A. A., 27
Diaghilev, Sergey, 307, 328
Dickens, Charles, 127, 190
Dietrich, Marlene, 308, 309
Dmitriev, Ivan, 130
Dodonov, Alexander, 99, 319, 324
Dolukhanova, Zara, xi, 82, 84, 246,
    303, 309, 312, 313, 322
Donaurov, Sergey, 104, 209
Dorliak, Nina, 139, 325
Dostoyevsky, Fyodor, 91, 127-8, 152
Dubuque, Alexander, 19, 56, 91, 93
Dumas, Alexandre (fils), 203
Dvořák, Anton, 251
Edward VII, 206
Eichenwald, Yuly, 161
Eisler, Hanns, 26
Everardi, Camillo, 198, 202, 297,
    301, 302, 307, 313, 318, 322, 325

Evlampios, Georgy, 47-9
Fellini, Federico, 197
Fesca, Alexander, 76
Fet, Afanasy, 1-2, 32, 40-1, 45, 52-4,
    84-5, 111, 210-11, 223, 225, 238,
    247, 270, 271
Fiedler, Arthur, 26
Field, John, 160
Figner, Nikolay, 249, 270, 271-82,
    303-4, 315
Fischer-Dieskau, Dietrich, 69, 304,
    326
Flaubert, Gustave, 128
Fontane, Theodor, 292
Franck, César, 257
Frank, Joseph, 152
Franz, Robert, 43
Gabel, Stanislav, 298, 307, 315, 327
Gaisberg, Fred, 255, 321, 325
Galvani, Giacomo, 297-8, 318
Garcia, Manuel, 99, 297, 319
Gawiński, Jan, 157
Gay, Delphine, 102-3
Gellert, Christian, 172
Gershwin, George, 35, 75
Gershwin, Ira, 130
Gippius, Zinaida, 152
Girardin, Emile, 102
Glavach, V. I., 124
Glazunov, Alexander, 47
Glière, Reinhold, 160, 178, 293
Glinka, Mikhail, 7, 10, 14, 18, 19, 45,
    51, 59, 67, 91-3, 96, 119, 130,
    252, 283
Goethe, Johann Wolfgang von, 25-8,
    64-6, 114, 116, 182, 197-8, 216
Gogol, Nikolay, 50, 152
Goldenweiser, Alexander, 293, 298,
    300, 305, 306, 327
Golitsyn, S. G., 93
Golovin, Dmitry, 99, 305
Gorchakova, Aleksandra, 251-2, 255,
    257-67, 324
Gorchakova, Galina, 297, 305
Gorky, Maxim, 199, 206, 302
Grant, Cary, 25
Gray, Thomas, 14
Grechaninov, Alexander, 35, 71, 293,
    308, 310

Grekov, Nikolay, 38-9, 77-8, 82-3, 94-5, 136
Grieg, Edvard, 251, 321
Grigoriev, Apollon, 71, 76
Grimm, Jacob, 216
Gurilyov, Alexander, 6, 45, 88, 130, 198, 283
Hartmann, Moritz, 14-16
Heine, Heinrich, 23-4, 52, 55-6, 75-6, 82, 100, 271
Hemans, Felicia, 42-4
Hensel, Fanny, 24
Herzen, Alexander, 79
Hofmann, Josef, 57-8
Hubert, Nikolay, 44
Hvorostovsky, Dmitri, 20, 60, 122, 207, 297, 301, 306
Igumnov, Konstantin, 301, 306, 317, 322
Ilina, Marya, 101
Ippolitov-Ivanov, Mikhail, 37, 121, 160, 205, 305
Iretskaya, Natalia, 297, 307, 313, 320, 323
Ivan the Terrible, 33, 72
Ives, Charles, 56
Jackson, David, 26, 112
Jeitteles, Aloys, 41
John of Damascus, 142-3
Jurgenson, Pyotr, 7, 8, 9, 10, 17, 21, 32, 51, 54, 56, 58, 76, 78, 81, 109, 127, 129, 147, 151, 153, 187, 205, 238, 246, 251, 269, 289
Kadmina, Yevlaliya, 107
Kalinnikov, Vasily, 236
Kamenskaya, Maria, 66
Karadžić, Vuk Stefanović, 214-17
Karr, Alphonse, 124
Kashkin, Nikolay, 16, 127, 328
Katenin, Pavel, 193
Katulskaya, Yelena, 199, 307, 315
Każyński, Wiktor, 99
Keneman, Fyodor, 135
Khomyakov, Aleksey, 206, 207-9, 233-4
Khromchenko, Solomon, 282, 308
Khrushchev, Nikita, 175
Khvostova, Alina, 25, 27
Klimenko, Ivan, 24, 25

Knipper, Olga, 228
Kochetova: see Aleksandrova-Kochetova
Koltsov, Aleksey, 71, 88, 148
Komissarzhevskaya, Vera, 193
Komissarzhevsky, Fyodor, 193
Kondratowicz: see Syrokomla
Konstantin Konstantinovich, Grand Duke (K. R.), 52, 135, 206, 210, 237-8, 239-50
Konstantin Nikolayevich, Grand Duke, 128
Koreshchenko, Arseny, 242
Korganov, G. O., 204
Korsov, Bogomir (Gottfried), 61, 105, 196
Kotek, Joseph, 109-110
Kovalyova, Galina, 35, 55, 309, 315
Kozel, Berta, 298, 303, 309
Kozin, Vadim, 283, 309
Kozlovsky, Ivan, 199, 309, 318
K. R.: see Konstantin Konstantinovich
Krutikova, Alexandra, 61, 105, 204
Kuprin, Alexander, 106
Kurenko, Maria, 203, 298, 310
Landowska, Wanda, 316
Larme, A. M., 61
Laroche, Hermann, 41, 50
Lavrovskaya, Elizabeth, 9, 17, 25, 58, 80-1, 83-93, 108, 128, 150, 297, 316, 323, 328
Lazhechnikov, Ivan, 241
Legostayeva, Lyudmila, 261, 311
Leibrok, Yu., 2, 8
Leiferkus, Sergei, 3, 122, 297, 311
Lemeshev, Sergey, 175, 180, 182, 211, 223, 309-11
Lenartowicz, Teofil, 88-90, 185-6
Lenin, Vladimir, 273, 321
Lensky, N. A., 243
Leoncavallo, Ruggero, 3
Lermontov, Mikhail, 18, 35, 67, 79, 117, 119, 122-4, 133, 199, 270, 281
Levik, Sergey, 128, 298
Levinsky, Ilya, 297, 312
Levinson, Gina, 144
Liadov, Anatoly, 49
Lischke, André, xiv

Lisitsian, Pavel, 63, 303, 312-13
Lisovsky, Konstantin, xi, 55, 214, 300, 313
Liszt, Franz, 33, 47, 51, 66
Llewellyn, Richard, 25
Lodii, Pyotr, 205-6, 313
Lodii, Zoya, 303, 313
Lomonosov, Mikhailo, 207
Maikov, Apollon, 35-7, 41, 47-8, 153, 238
Makarov, Abram, 298, 313-4, 321
Malinin, F. N., 146
Mandelstam, Osip, 271
Maria Fyodorovna, Empress, 190, 206, 209-36
Masetti, Umberto, 298, 300, 302, 308, 310, 316, 317, 319, 320
Massenet, Jules, 133
Massini, Yekaterina, 103
McBurney, Gerard, 97
McCormack, John, 26, 163, 315
Meck, Nadezhda Filaretovna von, 110-11, 122, 127-9, 148, 151, 154, 191, 197, 205, 218, 226, 268, 284, 289, 291
Medtner, Nikolay, 27, 62, 293, 305, 308
Medvedev, Mikhail, 298
Mei (Figner), Medea, 304, 315, 316
Melnikov, Ivan, 70
Mendelssohn, Felix, 24
Menshikova, Aleksandra, 13
Menuhin, Yehudi, 298, 313
Merezhkovsky, Dmitry, 152, 199-202
Mérimée, Prosper, 216
Messager, André, 95
Mey, Lev, 23-4, 25-7, 52, 67-76, 86-93, 96-101, 111, 197
Mickiewicz, Adam, 88, 90, 91-3, 136-8, 216
Migay, Sergey, 314, 315, 316, 321, 326
Mikhailov, Mikhail, 55-6, 158
Miller, Sofia, 139, 194
Milyukova, Antonina, 109-110
Moniuszko, Stanisław, 91, 93
Monteverdi, Claudio, 256
Mozart, Wolfgang Amadeus, 10, 17-18, 47, 112, 206, 245

Musorgsky, Modest, 9, 10, 25, 35, 71-3, 75-6, 135, 153, 283, 318, 322
Musset, Alfred, 94-5
Nabokov, Vladimir, xiii-xiv
Nápravník, Eduard, 91, 93, 109
Nekrasov, Nikolay, 38, 226-7
Neuhaus, Heinrich, 309, 327
Nezhdanova, Antonina, 297-8, 299, 316
Nicholas I, 79, 87, 152-3, 237
Nicholas II, 206
Nikolayev, Anton, 95
Nissen-Saloman, Henriette, 27, 61, 81, 128, 297, 301
Norman, Jessye, xviii, 253, 316
Oborin, Lev, 298, 300, 317
Obraztsova, Yelena, 148, 317
Obukhova, Nadezhda, 144, 258, 283, 298, 317, 322
Ogaryov, Nikolay, 79-81
Orlov, Dmitry, 63
Ostrovsky, Alexander, 9, 50, 59, 71
Ovchinnikov, Mikhail, xiv, 209
Pabst, Pavel, 305, 306
Panayeva, Alexandra, 128-9, 132-50
Panina, Varvara, 59, 248, 283, 309
Pasternak, Boris, 52, 181
Pater, Walter, 62
Patti, Adelina, 13, 33
Pavlovskaya, Emilia, 198, 309
Pears, Peter, 163, 318
Percy, Thomas, 292
Petrarch, Francesco, 136
Petrashevsky, Mikhail, 152
Petrovsky, Miron, 30
Piatigorsky, Gregor, 27, 318
Piccioli, Luigi, 7, 105
Pisemsky, Aleksey, 153
Pishchayev, Gennady, 153, 299, 300, 319
Pleshcheyev, Aleksey, 9, 14-16, 42-3, 52, 148, 151-3, 154-84, 203-4, 212-3, 235-6, 270
Plevitskaya, Nadezhda, 283
Podleś, Ewa, 297, 319
Poe, Edgar Allan, 269
Polonsky, Yakov, 205, 223-5, 228-32, 236, 238
Porter, Cole, 145

Poznansky, Alexander, 109, 284
Prigozhii, Yakov, 220, 223, 243
Prokofiev, Sergey, 308, 319
Prokunin, Vasily, 50
Pushkin, Alexander, xiii-xiv, 3-6, 14, 18, 52, 59, 67, 69, 77, 81, 108, 117, 119, 128, 130, 190, 199, 206, 214-7, 223, 228, 268, 270
Raab, Wilhelmina, 68
Rachmaninoff, Sergei, 3, 13, 35, 37, 47, 52, 62, 71, 211, 269, 300, 302, 305, 308, 310, 319, 320, 326
Raisky, Nazary G., 305, 311, 326
Ratgauz, Daniil, 268-70, 271-82
Ratisbonne, Louis, 178
Rautio, Nina, 3, 80, 297, 320
Rebikov, Vladimir, 158, 160, 162, 164, 170, 174, 176, 178, 182, 184, 240, 293
Reizen, Mark, 142, 273, 313-14, 320-1
Richter, Svyatoslav, 139
Rimskaya-Korsakova, Nadezhda, 34, 37
Rimsky-Korsakov, Nikolay, 10, 13, 33-4, 39, 50-1, 63, 67, 71, 91, 93, 114, 116, 121, 135, 141, 195-6, 226-7, 248, 283
Rodgers, Joan, 29, 297, 321
Rodgers, Richard, 57-8, 75
Romanov, Konstantin (K. R.): see Konstantin Konstantinovich
Rossini, Gioachino, 7, 33, 153
Rostopchina, Yevdokiya, 17-19
Rothstein, Robert A., 163
Rousseau, Jean Jacques, 127
Rozhdestvensky, Gennady, 299, 319, 322
Rubets, Aleksandr, 37, 85, 148
Rubinstein, Anton, 6, 9, 10, 56, 57-8, 67, 128, 132, 141, 151, 307, 326
Rubinstein, Nikolay, 9, 10, 33-4, 46, 49, 50, 57-8, 107, 110-11, 127-9, 151, 298, 328
Rublyov, Andrey, 15
Sakharov, Andrey, 233
Sakharov, Matvey, 298, 301, 317, 322
Santagano: see Gorchakova
Schiller, J. C. F. von, 197
Schoeck, Othmar, 24

Schopenhauer, Arthur, 122
Schubert, Franz, 27, 35, 66, 198, 271
Schumann, Robert, 10, 27, 51, 64, 66, 198
Schumann-Heink, Ernestine, 297, 322
Scott, Walter, 50
Selznick, David, 26
Shakespeare, William, 38, 50-1, 62, 77, 238, 251
Shaposhnikov, Sergey, 258, 264
Shcherbina, Nikolay, 59-61, 235
Shebalin, Vissarion, 119
Shenderovich, Yevgeny, 253
Shevchenko, Taras, 86-7, 96, 281, 294
Shilovsky, Konstantin, 108, 144
Shilovsky, Vladimir, 51, 108
Shostakovich, Dmitry, 47, 303, 317, 327
Shpiller, Natalia, 317, 320, 323
Siloti, Alexander, 305
Sinatra, Frank, 26, 323
Slonimsky, Nicolas, xiv, xvi, 29, 67, 114, 228, 307, 321
Smit, Leo, 145
Sobinov, Leonid, 99, 255, 297, 324
Sobolevsky, Aleksey, 72-3, 130
Söderström, Elisabeth, 3, 29, 53, 300, 324
Sollogub, Vladimir, 192-3
Solovyov, Vladimir, 14, 127
Solzhenitsyn, Alexander, 233
Spiro, A. A., 220, 222
Stalin, Joseph, 153, 175, 282, 302, 309
Stanislavsky, Konstantin, 193, 299, 311, 316, 318, 328
Stanyukovich, A. M., 124
Stasov, Vladimir, 10, 33, 50-1, 57, 127
Steshka, 130
Stoddard, Richard Henry, 163-5
Stokowski, Leopold, 282, 302, 325
Stracciari, Riccardo, 298, 302
Strakhov, Nikolay, 238
Strauss, Richard, 251
Stravinsky, Fyodor, 298
Stravinsky, Igor, 35, 69, 310, 319, 322, 323, 325

Strugovshchikov, Aleksandr, 197-8
Sully Prudhomme, René, 212-3
Surikov, Ivan, 148-50, 185-6, 270,
    289-90, 294, 296
Syrokomla, Władysław, 96-9, 157-8
Taneyev, Sergey, 16, 37, 85, 107, 127,
    129, 143, 153, 157, 169, 171, 184,
    185, 205, 225, 242, 250, 294, 305
Tartakov, Ioachim, 307, 321, 324
Tasso, Torquato, 69
Tauber, Richard, 26, 325
Tchaikovsky, Anatoly Ilyich, 109-111,
    113-26, 128, 237, 289
Tchaikovsky, Modest Ilyich, 1, 34,
    109, 128, 197, 285, 294
Tcherepnin, Nikolay, 37, 54, 200,
    202, 227, 293
Teyte, Maggie, 264, 325
Theophanes the Greek, 15
Titov, A. F., 144
Tolstaya, A. V., 211
Tolstaya, T. K., 210-11
Tolstoy, Aleksey, 11-13, 20-22, 104,
    111-21, 129-135, 139-43, 152,
    194-6, 237, 270, 291-2, 295
Tolstoy, Lev, 20, 30, 33, 52, 59, 62,
    67, 117, 127, 128, 194-5, 220, 235,
    285, 305
Tolstoy, M. L., 211
Tsereteli, Tamara, 283
Tsyganov, Nikolay, 59
Turgenev, Ivan, 25, 30, 32, 52, 77,
    107, 117, 128, 220-1, 223, 226
Turquety, Edouard, 252-5
Tyutchev, Fyodor, 62-6, 71, 111, 112,
    197, 293
Usatov, Dmitry, 165, 202, 297-8, 301
Varady, Julia, 252, 326
Varlamov, Alexander, 45, 59, 84-5, 283
Vasina-Grossman, Vera, xiv, 29, 71-2,
    122, 130, 149, 191, 223, 228, 271,
    277
Veisberg, Yulia, 63
Verdi, Giuseppe, 33, 47, 203
Verstovsky, Aleksey, 3, 6
Vertinsky, Alexander, 283
Vialtseva, Anastasia, 283
Viardot, Pauline, 6, 25, 81, 99, 128,
    153, 206, 243, 251, 297, 303

Vielgorsky, Mikhail, 3, 6
Vietinghoff-Schell, Boris, 132, 295
Vinogradov, Georgy, 53, 175, 182,
    211, 326-7
Vishnevskaya, Galina, 106, 327
von Meck: see Meck
Vyazemsky, Pyotr, 71
Wagner, Richard, 33, 237, 328
Westbrook, Arthur, 25-8
Whitman, Walt, 199
Wilde, Oscar, 32
Wolf, Hugo, 27, 66, 198
Wyatt, Thomas, 100
Yershov, Ivan, 249, 302, 306, 310,
    320, 327-8
Zamboni, Luigi, 7
Zarudnaya, Varvara, 205-6, 301, 306
Zhukovsky, Vasily, 14, 18, 59